Innovation Management and New Product Development

Paul Trott

FINANCIAL TIMES
PITMAN PUBLISHING

FINANCIAL TIMES
MANAGEMENT
LONDON • SAN FRANCISCO
KUALA LUMPUR • JOHANNESBURG

*Financial Times Management delivers the knowledge,
skills and understanding that enable students,
managers and organisations to achieve their ambitions,
whatever their needs, wherever they are.*

London Office:
128 Long Acre, London WC2E 9AN
Tel: +44 (0)171 447 2000
Fax: +44 (0)171 240 5771
Website: www.ftmanagement.com

A Division of Financial Times Professional Limited

First published in Great Britain in 1998

ISBN 0 273 63111 X

British Library Cataloguing in Publication Data
A CIP catalogue record for this book can be obtained from the British Library.

10 9 8 7 6 5 4 3 2 1

Typeset by Pantek Arts, Maidstone, Kent.
Printed and bound in Great Britain by Clays Ltd, St Ives plc.

The Publishers' policy is to use paper manufactured from sustainable forests.

Contents

Part Two: New Product Development

Part Three: Technology Management

Preface

Like many people I have been fascinated for a long time by new technology and new products, especially those that affect (and usually enhance) our daily lives, such as pharmaceutical drugs, personal computers, mobile telephones and compact discs. It is the continual stream of new materials and new designs, all of which are outputs of human creativity and the application of knowledge, which is so absorbing. Not all technical achievement would be classified as enhancing humanity. The development and subsequent use of the first atomic bomb at Hiroshima at the end of World War II or the Thalidomide drug that led to many birth defects in the 1960s are two notable examples of the potential problems with new technology.

In spite of this, the application of human knowledge to human problems is a fascinating subject. Indeed, the development of new products and the successful management of that process have always been of interest to both academics and businesses. Today's most successful companies rely on the ability continually to develop new and improved products, either through using the latest advances in scientific research and technology or using existing technology applied in a new and interesting way. This subject, however, has not previously been addressed by students of business and management.

Many students of business may be wondering how this subject relates to other subjects. The answer, as usual, depends on which perspective is taken: marketing, technology, legal, strategic management, commercialisation, or a multiple-perspective approach incorporating all of these. In any event, the management of innovation in general, and the development of new products in particular, require the expertise of all areas – finance, manufacturing, human resources, marketing and business strategy. The management of innovation is not a functional activity, solely the preserve of a single department. It is imperative to view innovation and product development as an internal *management process* rather than as a functional activity. This is the view taken by this book (*see* Figure 0.1). Indeed, many would argue that product innovation suffers seriously when it is subdivided into separate specialisations.

The objective of this book is to present a contemporary view of innovation management that focuses on the links and overlaps between groups (the corners of the triangle on Figure 0.1) rather than on a single perspective from, say, marketing or research and development. It attempts to do this from a business management perspective and aims to provide students with the knowledge to understand how to manage innovation. It is designed to be accessible and readable and is the first textbook to bring together the areas of innovation management and new product development for the student of business.

It is worthy of note that there are very few textbooks on the subject of innovation management and new product development. This may be because the subject is complex, with few simple solutions. In attempting to advance our understanding of the subject, emphasis has been placed in this book on viewing innovation as a manage-

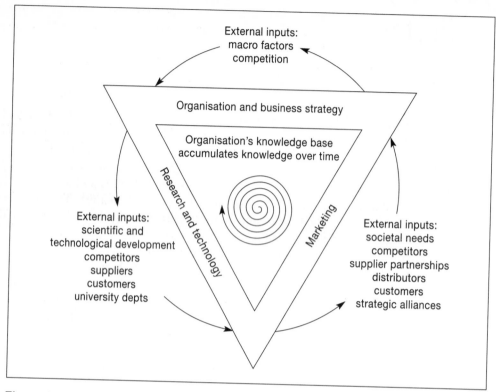

Figure 0.1 : Innovation management as a management process

ment process. The intention is to highlight the folly of thinking that the use of a few simple management tools can transform any company into the next 3M. Such simple approaches to complex management issues continually irritate and annoy experienced managers in industry.

It is the *raison d'être* of this book to emphasise that managing innovation involves analysing the culture and heritage of an organisation, the systems and routines that the organisation has in place and the knowhow that it has built up over its life. To attempt to understand how a business develops new products without taking these issues into consideration would be folly indeed. Hence the approach of this book is both practical and conceptual – it involves analysing both operational activities and long-term strategic issues and the linkages between the two. It is not intended to be a product management book. Indeed, there are many marketing management books that cover this area satisfactorily.

Innovation management is a new and exciting subject, yet its history already stretches over a half a century. The instruction of courses on the subject of the management of innovation can be traced back to the 1950s. During this decade enrolments in business schools (especially in the US) surged and one of the areas to receive attention was the management of innovation. By the 1990s a new product management and innovation discipline had evolved, supported by a variety of research and practitioner-based journals such as *The International Journal of Innovation Management, The Journal of Product Innovation Management, Technovation and R&D Management.*

The book is divided into three parts, indicated in the plan of the book. This framework is intended to operate as a navigational map to help students through the book. Part One explores the concept of innovation management and what needs to be managed. Part Two looks at the process of developing new products and examines many of the new product management issues faced by companies. Part Three examines the wide issue of technology management and in particular how companies manage research and development.

I hope you find the book both stimulating and exciting and that this is merely the start of a long journey exploring the subject of innovation management and new product development.

Paul Trott

Foreword

By Baroness Hogg

In 1997, I chaired an inquiry of the House of Lords Select Committee on Science and Technology into the innovation–exploitation barrier in the United Kingdom. One of our strongest recommendations was that 'business schools should play a greater role in teaching the management of innovation'. This followed a great deal of evidence from witnesses that, despite some remarkable progress in the five years since the committee last reviewed the topic, the level of management skills in new technology businesses was still a weakness in the chain of development from scientific idea to commercial success. We concluded that it was still important to promote education for the management of innovation and exploitation, and that this meant both increasing scientific and technological understanding among the financial community and general management, and increasing business, management and entrepreneurship skills among scientists and technologists.

Dr Paul Trott's book is a welcome response to such pleas, firmly rooted on the business studies side of the divide. The management of innovation is widely and thoroughly treated, filling a large gap in the existing range of textbooks but including a review of the existing literature. This gap exists not merely because, as Dr Trott says, that the subject is complex, with few simple solutions, but because the subject is often treated as a series of separate specialisms, rather than an integrated task. This book usefully brings together innovation management and new product development, the role of intellectual property and the management of research and development.

While courses on this subject have been run in business schools, both in the United Kingdom and the United States, for several decades, the quality of innovation management is still patchy. This is partly, of course, because the management of large organisations has inevitably attracted more attention than the evolution of small ones. Not that one should every make the mistake of equating the pace of innovation to the rate of start-up of new businesses. The links between leading companies in the pharmaceutical industry, for example, and the science base in the universities, are crucial to the successful exploitation of research and industrial success. The management of innovation is a topic of concern to businesses of all sizes, and indeed much of this book is more relevant to big companies than small. Nevertheless, to those start-up or young companies seeking to exploit the spin-off of scientific research, quality of management is an issue that time and again is identified as a critical element of success.

Baroness Hogg
Chairman, London Economics

Plan of the book

Part 1: The Concept of Innovation Management

Chapter 1	**Chapter 2**	**Chapter 3**
Innovation management: an introduction	Managing innovation within firms	Business strategy and organisational knowledge

Part 2: New Product Development

Chapter 4	**Chapter 5**	**Chapter 6**
Product strategy	New product development	Managing the new product development team

Part 3: Technology Management

Chapter 7	**Chapter 8**	**Chapter 9**	**Chapter 10**
Management of research and development: an introduction	Effective research and development management	The role of technology transfer in innovation	Strategic alliances and intellectual property

The Concept of Innovation Management

The purpose of this part of the book is to introduce and explore the concept of innovation management. Particular emphasis is placed on the need to view innovation as a management process. A conceptual framework is introduced which emphasises the importance of internal processes and external linkages. It is from this vantage point that the subject of managing innovation within firms is addressed. This raises the issue of the organisational context and this is the subject of Chapter Two.

Given that virtually all businesses are established to generate funds for their owners, the role of business strategy and how it affects the management of innovation is clearly an important consideration. Chapter Three examines business strategy and how the heritage and knowledge base of an organisation drive the development of business opportunities. It is these opportunities which are at the heart of new product ideas.

The principal message of this part is this: innovation is a management process that is heavily influenced by the organisational context.

1

Innovation management: an introduction

Introduction

There is extensive scope for examining the way innovation is managed within organisations. Most of us are well aware that good technology can help companies achieve competitive advantage and long-term financial success. But there is an abundance of exciting new technology in the world and it is the transformation of this technology into products that is of particular concern to organisations. There are numerous factors to be considered by the organisation. However, it is necessary to be clear about what is being examined and why it needs to be studied.

Learning objectives

When you have completed this chapter, you will be able to:

- Recognise the importance of innovation
- Explain the meaning and nature of innovation management
- Provide an introduction to a management approach to innovation
- Appreciate the complex nature of the management of innovation within organisations
- Describe the changing views of innovation over time
- Recognise the role of key individuals within the process
- Recognise the need to view innovation as a management process.

The importance of innovation

Corporations must be able to adapt and evolve if they wish to survive. Businesses operate with the knowledge that their competitors will inevitably come to the market with a product that changes the basis of competition. The ability to change and adapt is essential to survival.

Today, the idea of innovation is widely accepted. It has become part of our culture – so much so that it verges on becoming a cliché. For example, in 1994 and 1995, 275 books published in the US had the word 'innovation' in their title (Coyne, 1996). But even though the term is now embedded in our language, to what extent do we fully understand the concept? Moreover, to what extent is this understanding shared? A scientist's view of innovation may be very different to that of an accountant in the same organisation.

Celtec shares plummet on news that its latest drug has not performed well in recent clinical trials

The UK's fledgling biotechnology industry suffered a setback when Celltech announced that treatment for septic shock – a reaction to blood poisoning – was being dropped after disappointing trial results.

Celltech's shares almost halved in value, from 630p to 341p, and confidence in the whole sector was shaken. This latest development has raised serious doubt amongst the business community concerning not only the future of Celltech but also the whole biotechnology industry. The shock waves may yet reverberate around the world pharmaceuticals industry.

There is no effective treatment for septic shock, a severe reaction to blood poisoning which often follows surgery. It kills more than 200 000 people a year in the US and Europe. Analysts had forecast sales of up to $600m from the product.

Bayer, the German pharmaceutical company developing the product with Celltech, said it was stopping any future work in the area. It had invested $150m on the product to date.

Source: Financial Times May 22, 1997

The Celtec story puts into context the subject of innovation and new product development. Innovation is at the heart of many companies activities. But to what extent is this true of all businesses? And why are some businesses more innovative than others? What is meant by innovation? And can it be managed? These are questions that will be addressed in this book.

' . . . not to innovate is to die' wrote Christopher Freeman (1982) in his famous study of the economics of innovation. Certainly companies that have established themselves as technical and market leaders have shown an ability to develop successful new products. In virtually every industry from aerospace to pharmaceuticals and

Table 1.1 : Market leaders in 1996

Industry	Market leaders	Innovative new products
Aerospace	Boeing	Passenger aircraft
Pharmaceuticals	Glaxo-Wellcome	Ulcer treatment drug
Motor cars	Mercedes, Ford	Car design and associated product developments
Computers	Intel, IBM and Microsoft	Computer chip technology, computer hardware improvements and software developments respectively

from motor cars to computers, the dominant companies have demonstrated an ability to innovate (*see* Table 1.1).

A brief analysis of economic history, especially in the UK, will show that industrial technological innovation has led to substantial economic benefits for the innovating *company* and the innovating *country*. Indeed, the industrial revolution of the nineteenth century was fuelled by technological innovations (*see* Table 1.2). Technological innovations have also been an important component in the progress of human societies. Anyone who has visited the towns of Bath, Leamington and Harrogate will be very aware of how the Romans contributed to the advancement of human societies. The introduction over 2000 years ago of sewers, roads and elementary heating systems is credited to these early invaders of Britain.

Table 1.2 : Nineteenth-century economic development fuelled by technological innovations

Innovation	Innovator	Date
Steam engine	James Watt	1770–80
Iron boat	Isambard Kingdom Brunel	1820–45
Locomotive	George Stephenson	1829
Electromagnetic induction dynamo	Michael Faraday	1830–40
Electric light bulb	Thomas Edison and Joseph Swan	1879–90

The study of innovation

Innovation has long been argued to be the engine of growth. It is important to note that it can also provide growth almost regardless of the condition of the larger economy. Innovation has been a topic for discussion and debate for hundreds of years. Nineteenth-century economic historians observed that the acceleration in economic growth was the result of technological progress. However, little effort was directed towards understanding *how* changes in technology contributed to this growth.

Schumpeter (1939, 1942) was among the first economists to emphasise the importance of *new products* as stimuli to economic growth. He argued that the competition posed by new products was far more important than marginal changes in the *prices* of existing products. For example, economies are more likely to experience growth due to the development of products such as new computer software or new pharmaceutical drugs than owing to reductions in prices of existing products such as telephones or motor cars. Indeed, early observations suggested that economic development does not occur in any regular manner, but seemed to occur in 'bursts' or waves of activity, thereby indicating the important influence of external factors on economic development.

A review of the history of economic growth

The classical economists of the eighteenth and nineteenth centuries believed that technological change and capital accumulation were the engines of growth. This belief was based on the conclusion that productivity growth causes population growth, which in turn causes productivity to fall. Today's theory of population growth is very different to these early attempts at understanding economic growth. It argues that rising incomes slow the population growth because they increase the rate opportunity cost of having children. Hence, as technology advances productivity and incomes grow.

Joseph Schumpeter was the founder of modern growth theory and is regarded as one of the world's greatest economists. In the 1930s he was the first to realise that the development and diffusion of new technologies by profit-seeking entrepreneurs formed the source of economic progress. Robert Solow, who was a student of Schumpeter, advanced his professor's theories in the 1950s and won the Nobel Prize for economic science. Paul Romer has developed these theories further and is responsible for the modern theory of economic growth, sometimes called neo-Schumpeterian economic growth theory, which argues that sustained economic growth arises from competition among firms. Firms try to increase their profits by devoting resources to creating new products and developing new ways of making existing products. It is this economic theory that underpins most innovation management and new product development theories.

Adapted from: Parkin et al. (1997)

This macro view of innovation as cyclical can be traced back to the mid-nineteenth century. It was Marx who first suggested that innovations could be associated with waves of economic growth. Since then others such as Schumpeter (1939), Kondratieff (1935/51), Abernathy and Utterback (1978) have argued the long-wave theory of innovation. Kondratieff was unfortunately imprisoned by Stalin for his views on economic growth theories, because they conflicted with those of Marx. Marx suggested that capitalist economies would eventually decline, whereas Kondratieff argued that they would experience waves of growth and decline. Abernathy and Utterback (1978) contended that at the birth of any industrial sector there is radical product innovation which is then followed by radical innovation in production processes, followed, in turn, by widespread incremental innovation. This view was once popular and seemed to reflect the life cycles of many industries. It has, however, failed to offer any understanding of *how* to achieve innovative success.

After World War II economists began to take an even greater interest in the causes of economic growth (Harrod, 1949; Domar, 1946). One of the most important influences on innovation seemed to be industrial research and development. After all, during the war, military research and development (R&D) had produced significant technological advances and innovations, including radar, aerospace and new weapons. A period of rapid growth in expenditure by countries on R&D was to follow, exemplified by US President Kennedy's 1960 speech outlining his vision of getting a man on the moon before the end of the decade. But economists soon found that there was no *direct* correlation between R&D spending and national rates of economic growth. It was clear that the linkages were more complex than first thought (this issue is explored more fully in Chapter 7).

There was a need to understand *how* science and technology affected the economic system. The neo-classical economics approach had not offered any explanations. A series of studies of innovation were undertaken in the 1950s which concentrated on the internal characteristics of the innovation process within the economy. A feature of these studies was that they adopted a cross-discipline approach, incorporating economics, organisational behaviour and business and management. The studies looked at:

- the generation of new knowledge
- application of this knowledge in the development of products and processes
- commercial exploitation of these products and services in terms of financial income generation.

In particular, these studies revealed that firms behaved differently (*see* Simon, 1957; Woodward, 1965; Carter and Williams, 1959). This led to the development of a new theoretical framework that attempted to understand how firms managed the above, and why some firms appeared to be more successful than others. Later studies in the 1960s were to confirm these initial findings and uncover significant differences in organisational characteristics (Myers and Marquis, 1969; Burns and Stalker, 1961; Cyert and March, 1963). Hence, the new framework placed more emphasis on the firm and its internal activities than had previously been the case. The firm and how it used its resources was now seen as the key influences on innovation.

Neo-classical economics is a theory of economic growth that explains how savings, investments and growth respond to population growth and technological change. The rate of technological change influences the rate of economic growth, but economic growth does not influence technological change. Rather, technological change is determined by chance. Thus population growth and technological change are exogenous. Also, neo-classical economic theory tends to concentrate on industry or economy-wide performance. It tends to ignore differences among firms in the same line of business. Any differences are assumed to reflect differences in the market environments that the organisations face. That is, differences are not achieved through choice but reflect differences in the situations in which firms operate. In contrast, research within business management and strategy focuses on these differences and the decisions that have led to them. Furthermore, the activities that take place within the firm that enable one firm seemingly to perform better than another, given the same economic and market conditions, has been the focus of much research effort since the 1960s.

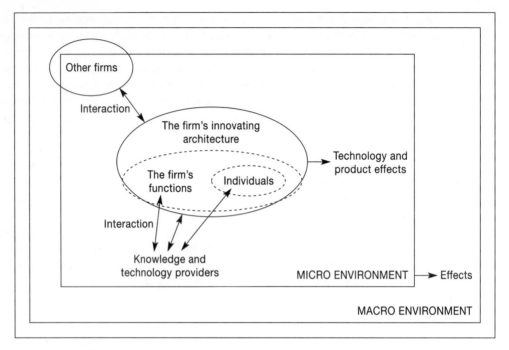

Figure 1.1 : General overview of the innovation process

The Schumpeterian view sees firms as different – it is the way a firm manages its resources over time and develops capabilities that influences its innovation performance. The varying emphasis placed by different disciplines on explaining how innovation occurs is brought together in the framework in Figure 1.1. This overview of the innovation process includes an economic perspective, a business management strategy perspective and organisational behaviour which attempts to look at the internal activities. It also recognises that firms form relationships with other firms and trade, compete and co-operate with each other. It further recognises that the activities of individuals within the firm also affect the process of innovation.

Each firm's unique organisational architecture represents the way it has constructed itself over time. This comprises its internal design, including its functions and the relationships it has built up with suppliers, competitors, customers etc. This framework recognises that these will have a considerable impact on a firm's innovative performance. So too will the way it manages its individual functions and its employees or individuals. These are separately identified within the framework as being influential in the innovation process.

Recent and contemporary studies

As the twentieth century draws to a close there is probably as much debate and argument concerning innovation and what contributes to innovative performance as a hundred years ago. This debate has, nonetheless, progressed our understanding of the area of innovation management. It was Schumpeter who argued that modern firms equipped with R&D laboratories have become the central innovative actors. Since his work others have contributed to the debate (Chandler, 1962; Nelson and Winter, 1982; Cohen and Levinthal, 1990; Hamel and Prahalad, 1990; Pavitt, 1990). This emerging Schumpeterian or evolutionary theory of dynamic firm capabilities is having a significant impact on the study of business and management today. Success in the future, as in the past, will surely lie, in the ability to acquire and utilise knowledge and apply this to the development of new products. Uncovering how to do this remains one of today's most pressing management problems.

The need to view innovation in an organisational context

During the early part of the nineteenth century manufacturing firms were largely family oriented and concentrated their resources on one activity. For example, one firm would produce steel from iron ore, another would roll this into sheet steel for use by, say, a manufacturer of cooking utensils. These would then be delivered to shops for sale. Towards the latter part of the century these small enterprises were gradually replaced by large firms who would perform a much wider variety of activities. The expansion in manufacturing activities was simultaneously matched by an expansion in administrative activities. This represented the beginnings of the development of the diversified functional enterprise. The world expansion in trade during the early part of the twentieth century saw the quest for new markets by developing a wide range of new products (Chandler, 1962).

Unfortunately, many of the studies of innovation have treated it as an artefact that is somehow detached from knowledge and skills and not embedded in knowhow. This inevitably leads to a simplified understanding, if not a misunderstanding, of what constitutes innovation. This section shows why innovation needs to be viewed in the context of organisations and as a process within organisations.

The diagram in Figure 1.1 shows how a number of different disciplines contribute to our understanding of the innovation process. It is important to note that firms do not operate in a vacuum. They trade with each other, they work together in some areas and compete in others. Hence, the role of other firms is a major factor in understanding innovation. As discussed earlier, economics clearly has an important role to play. So too does organisational behaviour as we try to understand what activities are necessary to ensure success. Studies of management will also make a significant contribution to specific areas such as marketing, R&D, manufacturing operations and competition.

As has been suggested, in previous centuries it was easier in many ways to mobilise the resources necessary to develop and commercialise a product, largely because the resources required were, in comparison, minimal. Today, however, the resources required, in terms of knowledge, skills, money and market experience, mean that significant innovations are synonymous with organisations. Indeed, it is worthy of note that more recent innovations and scientific developments, such as significant medical discoveries like DNA or computer software and hardware developments, are associated with organisations rather than individuals (*see* Table 1.3). Moreover, the

Table 1.3 : More recent technological innovations

Date	New product	Responsible organisation
1930s	Polythene	ICI
1945	Ballpoint pen	Reynolds International Pen Company
1950s	Manufacturing process: float glass	Pilkington
1970/80s	Ulcer treatment drug: Zantac	Glaxo
1970/80s	Photocopying	Xerox
1980s	Personal computer	Apple Computer
1980/90s	Computer operating system: Windows 95	Microsoft

increasing depth of our understanding of science inhibits the breadth of scientific study. In the early part of this century, for example, ICI was regarded as a world leader in chemistry. Now it is almost impossible for chemical companies to be scientific leaders in all areas of chemistry. The large companies have specialised in particular areas. This is true of many other industries. Even university departments are having to concentrate their resources on particular areas of science. They are no longer able to offer teaching and research in all fields. In addition, the creation, development and commercial success of new ideas require a great deal of input from a variety of specialist sources and often vast amounts of money. Hence, today's innovations are associated with groups of people or companies. Innovation is invariably a team game. This will be explored more fully in Chapter 3.

Individuals in the innovation process

Figure 1.1 identifies individuals as a key component of the innovation process. Within organisations it is individuals who define problems, have ideas and perform creative linkages and associations that lead to inventions. Moreover, within organisations it is individuals in the role of managers who decide what activities should be undertaken, the amount of resources to be deployed and how they should be carried out. This has led to the development of so-called key individuals in the innovation process such as inventor, entrepreneur, business sponsor, etc. These will be discussed in detail in Chapter 2.

Problems of definition and vocabulary

While there are many arguments and debates in virtually all fields of management, it seems that this is particularly the case in innovation management. Very often these centre on semantics. This is especially so when innovation is viewed as a single event. When viewed as a *process*, however, the differences are less substantive. At the heart of this book is the thesis that innovation needs to be viewed as a process. If one accepts that inventions are new discoveries, new ways of doing things, and that products are the eventual outputs from the inventions, that process from new discovery to eventual product is the innovation process. A useful analogy would be education, where qualifications are the formal outputs of the education process. Education, like innovation, is not and cannot be viewed as an event.

Arguments become stale when we attempt to define terms such as new, creativity or discovery. It often results in a game of semantics. First, what is new to one company may be 'old hat' to another. Second, how does one judge success in terms of commercial gain or scientific achievement? Are they both not valid and justified goals in themselves? Third, it is context dependent – what is viewed as a success today may be viewed as a failure in the future. We need to try to understand how to encourage innovation in order that we may help to develop more successful new products (this point is explored in Chapter 6).

Entrepreneurship

In the US the subject of innovation management is often covered in terms of 'entrepreneurship'. Indeed, there are many courses available for students in US business schools on this topic. In a study of past and future research on the subject of entrepreneurship, Low and MacMillan (1988) define it as 'the process of planning, organising, operating, and assuming the risk of a business venture'.

It is the analysis of the role of the individual entrepreneur that distinguishes the study of entrepreneurship from that of innovation management. Furthermore, it is starting small businesses and growing them into large and successful businesses that is the focus of attention of those studying entrepreneurship. For example, the *Sunday Times* recently reported the rise of a successful property entrepreneur, Minerva's Andrew Rosenfeld. He is responsible for building Minerva into a £200m property business in which he has a £50m stake (*Sunday Times*, 1998).

Innovation and invention

Many people confuse these terms. Indeed, if you were to ask people for an explanation you would collect a diverse range of definitions. It is true that innovation is the first cousin of invention, but they are not identical twins that can be interchanged. Hence, it is important to establish clear meanings for them.

Innovation itself is a very broad concept that can be understood in a variety of ways. One of the more comprehensive definitions is offered by Myers and Marquis (1969):

> **Innovation is not a single action but a total process of interrelated sub processes. It is not just the conception of a new idea, nor the invention of a new device, nor the development of a new market. The process is all these things acting in an integrated fashion.**

It is important to clarify the use of the term 'new' in the context of innovation. Rogers and Shoemaker (1971) do this eloquently:

It matters little, as far as human behaviour is concerned, whether or not an idea is 'objectively' new as measured by the lapse of time since its first use or discovery ... If the idea seems new and different to the individual, it is an innovation.

Most writers, including those above, distinguish innovation from invention by suggesting that innovation is concerned with the *commercial and practical application* of ideas or inventions. Invention, then, is the conception of the idea, whereas innovation is the subsequent translation of the invention into the economy (US Dept of Commerce, 1967). The following simple equation helps to show the relationship between the two terms:

Innovation = theoretical conception + technical invention + commercial exploitation

However, all the terms in this equation will need explanation in order to avoid confusion. The *conception* of new ideas is the starting point for innovation. A new idea by itself, while interesting, is neither an invention nor an innovation, it is merely a concept or a thought or collection of thoughts. The process of converting intellectual thoughts into a tangible new artefact (usually a product or process) is an *invention*. This is where science and technology usually play a significant role. At this stage inventions need to be combined with hard work by many different people to convert them into products that will improve company performance. These later activities represent *exploitation*. However, it is the *complete* process that represents *innovation*. This introduces the notion that innovation is a process with a number of distinctive features that have to be managed. This is the view taken by this book. To summarise, then, innovation depends on inventions but inventions need to be harnessed to commercial activities before they can contribute to the growth of an organisation. Thus:

> Innovation is the management of all the activities involved in the process of idea generation, technology development, manufacturing and marketing of a new (or improved) product or manufacturing process or equipment.

This definition of innovation as a management process also offers a distinction between an innovation and a product, the latter being the output of innovation. The following example should help to clarify the differences.

An example of an invention

Scientists and development engineers at a household cleaning products company had been working for many months on developing a new lavatory cleaning product. They had developed a liquid that when sprayed into the toilet pan, on contact with water, would fizz and sparkle. The effect was to give the impression of a tough, active cleaning product. The company applied for a patent and further developments and market research were planned.

However, initial results both from technical and market specialists led to the abandonment of the project. The preliminary market feedback suggested a fear of such a product on the part of consumers. This was because the fizz and sparkle looked too dramatic and frightening. Furthermore, additional technical research revealed a short shelf life for the mixture. This is a clear example of an invention that did not progress beyond the organisation to a commercial product.

It is necessary at this point to cross-reference these discussions with the practical realities of managing a business today. The senior vice-president for research and development at 3M, one of the most highly respected and innovative organisations, recently defined innovation as:

Creativity: the thinking of novel and appropriate ideas.
Innovation: the successful implementation of those ideas within an organisation.

Successful and unsuccessful innovations

There is often a great deal of confusion surrounding innovations that are not commercially successful. A famous example would be the Sinclair C5. This was a small, electrically driven tricycle or car. Unfortunately for Clive Sinclair, the individual behind the development of the product, it was not commercially successful. Commercial failure, however, does not relegate an innovation to an invention. Using the definition established above, the fact that the product progressed passed from the drawing board and into the marketplace makes it an innovation – albeit an unsuccessful one.

Different types of innovations

Industrial innovation does not only include major (radical) innovations but also minor (incremental) technological advances. Indeed, the definition offered above suggests that successful commercialisation of the innovation may involve considerably wider organisational changes. For example, the introduction of a radical technological innovation, such as Polaroid's Instamatic camera, invariably results in substantial internal organisational changes. In this case substantial changes occurred with the manufacturing, marketing and sales functions. The business decided to concentrate on the Instamatic camera market, rather than on that for the traditional 26mm and 35mm film, thus forcing changes on the production function. Similarly, marketing had to employ extra sales staff to educate and reassure retail outlets that the new product would not cannibalise their film-processing business. Furthermore, a new business had to be established to produce and distribute the unique film required by the instamatic camera – a service innovation?

Hence, technological innovation can be accompanied by additional managerial and organisational changes, often referred to as innovations. This presents a far more blurred picture and begins to widen the definition of innovation to include virtually any organisational or managerial change. Table 1.4 shows a typology of innovations.

Innovation was defined earlier in this section as the application of knowledge. It is this notion that lies at the heart of all types of innovations, be they product, process or service. It is also worthy of note that many studies have suggested that product innovations are soon followed by process innovations in what they describe as an industry innovation cycle (*see* Chapter 5). Furthermore, it is common to associate innovation with physical change, but many changes introduced within organisations involve very little physical change. Rather, it is the activities performed by individuals that change. A good example of this is the adoption of so-called Japanese management techniques by automobile manufacturers in Europe and the US.

Table 1.4 : A typology of innovations

Type of innovation	Example
Product innovation	The development of a new or improved product
Process innovation	The development of a new manufacturing process such as Pilkington's float glass process
Organisational innovation	A new venture division, a new internal communication system, introduction of a new accounting procedure
Management innovation	TQM (total quality management) systems, BPR (business process re-engineering), introduction of SAP R3
Production innovation	Quality circles, just-in-time (JIT) manufacturing system, new production planning software, e.g. MRP II, new inspection system
Commercial/marketing innovation	New financing arrangements, new sales approach, e.g. direct marketing
Service innovation	Telephone financial services

It is necessary to stress at the outset that this book concentrates on the management of product innovation. This does not imply that the list of innovations above are less significant; this focus has been chosen to ensure clarity and to facilitate the study of innovation.

Technology and science

We also need to consider the role played by *science and technology* in innovation. The continual fascination with science and technology at the end of the nineteenth century and subsequent growth in university teaching and research have led to the development of many new strands of science. The proliferation of scientific journals over the past thirty years demonstrates the rapidly evolving nature of science and technology. The scientific literature seems to double in quantity every five years (Rothwell and Zegveld, 1985).

Science can be defined as systematic and formulated knowledge. There are clearly significant differences between science and technology. Technology is often seen as being the application of science. It has been defined in many ways (Lefever, 1992). It is important to remember that technology is not an accident of nature. It is the product of deliberate action by human beings. The following definition is suggested:

Technology is knowledge applied to products or production processes.

No definition is perfect and the above is no exception. It does, however, provide a good starting point from which to view technology with respect to innovation. It is important to note that technology, like education, cannot be purchased off the shelf, like a can of tomatoes. It is embedded in knowledge and skills.

In a lecture given to the Royal Society in 1992 the former chairman of Sony, Akio Morita, suggested that, unlike engineers, scientists are held in high esteem. This, he suggested, is because science provides us with information which was previously unknown. Yet technology comes from employing and *manipulating science* into concepts, processes and devices. These, in turn, can be used to make our life or work more efficient, convenient and powerful. Hence, it is technology, as an *outgrowth of science*, that fuels the industrial engine. And it is *engineers* and not scientists who make technology happen. In Japan, he argued, you will notice that almost every major manufacturer is run by an engineer or technologist. However, in the UK, some manufacturing companies are led by CEOs who do not understand the technology that goes into their own products. Indeed, many UK corporations are headed by chartered accountants. With the greatest respect to accountants, their central concerns are statistics and figures of *past* performance. How can an accountant reach out and grab the future if he or she is always looking at *last* quarter's results (Morita, 1992)?

The above represents the personal views of an influential senior figure within industry. There are many leading industrialists, economists and politicians who would concur (Hutton, 1995). But there are equally many who would profoundly disagree. The debate on improving economic innovative performance is one of the most important in the field of political economics.

Popular views of innovation

Science, technology and innovation have received a great deal of popular media coverage over the years, from Hollywood and Disney movies to best-selling novels (*see* Figure 1.2). This is probably because science and technology can help turn vivid imaginings into a possibility. The end result, however, is a simplified image of scientific discoveries and innovations. It usually consists of a lone professor, with a mass of white hair, working away in his garage and stumbling, by accident, on a major new discovery. Through extensive trial and error, usually accompanied by dramatic experiments, this is eventually developed into an amazing invention. This is best demonstrated in the blockbuster movie *Back to the Future*. Christopher Lloyd plays the eccentric scientist and Michael J. Fox his young, willing accomplice. Together they are involved in an exciting journey that enables Fox to travel back in time and influence the future.

Cartoons have also contributed to a misleading image of the innovation process. Here, the inventor, an eccentric scientist, is portrayed with a glowing lightbulb above his head, as a flash of inspiration results in a new scientific discovery. We have all seen and laughed at these funny cartoons.

This humorous and popular view of inventions and innovations has been reinforced over the years and continues to occur in the popular press. Many industrialists and academics have argued that this simple view of a complex phenomenon has caused immense harm to the understanding of science and technology.

Figure 1.2 : The popular view of science

Models of innovation

Traditional arguments about innovation have centred on two schools of thought. On the one hand, the social deterministic school argued that innovations were the result of a combination of external social factors and influences, such as demographic changes, economic influences and cultural changes. The argument was that when the conditions were 'right' innovations would occur. On the other hand, the individualistic school argued that innovations were the result of unique individual talents and such innovators are born. Closely linked to the individualistic theory is the important role played by serendipity.

Serendipity

Many studies of historical cases of innovation have highlighted the importance of the unexpected discovery. The role of serendipity or luck is offered as an explanation. As we have seen, this view is also reinforced in the popular media. It is, after all, every one's dream that they will accidentally uncover a major new invention leading to fame and fortune.

On closer inspection of these historical cases, serendipity is rare indeed. After all, in order to recognise the significance of an advance one would need to have some prior knowledge in that area. Most discoveries are the result of people who have had a fascination with a particular area of science or technology and it is following extended efforts on their part that advances are made. Discoveries may not be expected, but in the words of Louis Pasteur, 'chance favours the prepared mind'.

Linear models

It was US economists after World War II who championed the linear model of science and innovation. Since then, largely because of its simplicity, this model has taken a firm grip on people's views on how innovation occurs. Indeed, it dominated science and industrial policy for 40 years. It was only in the 1980s that management schools around the world seriously began to challenge the sequential linear process. The recognition that innovation occurs through the interaction of the science base (dominated by universities and industry), technological development (dominated by industry) and the needs of the market was a significant step forward (*see* Figure 1.3). The explanation of the interaction of these activities forms the basis of models of innovation today.

There is, of course, a great deal of debate and disagreement about precisely what activities influence innovation and, more importantly, the internal processes that affect a company's ability to innovate.

Nonetheless, there is broad agreement that it is the linkages between these key components that will produce successful innovation. Importantly, the devil is in the detail. From a European perspective an area that requires particular attention is the linkage between the science base and technological development. The European Union (EU) believes that European universities have not established effective links with industry, whereas in the US universities have been working closely with industry for many years.

As explained above, the innovation process has traditionally been viewed as a sequence of separable stages or activities. There are two basic variations of this model for product innovation. First, and most crudely, there is the technology-driven model (often referred to as 'technology push') where it is assumed that scientists make unexpected discoveries, technologists apply them to develop product ideas and engineers and designers turn them into prototypes for testing. It is left to manufacturing to devise ways of producing the products efficiently. Finally, marketing and sales will promote the product to the potential consumer. In this model the marketplace was a passive recipient for the fruits of R&D. This technology-push model dominated industrial policy after World War II (*see* Figure 1.4). While this model of innovation can be applied to a few cases, most notably the pharmaceutical industry, it is not applicable in many other instances; in particular where the innovation process follows a different route.

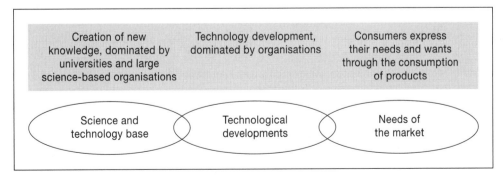

Figure 1.3 : Conceptual framework of innovation

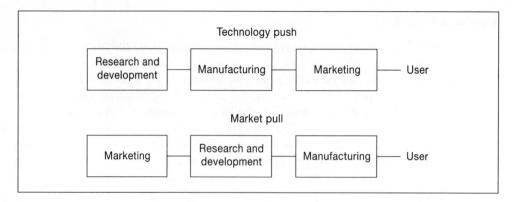

Figure 1.4 : Linear models of innovation

It was not until the 1970s that new studies of actual innovations suggested that the role of the marketplace was influential in the innovation process (von Hippel, 1978). This led to the second linear model, the 'market-pull' model of innovation. The customer need-driven model emphasises the role of marketing as an initiator of new ideas resulting from close interactions with customers. These, in turn, are conveyed to R&D for design and engineering and then to manufacturing for production.

Simultaneous coupling model

Whether innovations are stimulated by technology, customer need, manufacturing or a host of other factors, including competition, misses the point. The models above concentrate on what is driving the downstream efforts rather than on *how* innovations occur (Galbraith, 1982). The linear model is only able to offer an explanation of *where* the initial stimulus for innovation was born, that is, where the trigger for the idea or need was initiated. The simultaneous coupling model shown in Figure 1.5 suggests that it is the result of the simultaneous coupling of the knowledge within all three functions that will foster innovation. Furthermore, the point of commencement for innovation is not known in advance.

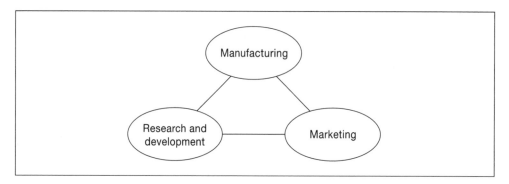

Figure 1.5 : The simultaneous coupling model

Interactive model

The interactive model develops this idea further (*see* Figure 1.6) and links together the technology-push and market-pull models. It emphasises that innovations occur as the result of the interaction of the marketplace, the science base and the organisation's capabilities. Like the coupling model, there is no explicit starting point. The use of information flows is used to explain how innovations transpire and that they can arise from a wide variety of points.

While still oversimplified, this is a more comprehensive representation of the innovation process. It can be regarded as a logically sequential, though not necessarily continuous, process that can be divided into a series of functionally distinct but interacting and interdependent stages (Rothwell and Zegveld, 1985). The overall innovation process can be thought of as a complex set of communication paths over which knowledge is transferred. These paths include internal and external linkages. The innovation process outlined in Figure 1.6 represents the organisation's capabilities and its linkages with both the marketplace and the science base. Organisations that are able to manage this process effectively will be successful at innovation.

At the centre of the model are the organisational functions of R&D, engineering and design, manufacturing and marketing and sales. While at first this may appear to be a linear model, the flow of communication is not necessarily linear. There is provision for feedback. Also, linkages with the science base and the marketplace occur between all functions, not just with R&D or marketing. For example, as often happens, it may be the manufacturing function which initiates a design improvement that leads to the introduction of either a different material or the eventual development by R&D of a new material. Finally, the generation of ideas is shown to be dependent on inputs from three basic components (as outlined in Figure 1.2): organisation capabilities; the needs of the marketplace; the science and technology base.

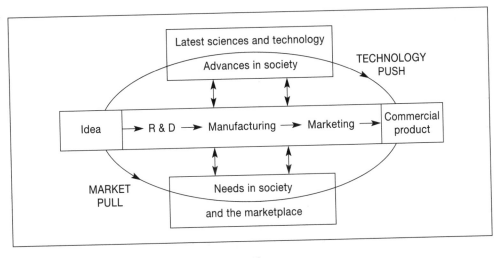

Figure 1.6 : Interactive model of innovation

Source: adapted from Rothwell and Zegveld (1985)

Table 1.5 : Table showing the chronological development of models of innovation

Date	Model	Characteristics
1950/60s	Technology push	Simple linear sequential process. Emphasis on R&D. The market is a recipient of the fruits of R&D.
1970s	Market pull	Simple linear sequential process. Emphasis on marketing. The market is the source for directing R&D. R&D has a reactive role.
1980s	Coupling model	Emphasis on integrating R&D and marketing.
1980/90s	Interactive model	Combinations of push and pull.

Source: based on Rothwell (1992)

Table 1.5 summarises the historical development of the dominant models of the industrial innovation process.

Innovation as a management process

The preceding sections have revealed that innovation is not a singular event, but a series of activities that are linked in some way to the others. This may be described as a process and involves (Kelly *et al.*, 1978):

1 a response to either a need or an opportunity that is context dependent

2 a creative effort that if successful results in the introduction of novelty

3 the need for further changes.

Usually in trying to capture this complex process the simplification has led to misunderstandings. The simple linear model of innovation can be applied to only a few innovations and is more applicable to certain industries than others. The pharmaceutical industry characterises much of the technology-push model. Other industries, like the food industry, are better represented by the market-pull model. For most industries and organisations innovations are the result of a mixture of the two. Managers working within these organisations have the difficult task of trying to manage this complex process.

A framework for the management of innovation

Industrial innovation and new product development have evolved considerably from their early beginnings outlined above. However, establishing departmental functions to perform the main tasks of business strategy, R&D, manufacturing and marketing does not solve the firm's problems. Indeed, as we have seen, innovation is extremely complex and involves the effective management of a variety of different activities. It is precisely how the process is managed that needs to be examined.

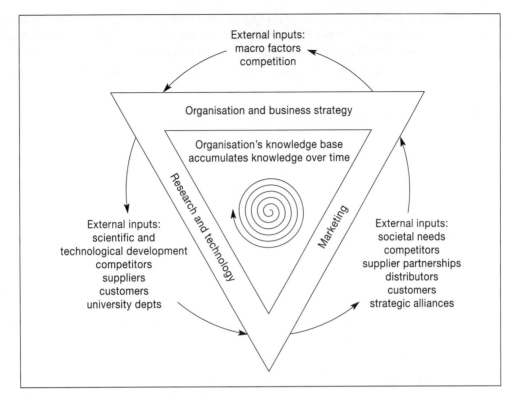

Figure 1.7 : Innovation management framework

A framework is presented in Figure 1.7 that helps to illustrate innovation as a management process. This is simply an aid in describing the main factors which need to be considered if innovation is to be successfully managed. It helps to show that while the interactions of the functions inside the organisation are important, so too are the interactions of those functions with the external environment. Scientists and engineers within the firm will be continually interacting with fellow scientists in universities and other firms about scientific and technological developments. Similarly, the marketing function will need to interact with suppliers, distributors, customers and competitors to ensure that the day-to-day activities of understanding customer needs and getting products to customers are achieved. Business planners and senior management will likewise communicate with a wide variety of firms and other external institutions, such as government departments, suppliers and customers. All these information flows contribute to the wealth of knowledge held by the organisation. Recognising this, capturing and utilising it to develop successful new products forms the difficult management process of innovation.

Within any organisation there are likely to be many different functions. Depending on the nature of the business, some functions will be more influential than others. The framework shown in Figure 1.7 identifies three main functions: marketing, research and manufacturing and business planning. Historical studies have identified these functions as the most influential in the innovation process. Whether one lists three or seven functions misses the point, which is that it is the interaction of these internal functions and the flow of knowledge between them that needs to be facilitated (Trott, 1993). Similarly, as shown on the framework, effective communication with the external environment also requires encouragement and support.

The need to share and exchange knowledge

The framework in Figure 1.7 emphasises the importance placed on interaction (both formal and informal) within the innovation process. Indeed, innovation has been described as an information-creation process that arises out of social interaction. In effect, the firm provides a structure within which the creative process is located (Nonaka and Kenney, 1991).

These interactions provide the opportunity for thoughts, potential ideas and views to be shared and exchanged. However, we are often unable to explain what we normally do; we can be competent without being able to offer a theoretical account of our actions (Polanyi, 1966). This is referred to as 'tacit knowledge'. A great deal of technical skill is knowhow and much industrial innovation occurs through on-the-spot experiments, a kind of action-oriented research with *ad hoc* modifications during step-by-step processes, through which existing repertoires are extended. Such knowledge can only be learned through practice and experience. This view has recently found support from a study of Japanese firms (Nonaka, 1991) where the creation of new knowledge within an organisation depends on tapping the tacit and often highly subjective insights, intuitions and hunches of individual employees and making those insights available for testing and use by the organisation as a whole. This implies that certain knowledge and skills, embodied in the term 'knowhow', are not easily understood; moreover they are less able to be communicated. This would suggest that to gain access to such knowledge one may have to be practising in this or related areas of knowledge. Cohen and Levinthal (1990) refer to this condition as 'lockout', suggesting that failure to invest in research and technology will limit an organisation's ability to capture technological opportunities: 'once off the technological escalator it's difficult to get back on'.

In addition to informal interactions, the importance of formal interactions is also highlighted. There is a substantial amount of research stressing the need for a 'shared language' within organisations to facilitate internal communication (Allen; 1977; Tushman, 1978). The arguments are presented along the following lines. If all actors in the organisation share the same specialised language, they will be effective in their communication. Hence, there needs to be an overlap of knowledge in order for communication to occur. Such arguments have led to developments in cross-functional interfaces, for example between R&D, design, manufacturing and marketing. Concurrent engineering is an extension of this; in this particular case a small team consisting of a member from each of the various functional departments manages the design, development, manufacture and marketing of a product (*see* Chapter 7 for more on concurrent engineering).

Such thinking is captured in the framework outlined in Figure 1.7. It stresses the importance of interaction and communication within and between functions and with the external environment. This networking structure allows lateral communication, helping managers and their staff unleash creativity. This framework emphasises the importance of informal and formal networking across all functions.

This introduces a tension between the need for diversity, on the one hand, in order to generate novel linkages and associations, and the need for commonality, on the other, to facilitate effective internal communication. Clearly, there will be an organisational trade-off between diversity and commonality of knowledge across individuals.

Introducing organisational heritage

Finally, the centre of the framework is represented as organisational heritage, sometimes referred to as the organisational knowledge base. This does not mean the culture of the organisation. It represents a combination of the organisation's knowledge base (established and built up over the years of operating) and the organisation's unique architecture (explained above). This organisational heritage represents for many firms a powerful competitive advantage that enables them to compete with other firms. For Marks and Spencer it is its customer service and customer relations, developed and built up over decades, that provides the company with a powerful competitive advantage. ICI's organisational heritage is dominated by its continual investment over almost a hundred years in science and technology and the high profile given to science and technology within its businesses. For Unilever, its organisational heritage can be said to lie in its brand management skills and knowhow developed over many years. These heritages cannot be ignored or dismissed as irrelevant when trying to understand how companies manage their innovative effort.

This framework will be used as a navigational map to help guide readers through this complex field of study. Very often product innovation is viewed from purely a marketing perspective with little, if any, consideration of the R&D function and the difficulties of managing science and technology. Likewise, many manufacturing and technology approaches to product innovation have previously not taken sufficient notice of the needs of the customer. Finally, the organisational heritage of the firm will influence its future decisions regarding the markets in which it will operate. The point here is that firms do not have a completely free choice. What they do in the future will depend to some extent on what they have done in the past.

CASE STUDY

Part one:

Responding to 'green' pressure and how innovation helped ICI[1]

This case study demonstrates why innovation should be viewed as a management process. It shows how a wide variety of internal and external inputs affect the process. The story presented shows how a business responds to an environmental threat by developing a new range of products.

▶

[1] This case has been written as a basis for class discussion rather than to illustrate effective or ineffective managerial or administrative behaviour. It has been prepared from a variety of published sources, as indicated, and from observations.

▶ *Introduction*

The headlines in the morning papers carried a now familiar story: 'The green challenge'. It was the morning after the spring 1989 European elections. The previous day 15 per cent of people in the UK had voted for the Green Party. Compared with the rest of Europe, most notably Germany, this was not unusual, but here in the UK nothing like this had happened before. Environmental concerns were no longer a fringe issue, important only to those who wore sandals and their hair long. This was now a mainstream issue that all political parties – and companies – would have to address.

Since the latter part of the nineteenth century the ICI plants based around Runcorn, Cheshire in the North West of England had been producing chlorine derivative products. These huge plants, that lit up the Cheshire coast at night like Christmas decorations, had delivered employment to generations of families in the area. Suddenly discussions in the local pubs and corner shops were dominated by talk of their closure.

Of all the ICI businesses it was the Chlor-chemicals businesses and the Solvents business in particular that was considered at most threat from the environmental legislation and mounting 'green' pressure. Mainly because the general public were unable immediately to recognise the need for these industrial solvents, the industry was receiving intense criticism from sections of the popular press. Much of this was inaccurate and very often out of date.

The solvents business: the background

The Chlor-chemicals business was the main business of the United Alkali Company Ltd which was one of four companies that founded Imperial Chemical Industries in 1926. The three other companies were at that time the largest British chemical companies of the day: Nobel Industries Ltd, Bruner Mond & Company Ltd and the British Dyestuffs Corporation Ltd.

During the 1980s the Chlor-chemicals business was the fourth largest producer of chlorine in the world and the second largest in Europe, with a turnover of almost £400 million in 1989. As a business it was one of the most successful of the whole ICI group of companies. It produces a range of commodity chemicals to meet essential industrial applications. Included in this are chlorine for water treatment, dry cleaning and engineering solvents, together with polyvinyl chloride (PVC) and chlorinated paraffins.

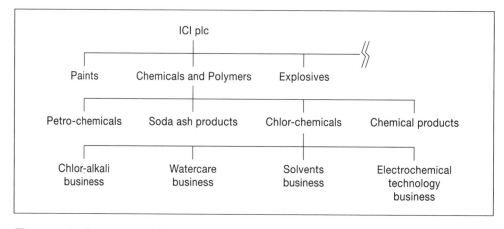

Figure 1.8 : Structure of Chlorine Chemicals business

The Solvents business has traditionally been a bulk chemical business supplying manufacturing industries. During periods of economic growth the business has been one of the most profitable within the ICI Chemicals and Polyners (C&P) group. In marketing terminology it is viewed as a successful 'cash cow'. That is, it requires minimal investment to produce high returns. The business operates in a very mature market. Consequently the market is highly competitive with many companies offering similar products. Within this type of environment the focus of the business is on increasing volume and attempting to protect, and where possible increase, profit margins on sales. Typically this would involve trying to reduce manufacturing and or distribution costs to try to generate larger profit margins.

Simply put, the operations of the Chlor-chemicals business involved taking rock salt, quarried from the local Cheshire hills, and turning this into chlorine and ethylene. The derivatives of these chemicals produced a wide range of chemical products that have been used in the UK for almost a hundred years. In particular, chlorine is used by the water industry to clean drinking water. Trichloroethylene is used by many manufacturers to clean components prior to welding or joining by industrial adhesives.

Around the world other chemical companies manufactured chlorine, for example Hoechst in Germany and Du Pont in the US. Partly due to high transportation costs, ICI was the market leader in the UK. One of its largest customer groups was the dry-cleaning industry which used large quantities of solvents in cleaning processes.

What could be done about 'green' pressure?

In an office at the corner of a three-storey glass building senior managers from ICI tossed the newspapers to one side and nodded in agreement. Whereas before they had only thought that the growing environmental pressure would force changes, now they were not only certain of change but also that the changes would be far reaching. Legislation in the 1980s and 1990s would have a significant impact on the range of products manufactured by chemical companies. The Montreal Protocol, to be implemented in 1996, was a case in point.

While many political and social commentators on television and radio were discussing their surprise at the level of support for environmental concerns, senior managers at ICI were not in a state of panic. ICI had operations all over the world, so they were well aware of the powerful 'green' lobby in other parts of Europe. This was especially so in Germany where the lobby is an influential political force with elected politicians. They were nonetheless concerned about 'knee-jerk reactions' on the part of government or other policy makers. Such reactions and subsequent legislation could imperil the future of the business, despite their best efforts. They tried to continue discussions without alarm and within an atmosphere of calm.

One of the managers continued to stare out of the window and suggested that maybe now was an appropriate time to withdraw from the solvents industry, especially as the public seemed opposed to such operations. This argument had been voiced before. Moreover, ICI had shut down businesses and withdrawn from many different markets over the years. Hence, the continuing discussions were balanced and forceful but not excited.

The impact of the legislation and the strength of the environmental lobby forced ICI senior managers to look closely at the long-term future prospects for the business. The damaging publicity arising from the manufacture of a product that is seen as harmful to the environment certainly did not fit easily with ICI's corporate image of being 'world class'. The arguments for withdrawing gracefully from this market were obvious. However, there is a less clear argument, but nevertheless a compelling one, to remain in the Solvents business. This hinges on the fact that, as one of the world's leading suppliers of solvents, ICI had an extremely large ▶

▶ customer base. Companies usually work extremely hard to build a customer base of this size and ICI's Solvents business was no exception. Yet the business was considering walking away from this loyal market. One could argue that these customers rely on ICI for many of their supplies; for example the dry-cleaning industry and many manufacturing industries which require the removal of oil and grease during manufacture. These customers would look to ICI Solvents to develop alternative cleaning products that they could use.

To remain in the business or to withdraw was the stark choice – or was there another alternative? Discussions, arguments and debate followed. Arguments did not polarise along functional lines, as is very often the case in science or knowledge based industries, where individuals are expected to contribute. Within each function views were divided. In the marketing function there were arguments for continuing to support a successful 'cash cow'. There were also arguments in favour of withdrawal because of the potential harm likely to be experienced by being associated with such a business. Arguments from within the Solvents business were less objective; after all, its future was at stake. Research and technology were equally divided, although there was support for remaining in the business by trying to develop more environmentally friendly products. This clearly had cost implications and would not solve the immediate problem of trying to manage the impending onslaught of criticism likely to be levelled at the company for being involved in the manufacture of so-called environmentally damaging products.

The senior management team listened carefully to what people said. In line with the management style within the organisation, part of its culture, they searched for consensus, but this proved difficult to find. Most of the senior management team were by now either staring at the notes in front of them or looking towards the Solvents business manager. His view was of particular significance. He, after all, knew the business better than anyone. The wider implications were clear.

A few concluding comments from around the table suggested a growing interest in the possibility of developing cleaner replacement products. This was partly influenced by the uncertainty of the long-term effects of the environmental lobby. There was some agreement that while the current, high-profile environmental concern would not go away it would probably fade. This should enable sufficient time for the Solvents business to develop some new products, providing it was able to fend off the onslaught from the environmental lobby. This decision would clearly not please everyone, but would enable the business to continue and provide an opportunity to secure a better future.

Interestingly, the managers went on to discuss not only the threats that the announcement of this news would bring to their business but also the benefits. Indeed, one of the problems the business had faced was trying to convince its customers of the need to consider some of the newer, 'cleaner' prototype products that ICI was developing. To date its customers had resisted change and rejected the new prototypes, insisting that while the solvents might damage the environment they also needed them for their manufacturing operations. The managers in the meeting were also aware that there were many in ICI who were also resistant to change. But if one thing was certain, it was that change was imminent.

How organisational heritage influences the future

Over the following few months senior managers within the Chlor-chemicals business continued discussions on what their choice of strategy should be. Several suggestions emerged:

1 Withdraw from the solvents market.

2 Try to develop a new range of 'green' cleaning products.

3 Continue with existing products until they are removed by legislation.

However, what a business decides to do in the future is partly influenced by what it has done in the past. Over the previous hundred years the Solvents business had built up in-depth knowledge of the solvents industry, including how it worked, customer requirements, the key players in the industry and how competitors operated. Customers had admitted in the past that they relied on ICI to provide them with effective, safe cleaning products. Indeed, the few weeks leading up to the crisis had witnessed a huge number of enquiries from customers concerned about rumours that ICI was pulling out of the business. In addition, the research and technology department had already considered different and alternative technologies. However, previously there had been insufficient demand for change and the new products it developed were not considered to offer any improvement, so customers had dismissed them. Nonetheless, the R&T function possessed research projects and technologies in this area, although many had turned out to be unworkable or ineffective. However, a considerable amount of knowledge had been gathered in this subject area. Furthermore, over the many years of working in this industry the company had built up relationships with other research groups and manufacturers in similar areas. The company was aware of technology that other companies and university research departments had been working on. At the very least, these other research projects should form the basis of new projects or joint development ventures with ICI. There was even the possibility that the technology ICI required to develop a new product was available in a university research department but had not yet been fully developed.

Armed with this knowledge, the business was in a position to reach out for the future and build on its past success. The combination of previous technical knowledge with strong motivation for change provided an opportunity to develop a new range of products for the solvents industry.

The development of a new range of aqueous cleaning products

The research and technology function within ICI had a long history of innovation and developing new products. Although recent successes had been scarce, research projects into alternative cleaning products had been undertaken. There was now, however, much more urgency. Indeed, it was thought that for the business to have a future the new products would have to be out in the market well ahead of the 1996 deadline.

The Solvents business's long association with the industry and its thorough understanding of the needs of the customer ensured that the business had a wealth of knowledge on which to draw. Even if the technology could not be developed internally, this combination of commercial and technical knowledge would enable it to access technology externally. Indeed, this was one area of research that received a great deal of attention. Existing patent databases were searched for possible technologies that could be used, adapted and modified to develop new cleaning products.

After only six months of concerted effort the results were promising. A combination of in-house and externally developed technology obtained through the use of licences and several joint ventures had led to several new prototype products. These were aqueous products, that ▶

▶   is, the cleaning product was a water-based solution. Additional research projects looked promising for the future. The reaction from customers had also been encouraging: at long last they were keen to test these new products. The long-term future of the business, while not secure, looked far more promising. The threat of closing the business had been removed, for the moment at least.

Discussion

This case study illustrates the numerous information flows that continually exist in the activities of virtually all businesses. The internal communication between functions and senior management was clearly evident. In situations of uncertainty it is only through accessing the relevant information that rational and informed decisions about the future can be made. Much of this information exists within the networks of relationships that businesses have built up over time. This information is collected and absorbed into the organisation via a wide variety of actors in a huge 'osmosis' process. Similarly, vast amounts of information flow between functions and within the same function. The ability to capture this information, recognise a commercial opportunity and associate it with technical capabilities demonstrates why innovation should be viewed as a management process.

Chapter summary

This initial chapter has sought to introduce the subject of innovation management and place it in context together with the theory of economic growth. One can quickly become snarled in stale academic debates about semantics if innovation is viewed as a single event, hence it is important to view it as a process. The chapter has also stressed the importance of understanding how firms manage innovation and how this can be more effectively achieved by adopting a management perspective.

The level of understanding of the subject of innovation has improved significantly over the past 50 years and a variety of models of innovation have emerged. The strengths and weaknesses of these were examined and a conceptual framework was presented that stressed the linkages and overlaps between internal departments and external organisations.

Questions for discussion

1   Many innovations today are associated with companies as opposed to individuals. Why is this, and what does it tell us?

2   What is wrong with the popular view of innovation as the creations of eccentric scientists?

3   Explain how organisational heritage influences the innovation process.

4   Explain how technology differs from science, yet still does not equal innovation.

5   What is the difference between an unsuccessful innovation and an invention?

6 To what extent do you agree with the controversial view presented by the chairman of Sony?

7 To what extent are industry standards (such as the VHS format) beneficial?

8 To what extent does Microsoft dictate prices and choice of software?

References

Abernathy, W.J. and Utterback, J. (1978) 'Patterns of industrial innovation', in Tushman, M.L. and Moore, W.L. *Readings in the Management of Innovation*, 97–108, HarperCollins, New York.

Allen, T.J. (1977) *Managing the Flow of Technology*, MIT Press, Cambridge, MA.

Burns, T. and Stalker, G.M. (1961) *The Management of Innovation*, Tavistock, London.

Carter, C.F. and Williams, B.R. (1959) 'The characteristics of technically progressive firms', *Journal of Industrial Economics*, March, 87–104.

Chandler, A.D. (1962) *Strategy and Structure: Chapters in the History of American Industrial Enterprise*. MIT Press: Cambridge, MA.

Cohen, W.M. and Levinthal, D.A. (1990) 'A new perspective on learning and innovation', *Administrative Science Quarterly*, 35 (1), 128–52.

Coyne, W.E. (1996) Innovation lecture given at the Royal Society, 5 March.

Cyert, R.M. and March, J.G. (1963) *A Behavioural Theory of the Firm*, Prentice-Hall, Englewood Cliffs, NJ.

Domar, D. (1946) 'Capital expansion, rate of growth and employment', *Econometra*, 14.

Freeman, C. (1982) *The Economics of Industrial Innovation*, 2nd edn, Frances Pinter, London.

Galbraith, J.R. (1982) 'Designing the innovative organisation', *Organisational Dynamics*, Winter, 3–24.

Harrod, R.F. (1949) 'An essay in dynamic theory', *Economic Journal*, 49 (1).

Hutton, W. (1995) *The State We're In*, Vintage, London.

Kelly, P. and Kranzberg, M. (eds) (1978) *Technological Innovation: A Critical Review Of Current Knowledge*, San Francisco Press.

Kondratieff, N.D. (1935/51) 'The long waves in economic life', *Review of Economic Statistics*, XVII, 6–105 (1935), reprinted in *Readings in Business Cycle Theory*, Richard D Irwin, Homewood, IL (1951).

Lefever, D.B. (1992) 'Technology transfer and the role of intermediaries'. PhD thesis, INTA, Cranfield Institute of Technology.

Low, M.B. and MacMillan, I.C. (1988) 'Entrepreneurship: past research and future challenges', *Journal of Management*, June, 139–59.

Morita, A. (1992) '"S" does not equal "T" and "T" does not equal "I"', Royal Society, February.

Myers, S. and Marquis, D.G. (1969) 'Successful industrial innovation: a study of factors underlying innovation in selected firms', National Science Foundation, NSF 69–17, Washington.

Nelson, R.R. and Winter, S. (1982) *An Evolutionary Theory of Economic Change*, Harvard University Press, Boston, MA.

Nonaka, I. (1991) 'The knowledge creating company'. *Harvard Business Review*, November–December, 96–104.

Nonaka, I. and Kenney, M. (1991) 'Towards a new theory of innovation management: a case study comparing Canon, Inc. and Apple Computer, Inc.', *Journal of Engineering and Technology Management*, 8, 67–83.

Parkin, M., Powell, M. and Matthews, K. (1997) *Economics*, 3rd edn, Addison-Wesley, Harlow.

Pavitt, K. (1990) 'What we know about the strategic management of technology', *California Management Review*, 32, 3, 17–26.

Polanyi, M. (1966) *The Tacit Dimension*, Routledge and Kegan Paul, London.

Prahalad, C.K. and Hamel, G. (1990) 'The core competence of the corporation', *Harvard Business Review*, 68(3) 79–91.

Rogers, E. and Shoemaker, R. (1972) *Communications of Innovations*, Free Press, New York.

Rothwell, R. and Zegveld, W. (1985) *Reindustrialisation and Technology*, Longman, London.

Rothwell, R. (1992) 'Successful industrial innovation: critical factors for the 1990s'. *R&D Management* (22) 3, 221–39.

Schumpeter, J.A. (1934) *The Theory of Economic Development*, Harvard University Press, Boston, MA.

Schumpeter, J.A. (1939) *Business Cycles*, McGraw-Hill, New York.

Schumpeter, J.A. (1942) *Capitalism, Socialism and Democracy*, Allen & Unwin, London.

Simon, H. (1957) *Administrative Behaviour*, The Free Press, New York.

Sunday Times (1998) 'Property whiz-kid who was to his manor born', Business 5, 25 January.

Trott, P. (1993) 'Inward technology transfer as an interactive process: a case study of ICI', PhD thesis, Cranfield University.

Tushman, M.L. (1978) 'Task characteristics and technical communication in research and development', *Academy of Management Review* 21, 624–45.

von Hippel, E. (1978) 'Users as innovators', *Technology Review*, 80 (3), 30–4.

Woodward, J. (1965) *Industrial Organisation: Theory and Practice*, 2nd edn, Oxford University Press.

Further reading

Byron, K. (1998) 'Invention and innovation', *Science and Public Affairs*, Summer, Royal Society.

Badden-Fuller, C. and Pitt, M. (eds) (1996) *Strategic Innovation*, Routledge, London.

Tidd, J., Bessant, J. and Pavitt, K. (1997) *Managing Innovation*, John Wiley & Sons, Chichester.

Tushman, M.L. and Moore, W.L. (eds) (1988) *Readings in the Management of Innovation*, HarperCollins, New York.

2

Managing innovation within firms

Introduction

Virtually all innovations, certainly major technological innovations such as pharmaceutical and automobile products, occur within organisations. The management of innovation within organisations forms the focus for this chapter. The study of organisations and their management is a very broad subject and no single approach provides all the answers. The identification of those factors and issues that affect the management of innovation within organisations are addressed in this chapter.

Learning objectives

When you have completed this chapter, you will be able to:

- Identify the main trends in the development of the management of organisations
- Explain the dilemma facing all organisations concerning the need for creativity and stability
- Recognise the difficulties of managing uncertainty
- Identify the activities performed by key individuals in the management of innovation
- Recognise the relationship between the activities performed and the organisational environment in promoting innovation.

Theories about organisations and innovation

The previous chapter outlined some of the difficulties in studying the field of innovation. In particular, it emphasised the need to view innovation as a management process within the context of the organisation. This was shown to be the case especially in a modern industrialised society where innovation is increasingly viewed as an *organisational activity*. This chapter tackles the difficult issue of managing innovation within organisations. To do this, it is necessary to understand the patterns of interaction and behaviour which represent the organisation.

The theory of organisations is a set of ideas drawn from many disciplines and lies beneath much of the study of innovation. In many ways organisation theory bridges pure social and behavioural sciences and management practices at the level of the organisation. As an applied science it examines the behaviour of organisations and provides useful information about how organisations respond to different management techniques and practices, hence its importance in understanding how the process of innovation is managed.

Given the diversity of the literature in this field, there are few clear prescriptions on what organisations need to do in order to manage innovation successfully. Nonetheless, there are numerous analytical frameworks and organisation-specific models of innovation. The literature can be classified into four dominant strands (Perrow, 1970) as shown in Figure 2.1.

Classical or scientific management perspective

The classical view of organisations took hold after the industrial revolution and the huge increase in world trade at the beginning of the twentieth century. It is built around traditional management concepts, bureaucratic theory (Weber, 1964) and scientific management (Taylor, 1947). This school of thought tends to view the organisation as an instrument for achieving established goals, in which members of

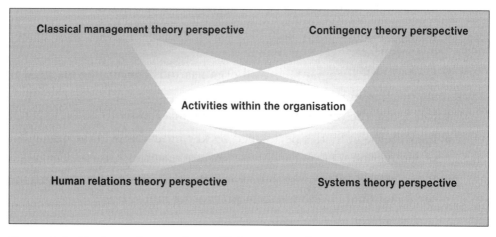

Figure 2.1 : The importance of a multiple-perspective approach

the organisation can be made to serve these goals by management's use of reward and motivation techniques. It assumes that all tasks confronting the organisation can be rationalised. Hence, organisations should be designed to ensure a predictable flow of work. Specialisation of tasks is employed to maximise efficiency and there is emphasis on rules to achieve co-ordination between units. This view assumes that people can be combined with machines to produce an orderly output. Within this framework innovation is a series of rational decisions leading to a clearly defined outcome. Indeed, this school of thought contributed to the dominance of the 'technology-push' model of innovation (*see* Chapter 1).

Human relations approach

It was following extensive questioning of the classical view in the 1930s that the human relations school evolved. Much of the original impetus was provided by the Hawthorn Studies at Western Electric (Roethlisberger and Dickinson, 1939). These new approaches identified informal and non-legitimised group processes within the organisation. Informal communications and activities were unearthed by social scientists and found to influence organisational behaviour. This school of thought also led to the development of the contingency theory (*see* below).

A slightly different perspective views the organisation as a political system and suggests that change will result in some conflict between different units in the organisation when a unit perceives that the innovation or change might reduce its influence (Harvey and Mills, 1970). This also introduces the notion of routine and innovative solutions. It is argued that problem situations and problem solutions are arranged along a routine–innovative dimension. A routine solution is defined as 'a solution that has been used before while an innovative solution is defined as a solution that has not been used before and for which there are no precedents in the organisation' (189–90). Harvey and Mills (1970) argue that an organisation will tend to impose routine solutions unless there is pressure on the organisation's structural arrangements. These arrangements reinforce the continuation of routine patterns around which interests have formed. Innovative solutions will only be imposed when the organisation is in a higher stress-threat situation, which is more likely to demand innovative behaviour if the organisation is to adapt. This model builds on the work of Burns and Stalker (*see* below), who indicate that there are different types of solutions, mechanistic routine and organic innovative, that are appropriate for different situations.

Contingency approach

The third main strand of literature is represented by organisation contingency theories. These posit the view that there is not necessarily a *single best* organisational structure, but rather that the structure should be adapted to the activities being performed. Organisational activities or tasks are the things that individuals do as part of groups in order for the organisation to achieve its purposes. This emphasis on internal activities rather than structure is an important factor with regard to innovation. This book takes the view that the process of innovation is made up of a *series of linked activities within an organisation.*

Research in this field (Thompson, 1967; Perrow, 1970; Hull and Haige, 1981) has identified a range of different characteristics that organisations have exhibited that, it is argued, more accurately describe the range of different organisational environments. The following list represents a typology of characteristics that have been identified within certain organisations:

certainty vs uncertainty

stability vs instability

uniform vs non-uniform

few exceptions vs many exceptions

many repetitive events vs few repetitive events

In general, contingency theory argues that tasks that are certain, stable, uniform, have few exceptions and many repetitive events are compatible with bureaucratic organisational forms, which stress formality. At the other end of the task continuum, tasks that are uncertain, unstable, non-uniform, have many exceptions and few repetitive events are compatible with organic flexible organisational forms (*see* Table 2.1).

Systems theory

The fourth set of ideas developed concurrently with contingency theory during the 1960s and 1970s. However, systems theory emphasises processes and dynamic analysis rather than characteristic and structural analysis (Checkland, 1989; Thompson, 1967; Katz and Khan, 1966). The origins of the theory can be traced back to the 1950s when Ludvig von Bertalanffy, a biologist, first used the term 'systems theory' (Bertalanffy, 1951). Systems theorists analyse the commercial organisation from the perspective of complex organic systems.

A system is defined as any set of elements linked in a pattern which carries information ordered according to some pre-determined rules. Organisations are seen as goal-directed systems. All systems have both structures and processes. Structures are the relatively stable elements, whereas processes are the dynamic relationships among system elements over time.

Table 2.1 : Issues identified by systems theory that need to be managed

Issue	Characteristics
Adaptation	The ability to alter ways of working to meet the changing environment
Co-ordination	Enabling the different parts of the organisation to function as one
Integration	The ability to harmonise a diverse range of activities and people
Strain	Coping with friction between organisational parts
Output	Achieving purposes and goals
Maintenance	Keeping elements in the system active

Table 2.2 : Organisational characteristics that facilitate the innovation process

Organisational requirement	Characterised by
1 Growth orientation	A commitment to long-term growth rather than short-term profit
2 Vigilance	The ability of the organisation to be aware of its threats and opportunities
3 Commitment to technology	The willingness to invest in the long-term development of technology
4 Acceptance of risks	The willingness to include risky opportunities in a balanced portfolio
5 Cross-functional co-operation	Mutual respect among individuals and a willingness to work together across functions
6 Receptivity	The ability to be aware of, to identify and to take effective advantage of externally developed technology
7 'Slack'	An ability to manage the innovation dilemma and provide room for creativity
8 Adaptability	A readiness to accept change
9 Diverse range of skills	A combination of specialisation and diversity of knowledge and skills

This school of thought has led to a richer and better understanding of organisational activities. For example, the issues in Table 2.2 are said to be continually addressed by organisations. They should be viewed as issues that need to be managed rather than problems that can be solved (Georgopoulos, 1972).

In addition, systems theory has also highlighted the importance of the organisation's interaction with the external world. Indeed, this interaction is identified as an important element of the innovation process. It is precisely the way in which organisations manage and capture the benefits from the knowledge flows, which are the product of these interactions, that will affect their ability to innovate.

Together these four schools of thought have contributed enormously to the understanding of the management of innovation. Some of the more significant issues will now be addressed in more detail.

The dilemma of innovation management

Within organisations there is a fundamental tension between the need for stability and the need for creativity. On the one hand, companies require stability and static routines to accomplish daily tasks efficiently and quickly. This enables the organisation to compete today. For example, the processing of millions of cheques by a bank every day, or the delivery of food by multiples to their retail outlets all over the country, demands high levels of efficiency and control. On the other hand, companies also need to develop new ideas and new products to be competitive in the future. Hence they

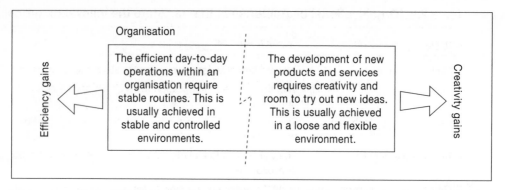

Figure 2.2 : Managing the tension between the need for creativity and efficiency

need to nurture a creative environment where ideas can be tested and developed. This poses one of the most fundamental problems for management today (*see* Figure 2.2).

Take any medium to large company and examine its operations and activities. From Mars to Ford, and from P&G to Sony, these companies have to ensure that their products are carefully manufactured to precise specifications and that they are delivered for customers on time day after day.

Managing uncertainty

It is becoming clear that product innovation is a complex process. Figure 1.6 highlighted the main areas of attention, but each of these represents a complex area in itself. Innovation involves numerous factors acting separately but often influencing one another. Organisations have to respond to internal and external events, some of which are beyond their control. While management in general involves coping with uncertainty, sometimes trying to reduce uncertainty, the *raison d'être* of managers involved in innovation is to develop something different, maybe something new. The management of the innovation process involves trying to develop the creative potential of the organisation. It involves trying to foster new ideas and generate creativity. Managing uncertainty is a central feature of managing the innovation process.

Pearson's uncertainty map

Pearson's uncertainty map (Pearson, 1991) provides a framework for analysing and understanding uncertainty and the innovation process. The map was developed following extensive analysis of case studies of major technological innovations, including Pilkington's float glass process, 3M's Post-It notes and Sony's Walkman (Henry and Walker, 1991). In these and other case studies a great deal of uncertainty surrounded the project. If it involves newly developed technology this may be uncertainty about the type of product envisaged. For example, Spencer Silver's unusual

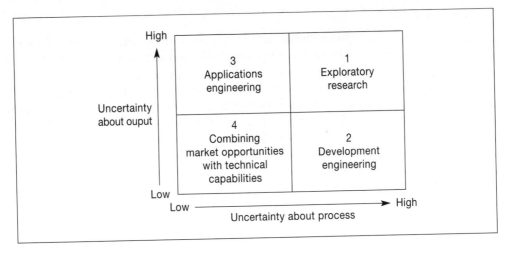

Figure 2.3 : Pearson's uncertainty map

Reproduced with kind permission from A.W. Pearson (1991) 'Managing innovation: an uncertainty reduction process', Sage/OU.

adhesive remained unexploited within 3M for five years before an application was found. Similarly, if a market opportunity has been identified the final product idea may be fairly well established, but much uncertainty may remain about how exactly the company is to develop such a product. For example, the case study at the end of Chapter 1 discussed the development of a new range of aqueous based cleaning products. Here the market was identified but at the time there was uncertainty about how to develop a product for this market.

So Pearson's framework divides uncertainty into two separate dimensions:

■ uncertainty about ends (what is the eventual target of the activity or project)

■ uncertainty about means (how to achieve this target).

The case study at the end of Chapter 7 deals with the development of 'Guinness's in-can system'. This clearly highlights the problems of managing uncertainty about means. Several projects were unsuccessful and there were probably several occasions where decisions had to be taken regarding future funding. Decisions had to be made such as whether to cancel, continue or increase funding. In these situations, because the degree of uncertainty is high, senior managers responsible for million-dollar budgets have to listen carefully to those most closely involved and those with the most information and knowledge. Further information and knowledge are usually available with the passage of time, so time is another element that needs to be considered. Indeed, it is because time is limited that decisions are required. It is clear, however, that many decisions are made with imperfect knowledge, thus there is usually an element of judgement involved in most decisions.

Pearson's framework, shown in Figure 2.3, addresses the nature of the uncertainty and the way it changes over time. The framework is based on the two dimensions discussed above, with uncertainty about ends on the vertical axis and uncertainty about means on the horizontal axis. These axes are then divided, giving four quadrants.

Quadrant 1

Quadrant 1 represents activities involving a high degree of uncertainty about means and ends. The ultimate target is not clearly defined and how to achieve this target is also not clear. This has been labelled 'exploratory research' or 'blue sky' research, because the work sometimes seems so far removed from reality that people liken it to working in the clouds! These activities often involve working with technology that is not fully understood and where potential products or markets have also not been identified. This is largely the domain of university research laboratories, which are usually removed from the financial and time pressures associated with industry. Some science-based organisations also support these activities, but increasingly it is only large organisations who have the necessary resources to fund such exploratory studies.

Quadrant 2

In this area the end or target is clear. For example, a commercial opportunity may have been identified but as yet the means of fulfilling this has yet to be established. Companies may initiate several different projects centred around different technologies or different approaches to try to achieve the desired product. Also additional approaches may be uncovered along the way. Hence, there is considerable uncertainty about precisely how the company will achieve its target. This type of activity is often referred to as development engineering and is an on-going activity within manufacturing companies which are continually examining their production processes, looking for efficiencies and ways to reduce costs. A good example of a successful development in this area is the Guinness 'in-can system'. The company was clear about its target – trying to make the taste of Guinness from a can taste the same as draught Guinness. Precisely how it was to achieve this was very uncertain and many different research projects were established.

Quadrants 3 and 4 deal with situations where there is more certainty associated with how the business will achieve the target. This usually means that the business is working with technology it has used before.

Quadrant 3

In this area there is uncertainty regarding ends. This is usually associated with attempting to discover how the technology can be most effectively used. Applications engineering is the title given to this area of activity. Arguably many new materials fall into this area. For example, the material kevlar (used in the manufacture of bullet-proof clothing) is currently being applied to a wide range of different possible product areas. Many of these may prove to be ineffective due to costs or performance, but some new and improved products will emerge from this effort.

Quadrant 4

This area covers innovative activities where there is most certainty. In these situations activities may be dominated by improving existing products or creating new products through the combination of a market opportunity and technical capability. With so much certainty similar activities are likely to be being undertaken by the competition. Hence, speed of development is often the key to success here. New product designs that use minimal new technology but improve, sometimes with dramatic effect, the appearance or performance of an existing product are examples of product innovations in this area.

Applying the uncertainty map to avoid promising success and delivering failure

The uncertainty map's value is partly the simplicity with which it is able to communicate a complex message, that of dealing with uncertainty, and partly its ability to identify the wide range of organisational characteristics that are associated with managing uncertainty with respect to innovation. The map conveys the important message that the management of product and process innovations is very different. Sometimes one is clear about the nature of the target market and the type of product required. In contrast, there are occasions when little, if anything, is known about the technology being developed and how it could possibly be used. Most organisations have activities that lie between these two extremes, but such differing environments demand very different management skills and organisational environments. This leads the argument towards the vexed question of the organisational structure and culture necessary for innovation, which will be addressed in the following section. First, it is necessary to explore the innovation process through the uncertainty map.

The map helps managers to consider how ideas are transformed into innovations; a very simplistic view of the innovation process. Moreover, it provides a way of identifying the different management skills required. Quadrant 1 highlights an area of innovative activity where ideas and developments may not be immediately recognisable as possible commercial products. There are many examples of technological developments that occurred within organisations that were not recognised. In Xerox's Palo Alto laboratories, the early computer software technology was developed for computer graphical interface as far back as the early 1970s. Xerox did not recognise the possible future benefits of this research and decided not to develop the technology further. It was later exploited by Apple Computer and Microsoft in the 1980s. This raises the question of how to evaluate research in this area. Technical managers may be better able to understand the technology, but a commercial manager may be able to see a wide range of commercial opportunities. Continual informal and formal discussions are usually the best way to explore all possibilities fully, in the hope that the company will make the correct decision regarding which projects to support and which to drop. This is a problem that will be returned to in Chapter 8.

At the other extreme is Quadrant 4, where scientists often view this type of activity as merely tinkering with existing technology. However, commercial managers often get very excited because the project is in a 'close-to-market' form with minimal technical newness.

Between these two extremes lie Quadrants 2 and 3. In the applications engineering quadrant where the business is exploring the potential uses of known technology, management efforts centre on which markets to enter; whereas in the development engineering quadrant special project-management skills are required to ensure that projects either deliver or are cancelled before costs escalate.

In all of the above particular organisational environments and specialist management skills are required depending on the type of activity being undertaken. These will be determined by the extent of uncertainty involved.

Organisational characteristics that facilitate the innovation process

The innovation process, outlined at the end of Chapter 1, identified the complex nature of innovation. It also emphasised the need to view innovation within the context of the organisation. Table 2.3 represents a classification of the main *organisational characteristics* that are continually identified in the literature as necessary for successful innovation.

Growth orientation

It is sometimes surprising to learn that not all companies' first and foremost objective is growth. Some companies are established merely to exploit a short-term opportunity. Other companies, particularly family-run ones, would like to maintain the company at its existing size. At that size the family can manage the operation without having to employ outside help. Companies that are innovative are those companies whose objective is to grow the business. This does not imply that they make large profits one year then huge losses the next, but they actively plan for the long term. There are many companies who make this explicit in their annual reports, companies such as J. Sainsbury, ICI, BMW, Renault and Mercedes-Benz.

Vigilance

Vigilance requires continual external scanning, not just by senior management but also by all other members of the organisation. Part of this activity may be formalised. For example, within the marketing function the activity would form part of market research and competitor analysis. Within the research and development department scientists and engineers will spend a large amount of their time reading the scientific literature in order to keep up to date with the latest developments in their field. In other functions it may not be as formalised but it still needs to occur. Collecting valuable information is one thing, but relaying it to the necessary individuals and acting on it are two necessary associated requirements. An open communication system will help to facilitate this.

Commitment to technology

Most innovative firms exhibit patience in permitting ideas to germinate and develop over time. This also needs to be accompanied by a commitment to resources in terms of intellectual input from science, technology and engineering. Those ideas that look most promising will require further investment. Without this long-term approach it would be extremely difficult for the company to attract good scientists. Similarly, a climate that invests in technology development one year then decides to cut investment the next will alienate the same people in which the company encourages creativity. Such a disruptive environment does not foster creativity and will probably cause many creative people to search for a more suitable company with a stronger commitment to technology.

Acceptance of risks

Accepting risks does not mean a willingness to gamble. It means the willingness to consider carefully risky opportunities. It also includes the ability to make risk-assessment decisions, to take calculated risks and to include them in a balanced portfolio of projects, some of which will have a low element of risk and some a high degree of risk.

Cross-functional co-operation

Inter-departmental conflict is a well-documented barrier to innovation. The relationship between the marketing and R&D functions has received a great deal of attention in the research literature. This will be explored further in Chapter 6, but generally this is because the two groups often have very different interests. Scientists and technologists can be fascinated by new technology and may sometimes lose sight of the business objective. Similarly, the marketing function often fails to understand the technology involved in the development of a new product. Research has shown that the presence of some conflict is desirable, probably acting as a motivational force (Souder, 1981). It is the ability to confront and resolve frustration and conflict that is required.

Receptivity

The capability of the organisation to be aware of, identify and take effective advantage of externally developed technology is key. Most technology-based innovations involve a combination of several different technologies. It would be unusual for all the technology to be developed in-house. Indeed, businesses are witnessing an increasing number of joint ventures and alliances (Hinton and Trott, 1996), often with former competitors. For example, IBM and Apple have formed a joint venture to work on mutually beneficial technology. Previously these two companies fought ferociously in the battle for market share in the personal computer market.

'Slack'

While organisations place great emphasis on the need for efficiency, there is also a need for a certain amount of 'slack' to allow individuals room to think, experiment, discuss ideas and be creative (Cordey-Hayes *et al.*, 1997). In many R&D functions this issue is directly addressed by allowing scientists 10–15 per cent of their time to spend on the projects they choose. This is not always supported in other functional areas.

Adaptability

The development of new product innovations will invariably lead to disruptions to established organisational activities. Major or radical innovations may result in significant changes, although the two are not necessarily linked. The organisation must be ready to accept change in the way it manages its internal activities. Otherwise proposed innovations would be stifled due to a reluctance to alter existing ways of working or to learn new techniques. In short, organisations need the ability to adapt to the changing environment.

Diverse range of skills

Organisations require a combination of specialist skills and knowledge in the form of experts in, say, science, advertising or accountancy and generalist skills that facilitate cross-fertilisation of the specialist knowledge. In addition they require individuals of a hybrid nature who are able to understand a variety of technical subjects and facilitate the transfer of knowledge within the company. Similarly, hybrid managers who have technical and commercial training are particularly useful in the area of product development (Trott, 1993). It is the ability to manage this diversity of knowledge and skills effectively that lies at the heart of the innovation process.

Industrial firms are different: a classification

A brief look at companies operating in your town or area will soon inform you that industrial firms are very different. You may say that this is axiomatic. The point is, however, that in terms of innovation and product development it is possible to argue that some firms are users of technology and others are providers. For example, at the simplest level most towns will have a range of housebuilding firms, agricultural firms, retail firms and many others offering services to local people. Such firms tend to be small in size, with little R&D or manufacturing capability of their own. They are classified by Pavitt (1984) as *supplier-dominated firms*. Many of them are very successful because they offer a product with a reliable service. Indeed, their strength is that they purchase technologies in the form of products and match these to customer needs. Such firms usually have limited, if any, product or process technology capabilities. Pavitt offers a useful classification of the different types of firms with regard to technology usage; this is shown in Figure 2.4.

At the other end of the scale are *science-based firms* or technology-intensive firms. These are found in the high-growth industries of the twentieth century: chemicals, pharmaceuticals, electronics, computing etc. It is the manipulation of science and technology usually by their own R&D departments that has provided the foundation for the firms' growth and success. Unlike the previous classification, these firms tend to be large and would include corporations such as Bayer, Hoechst, ICI, Glaxo-Wellcome, Siemens, Rhone-Poulenc and 3M.

The third classification Pavitt refers to as scale-intensive firms, which dominate the manufacturing sector. At the heart of these firms are process technologies. It is their ability to produce high volumes at low cost that is usually their strength. They tend to have capabilities in engineering, design and manufacturing. Many science-based firms are also scale-intensive firms, so it is possible for firms to belong to more than one category. Indeed, the big chemical companies in Europe are a case in point.

The final classification is *specialist equipment suppliers*. This group of firms is an important source of technology for scale-intensive and science-based firms. For example, instrumentation manufacturers supply specialist measuring instruments to the chemical industry and the aerospace industry to enable these firms to measure their products and manufacturing activities accurately.

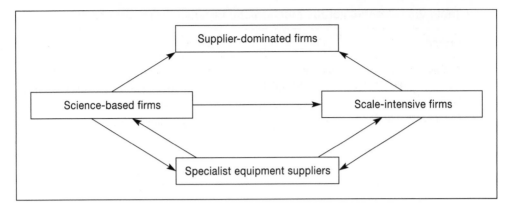

Figure 2.4 : Technological linkages among different types of firms
Source: Pavitt (1994)

This useful classification highlights the flows of technology between the various firms. This is an important concept and is referred to in later chapters to help explain the industry life cycle in Chapter 5, the acquisition of technology in Chapter 8, the transfer of technology in Chapter 9 and strategic alliances in Chapter 10.

Organisational structures and innovation

The structure of an organisation is defined by Mintzberg (1978) as the sum total of the ways in which it divides its labour into distinct tasks and then achieves co-ordination among them. One of the problems when analysing organisational structure is recognising that different groups within an organisation behave differently and interact with different parts of the wider external environment. Hence, there is a tendency to label structure at the level of the organisation with little recognition of differences at group or department level. Nonetheless, there have been numerous useful studies exploring the link between organisational structure and innovative performance.

The seminal work by Burns and Stalker (1961) on Scottish electronic organisations looked at the impact of technical change on organisational structures and on systems of social relationships. It suggests that 'organic', flexible structures, characterised by the absence of formality and hierarchy, support innovation more effectively than do 'mechanistic' structures. The latter are characterised by long chains of command, rigid work methods, strict task differentiation, extensive procedures and a well-defined hierarchy. Many objections have been raised against this argument, most notably by Child (1973). Nevertheless, flexible rather than mechanistic organisational structures are still seen, especially within the business management literature, as necessary for successful industrial innovation. In general, an organic organisation is more adaptable, more openly communicating, more consensual and more loosely controlled. As Table 2.4 indicates, the mechanistic organisation tends to offer a less

Table 2.3 : Organic versus mechanistic organisational structures

Organic	Mechanistic
1 Channels of communication Open with free information flow throughout the organisation	**1 Channels of communication** Highly structured, restricted information flow
2 Operating styles Allowed to vary freely	**2 Operating styles** Must be uniform and restricted
3 Authority for decisions Based on the expertise of the individual	**3 Authority for decisions** Based on formal line management position
4 Free adaptation By the organisation to changing circumstances	**4 Reluctant adaptation** With insistence on holding fast to tried and true management principles despite changes in business conditions
5 Emphasis on getting things done Unconstrained by formally laid out procedures	**5 Emphasis on formally laid down procedures** Reliance on tried and true management principles
6 Loose, informal control With emphasis on norm of co-operation	**6 Tight control** Through sophisticated control systems
7 Flexible on-job behaviour Permitted to be shaped by the requirements of the situation and personality of the individual doing the job	**7 Constrained on-job behaviour** Required to conform to job descriptions
8 Participation and group consensus used frequently	**8 Superiors make decisions with minimum consultation and involvement of subordinates**

Source: Slevin and Covin (1990)

suitable environment for managing creativity and the innovation process. The subject of organisation structures is also discussed in Chapter 6 in the context of managing new product development teams.

Formalisation

Following Burns and Stalker, there have been a variety of studies examining the relationship between formalisation and innovation. There is some evidence of an inverse relationship between formalisation and innovation. That is, an increase in formalisation of procedures will result in a decrease in innovative activity. It is unclear, however, whether a decrease in procedures and rules would lead to an increase in innovation. Moreover, as was argued above, organisational planning and routines are necessary for achieving efficiencies.

Complexity

The term complexity here refers to the complexity of the organisation. In particular, it refers to the number of professional groups or diversity of specialists within the organisation. For example, a university, hospital or science-based manufacturing company would represent a complex organisation. This is because within these organisations there would be several professional groups. In the case of a hospital, nurses, doctors and a wide range of specialists represent the different areas of medicine. This contrasts sharply with an equally large organisation that is, for example, in the distribution industry. The management of supplying goods all over the country will be complex indeed; but it will not involve the management of a wide range of highly qualified professional groups.

Centralisation

Centralisation refers to the decision-making activity and the location of power within an organisation. The more decentralised an organisation the fewer levels of hierarchy usually required. This tends to lead to more responsive decision making closer to the action.

Organisational size

Size is a proxy variable for more meaningful dimensions such as economic and organisational resources, including number of employees and scale of operation. Below a certain size, however, there is a major qualitative difference. A small business with fewer than 20 employees differs significantly in terms of resources from an organisation with 200 or 2000 employees.

The role of the individual in the innovation process

The innovation literature has consistently acknowledged the importance of the role of the individual within the industrial technological innovation process. (Rothwell *et al.*, 1974; Szakastis *et al.*, 1974; Langrish *et al.*, 1972; Schock, 1974; Utterback, 1975; Rothwell, 1976). Furthermore, a variety of *key roles* have developed from the literature stressing particular qualities (*see* Table 2.4).

Rubenstien *et al.* (1976) went further, arguing that the innovation process is essentially a *people process* and that organisational structure, formal decision-making processes, delegation of authority and other formal aspects of a so-called well-run company are not necessary conditions for successful technological innovation. Their studies revealed that certain individuals had fulfilled a variety of roles (often informal) that had contributed to successful technological innovation.

In a study of biotechnology firms, Sheene (1991) explains that it is part of a scientist's professional obligation to keep up to date with the literature. This is achieved by extensive scanning of the literature. However, she identified feelings of guilt associ-

Table 2.4 : Key individual roles within the innovation process

Key individual	Role
Technical Innovator	Expert in one or two fields. Generates new ideas and sees new and different ways of doing things. Also referred to as the 'mad scientist'.
Technical/Commercial Scanner	Acquires vast amounts of information from outside the organisation, often through networking. This may include market and technical information.
Gatekeeper	Keeps informed of related developments that occur outside the organisation through journals, conferences, colleagues and other companies. Passes information on to others, finds it easy to talk to colleagues. Serves as an information resource for others in the organisation.
Product Champion	Sells new ideas to others in the organisation. Acquires resources. Aggressive in championing his or her cause. Takes risks.
Project Leader	Provides the team with leadership and motivation. Plans and organises the project. Ensures that administrative requirements are met. Provides necessary co-ordination among team members. Sees that the project moves forward effectively. Balances project goals with organisational needs.
Sponsor	Provides access to a power base within the organisation: a senior person. Buffers the project team from unnecessary organisational constraints. Helps the project team to get what it needs from other parts of the organisation. Provides legitimacy and organisational confidence in the project.

Source: Based on Roberts and Fushfield (1981)

ated with browsing in the library by some scientists. This was apparently due to a fear that some senior managers might not see this as a constructive use of their time. Many other studies have also shown that the role of the individual is critical in the innovation process (Allen and Cohen, 1969; Allen, 1977; Tushman, 1977; Burgelman, 1983).

Establishing an innovative environment and propagating this virtuous circle

This chapter has highlighted the role of the organisational environment in the innovation process. It has also shown how many different factors influence this environment. Given the importance of innovation, many businesses have spent enormous sums of money trying to develop an environment that fosters innovation. Each year *Fortune* produces a list of the most innovative companies in the US. For the past few years the following companies have finished at or near the top: 3M, Rubbermaid, Merck and Motorola (*Fortune*, 1994). Developing a reputation for innovation helps propagate a virtuous circle that reinforces a company's abilities (*see* Figure 2.5).

The concept of a virtuous circle of innovation can be viewed as a specific example of Michael Porter's (1985) notion of competitive advantage. Porter argued that those companies who are able to achieve competitive advantage – that is, above-average performance in an industry sector – are able to reinvest this additional profit into the activities that spawned the advantage in the first place, thus creating a virtuous circle of improvement, or so-called competitive advantage.

Reputation of the organisation

The reputation of a company for innovation takes many years to develop. It is also strongly linked to overall performance. However, within a selection of successful companies there will inevitably be some that are regarded as more innovative than others. This may be due to several factors, including recent product launches; recent successful programmes of research; high levels of expenditure on R&D. Depending on topical media events at the time, some companies are able to achieve wide exposure of new products or new research. Such exposure is often dependent on effective publicity but also serendipity.

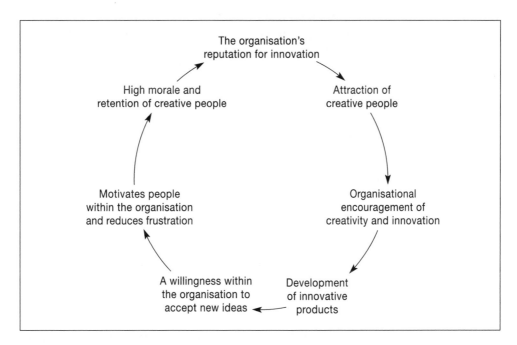

Figure 2.5 : Propagating a virtuous circle of innovation

Promoting VW's reputation for innovation

In 1993, following several environmental disasters, the Volkswagen Audi Group benefited from an enormous amount of publicity concerning the new engine–gearbox system that it had recently developed. This Ecomatic system was of particular interest to the media because of its reduced emissions into the environment. The system switched the engine off whenever the driver took his or her foot off the accelerator. For example, in a queue of traffic or when going down hill the engine would switch off. The engine restarted when the accelerator was depressed. The Ecomatic promised to slash fuel bills by a quarter. Clearly, this new technology was interesting in its own right and would have gained coverage in the motoring pages. However, it gained additional coverage all over Europe due to the environmental debates at the time.

Source: *European* (1993)

Attraction of creative people

Creative people will be attracted to those companies that themselves are viewed as creative. In much the same way as undergraduates apply for positions of employment with those companies viewed as successful, top scientists will seek employment from those companies which have a reputation for innovation and scientific excellence (Jones, 1992).

Organisation encourages creativity

Many organisations pay lip service to creativity without putting in place any structures or plans to encourage innovation. It has to be supported with actions and resources. The organisation has to provide people with the time to be creative. This can be in a formalised way, as used in much of the chemical industry. For example, 15 per cent of a research scientist's time may be dedicated to projects of personal interest. Alternatively, organisations can try to build sufficient slack into the system to allow for creative thinking (*see* above).

In addition, the organisation should try to build an environment that tolerates errors and mistakes. This will encourage people to try new ideas and put forward suggestions. Successful new ideas need to be rewarded in terms of publicity for the people involved. This is usually most easily achieved through internal newsletters or company magazines. In addition, financial rewards – promotions, gifts or holidays – may be offered.

Some organisations also use creativity-stimulation techniques such as a weekend away at a country retreat to discuss new ways of working, new ideas, etc. These activities collectively will help send a clear message that the organisation is serious about innovation.

Development of innovative products

This does not mean the ability to develop products incorporating the latest technology, although this may be an output. It means developing new products that are genuine improvements compared to products currently available. Moreover, it is success in the marketplace that very often leads to further success.

A willingness to accept new ideas

Many organisations suffer from an inability to implement changes and new ideas, even after rewarding the people involved in developing the new idea. Once a new product idea has been accepted it is important that it is carried through to completion.

Increased motivation and reduced frustration

If individuals within the organisation can see their ideas and efforts contributing to the performance of the business, they will be encouraged still further. On the other hand, if seemingly good ideas are constantly overlooked, this will lead to increased frustration.

High morale and retention of creative people

All of the proceeding activities will help contribute to increased morale within the organisation. A rewarding and enjoyable working environment will help to retain creative people. This in turn should reinforce the company's innovative capabilities.

CASE STUDY

The birth of a new business from within ICI[1]

This case study describes how a new business was formed from within an old established business. It highlights the important role of senior managers in the innovation process and how a business proposal was accepted not least because it matched the company's longer-term strategy.

Introduction

This case study tells part of the story of ICI's overall strategy to move away from the bulk chemicals business into new speciality, lower-volume businesses that offer greater opportunity to add value. The sale of its fertilisers business to Terra Industries, Iowa, represented a complete transformation for the company that was founded in 1926 with fertilisers as one of its core businesses (*Financial Times*, 1997). ICI's decision to purchase Unilever's speciality chemicals business for £4.9 billion was the final piece in the jigsaw (*Financial Times*, 1997).

At the same time as the results of the European elections were announced, a group of senior managers were looking at a new business proposal that had been delivered from a group of managers from the Chlor-Chemicals business. This proposal had taken almost a year to produce and the managers had invested many hours rechecking their figures and adding flesh to the bones of the original concept. As they walked away from the conference room, where they had just delivered their presentation, the three of them smiled nervously at one another. No one uttered a sound but they were content that the presentation had gone well. They hoped the directors and senior managers they had just left would agree with them and invest the £50 million required for this new venture.

---

[1] This case has been written as a basis for class discussion rather than to illustrate effective or ineffective managerial or administrative behaviour. It has been prepared from a variety of published sources, as indicated, and from observations.

▶ *Gathering support for a business idea*

In 1988 a study group within ICI was looking at the public health market. It was considering opportunities in water treatment and was interested in the possibility of offering solutions to problems rather than simply chemical treatments. This study group identified a latent market need for water treatment, especially in the area of sewerage treatment prior to discharge and the much wider area of treating water for domestic and industrial use. The concept of a business developed from a combination of this report and the realisation that ICI had a number of related areas of technical competence within its group of businesses.

Indeed, over the previous year much of the efforts of the three strong new business group had been directed towards identifying areas of ICI that sell their separate wares to the water industry. This group had identified 17 separate parts (ICI, 1993). Thus, the concept of a new business was born by combining this market opportunity with internal technical capabilities.

The thrust of the idea was to establish a new business focused on the needs of the water treatment market, in particular all those businesses that use water within their manufacturing operations. The concept was developed further through discussions with business managers and scientists within a range of ICI businesses. These discussions led to the uncovering of a collection of research projects that were being undertaken throughout the ICI group on a variety of water treatment type products. Hence, the new business group was beginning to build support within the company for a business based on in-house technology and products to serve the growing market of waste treatment. Further discussions revealed that within this area of science, technology existed in other external companies and universities. The combination of internal knowhow and external technology would provide the technological uniqueness that ICI sought in order to compete and build a business that offered the potential for high added-value products and services.

Long-term corporate strategy

In order to compete in today's highly competitive markets, companies do not only have to be efficient and competent in what they do. They have to offer uniqueness, whether this is in the form of service benefits or technical attributes or more usually a combination of these.

Furthermore, ICI Chemicals and Polymers has a long-term strategy of developing and building high added-value businesses. Essentially, this means a move away from the traditional business activities of the company's past that had focused on large-scale production of commodity chemical products such as chlorine and solvents. These were now regarded as 'low-technology' products and competition was focused on price, with little if any room for differentiating one product from the competition. Many smaller chemical companies all over the world were able to manufacture these commodity chemicals under licence from one of the multinational chemical companies. ICI's strategy was to search for business opportunities where the company could build a business around a product that could be differentiated from the competition and would provide the opportunity to add value.

Two of the most common ways of developing added-value businesses are through unique technology, ideally protected through patents, and branding. This is where a company attempts to differentiate its product from that of the competition through influencing perceptions and is more common in consumer than industrial markets.

The business concept – technology products and markets

Initial discussions were positive and a further opportunity emerged. Not only were these manufacturing businesses interested in treating their waste water prior to discharge, but during discussions with ICI scientists it became obvious that manufacturing operations that used water could be improved if the water was treated before use. ICI technologists had discovered that ICI could improve the water used prior to use *and* after use (*see* Figure 2.6).

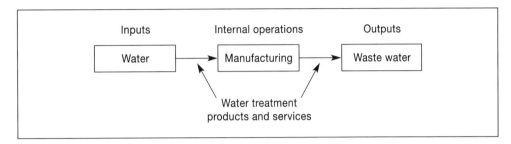

Figure 2.6 : The business concept

Additional factors were being uncovered that seemed to support the reasoning behind the new business idea. In particular, the manufacturing environment was changing and most analysts agreed that environmental legislation would probably become ever tougher. Increased participation with Europe would also probably mean a more forceful environmental lobby. There was a growing consensus in several ICI businesses that a wide range of manufacturers were concerned that legislation may force changes on their operations. Moreover, consumer companies such as Marks and Spencer and McDonald's, which pride themselves on excellent customer relations, were demanding tougher, 'greener' ways of working from their suppliers. Many small manufacturers which supplied these large organisations with packaging, foodstuffs, paper etc. were expressing concern that they would lose vital business if they failed impending inspections of their operations from these major customers.

An opportunity was clearly emerging for a business that could offer to manufacturing businesses, not just in the UK but around the world, a complete service that focused on how they deal with the water they use during their operations. In particular, this would include technical advice and products to improve and treat the water, at both the input stage to improve operations and at the output stage prior to discharge of waste water.

To be successful in this market any business offering products and services would need credibility and would also need to be technology literate, to be seen as knowledgable in the field. ICI had this credibility due to its long association with the water industry built up over 60 years of providing chlorine. In addition, it is also recognised as a serious player in the field of science and technology, largely through its heritage of investing in technology, research and development in particular.

The new Watercare business

It was unusual for a new business in ICI to start life without any assets. This is because ICI has been built on the manufacture of chemicals and businesses usually start with building a new chemical plant to manufacture a new product. The Watercare business, as it was christened, started with no assets of its own but acted as a channel to the water treatment market. It took over a sales portfolio of existing chemicals, essentially chlorine-based ▶

▶ products for the water industry. This provided the business with a small but steady income that it would use to meet its running costs. In addition, the products provided the business with channels into the marketplace where they could better understand consumer needs. Funding for the development of new products would be provided by central R&D funds. The intent was to add value to the existing offerings through formulation and packaging, providing complete treatment systems. From the outset the business maintained that, as one of the world's major scientific groups, ICI had the resources and unrivalled expertise in the formulation, manufacture and distribution of specialist water treatment products world-wide to be successful in this market (ICI, 1993).

Within the first two years of operating several new products had been developed. One of these, called Coastguard, was developed for North West Water. This was essentially a treatment process for breaking down solids in sewerage. There were already chemical products that performed this function, but this was specifically for previously untreated sewage that was discharged away from the shore. Another product was developed for the electricity generating industry which required help with treatment of water within cooling towers.

A product was also developed for the treatment of water at the input stage of operations of a major brewer in the UK. Following extensive research and trials with the brewer, the Watercare business was able to offer a water treatment system that improved the efficiency of the brewing process through reducing costs later in the operation.

Discussion

This case demonstrates some of the internal processes involved in transforming an idea into a business, especially the role played by internal and external technical and commercial knowledge in developing a genuine business opportunity. It is a good example of how large companies build new businesses and highlights the role played by individuals within the organisation, in particular the process of generating support for an idea. This form of gathering support and building consensus is very common in large organisations. It is extremely rare for a single person to generate the idea for a business and then become leader of that business. It usually involves many different people with a variety of skills and capabilities, who together push the idea and transform it into a business opportunity. However, many business opportunities are also rejected by senior managers at the final stages, for a wide range of reasons.

Chapter summary

Before the Industrial Revolution many innovations were the result of lone inventors and entrepreneurs. Today the situation is very different. The overwhelming majority of innovations come from organisations and this was the focus of this chapter. In particular, it explored the organisational environment and the activities performed within it that are necessary for innovation to occur. These, of course, are dependent on the extent to which an organisation recognises the need for and encourages innovation.

All organisations have to manage the dilemma of innovation. It is not something that can be removed; it will always be present. Successful companies, however, are able to manage this dilemma. It was shown that successful companies also need to be able to manage uncertainty. In addition, several roles were identified as necessary for innovation to occur and it was stressed that these are often performed by key individuals.

Questions for discussion

1 What are the three main schools of thought that have contributed to our understanding of managing innovation within organisations?

2 Can organisations operate across the entire spectrum of innovation activities?

3 Explain the fundamental dilemma facing organisations and the tensions it creates.

4 How can the uncertainty map help managers?

5 Discuss the main organisational characteristics that facilitate the innovation process.

6 Explain the key individual roles within the innovation process and the activities they perform.

7 Explain the rationale behind ICI's change in corporate strategy.

8 Describe how support for ICI's new business idea was gathered.

9 Discuss the influence of ICI's knowledge base on the decision to develop this business idea further.

References

Allen, T.J. (1977) *Managing the Flow of Technology*, MIT Press, Cambridge, MA.

Allen, T.J. and Cohen, W.M. (1969) 'Information flow in research and development laboratories', *Administrative Science Quarterly*, 14 (1) 12–19.

Bertalanffy, L. von (1951) 'Problems of general systems theory: the skeleton of science', *Management of Science, Human Biology*, 23 (4), December.

Burgelman, R.A. (1983) 'A process model of internal corporate venturing in the diversified major firm', *Administrative Science Quarterly*, 28, 225–44.

Burns, T. and Stalker, G.M. (1961) *The Management of Innovation*, Tavistock, London.

Checkland, P. (1989) 'Soft systems methodology', *Human Systems Management*, 8, 273–89.

Child, J. (1988) *Organisation: A Guide to Problems and Practice*, Second edition, Harper & Row, London.

Cordey-Hayes, M., Trott, P. and Gilbert, M. (1997) 'Knowledge assimilation and learning organisations, in Butler, J. and Piccaluga, A. (eds) *Knowledge, Technololgy and Innovative Organisations*, Guerini E. Associati, Italy.

European (1993) 'Golf's free wheeler laps up the quiet side of life', October 14–17, 46.

Financial Times (1977) 'A cultural exchange', May 8, 25.

Financial Times (1997) 'ICI to sell UK fertilisers business', November 21, 19.

Fortune (1994) 'America's most admired companies', February 7, 50–66.

Harvey, E. and Mills, R. (1970) 'Patterns of organisational adaptation: a political perspective', in Mayer, N. Zald (ed.) *Power in Organisations*, Vanderbilt University Press, Nashville, Tenn.

Henry, J. and Walker, D. (eds) (1991) *Managing Innovation*, Sage/OU Press, London.

Hinton, M. and Trott, P. (1996) 'The changing nature of R&D management and why I.T. is not a panacea', paper presented at *R&D Management Conference*, Switzerland, September.

ICI (1993) Promotional literature on the new Watercare business, Cheshire.

Jones, O. (1992) 'Postgraduate scientists and R&D: the role of reputation in organisational choice', *R&D Management*, 22, 4.

Katz, D. and Kahn, R.L. (1966) 'The Social Psychology of Organisations', Wiley & Sons, New York.

Langrish, J., Gibbons, M., Evans, W.G. and Jevons, F.R. (1972) *Wealth from Knowledge*, Macmillan, London.

Mintzberg, H. (1978) 'Patterns in strategy formulation', *Management Science*, 24, 934–48.

Pavitt, K. (1994) 'Sectoral patterns of technological change: towards a taxonomy and theory', *Research Policy*, 13, 343–73.

Pearson, A. (1991) 'Managing uncertainty: an uncertainty reduction process', in *Managing Innovation*, Henry, J. and Walker, D. (eds) Sage/OU Press, Chapter 2, 18–27.

Perrow, C. (1970) *Organisational Analysis: a Sociological View*, Tavistock Publications, London.

Porter, M.E. (1985) *Competitive Advantage*, Harvard University Press, Boston, MA.

Roberts, E.B. and Fushfield, A.R. (1981) 'Staffing the innovative technology-based organisation', *Sloan Management Review*, Spring, 19–34.

Roethlisberger, F.J. and Dickinson, W.J. (1939) *Management and the Worker*, Harvard University Press, Boston, MA.

Rothwell, R. (1976) 'Innovation in the UK textile industry: some significant factors in success and failure', Science Policy Research Unit, Occasional paper series, 2, June.

Rothwell, R., Freeman, C., Horlsey, A., Jervis, V.T.P., Robertson, A.B. and Townsend, J. (1974) 'SAPPHO updated: Project SAPPHO phase II', *Research Policy*, 3, 258–91.

Rubenstien, A.H. (1976) 'Factors influencing success at the project level', *Research Management*, XIX (3) 15–20.

Schock, G. (1974) 'Innovation processes in Dutch industry', TNO Industrial Research Organsiation, Netherlands.

Sheene, M.R. (1991) 'The boundness of technical knowledge within a company: barriers to external knowledge acquisition', paper presented at R&D Management Conference on *The Acquisition of External Knowledge*, Kiel, Germany.

Slevin, D.P. and Covin, J.G. (1990) 'Juggling entrepreneurial style and organizational structure: how to get your act together', *Sloan Management Review*, Winter, 43–53.

Souder, W.E. (1987) *Managing New Product Innovations*, Lexington Books, Lexington, MA.

Szakastis, G.D. (1974) 'The adoption of the SAPPHO method in the Hungarian electronics industry', *Research Policy*, 3.

Taylor, F. (1947) *Scientific Management*, Harper & Row, New York.

Thompson, J.D. (1967) *Organisations in Action*, John Wiley & Sons, New York.

Trott, P. (1993) 'Inward technology transfer as an interactive process: a case study of ICI', PhD thesis, Cranfield University, November.

Tushman, M.L. (1977) 'Communication across organisational boundaries: special boundary roles in the innovation process', *Administrative Science Quarterly*, 22, 587–605.

Tushman, M.L. and Nadler, D. (1978) 'An information processing approach to organisational design', *Academy of Management Review*, 3, 613–24.

Utterback, J.M. (1971) 'The process of technological innovation within the firm', *Academy of Management Review*, 12, 75–88.

Weber, M. (1964) *The Theory of Social and Economic Organisation*, Collier Macmillan, London.

Further reading

Chesbrough, H.W. and Teece, D. (1996) 'When is virtual virtuous? Organising for innovation', *Harvard Business Review*, Jan–Feb, 11, 65–73.

Clark, P. and Staunton, N. (1993) *Innovation in Technology and Organisation*, Routledge, London.

Rothwell, R. (1992) 'Successful industrial innovation: critical factors for the 1990s', *R&D Management*, 22 (3) 221–39.

van de Ven, A.H. (1986) 'Central problems: the management of innovation', *Management Science*, 32 (5) 590–607.

Wolfe, R.A. (1994) 'Organisational innovation: review and critique and suggested research directions', *Journal of Management Studies*, 31 (3) 405–31.

3

Business strategy and organisational knowledge

Introduction

Business strategy is concerned with an organisation's basic direction for the future. This involves careful consideration of its purpose, its resources and how it interacts with the environment in which it operates. When it comes to managing innovation, the strategy of a business has an enormous impact. This chapter examines how strategy affects the management of innovation. The case study at the end of the chapter shows how high-level strategic decisions often influence whether a product is developed or not.

Learning objectives

When you have completed this chapter, you will be able to:

- Provide an understanding of the role of an organisation's knowledge base in determining innovative capability
- Recognise the importance of organisational heritage for a company's strategic planning process
- Provide an understanding of the concept of the learning organisation
- Recognise the importance of technical and commercial capabilities in innovation management
- Recognise a variety of different innovation strategies.

The battle of Trafalgar

The battle of Trafalgar in 1805 may not seem like an appropriate place to begin the study of strategy and technological innovation. It does, however, provide an interesting historical example of how strategy (in this case military strategy) is often linked to new technological developments.

For those who are unable to recall their eighteenth and nineteenth century maritime history, Nelson defeated the French and Spanish fleets in the battle of Trafalgar. Today Nelson's ship, *HMS Victory*, stands in a drydock in Portsmouth harbour. The battle was fought off the south-west coast of Spain and the sailing ships of the day were armed with cannons that used gunpowder to launch cannon balls at the enemy's ships, the aim being to hole the ship so that it would ultimately sink. Failure to achieve this would either result in being 'holed' oneself or being invaded by the enemy's crew if they were able to get alongside.

Nelson's fleet, while composed of fewer vessels, had a crucial strategic advantage. It possessed a simple but important piece of technology that, arguably, was instrumental in securing victory. The Spanish and French armadas were armed with cannons, but theirs were fired by lighting a short fuse that burned and then ignited the gunpowder. There were several limitations to this ignition process. First, the fuse would not always burn; and secondly, valuable time was being wasted while waiting for it to burn. Nelson's ships, on the other hand, had overcome this limitation through the development of a simple hammer-action ignition system that ignited the gunpowder. The firing process involved placing a cannon ball in the cannon and rolling it into position, with its nose poking through the aperture in the side of the ship. A cord would be pulled to trigger the hammer action and ignite the gunpowder, causing an explosion that would force the cannon ball out towards the target. Nelson's ships were able to load and fire several cannon balls while the enemy's fleet were waiting for fuses to burn.

Strategic innovation: an overview of the strategic management literature

The battle of Trafalgar also provides an appropriate link to the study of strategic management. The study of strategy, after all, can be traced back to military origins (*see* Figure 3.1). We need to be clear from the beginning about what is meant by strategy. Most dictionaries define strategy in military terms, for example, 'Strategy is the imposition upon an enemy of a place and time and conditions for fighting preferred by oneself.'

There is a clear similarity in competition between armed forces and competition between companies. Businesses have to decide which is the best way forward given the resources available and present and future environmental conditions.

At the beginning of the twentieth century management thinking was dominated by scientific management, in particular the writings of F. W. Taylor (1947). This approach to the management of resources and organisations was largely responsible for the division of labour and the production line or Fordist approach. Control was top down, the man with the pen telling the man with the screwdriver what to make. Control was achieved on the basis of raw positional power. Successful companies, however, realised that respect was never achieved in the same way. The creation of new products was dominated by new scientific developments – the so-called 'technology-push' approach.

By the middle of the century the behaviourists dominated management thinking and the importance of teamwork and improved working conditions received much greater attention (Maslow, 1954; Drucker, 1954). Increased competition during the 1950s led to increased influence for the strategists. Up to this point it was largely possible for companies to sell all the products they could produce. Competition issues raised the importance of market knowledge and the need to understand more about the consumer's requirements. The creation of new opportunities was dominated by 'market-pull' approaches to new product development.

The idea that sustained organisational success was the result of extensive logical sequential planning mechanisms continued to dominate strategic management thinking in the 1950s and 1960s. Chandler's (1962) influential work popularised the notion of strategy, hence the increased use by many multinational organisations of strategic planners at this time. This view was criticised by Lindblom (1959), who argued that it was unrealistic to suggest that managers could manage all the changes they have to deal with through logical, sequential planning mechanisms. The management of organisations, he argued, involved dealing with many uncertainties for which it was not possible to plan, such as external political and economic changes. This led to an evolutionary view of management theory, whereby the process involves continual iteration over time between the various parts of the organisation until a strategy emerges. Mintzberg's (1978) historical studies of organisations showed the importance of incremental change. Similarly, Quinn (1978) argued that decisions are taken via logical incrementalism. This is where decision making is based on adaptation to the changing environment. That is, managers experiment with a range of different decisions before eventually selecting a particular one, the next decision following on from the previous one in an incremental fashion. This *dynamic view* of decision making, based on learning from experience and the emergence of strategies over time, accommodates an interactive model of innovation whereby market considerations interact with the organisation's science and technology base (*see* Chapter 1).

Content and process views of strategic management

The literature on strategic management has evolved into two main streams. The dominant stream, in terms of quantity, is the '*content*' view. This body of literature is dominated by industrial economics and marketing and is mainly concerned with strategies formed through analysis of the external environment. In particular, it is concerned with strategic analysis of what should be done at different levels within the organisation or different business units of analysis (for example Ansoff, 1968;

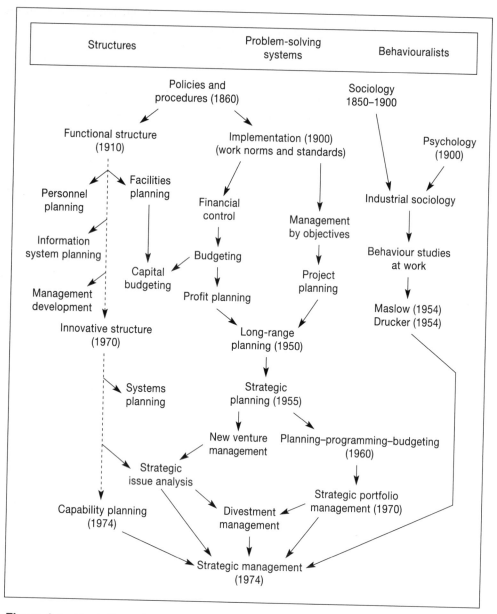

Figure 3.1 : Evolution of strategic management
Source: adapted from Bennett (1996)

Abernathy and Utterback, 1988; Porter, 1985; Roussel *et al.*, 1991). It is argued that successful strategies can be identified and selected in advance to deliver success.

A major criticism of the content view of strategy is that it reflects a static approach and neglects the context within which, and the processes whereby, strategies are generated, chosen and implemented. Furthermore, in practice, the formulation of strategy is often not clearly defined.

The content approach has also been used to identify *internal* factors that are seen as necessary for success (van de Ven, 1986; Buzzell and Gale, 1987; Rothwell, 1992). This body of literature is responsible for identifying key individuals in the innovation process such as Product Champions; Gatekeepers and Business Sponsors. The use of these key individuals can be said to be necessary but insufficient in itself to ensure continued innovative success. Rather, it is the *activities* performed by these individuals which should be the focus of management studies. This is the approach used by the *process* theorists and represents the other main body of literature within strategic management.

This approach is mainly concerned with the process of managing change. The process theory approach tends to produce models that identify conditions necessary to cause an outcome. It is the combination of these conditions that tells the story of how an outcome occurs. Process models provide a richer explanation of how and why the outcomes occur.

From an external perspective the process theory approach has concentrated on uncovering how companies compete. Within this stream of literature are inter-organisational networks, game theory and resource-dependency themes (Ansoff, 1982; Grindley, 1991). In analysing how strategies are implemented from within, research has uncovered a series of activities that together represent a process explaining how an outcome is achieved (Child, 1973; Burgelman, 1983; Pavitt, 1990; Trott *et al.*, 1995), for a review of different schools of thought in strategic management *see* Venkatraman and Camillus, 1984; Van de Ven, 1992.

There are several limitations to the process view. In particular, attention focuses on the factors involved and how they influence strategy, not on whether the intended strategy is itself worthwhile. Hence, there is limited consideration of the effects of strategies.

The strategic planning process

There have been numerous publications and much has been said about the formulation of business strategy. In practice, as Figure 3.2 illustrates, the formulation of business strategy is often not clearly defined. The process involves continual iteration over time between the various parts until strategy emerges. The elements in Figure 3.2 represent a simplified overview of the key elements:

1 The organisation's and senior management's long-term aspirations which will clearly have a significant impact on the eventual strategy.

2 The organisation's capabilities and heritage, that is, the skills acquired and developed over its history. In addition, this will include analysis of the organisation's resources in terms of finance, people etc.

3 The operating environment in which the organisation competes. The analysis here will need to take account of technological developments, strategies of competitors, changing market conditions etc.

It is the iteration over time of these elements that leads to the development of business strategy. For a more detailed explanation of the development of business strategy *see* Stacey (1997), Johnson and Scholes (1997), Lynch (1997).

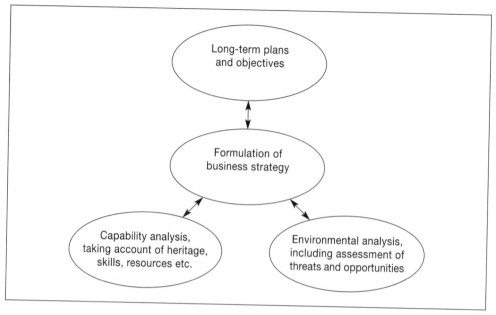

Figure 3.2 : The key elements in the process of formulating business strategy

Uncovering innovative capability

The field of strategic innovation management is characterised by a wide variety of conceptual frameworks and paradigms, including experience curves, growth-share matrices, industry structures and game theory. There has, however, been limited research that attempts to address both the external and internal considerations. However, the emerging theory within strategic management, the *dynamic competence-based theory of the firm*, attempts to address this limitation.

The new theory sees both the external and internal environments as dynamic: external environment is constantly changing as different players manoeuvre themselves and a company's internal environment is also evolving. The management of this internal process of change together with an understanding of the changes in the external environment offers a more realistic explanation of the challenges facing senior management. In addition, firms are seen as different (Nelson, 1991) and hence compete on the basis of competencies and capabilities (Tushman and Anderson, 1986; Nelson and Winter, 1982; Hamel and Prahalad, 1990; Pavitt, 1990; Cohen and Levinthal, 1990; Seaton and Cordey-Hayes, 1993; Hamel and Prahalad, 1994). This literature presents a related theoretical view that centres around an organisation's ability to develop specific capabilities. These capabilities tend to be dependent on the organisation's incremental and cumulative historical activities. In other words, a company's ability to compete in the future is dependent on its past activities. This view of an organisation's heritage is developed by Cohen and Levinthal (1990) in the context of the management of research and development. In their research, they developed the notion of 'absorptive capacity'.

In their study of the US manufacturing sector Cohen and Levinthal reconceptualise the traditional role of R&D investment, which was viewed simply as a factor aimed at creating specific innovations. They see R&D expenditure as an investment in an organisation's absorptive capacity. They argue that an organisation's ability to evaluate and utilise external knowledge is related to its *prior knowledge* and expertise and that this prior knowledge is, in turn, driven by prior R&D investment. Similarly, the notion of 'receptivity', advocated by Seaton and Cordey-Hayes (1993), is defined as an organisation's overall ability to be aware of, identify and take effective advantage of technology. This is explored in Trott and Cordey-Hayes (1996), who present a process model of receptivity showing the activities necessary for innovation to occur.

The issue of an organisation's capacity to acquire knowledge was also addressed by Nelson and Winter (1982) who emphasised the importance of 'innovative routines'. They argue that the practised routines that are built into the organisation define a set of competencies that the organisation is capable of doing confidently. These routines are referred to as an organisation's core capabilities. It is important to note that the notion of routines here does not necessarily imply a mechanistic, bureaucratic organisational form (*see* Chapter 2). The potential for controversy is resolved by Teece (1986), who distinguishes between 'static routines', which refer to the capability to replicate previously performed tasks, and 'dynamic routines', which enable a firm to develop new competencies. Indeed, dynamic organisational routines are very often those activities that are not easily identifiable and may be dominated by tacit knowledge (*see* Figure 3.3).

The point here is that over long periods organisations build up a body of knowledge and skills through experience and learning-by-doing. In addition to these internal organisational processes, Kay (1993) suggests that the *external linkages* that a company has developed over time and the investment in this network of relationships (generated from its past activities) form a distinctive competitive capability. Moreover, this can be transformed into competitive advantage when added to additional distinctive capabilities such as technological ability and marketing knowledge.

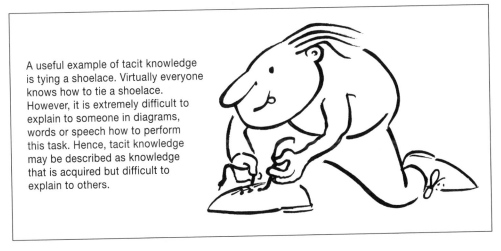

A useful example of tacit knowledge is tying a shoelace. Virtually everyone knows how to tie a shoelace. However, it is extremely difficult to explain to someone in diagrams, words or speech how to perform this task. Hence, tacit knowledge may be described as knowledge that is acquired but difficult to explain to others.

Figure 3.3 : Tacit knowledge

The knowledge base of an organisation

Many organisations have shown sustained corporate success over many years. This does not only mean unbroken periods of growth or profit, but also combinations of growth and decline that together represent sustained development and advancement. Research by Pavitt *et al.* (1991) on innovative success led him to remark:

> Large innovating firms in the twentieth century have shown resilience and longevity, in spite of successive waves of radical innovations that have called into question their established skills and procedures . . . Such institutional continuity in the face of technological discontinuity cannot be explained simply by the rise and fall of either talented individual entrepreneurs or of groups with specific technical skills. The continuing ability to absorb and mobilise new skills and opportunities has to be explained in other terms.

Pavitt identifies a number of properties of innovative activities in large firms. He places a great deal of emphasis on the concept of firm-specific competencies that take time to develop and are costly to initiate. Key features of these competencies are the ability to convert technical competencies into effective innovation and the generation of effective *organisational learning*. The observations made earlier suggest a need to analyse organisational knowledge and the processes involved in realising that knowledge rather than analysing organisational structure. If we can uncover the internal processes that determine a company's response to a given technology, this may help to explain the longevity of large innovating companies.

But what is meant by organisational knowledge? One may be tempted to think that the collective talents and knowledge of all the individuals within an organisation would represent its knowledge base. It is certainly the case that one individual within an organisation, especially within a large organisation, rarely sees or fully understands how the entire organisation functions. Senior managers in many large corporations have frequently said, with some amusement, when addressing large gatherings that they do not understand how the organisation operates! The following quote is typical:

> I am constantly being surprised as I travel around the many different parts of this organisation; while I know that we are in the car production business I am constantly amazed at the wide range of activities that we perform and how we do what we do. We regularly convert our raw materials of steel and many different component parts into fine automobiles, and then get them all over the world all within a matter of days. It's amazing and difficult to explain how we do it.
>
> *(Senior executive from a US car producer)*

This statement highlights the notion that *an organisation can seem to have knowledge itself.* That is, no one individual, even those people charting the course of the company, actually fully understands how all the internal activities and processes come together and function collectively. This concept of the organisation retaining knowledge is developed by Willman (1991), who argues that 'the organisation itself, rather than the individuals who pass through it, retains and generates innovative capacity, even though individuals may be identified who propagate learning'.

The whole can be more than the sum of the parts

It is important to recognise that the knowledge base of an organisation is not simply the sum of individuals' knowledge bases. If this were the case, and knowledge was only held at the individual level, then an organisation's expertise and acquired abilities would change simply by employee turnover. The wealth of experience built up by an organisation through its operations is clearly not lost when employees leave. The employment of new workers and the retirement of old workers does not equate to changing the skills of a firm. Figure 3.4 attempts to show how a collective knowledge base is larger than the sum of individual knowledge bases.

Organisational heritage

Organisational knowledge is distinctive to the firm. That is, it is not widely available to other firms. Hence, the more descriptive term organisational heritage. It is true that technical knowledge, in the form of patents, or commercial knowledge, in the form of unique channels of distribution, although used by an organisation is available to other firms. However, organisational knowledge includes this and more. For example, a vehicle manufacturer may use a wide variety of technologies and patents. This knowledge will not necessarily be unique to the organisation, that is, other companies will be aware of this technology. But the development and manufacture of the vehicle

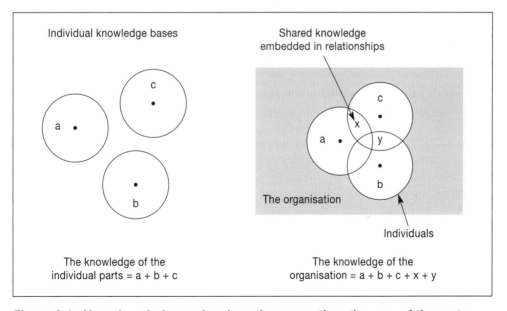

Figure 3.4 : How the whole can be viewed as more than the sum of the parts

will lead to the accumulation of skills and competencies that will be unique to the organisation. Hence, it is the individual ways in which the technology is applied that lead to organisation-specific knowledge.

To explore the above example further, groups or teams of people will develop specific skills required in the manufacture of a product. Over time, the knowledge, skills and processes will form part of the organisation's routines, which it is able to perform repeatedly. Individuals may leave the organisation and take their understanding to other organisations. But even if large groups of people leave, it is likely that understanding will have been shared with others in the organisation and it will have been recorded in designs or production planning records for use by others.

When the performance of the organisation is greater than the abilities of individuals

The notion of organisational knowledge was popularised by Kay (1993) who puts forward the idea of 'architecture' as a source of distinctive capability. This builds on the work of Nelson and Winter (1982); Pavitt (1990); Hamel and Prahalad (1990). These authors present an emerging theory concerned with the importance of accumulated knowledge and competencies within industrial companies. They argue that a firm's innovative capability is dependent on its incremental and cumulative historical activities. Elster (1983) refers to this notion as 'technological trajectories' within an organisation.

Kay uses the example of Liverpool football club, which, he argues, has consistently performed well but also better than the combined abilities of its players would seem to allow. This can also be said of many industrial organisations who have been able to generate exceptional long-term success from relatively ordinary employees. This, argues Kay (1993), is the result of the organisation's architecture. Whatever label one chooses, it seems clear that a firm's organisational knowledge plays a significant role in its firms ability to innovate and survive in the long term.

Organisational knowledge represents internal systems, routines, shared understanding and practices (*see* Figure 3.5). In the past it was loosely described as part of an organisation's culture, along with anything else that could not be fully explained. Organisational knowledge, however, represents a distinctive part of the much broader concept of organisational culture.

There are several tangible representations of this knowledge, such as minutes of meetings, research notebooks, databanks of customers, operating procedures, manufacturing quality control measures, as well as less tangible representations such as tried and tested ways of operating. Nelson and Winter (1982) argue that such learning-by-doing is captured in organisational routines. It is evident that the knowledge base of an organisation will be greater, in most cases, than the sum total of the individual knowledge bases within it. Willman (1991) argues that this is because knowledge is also embedded in social and organisational relationships (*see* Figure 3.5). At its simplest level suggests Kay, organisational knowledge is where each employee knows one digit of the code which opens the safe; clearly, this information is only of value when combined in the correct sequence with the information held by all the others.

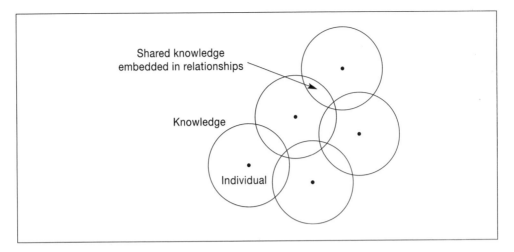

Figure 3.5 : Knowledge embedded in relationships

Japanese organisations and the role of organisational knowledge

It has been argued that western managers fail to understand the nature and concept of organisational knowledge and consequently they are unable to manage it, let alone exploit it. This is because the traditions of western management have become ingrained with writings and theories, from Frederick Taylor to Herbert Simon, which see the organisation as merely a machine to process information (Nonaka, 1991). According to this view, the only useful knowledge is formal and systematic: hard data and codified procedures. Similarly, the measurement of this knowledge is hard and quantifiable: increased efficiency, lower costs, improved return on investment etc. Nonaka suggests that there is another way to consider organisational knowledge found most commonly in highly successful Japanese companies. He explains:

> The centre-piece of the Japanese approach is the recognition that creating knowledge is not simply a matter of processing objective information. Rather, it depends on tapping the tacit and often highly subjective insights, intuitions, and hunches of individual employees and making those insights available for testing and use by the company as a whole.

The knowledge base of an organisation is defined in this view as 'the accumulation of the knowledge bases of all the individuals within an organisation *and* the social knowledge embedded in relationships between those individuals'. These relationships are often recognised as organisational processes and procedures (Kogut and Zander, 1992; Nonaka, 1991). The interactions and relationships between individuals may be said to represent a form of 'organisational cement' that performs two functions. First, it combines individual knowledge bases into a larger body of knowledge. Second, it enables individual knowledge bases to be accessed by the organisation, effectively via interaction with other individuals.

Characterising the knowledge base of an organisation

Discussions concerning the knowledge base of an organisation tend to focus on R&D activities and other technical activities. However, an organisation's ability to develop new products that meet current market needs, to manufacture these products using the appropriate methods and to respond promptly to technological developments, clearly involves more than technical capabilities. Nelson (1991) has argued that in industries where technological innovation is important firms need more than a set of core capabilities in R&D:

> These capabilities will be defined and constrained by the skills, experience, and knowledge of the personnel in the R&D department, the nature of the extant teams and procedures for forming new ones, the character of the decision making processes, the links between R&D and production and marketing, etc.
>
> *(Nelson, 1991)*

The wide range of skills mentioned by Nelson implies that the commonly held view of an organisation's knowledge base comprising only technical matters is too narrow. This is supported by Adler and Shenhar (1990), who suggest that an organisation's knowledge base is made up of several dimensions. The following five dimensions can be considered (*see* Figure 3.6):

- *Individual assets* – the skills and knowledge of the individuals that form the organisation. It is the application of these that influences corporate success.

- *Technological assets* – the most immediately visible elements of the technological base, the set of reproducible capabilities in *product, process* and *support areas*. Technological assets can be more or less reliably reproduced; the other elements are, by contrast, fundamentally relational, which makes them much more difficult to replicate.

- *Administration assets* – the resources that enable the business to develop and deploy individual and technological assets. These are specifically the skill profile of employees and managers, the *routines, procedures and systems* for getting things done, the organisational structure, the strategies that guide action, and the culture that shapes shared assumptions and values.

- *External assets* – the relations that the firm establishes with current and potential allies, rivals, suppliers, customers, political actors and local communities, e.g. joint ventures, distribution channels etc.

- *Projects* – the means by which technological, organisational and external assets are both deployed and transformed. Projects should be considered as part of the knowledge base in so far as the organisation's *modus operandi* is a learned behavioural pattern that can contribute to or detract from technological and business performance.

This more realistic assessment of an organisation's knowledge base shows how the various components of an organisation are inter-related. The inclusion of external networks is an important point. The formal and informal links an organisation has developed, often over many years, are a valuable asset. Pennings and Harianto (1992)

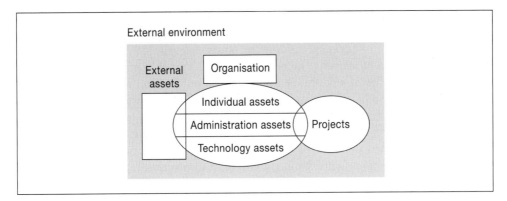

Figure 3.6 : The knowledge base of an organisation

Source: adapted from Adler and Shenar (1990)

include history of technological networking within the organisational skills necessary for innovation. At this point one may argue that it would be more appropriate to consider an organisation's knowledge base rather than select individual parts for analysis, which may be compared to trying to establish a racing car's performance by only analysing the engine. There are clearly other factors that will also have a dramatic impact on the car's performance.

The suggestion that an organisation's knowledge base is also time dependent, that the acquisition of knowledge takes place over many years, introduces the notion of organisational heritage, discussed above. If we accept the notion of organisational knowledge, this leads to the question of whether it is possible for organisations to learn.

The learning organisation

The concept of the learning organisation has received an unprecedented level of attention in the management literature. A special edition of *Organisational Science* was dedicated to the subject and it has received the attention of mainstream economics (Malbera, 1992). The emphasis of much of the early literature on this subject was on the past history of the organisation, and the strong influence of an organisation's previous activities and learning on its future activities. That is, the future activities of an organisation are strongly influenced by its previous activities and what it has learned (Pavitt *et al.*, 1991; Dosi, 1982; Nelson and Winter, 1982).

Unfortunately, the term organisational learning has been applied to so many different aspects of corporate management, from HRM to technology management strategies, that it has become a particularly vague concept. At its heart, however, is the simple notion that successful companies have an ability to acquire knowledge and skills and apply these effectively, in much the same way as human beings learn. Arguably, companies that have been successful over a long period have clearly demonstrated a capacity to learn. Cynics have argued that this is just another management fad with a new label for what successful organisations have been doing for many years. However, according to Chris Argyris (1977), organisations can be extremely bad at learning. Indeed, he suggests that it is possible for organisations to lose the benefits of experience and revert to old habits. It is necessary to engage in double-loop rather than single-loop learning, argues Argyris, since the second loop reinforces understanding. At its most simple level, single-loop learning would be the adoption of a new set of rules to improve quality, productivity etc. Double-loop learning occurs when those set of rules are continually questioned, altered and updated in line with experience gained and the changing environment.

A process of knowledge accumulation and application in innovative firms

The accumulation of knowledge and the effective assimilation and application of this knowledge are what appear to distinguish innovative firms from their less successful counterparts. This capability is popularly referred to as organisational learning. However, it is the internal processes that lead to this ability that need to be the focus of management attention. One would expect that a review of the organisational innovation literature would help in revealing these activities. However, this body of literature tends to use a structural approach when exploring the ability of organisations to innovate. Hence, discussions are dominated by how organisational structures and management strategies affect an organisation's ability to innovate. For example, Burns and Stalker (1961) supported the view that flexible organisational forms will sustain innovation but bureaucratic firms will not. Ansoff (1968) suggests the need for forecasting and environmental analysis techniques at the strategic management level. Daft (1986) emphasises the need for stable knowledge bases enhanced through stable communication. Rothwell (1975) discusses the importance of key individuals in the process, in this case the business innovator. Rothwell (1992) offers a list of 'critical success factors' necessary for successful industrial innovation, including company interaction with technology sources and markets; innovation as strategy; and internal control systems. All of these studies emphasise the presence or absence of certain factors rather than describing the actual activities or processes that are required. Recent studies by Japanese scholars on the development of new products have shown that to develop competencies companies have to uncover and understand their 'dynamic routines', which will invariably be built on tacit knowledge (Nonaka, 1991). These ideas are developed further by Trott (1993) who identifies an internal knowledge-accumulation model (see Figure 3.7). The process illustrated in this model highlights individual non-routine activities that contribute to the generation of genuine business opportunities.

Specialist functional departments in large organisations usually possess a wealth of idiosyncratic knowledge and experience. One of their important but unappreciated roles is constantly imparting specialist knowledge to colleagues concerning technical or commercial ideas. This 'informal internal consultancy' activity is often described as 'the informal testing of ideas on people in their functional capacity' (Trott, 1993). For example, a technical idea will often be informally discussed with colleagues from

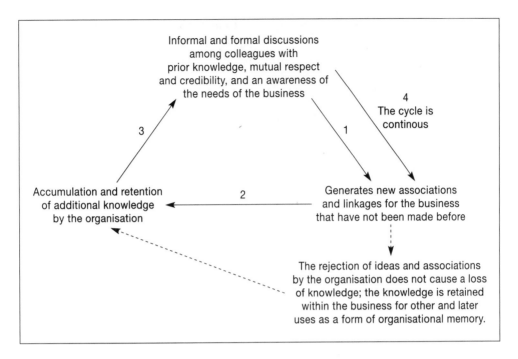

Figure 3.7 : The internal knowledge accumulation process

marketing to get informed commercial advice. This valuable informal activity is often unrecognised. The process has as a dual role: not only does it serve as an informal testing device whereby ideas can be presented to a variety of in-house specialists who are then able to assess the idea, it is also a support-gathering device. If the general feedback is positive and sufficient people are made aware of the idea, this will increase the likelihood of its eventually receiving formal backing from the business team. If, on the other hand, the feedback is broadly negative, this will alert individuals to the fact that the idea will probably not receive formal support. They will either develop the idea further by gaining additional information or decide that it is not suitable, for whatever reason, as an opportunity for the business.

Combining commercial and technological strengths: a conceptual approach to the generation of new business opportunities

In examining ways to generate new opportunities, the focus has been on recognising the importance of external organisational linkages, often called networks, as sources of external knowledge, *and* the process of associating these with the internal knowledge base of the company. It is this notion (shown diagrammatically in Figure 3.8) that helps identify a different approach to how companies can generate new business opportunities. It shows how these external linkages lower the threshold level for the process of 'osmosis' of external knowledge (Trott, 1993). Figure 3.8 highlights the role played by the knowledge base of the company and the need to view this as a dynamic entity made up of skills, knowhow and expertise, much of which is tacit, that is to say difficult to articulate and capture, but nonetheless present in all companies.

The conceptual framework shown in Figure 3.8 represents the role played by the knowledge bases of the firm in generating genuine business opportunities. A key activity is the continual external scanning undertaken by the organisation's commercial and technical arms shown at the furthest right- and left-hand sides. Towards the centre of the diagram is the process of assimilating internal knowledge from the organisation's knowledge bases. It is the assimilation of knowledge from the external environment via the company's external linkages with its internal capabilities that leads to new business opportunities being created. The successful combination of all of these activities can lead to the generation of genuine business opportunities (GBOs). This comprises a commercial opportunity (essentially commercial knowledge such as the identification of a new market, improving distribution through a strategic alliance, effective pricing strategies, etc.) with a technical opportunity (essentially technical knowledge such as the improvement in performance of a new material, the identification of an interesting new patent, the development of a new manufacturing process etc.) where this is aligned with existing commercial and technical competencies to ensure that the company genuinely has the ability turn the opportunity into a product (even if it decides not to). The complexity of the process may help to explain why creating genuine business opportunities is so difficult to achieve, since a wide range of activities need to be in place in order for associations to be made.

One company that seems not only to have recognised the importance of actively generating new business opportunities and new products but also to be extremely successful in this practice is Rubbermaid. It is widely known in the US for manufacturing a variety of plastic products from trash cans to mail boxes. A review of the *Fortune 500* companies reveals that Rubbermaid was the most respected company in 1994. It has built its success on generating new products (at a rate of almost one a day) and in

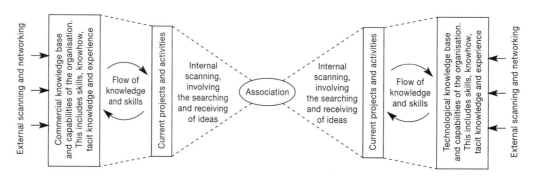

Figure 3.8 : Conceptual framework for generating Genuine Business Opportunities

many ways its strategy is relatively straightforward. It examines a wide variety of existing products on the market and sees to what extent they meet customers' needs and how Rubbermaid can improve the product. A host of ideas, from drip-proof drinking bottles to vandal-proof mail boxes, have provided the company with a stream of successful products. However, simplifying Rubbermaid's formula for success fails to acknowledge the environment that the company has created. It has been successful where many others have failed. Rubbermaid has long recognised the value of its external linkages, including customers and suppliers, and has developed a range of competencies based on the ability to capture opportunities from these linkages, associate these with its knowledge base and generate business opportunities and new products (Farnham, 1994). The company has thus facilitated the creation of genuine business opportunities by increasing the richness of the information received in terms of detail and breadth.

It is necessary to counsel caution at this point, because the process of turning these genuine business opportunities into commercial success is one of the most long-standing and fundamental issues facing businesses. We do not have to look too hard to uncover examples where companies have developed ideas and identified business opportunities yet failed to turn these into commercial successes. Xerox, which over the years has created numerous new product ideas including much of the technology behind the icon-driven computer operating system, did not recognise the potential of the opportunities it had created and did not benefit financially from the commercial success of what has turned out to be one of the most important developments in computing. It is significant, however, that the company has continued to generate business opportunities for itself and commercial success, while others have not.

The degree of innovativeness

The framework outlined in Chapter 1 emphasises the interaction that any firm has with the external environment, both in terms of markets and science and technology. The developments taking place in these external environments will continue largely independent of the individual firm. Any firm's ability to survive is dependent on its capability to adapt to this changing environment. This suggests that a firm has a range of options open to it. A company will attempt to look ahead and try to ensure that it is prepared for possible forthcoming changes and in some instances a firm can modify world science and technology. But mostly the future is unknown – some firms will prosper; others will not. In virtually all areas of business it is not always clear who are the players in the innovation race. Very often contenders will emerge from the most unexpected places. Furthermore, companies often find themselves in a race without knowing where the starting and finishing lines are! Even when some of these are known, companies often start out with the aim of becoming a leader and end up being a follower (Pavitt et al., 1990).

The development of new products and processes has enabled many firms to continue to grow. However, there is a wide range of alternative strategies which they may follow, depending on their resources, their heritage, their capabilities and their aspirations. Collectively these factors should contribute to the direction that the corporate strategy takes. Unfortunately, technology is rarely an explicit element of a firm's corporate strategy. This is so even in science- and technology-intensive firms. Very often, along with manufacturing, technology is the missing element in the corporate strategy. Until very recently technological competencies were not viewed as an integral part of the strategic planning process. They were seen as things to be acquired if required. As was discussed earlier, scientific knowledge cannot be bought like a can of tomatoes, off the shelf. By definition (*see* Chapter 1), technology is embedded in products and, processes and, while it is possible to acquire a patent, for example, this does not necessarily mean that the company will also possess the technological capability to develop products and processes from that patent. This has been an expensive lesson learned by many international chemical companies which have acquired licences from other chemical companies to develop a chemical process, only to experience enormous difficulties in producing the product. In one particular case the company abandoned the plant, having already sunk several million pounds into the project.

The innovation policy pursued cuts a wide path across functions such as manufacturing, finance, marketing, R&D and personnel, hence the importance attached to its consideration. The four broad innovation strategies commonly found in technology-intensive firms (Freeman, 1982; Maidique and Patch, 1988) are discussed below and in Table 3.1). These are not mutually exclusive or collectively exhaustive. A wide spectrum of other strategies are logically possible; indeed, very often a firm adopts a balanced portfolio approach with a range of products.

Leader/offensive

The strategy here centres on the advantages to be gained from a monopoly, in this case a monopoly of the technology. The aim is to try to ensure that the product is launched into the market before the competition. This should enable the company either to adopt a price-skimming policy, or to adopt a penetration policy based on gaining a high market share. Such a strategy demands a significant R&D activity and is usually accompanied by substantial marketing resources to enable the company to promote the new product. This may also involve an element of education about the new product, for example Polaroid's instant film and Apple's personal computer.

Fast follower/defensive

This strategy also requires a substantial technology base in order that the company may develop improved versions of the original, improved in terms of lower cost, different design, additional features etc. The company needs to be agile in manufacturing, design and development and marketing. This will enable it to respond quickly to those companies that are first into the market. Most of the major UK breweries were able to respond quickly to Guinness's 'In-can system' by developing their own versions. Without any in-house R&D their response would have been much slower, as this would have involved substantially more learning and understanding of the technology.

Very often both the first two strategies are followed by a company, especially when it is operating in fierce competition with a rival. Sometimes one is first to the market with a product development, only to find itself following its rival with the next product development. This is commonly referred to as healthy competition and is a phenomenon that governments try to propagate.

Cost minimisation/imitative

This strategy is based on being a low-cost producer and success is dependent on achieving economies of scale in manufacture. The company requires exceptional skills and capabilities in production and process engineering. This is clearly similar to the defensive strategy, in that it involves following another company, except that the technology base is not usually as well developed as for the above two strategies. Technology is often licensed from other companies. However, it is still possible to be extremely successful and even be a market leader in terms of market share. Arguably Compaq has achieved this position in the PC market. Originally its PCs were IBM clones but were sold at a cheaper price and are of a superior quality to many of the other competitors.

This is a strategy that has been employed very effectively by the rapidly developing Asian economies. With lower labour costs these economies have offered companies the opportunity to imitate existing products at lower prices, helping them enter and gain a foothold in a market, for example footwear or electronics. From this position it is then possible to incorporate design improvements to existing products.

Table 3.2 : Innovative strategies in the personal computer industry

Strategy	Characteristics	Examples of companies	Products
1 Leader/offensive	Science/technology intensive	Intel	Microchip
	High risk	Apple	Macintosh and graphical-user interface operating system
2 Follower/defensive	Srong technology base	IBM	Personal computer (leader in mainframe)
	Agility in design and manufacturing	Compaq	Regarded as market leader largely due to its range of PCs and additional features
3 Cost minimisation/ imitative	Low-cost manufacture	Research Machines	Low-cost PC
	Limited technology base	Research Machines	Focus is on assembly of component parts
4 Market segmentation specialist/traditional	Niche market	Apple	Graphic design and education markets
	Minimal technological change	n/a in this particular industry	n/a

Market segmentation specialist/traditional

This strategy is based on meeting the precise requirements of a particular market segment or niche. Large-scale manufacture is not usually required and the products tend to be characterised by few product changes. They are often referred to as traditional products. Indeed, some companies promote their products by stressing the absence of any change, for example Scottish whisky manufacturers.

A technology strategy provides a link between innovation strategy and business strategy

For each of the strategies discussed above there are implications in terms of the capabilities required. When it comes to operationalising the process of innovation, this invariably involves considering the technology position of the firm. Hence, the implementation of an innovation strategy is usually achieved through the management of technology.

Many decisions regarding the choice of innovation strategy will depend on the technology position of the firm with respect to its competitors. This will be largely based on the heritage of the organisation (*see* Chapter 1). In addition, the resource implications also need to be considered. For example, a manufacturer of electric lawn-mowers wishing to adopt an innovation leadership strategy would require a high level of competence in existing technologies such as electric motors, blade technology and injection moulding relative to the competition, as well as an awareness of the application of new technologies such as new light-weight materials and alternative power supplies. Adopting a follower strategy, in contrast, would require more emphasis on development engineering and manufacture.

In terms of resource expenditure, while the figures themselves may be very similar it is where the money is spent that will differ considerably, with the leader strategy involving more internal R&D expenditure and the follower strategy involving more emphasis on design or manufacturing. This area of technology strategy and the management of technology is explored in more detail in Chapters 7, 8 and 9.

CASE STUDY

Unilever garbage bags[1]

Although this case dates back to the mid-1970s, it is not widely known and is an excellent example of strategic planning, the generation of business opportunities and the evaluation of a business opportunity with respect to the stated corporate strategy.

▶

---

[1] This case has been written as a basis for class discussion rather than to illustrate effective or ineffective managerial and administrative behaviour. It has been prepared from a variety of published sources, as indicated, and from observations.

Introduction

Unilever plc is an Anglo-Dutch international brand management organisation specialising in the development of worldwide international brands. In particular it focuses its activities on the management of commodity products in three main areas: food products, such as margarine and tea; personal care products, such as shampoo and toothpaste; and household cleaning products, such as detergents and lavatory cleaners.

The company was formed in 1930 with the merger of Lever Brothers of the UK and Unie of the Netherlands. Lever Brothers had a long history of manufacturing soap and soap powders and X had built up a portfolio of products around the manufacture of margarine. Since this time Unilever has built businesses on this heritage and developed new capabilities and strengths.

Background

During the 1960s UK government planning had seen a huge increase in the development of high-rise housing. Although viewed today as flawed, the idea behind the building of tower blocks was to provide much needed inexpensive accommodation on limited available land. In addition, the population explosion in the 1960s caused many people involved with public policy to express concern about the shortage of housing for the future. High-rise housing was seen as a possible solution to these problems. Numerous city councils, supported by central government, decided to develop housing of this type and the construction of high-rise tower blocks continued into the early 1970s.

It was at this time that a consumer research group at Unilever uncovered what at first seemed to be merely a latent consumer need. This later turned into a multimillion-pound business opportunity.

A variety of different techniques were used at the time by consumer research groups to garner information from housewives. (Although the use of such terms as housewife may be inappropriate today, in the mid-1970s dual-income families were rare and household cleaning was largely the preserve of the female partner in a marriage.) The Household Cleaning Products business within Unilever would either invite housewives into the research laboratories at Port Sunlight Village, near Liverpool, or visit consumers at home. At that time the business was responsible for several well-known brands including Flash floor cleaner and Domestos lavatory cleaner.

A wide range of consumers from across the socioeconmic spectrum were involved in this research. However, it was during discussions with housewives in high-rise tower blocks that the need was uncovered. After several exchanges about cleaning bathrooms and sinks, the women expressed their frustration with having to clean up food remains from around the toilet. This puzzled the researcher, who for a brief second thought she had misunderstood what had been said. Further questioning revealed that for this woman a common cleaning chore was having to clean up spilt food from around the base of the toilet. This was because any liquid/semi-liquid food that was not eaten by her family had to be disposed of down the toilet. The researcher continued to enquire further about what happened with solid food waste. This, replied the woman, could be dealt with in a much more satisfactory way by wrapping the food in old newspaper and placing it in the kitchen wastebasket.

The researcher explored this problem with other housewives in high-rise tower blocks who expressed similar concerns. They also showed additional frustrations, in particular about odours from food sitting in kitchen wastebaskets until the weekly refuse collection. ▶

▶ This problem had not been mentioned by those living in more conventional single- or two-storey housing, largely because food waste was placed in dustbins outside the house.

A business opportunity

Extensive exploration of this issue was undertaken with consumers over the following few weeks. This revealed that this was an inconvenience for many and a problem for a few. One or two households explained that they placed plastic carrier bags inside their kitchen waste basket to avoid having to clean it after each use. They acknowledged, however, that this was a luxury. This was due to the effect of the oil crisis of the early 1970s. Petroleum and petroleum-derivative products, such as polythene, were relatively expensive. At that time the multiples (such as Sainsbury, Tesco and the Co-op) charged consumers for carrier bags (equivalent to approximately 21p in 1998). Most households used cardboard boxes to carry their groceries home or their own shopping bags, so unlike today, they did not have a drawer full of carrier bags.

The consumer research group presented their findings to a group of brand managers and R&D managers in the Household Cleaning business. Enormous excitement was generated as their thoughts immediately turned to a new product idea. Potentially the market was huge – virtually every household in the country. This was because, even though people in single- and two-storey housing did not currently identify kitchen wastebasket liners as a need, consumer products companies were experienced in highlighting problems to consumers and then offering solutions using sophisticated marketing communications. The meeting agreed to set up a new product group to explore the idea further. In particular, they looked at estimates of market size, manufacturing costs, technical input and marketing requirements.

Corporate strategy

A brief analysis of Unilever's history will reveal its consistent approach to the careful management and nurture of successful brands. Persil, Domestos and PG Tips have extremely long histories. The business has invested heavily over the years to build brand awareness and brand loyalty through a wide variety of promotional campaigns. This represents, albeit simplified, Unilever's corporate strategy – to build and develop international brands that will enable the group to provide added-value, long-term growth.

At the Household Cleaning Products division this translated into a portfolio of existing brands such as Flash, Domestos and Persil. The division had to decide whether the proposed new product concept would fit this strategy.

Evaluation of the opportunity

The results of the initial market research were placed in front of everyone. Around the table sat senior managers from the Household Cleaning division, senior research and development managers and the new product group (NPG). The initial discussions were very positive about the idea of a new business. This was largely due to the encouraging market research data which pointed to the enormous potential of such a product.

Discussions moved on to expected margins, that is, what were the expected costs and profits. At this point doubts began to creep into the minds of a few people – not because the margins were unhealthy, but because discussions began to focus on the manufacture of polythene, an area in which Unilever did not have a wealth of knowledge. The NPG began to realise that if this business opportunity was to develop it would be necessary to take the business into an area of technology with which it had little experience. However, as several people made clear, many companies have diversified into other areas with great success. The oil crisis and cost of polythene were also mentioned.

The discussions around the table switched to building a brand, the core of Unilever's strategy and the activity that is most readily associated with the company. It was at this juncture that several doubts emerged about the ability of the business to build a brand around such a product. One marketing manager argued that Bowater Scott had been able to build a brand around, of all things, toilet paper (Andrex). Surely Unilever could do it with liners for wastebaskets. Others in the group were not so certain. One senior research and development manager enquired about the group's preliminary technical investigations and in particular whether there were any possibilities of technical leadership. One member of the NPG explained that a research team had been established with the R&D department to look at this issue. Initial findings revealed the following technical possibilities:

- variety of different-size liners
- variety of different colours
- variety of different textures of material
- limited scope for design, but sealing the opening of the liner presented a few opportunities
- possibilities of incorporating fragrances within the liner.

As the meeting drew to a close there were several other discussions about the enormous market potential. The final point concerned competition and most around the table agreed that it would be fast and fierce as soon as this market opportunity was discovered. The potential competitors were likely to be the chemical and polythene manufacturers and polythene product manufacturers.

Walking away from a huge business opportunity

It slowly began to dawn on the NPG that it was increasingly unlikely that the investment required for this new business would be forthcoming. Eventually the meeting was closed and the decision was taken not to develop a new business. The NPG was given the opportunity to continue with its investigations and present its findings a year later. Most realised, however, that over the year many additional business opportunities were likely to emerge and this was probably the end for wastebasket liners at Unilever.

Discussion

This case provides an interesting example of a seemingly excellent business opportunity not being developed further because of lack of 'fit' with the business's capabilities, both in terms of commercial and technical knowhow. The lack of 'brand potential' and insufficient technical knowledge of the product area, in the end proved to be persuasive arguments. The role of the marketplace and the market research group in particular in generating business opportunities is clearly illustrated. Indeed, co-operation between marketing and R&D led to several suggestions for technical innovations and possible new product ideas.

Chapter summary

This chapter examined how business strategy affects the management of innovation. In so doing it introduced the notion of an organisation's knowledge base and how this links strategy and innovation. The heritage of a business was also shown to form a significant part of its knowledge base. Moreover, a firm's knowledge base largely determines its ability to innovate and certainly has a large influence on the selection of any innovation strategy.

Questions for discussion

1 Explain why a business's heritage needs to be considered in planning future strategy.

2 Explain the difference between individual knowledge and organisational knowledge and show how an organisation's knowledge can be greater than the sum of individual knowledge bases.

3 How would you compare the knowledge bases of two organisations?

4 Explain how Unilever's heritage influenced the decision not to develop further the wastebasket liner business opportunity.

5 Discuss the role of consumer research in the development of a new business opportunity for Unilever.

References

Abernathy, W.J. and Utterback, J. (1988) 'Patterns of industrial innovation' in Tushman, M.L. and Moore, W.L., *Readings in the Management of Innovation*, HarperCollins, New York, 97–108.

Adler, P.S. and Shenhar, A. (1990) 'Adapting your technological base: the organizational challenge', *Sloan Management Review*, Fall, 25–37.

Ansoff, H.I. (1968) *Corporate Strategy*, Penguin, Harmondsworth.

Ansoff, H.I. (1982) 'Societal strategy for the business firm', in Ansoff H.I., Bosman, A. and Storm, P.M. (eds) *Understanding and Managing Strategic Change*. North-Holland, New York, 83–109.

Argyris, C. (1977) 'Double loop learning in organizations', *Harvard Business Review*, Sept/Oct, 55.

Bennett, R. (1996) *Corporate Strategy and Business, Planning*, Financial Times Pitman Publishing, paper presented to R&D Management Conference, London.

Burgelman, R.A. (1983) 'Internal corporate venturing', *Administrative Science Quarterly*, 28, 223–44.

Burns, T. and Stalker, G.M. (1961) *The Management of Innovation*, Tavistock, London.

Buzzell, R.D. and Gale, B.T. (1987) *The PIMS Principle: Linking Strategy to Performance*, Macmillan, New York.

Chandler, A.D. (1962) *Strategy and Structure: Chapters in the History of American Industrial Enterprise*, MIT Press, Cambridge, MA.

Child, J. (1973) 'Predicting and understanding organisational structure', *Administrative Science Quarterly*, 18, 168–85.

Cohen, W.M. and Levinthal, D.A. (1990) 'A new perspective on learning and innovation', *Administrative Science Quarterly*, 35 (1) 128–52.

Daft, R. (1986) 'Bureaucratic versus non-bureaucratic structures and the process of innovation and change', in Bacharach, S. (ed.) *Research in Sociology of Organisations*, JAI, Greenwich.

Dosi, G. (1982) 'Technical paradigms and technological trajectories: a suggested interpretation of the determinants and directions of technical change', *Research Policy*, 11 (3).

Drucker, P. (1954) *The Practice of Management*, Harper & Row, New York.

Elster, J. (1983) *Explaining Technical Change*, Cambridge University Press, Cambridge.

Farnham, A. (1994) 'America's most admired company', *Fortune*, February 7.

Freeman, C. (1982) *The Economics of Industrial Innovation*, 2nd edn, Frances Pinter, London.

Grindley, P. (1991) 'Turning technology into competitive advantage', *Business Strategy Review*, Spring, 35–48.

Hamel, G. and Prahalad, C.K. (1990) 'The core competence of the corporation', *Harvard Business Review*, May/June, 79–91.

Hamel, G. and Prahalad, C.K. (1994) 'Competing for the future', *Harvard Business Review*, 72 (4) 122–28.

Johnson, G. and Scholes, K. (1997) *Exploring Corporate Strategy*, 4th edn, Prentice Hall, Hemel Hempstead.

Kay, J. (1993) *Foundations of Corporate Success*, Oxford University Press, Oxford.

Kogut, B. and Zander, U. (1992) 'Knowledge of the firm, combinative capabilities, and the replication of technology', *Organisation Science*, 3, (3), August.

Lindblom, L. (1959) 'The science of muddling through', *Public Administration Review*, 19, 79–88.

Lynch, R. (1997) *Corporate Strategy*, Financial Times Pitman Publishing, London.

Maidique, M. and Patch, P. (1988) 'Corporate strategy and technology policy' in *Readings in the Management of Innovation*, Tushman, M.L. and Moore, W.L. (eds) HarperCollins, New York.

Malbera, F. (1992) 'Learning by firms and incremental technical change', *The Economic Journal*, 102, 845–59.

Maslow, A. (1954) *Motivation and Personality*, Harper & Brothers, New York, 934–48.

Mintzberg, H. (1978) 'Patterns in strategy formulation', *Management Science*, 24.

Nelson, R.R. (1991) 'Why do firms differ, and how does it matter?' *Strategic Management Journal*, 12 (1) 61–74.

Nelson, R.R. and Winter, S. (1982) *An Evolutionary Theory of Economic Change*, Harvard University Press, Boston, M.A.

Nonaka, I. (1991) 'The knowledge creating company', *Harvard Business Review*, Nov/Dec 69 (6) 96–104.

Pavitt, K. (1990) 'What we know about the strategic management of technology', *California Management Review*, 32 (3) 17–26.

Pavitt, K. (1991) 'Key characteristics of the large firm', *British Journal of Management*, 2 (1) 41–8.

Pavitt, K., Robson, M. and Towsend, J. (1990) 'Technological accumulation, diversification and organisation in UK companies, 1945–1983', *Management Science*, 35 (1) 81–99.

Pennings, J.M. and Harianto, F. (1992) 'Technological networking and innovation implementation', *Organisational Science*, 3 (3), 356–82.

Porter, M.E. (1985) *Competitive Advantage*, Harvard University Press, Boston, MA.

Quinn, J.B. (1978) 'Strategic change: logical incrementalism', *Sloan Management Review*, 1 (20), Fall, 7–21.

Rothwell, R. (1975) 'Intracorporate entrepreneurs', *Management Decision*, 13 (3).

Rothwell, R. (1992) 'Successful industrial innovation: critical factors for the 1990's', *R&D Management*, 22 (3) 221–39.

Roussel, P.A., Saad, K.N. and Erikson, T.J. (1991) *Third Generation R&D: Managing the Link to Corporate Strategy*, Harvard Business School Press, Cambridge, MA.

Seaton, R.A.F. and Cordey-Hayes, M. (1993) 'The development and application of interactive models of technology transfer', *Technovation*, 13 (1), 45–53.

Simon, H. (1957) *Administrative Behavior*, Free Press, New York.

Stacey, R.D. (1997) *Strategic Management and Organisational Dynamics*, 2nd edn, Financial Times Pitman Publishing, London.

Taylor, F. (1947) *Scientific Management*, Harper & Row, New York.

Teece, D. (1986) 'Profiting from technological innovation: implications for integration, collaboration, licensing and public policy', *Research Policy*, 15, 285–305.

Trott, P. and Cordey-Hayes, M. (1996) 'Developing a receptive R&D environment: a case study of the chemical industry', *R&D Management*, 26 (1) 83–92.

Tushman, M. and Anderson, M. (1986) 'Technological discontinuities and organisational environments', *Administrative Science Quarterly*, 31 (3) 439–65.

van de Ven, A.H. (1986) 'Central problems in the management of innovation', *Management Science*, May, 32 (5) 590–607.

van de Ven, A.H. (1992) 'Suggestions for studying strategy process: a research note', *Strategic Management Journal*, 13, 169–88.

Part one : The concept of innovation management

Venkatraman, N. and Camillus, J.C. (1984) 'Exploring the concept of fit in strategic management', *Academy of Management Review*, 9 (3), 513–25.
Willman, P. (1991) 'Bureaucracy, innovation and appropriability', paper given at ESRC Industrial Economics Study Group Conference, London Business School, November 22.

Further reading

Henry, J. and Walker, D. (eds) (1991) *Managing Innovation*, Sage/OU Press, London.
Johnson, G. and Scholes, K. (1997) *Exploring Corporate Strategy*, Prentice Hall, Hemel Hempstead.
Kay, J. (1993) *Foundations of Corporate Success*, Oxford University Press, Oxford.
Lynch, R. (1997) *Corporate Strategy*, Financial Times Pitman Publishing, London.
Nonaka, I. and Takeuchi, H. (1995) *The Knowledge Creating Company*, Oxford University Press, Oxford.
Stacey, R.D. (1993) *Strategic Management and Organisational Dynamics*, Financial Times Pitman Publishing, London.

80

PART TWO

New Product Development

This part reviews and summarises the nature and techniques of new product development. It looks at the process of developing new products and examines many of the new product management issues faced by companies.

Product strategy is the subject of Chapter Four, building on many of the strategy issues discussed in Chapter Three. In particular, it examines the influences on product planning decisions and the role of marketing management. All of these heavily influence any decision to develop new products.

Our understanding of the new product innovation process has improved significantly in the past thirty years. During this period numerous models have been developed to help explain the process. These are examined in Chapter Five.

*Chapter Six moves from the conceptual to the operational level and analyses the particular challenges faced by the new product manager. Taking a practitioner view-point, it investigates the activities that need to be undertaken and how companies organise the process. Emphasis is placed on the role of the **new product team**.*

4

Product strategy

Gordon Oliver

Introduction

The products developed by an organisation provide the means for it to generate income. But there are many factors to consider in order to maximise the product's chance of success in competitive environments. A company has to identify the specific ways it can differentiate its products in order to gain competitive advantage. It has to consider the market in which it is competing, the nature of the competition and how its capabilities will enable its products to be successful. The positioning of the product and the brand strategy selected are of particular importance.

Learning objectives

When you have completed this chapter, you will be able to:

- Recognise that new products serve a variety of purposes depending on what is seen to be the strategic imperative
- Examine the concept of platforms in new product development
- Assess the importance of brand strategy in product development
- Explain how differentiation and positioning contribute to a product's success in the marketplace
- Recognise the importance of marketing research in the effective development of new products.

Customer satisfaction through products or services

Organisations choose to compete in one or more product-markets using a specified range of technologies. They seek to have a set of balanced capabilities that will enable them to match market opportunities by developing attractive market offerings which customers perceive as conveying valuable benefits. How well they accomplish this, compared with competitors, is a major determinant of success.

Products, or services, are the vital ingredients of the market offering and are the vehicles for providing customer satisfaction. Deriving a set of products which customers perceive as useful and worth buying may be fortuitous, but more often it is the result of deliberate, systematic endeavour. Some understanding of the nature of that endeavour can be gained from studying the interaction of three key factors: the organisation's capabilities, its strategies and the environment within which it operates. Additional insights can come from considering positioning and brand strategies, market entry strategies and the contribution of marketing research.

Capabilities, networks and platforms

The company's core capabilities, and those that it can develop or acquire, from the boundaries of what it can accomplish. However, a broader view brings in the notion of distinctive capabilities. This is wider than technical or operations competence. As we saw previously, Kay (1993) suggests that these broader capabilities include an organisation's 'architecture' and this embraces the network of relationships within or around the firm. These relationships might cover customers, suppliers, distributors or other firms engaged in related activities. This leads to the perspective that product development, and the competitive rivalry of which it is usually a part, can sometimes be better understood as undertaken by networks of partnerships and alliances rather than by individual, isolated producers (Doyle, 1995).

The composition of the network can vary widely. In some high-technology industries a horizontal alliance of competitors or firms might dominate and perhaps form a consortium for the research and development of a technology. For example, Kodak, Fujifilm, Minolta, Nikon and Canon were allied in the development of the Advanced Photo System. In other industries it might be a vertical arrangement between suppliers, manufacturers, distributors and possibly even customers. It can be a formal agreement, a loose collection of understandings or a system 'managed' by a powerful member.

Saying this of capabilities leads to complications. If networks are competing, rather than individual firms, then the activities across the network need to be co-ordinated. Sometimes it is the manufacturer which is dominant and leads and controls the network, as in the motor industry. Sometimes it is a distributor which takes the lead and initiates new product categories, as in food retailing. On occasion a large customer can dominate, show the need for a new product and encourage suppliers to innovate, as in the health service or defence industries. How effectively this leadership and co-ordination are undertaken influences substantially what products are developed and how they are developed. Another consideration is that the network members may have a collection of varied motives for being party to the relationship. Through time they may come to stress other motives that may result in their becoming less interested in the network's aims and less willing to co-operate. The network leader therefore needs to spend some time monitoring motives and encouraging, or inducing, full co-operation by all network members. If the network is established for the development of a technology then the partners have other sets of problems once the technology is available. How do they share the results and how do they each go on to establish distinctive, competitive products?

Choosing appropriate partners for the network and keeping them focused are important attributes for network leadership. Developing and refining the network's innovative ability is crucial; this is not restricted to technical innovation, because innovation in business processes and in distribution can also have large impact.

Capabilities change. Without continuous attention they can become ineffectual or redundant, as the technology or the market requirement moves on. Alternatively, capabilities may be enhanced through internal development, through external acquisition and through the bringing together of new partnerships and alliances so that the network's capability is deeper or wider. Most capabilities thrive through continuity, through continuous, incremental enhancement around a technology or a set of related technologies. This is in keeping with the idea of organisational heritage introduced in Chapter 2.

Product platforms

Emphasis on continuity in the development of capabilities is also consistent with the idea of an evolving product platform that a 'product family' shares. Meyer and Utterback (1993) use the car industry as the classic example of this idea, where several individual models may share the same basic frame, suspension and transmission. As they say, 'a robust platform is the heart of a successful product family, serving as the foundation for a series of closely related products' (31). The Sony Walkman provides another illustration, with its 160 variations and four major technical innovations between 1980 and 1990, all of which were based on the initial platform (Jones, 1997). Black & Decker rationalised its hundreds of products into a set of product families, with consequent economies throughout the chain from procurement to distribution and after-sales service. In all these cases the evolution of the product platform, along with the evolution of the requisite capabilities, is central to the product development strategy.

This notion may have originated in engineering but it can be applied widely. Food, cosmetics, clothing and furniture manufacturers can be seen to have product platforms and families. Johnson & Johnson and its development of the Acuvue disposable contact lenses provides another example. Thomas (1995) points out that many people needing vision correction did not wear traditional hard or soft contact lenses because of the discomfort and the cleaning requirements. Acuvue uses high-quality soft contact lenses sold at a sufficiently low price to allow disposal after a week, without cleaning. This distinctive advantage, which was clearly relevant to many consumers, led to a successful launch in 1987 that defined a new market segment. The original product became the basic platform for continuing innovation that is leading to other new offerings in Johnson & Johnson's vision care product family.

Sometimes entirely new platforms and entirely new capabilities are required. Step changes in the product or manufacturing technology, in the customer need or in what the competition offers and how it offers it can demand radical rather than incremental change. The risk is all the more if that means the adoption of new technologies, outside the firm's traditional arena.

Strategy contexts

New product strategy is part of a web of strategies. It is linked to, and its objectives are derived from, marketing strategy, technology strategy and the overall corporate strategy. These other strategies provide the role, the context, the impetus and the definition of the scope of new product strategy.

Competitive strategy

New products are not required just because they are new products. They are required because they serve a customer need and an organisational need. The organisational need will be articulated in the organisation's strategy and there might be comments in its mission statement about striving to lead in the technology, or to be the key innovator. However, much new product development (NPD) is not concerned with new-to-the-world innovations, partly because many companies are followers and not leaders in their technology. NPD for a follower can be very different to NPD for a leader. New products perform different roles at different times for different companies. They serve a variety of purposes depending on what is seen to be the strategic imperative.

Competitive strategy may drive new product planning on a short-term or long-term basis. In the shorter term a defensive posture may suggest that product variants are needed to shore up a declining market share, which is perhaps attributed to a competitor's aggressive new product activities. A reactive strategy could entail filling out product lines with different product sizes or added features that may be intended to deter a new entrant to the market, by not leaving unattended small market segments to be used as an entry point by the new competitor. Such minor product changes could also be employed to secure distributors' loyalty, because they are then able to carry a full range of the product and so be less inclined to stock rival offerings. Imitative products may be brought out, copying competitors, for similar reasons. In these kinds of situations where the new product is a minor modification, however new the advertising proclaims it to be, it is unlikely that the full, classic NPD process would be engaged. There may be little or no research and market testing may be restricted to determining acceptable price levels or to choosing between alternative advertising messages.

In the longer run competitive strategy may seek a more profound contribution from new products. A strategy may look for new product categories to be developed, within the same or a related technology or in a new technology area. These new products may appeal to the organisation's traditional customer base or seek new customer segments. This more radical product development would be more likely to be subject to thorough marketing and technical research, development and testing.

New products can also perform a learning function for the organisation. The development of a pioneering new product platform may at first be tentative and several alternative concepts for new platforms may be investigated simultaneously. Uncertainties surround such ventures because the new platform may require the development of costly new competences, while simultaneously the nature and the scale of the market opportunity are illusory. The firm may need to develop both new knowledge and new skills in technical, operations and marketing areas. The adequacy of the search for, and the acquisition of, these new skills and knowledge will mark out the leaders.

Product portfolios

Another set of strategic considerations concerns the overall portfolio of products. Analysing the organisation's total collection of products by viewing it as a portfolio, as in an investment portfolio, may give fresh insights. This approach was initiated by the share-growth matrix, or Boston box, which used market share and market growth as dimensions against which to plot the positions of products. A typology was derived with high and low values for each of the two dimensions so that the four quadrants could be contrasted. For example, products classified as high share/high growth could be contrasted with those deemed to be low share/low growth. Prospects could also be investigated by comparing where products are positioned presently, where they might be in the future with no change in strategy and some desired positions. Analyses of this kind might suggest some strategic issues. A clustering of the portfolio in one quadrant might be viewed as unbalanced and an absence of any products in the two high-growth quadrants might be thought to be unhealthy.

Such a simple depiction has attracted controversy and alternative models have been suggested using multifactor dimensions that are composites of variables, such as business strength and market attractiveness. Most of the derivations still employ two dimensions because they can be displayed with ease, but more complex, and some say more realistic, models are multidimensional. All these models share a similar aim: to give the strategist an overview that could reveal current or potential problems or opportunities in the product strategy.

This portfolio approach might also be applied to the product families and the platforms on which they are built, although the selection of appropriate variables to describe the space can be a problem. Thought might be given to the extent to which a wide range of words might be usefully employed to indicate the dimensions, such as robust, innovative, sophisticated, flexible, generic, evolving, traditional. For example, using relative sophistication (ranging from very sophisticated to unsophisticated) and flexibility (from very flexible to very inflexible) as descriptors of the two dimensions might show the majority of product platforms to be unsophisticated and inflexible, with possibly one isolated product that is sophisticated and flexible. Without qualification that probably means little and it leads to no great revelation. Being unsophisticated is not necessarily a bad thing; it may be just what the customer needs. Regarding the other dimension a very flexible product platform is not necessarily a good thing; it may result in too many compromises that lead to products that are not specialised enough for customer applications. Several of these 'mapping' exercises might be tried using different descriptors. A supplementary analysis might trace connections between platforms, any spin-off from them and in addition bring in a time dimension.

Nothing conclusive can be expected from these analyses: they are probing and investigative. The process of taking this broader view of the portfolio draws attention to issues that, with deeper analysis, could be significant. It is this identification of issues that can be critical and creative. It can flout any fixation with norms and conventions that can flourish readily within organisations; and it can underline the point that approaches to product strategy development must be original if they are to lead to distinctive new market offerings.

Environments

The external environment constrains what can be done, for example within the bounds of current understanding of a technology. Sometimes the external environment dictates what must be done, for example following the introduction of a new piece of legislation protecting an aspect of the natural environment, as was seen in the case study in Chapter 1. It can present possibilities and opportunities, such as a breakthrough in an enabling technology or the new affluence of consumers that allows them to be prepared to pay more for products in a particular category. The external circumstance can also pose threats and problems, as when a competitor introduces a significant product advance, or when another rival closes access to materials, or to distributors, through its acquisition of companies in those activities.

Gillette Sensor

The introduction of the Gillette Sensor shaving system provides an example of the importance of monitoring the environment and preparing product strategy as a response to crucial developments in the market.

During the 1980s disposable razors became a significant threat to the company's business and by 1988 they took half of the overall wet shaving market. Although Gillette brought out its own disposable shaver, it believed that these disposable products were undermining its more profitable lines in shaving systems, razors that can be refilled with blades. The problem was that competition in disposable razors focused on price, with many promotions based on price discounts. In some countries, like the UK, own-label disposable razors from retailers were pushing the product towards a commodity status where branding would be irrelevant. Gillette's response, through substantial R&D throughout the 1980s, was the idea of a blade in a suspension system that allowed it to 'float', to contour the face for a closer shave. These blades were incorporated into a cartridge that could reload the razor. Extensive in-use testing followed and the new product was launched in 1990. In 1991 its sales exceeded $300 million and in 1992 the same product platform was used for a brand extension with the introduction of Sensor for Women. This product has a wider handle and distinctive colours, but it employed the same suspension technology.

These new products enabled Gillette effectively to counter the threatening environment in which it was placed. Nevertheless, the company cannot be complacent because competitors have attempted to follow its move into this new technology and disposable razors with some form of suspension system have appeared. Constant monitoring of the way the market is developing is demonstrably required.

Source: Thomas, 1995, 253–65

Close analysis of the present situation in the market is fundamental, along with speculations about how it might progress. Because of the potential importance of external events and conditions, some type of environmental monitoring, in a strategic sense, has become a key exercise in strategy search. Assessments of the present situation can be extended to conjectures about future environments and in some industries, such as aerospace or pharmaceuticals, this may require a very long-term view. A range of alternative future scenarios may be built around these conjectures, indicating guesses about what the organisation sees to be the aspects of its environment carrying the most stress. These speculations might deal with some of the following issues:

1 Estimates would be needed about the way the technology will change and this could be more or less rigorous. It could involve some brainstorming within the organisation and it could seek various forms of external advice from government agencies, research centres, consultants and universities.

2 Estimates might also be made about how the industry's competitive structure may alter. Are the same competitors likely to be contending in the market in the future? Are there any indications that any are preparing some kind of strategic shift? Will any withdraw or reduce their activities within the industry? Will there be changes in how companies compete and the positioning they seek in the market? Will there be any new entrants from other industries or from other countries? Unexpected arrivals in the industry, especially if they are well funded, well managed and they come with a significant innovation, can be particularly troublesome. That was the case when Mars entered the ice-cream business and quickly secured a significant market share.

3 Another area of concern could be how any regulatory framework might evolve and this could include the extent to which it would limit activities in the future or open new possibilities.

4 Customer needs may be a further area in which to speculate. Will they become more demanding and require better materials and better performance in the products they use? Will they perceive some emerging technology as a substitute? Will they have new kinds of needs and will there be new kinds of customers?

Taking various combinations of these factors could yield a series of scenarios and investigating the implications for the organisation of each of them could indicate important issues requiring attention. Such future scenarios may throw up attractive or unattractive situations and the organisation may then attempt to do what it can to prepare itself and to increase the likelihood of the former while inhibiting the later. This will help shape ideas about the potential role for new products and the scope of the problems and opportunities that they are intended to address.

Differentiation and positioning

Product strategy will express how the organisation seeks to differentiate itself, and distance itself, from its competitors and it will be the bedrock of its market positioning. It is axiomatic that for new products to be successful in the market they need to be perceived to be beneficial by prospective buyers. The benefit needs to stand out, to be distinctive and attractive. This distinction needs to be relevant to buyers and it needs to be *seen* to be relevant by them. It is pointless being distinctive in a way that consumers believe to be irrelevant or incomprehensible. This point is illustrated in the case study at the end of this chapter.

Differentiation

Broadly, the differentiation sought by competitors could be based on cost, with a value-for-money proposition, or it could be based on superior quality, which might encompass better materials, better performance, new features, uncommon availability or better service. A useful perspective on product differentiation is provided by Levitt's idea of product augmentation (Levitt, 1986). He suggests that there are four levels on which products can be considered:

1 The *core product* comprises the essential basics needed to compete in a product-market; a car needs wheels, transmission, engine and a rudimentary chassis.

2 The *expected product* adds in what customers have become accustomed to as normal in the product-market; for a car this would be a reasonably comfortable interior and a range of accessories.

3 The *augmented product* offers features, services or benefits that go beyond normal expectations.

4 The *potential product* would include all the features and services that could be envisaged as beneficial to customers.

An interesting implication of this categorisation is that it can demonstrate that the position is dynamic because customer expectations change. In the example of the car, where would air conditioning be placed in these categories? Until recently it would have been an augmentation for mass-market vehicles, but it has now become a standard expectation in new cars. Competition drives up consumer expectations. One rival introduces something new and, if it finds customer acceptance, other rivals follow. As a consequence augmentations become expectations and this ratchet effect means that there is no equilibrium until the full potential has been realised. Even then, changes to the technology, or to another technology, might release an entirely new kind of potential so that the process continues.

Another implication is that as firms migrate upwards in this process they leave market opportunities for others to exploit. There may be niche markets left for 'unbundled' products or services making low-cost, basic offers with no frills. Airlines are an example.

The choice of differentiation strategy is pivotal (*see* Figure 4.1). It reaches back to core capabilities and it reaches forward to positioning strategy. The differentiation

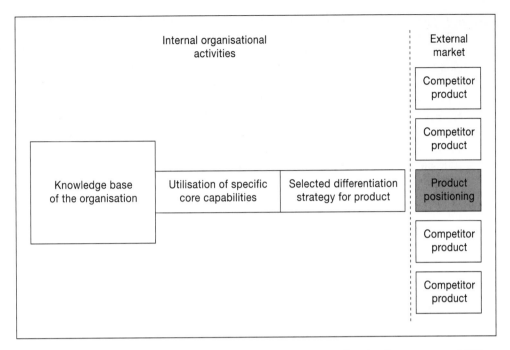

Figure 4.1 : The differentiation strategy links the organisation's core capabilities with external competitors

will not be effective unless it is rooted firmly in the organisation's capabilities, or in the capabilities of the network delivering the new product. Similarly, the positioning of the product in the market needs to be built on, and consistent with, the differentiation strategy.

Product positioning

Product positioning refers to the perceptions that customers have about the product. It is a relative term that describes customer perceptions of the product's position in the market relative to rival products. It is founded on understanding how customers discriminate between alternative products and it considers the factors customers use in making judgements or choices between products in the market being investigated. These are referred to as the customer's evaluative criteria and they may be the product's physical attributes, but they can include customer assessments about whom the product is meant for, when, where and how it is used and aspects of the brand's 'personality' (e.g. innovative, functional, old-fashioned, exclusive, frivolous, fun).

Positioning studies begin with determining a relevant set of products. The criterion for inclusion is that they must be perceived by customers to be alternatives. Then a list of determinant attributes is generated; that is, a list of attributes that are salient or the most important to customers in discriminating between the alternatives. With this framework customers' perceptions and preferences are collected. This could be by survey using a structured questionnaire. Respondents would be asked to scale their feelings about each product on each attribute. They could also be asked their preferred level for each attribute. The output can be portrayed in a diagram (sometimes called a brand map or perceptual map) showing the locations of each product against the attributes (the dimensions) and relative to the preferred level (the ideal point). This is most readily understood if the analysis is restricted to two dimensions. For example, for a food product the dimensions might be nourishment and calory count and respondents could rate all the brands they know in the category from high to low on these. Some brands may be seen to be highly nourishing with a high calory count and some not so nourishing with a low calory count. Illustrations can be found in Moore and Pessemier (1993) and Urban and Hauser (1993).

Such a study would show the proximity of, or the distance between, the perceived positions of the products considered. This might show the positions to be crowded in one area or well spaced. If an ideal point, that is, the customers' preferred position, is introduced then the relative distance of each product from this ideal can be measured. If these relative distances accord reasonably with the relative market shares of the products then it could be assumed that the dimensions chosen are a fair representation of the way customers choose in this market. Generally, it would be expected that the higher market shares would be won by products nearer to the ideal point.

Customers may be far from unanimous about these perceptions and preferences. If the observations were widely scattered, then further research would be needed to understand how customers make their evaluations and perhaps other dimensions might be tried. If there were several clusters of preferences, each in a different part of the map, this might indicate different market segments. In the food example above there could be one group preferring a very nourishing product with a low calory count, and another group wanting something nourishing with a high calory count. Mapping product positions against these two ideal points might then reveal one segment to be well served with many products, but an opening for a new product near the other ideal point where there may be no major existing brands.

Positioning strategy depends on the choice of an appropriate base. This base must be relevant and important to customers and related to how they make choices in that product field. It should also attempt to distance the brand from the positions of rivals. Wind (1982) offers six bases: product feature, benefits, use occasion, user category, against another product or by dissociation from all the other products. Crawford (1997) adds parentage (because of where it comes from), manufacture (because of how it is made) and endorsement (because people you respect say it is good).

Selecting an appropriate positioning can make the difference between success and failure. It determines what the organisation tells the market about the product, whom it tells and how it tells it. Motorcycle producers take various positions, for example. Piaggio's Vespa scooter is aimed at young riders and latterly at women. Suzuki is also now targeting women as a distinctive segment. Some of the most expensive machines are aimed at older men with a revived interest in motorcycling and higher discretionary income.

For most products there may be a host of features, benefits and applications; few, if any, products have a single feature, a singular benefit and one narrow application. Choosing from among the possibilities can lead to creative and unique solutions and consequentially to a highly differentiated strategy. It can also result in costly mistakes, with products being positioned in strange ways that consumers neither understand nor find credible.

As the market grows and matures it may become necessary to consider repositioning. The original differentiation could become less effective as competitors crowd in, or as new types of buyers with different expectations adopt the product. A repositioning exercise could focus on some reformulation of the product, some change to the image projected, a realignment of the segments targeted or a change to the distribution channels employed.

Brand strategy

Brand strategy is the spearhead of the organisation's competitive intentions. It carries the company or product name into the market and shows how it is positioning itself to compete. It involves choices between having no brand name at all, so that the product is sold as a commodity, and the attempt to develop a distinctive brand name with a distinctive set of associations and expectations. In the latter case there are further options. The product could be sold to another party for it to place its trademark or branding on it, or alternatively the complete product, or major components, could be bought in and then company branded. There are more choices with the brand name itself. Should the company have a single brand for all its products, such as Kellogg, or a range of apparently unconnected brands, such as Procter & Gamble? Should it establish a corporate brand as an umbrella with a series of subbrands under the umbrella, such as Ford? Or should it have a mixed brand strategy with elements of all these approaches?

On one level such consideration might appear to be quite trivial. What's in a name? Think back to the Gillette Sensor case referred to earlier. If that product was called, say, the Suspension Razor with no Gillette identification, then would market acceptance have been achieved so rapidly, if at all? Would consumers have trusted it? Would they have taken the risk and made a first purchase? In any event, they would probably not have been given the chance to buy because it would not have gained sufficient acceptance by distributors. It might have achieved limited distribution but it would have taken a great deal of time to reach full national, let alone international, distribution.

The brand name itself is really a summary; it can stand for a great deal more. It can represent the sum of what people know about the product and its usefulness, quality and availability. It can be surrounded with associations, negative or positive, about how it can be used, where it can be used and the occasions on which it is used. It can be symbolic and loaded with imagery about the kinds of people who use the brand. For some well-known brands the few letters in their names can be triggers to wide-ranging perceptions. Focus groups can talk for hours with just the prompt of a few brand names.

It is not just in consumer markets that this power of the brand name is apparent. Inspection of any trade magazine reveals its prevalence in all kinds of markets, and component makers now also attempt to ensure that their brand is evident in advertising and packaging.

Brand extensions

A brand extension is the use of an established brand name on a new product in the same product field or in a related field. The brand name might also be stretched to an unrelated product field. A simple brand extension would be when a new or unconventional size is brought out, so that the original brand name is given a prefix (e.g. Giant, Jumbo, Fun), or for some technical products this could be a new alphanumeric code. Operating within the same product field, but attempting to attract a new market segment, the extension might have a modified design and there could be words added to the brand name indicating for whom it is intended, such as men or women. Daily newspapers extended publication to Sunday and have branded sections, all carrying the original brand name in some way. In the case of an extension to a business computer package it could specify a new application type in the branding.

More radical extensions occur when the brand is stretched or carried into unrelated product fields. Some newspapers, such as the *Daily Telegraph*, have started direct marketing operations selling their own brand of clothing. Several fashion houses place their brand name wide and far across a range of luxury goods. Wilkinson Sword sells razors and gardening tools under the same brand. Canon markets cameras and copiers. Philips uses its brand name in diverse electrical and electronic industries. And the Virgin brand name is carried on an airline, a railway, a cola, a retail chain and in insurance.

The rationale behind a brand extension strategy is to take advantage of potential carry-over effects from the original brand. If the original is both well known and well regarded, then it probably has a pool of goodwill among consumers and distributors. The extension would be planned to dip into that pool. Three kinds of carry-over effects may be relevant:

Expertise

If the original had established and maintained itself, probably over a fairly long period, as the best available for that application or usage, then it is likely to have accrued a reputation for high-level competence in its field. Users may feel very comfortable and assured in making repeat buys. This may have been promoted actively and the company may have sought to have itself perceived as the acknowledged consultant in its area.

An extension that was complementary to the original, and of the same quality, would have its introduction eased owing to a halo effect. Consumers would know the name already and would have positive expectations, and they may believe that the company they trusted would not bring out a poor new product. The extension benefits from a trusting relationship established by the original.

Prestige

Some brands have enviable images and some consumers may believe that these images confer status on those who use them. Some brands benefit from particular kinds of associations and symbolism and they may have become, for some people, the only acceptable product to have in some situations. This does not just apply to consumer markets: organisational buyers can sometimes be just as subjective.

Access

A well-established original may have developed and held good access to the best suppliers and to the best distributors. An extension would capitalise on these relationships and it may have a better reception to its initial launch than a new brand that had no reputation.

But brand extensions can also be problematic. The connection with the original brand can be strained and the carry-over effects diminished or eliminated. Bic was famous for its ballpoint pens. Its extension to disposable lighters worked because people still saw them as consistent with the original in being inexpensive, disposable, functional products. But its extension into perfumes failed. Guinness is withdrawing its Guinness Bitter and once it tried an apparently contradictory idea with a new version of its original stout called Guinness Light.

In some markets brand extensions are added which contribute little and at times they can be harmful to the original. They can clutter the market and confuse the consumers. A series of lacklustre extensions, and no really new product development, can undermine the credibility of the company among distributors, customers and city analysts.

Market entry

Decisions about how and when to enter the market can make a substantial difference to the new product's prospects. Timing the entry to the market can make or break an innovation. Thoughtless positioning, with little or no distinction, can be harmful to long-term prospects, whereas astute positioning can have a very positive effect. Entry scale, and in particular obtaining and maintaining a strong market presence with high levels of market exposure, can ease the product's introduction and stimulate the market's evolution. These three factors are explored in this section.

Entry timing has received particular attention. It is commonly assumed that early entry is desirable and there is evidence that pioneers accrue 'first-mover advantages'. They are able to influence customer expectations and shape how customers make evaluations of products in the new field. They can suggest to consumers the criteria that they should employ in making their judgements and products that are later entrants are then evaluated on that basis. Pioneers can set the standards, establish a distinctive quality position, take the lead in the continuing evolution of the technology and gain valuable experience in manufacturing and distribution (Buzzell and Gale, 1987). In many mature markets the leaders are those that were the pioneering entrants. However, being too early can be as much of a disadvantage as being too late. A weak, tentative first mover, without the motivation or resources to grow the market, can spend years making losses only to be superseded by a stronger 'fast follower'. Green *et al.* (1995) caution that 'simple nostrums, such as early entry is best, can be dangerous oversimplifications'.

Those that come to the market early, but after the pioneer, can be successful. Procter & Gamble was not the pioneer in disposable napkins nor in biological washing powders, but its Pampers and Ariel brands dominate these markets. Japanese competitors displaced Ampex, the pioneer in VCR technology. Commenting on this *The Economist* (1996) said:

> In many cases, including Ampex's, the first mover was content to have pioneered the technology, believing its breakthrough was enough to bring market leadership. Micro Instrumentation and Tele-metry Systems invented the PC in the mid-1970s, but ceded market leadership to latecomers (such as Apple Computer and IBM) that invested heavily to turn the PC into a mass-market product.

Positioning decisions can be influential and the reprographics industry illustrates this point. Rank-Xerox pioneered and dominated this market until the late 1970s. It targeted high- and medium-volume users of photocopiers and developed a wide product range with continuous innovations around the basic platform. In the early 1970s IBM, Gestetner, Agfa-Gevaert and 3M all entered the medium-volume segment of the market with single products and almost all their installations were on rental, reducing cash flow. There was little to distinguish these brands and little or no reason for buyers to move from Rank-Xerox; eventually they all left the industry. A more distinctive and successful move was made in the late 1970s by several Japanese firms that targeted low-volume users with fairly basic machines sold at relatively low prices. Only after having established strong positions in this segment did they attempt to move into the medium-volume segment to compete more directly with Rank-Xerox.

The market for facsimile machines developed in a similar way with Rank-Xerox as the pioneer, followed by Burroughs and 3M. All these companies had sophisticated, high-cost products. Sharp and other Japanese firms entered later with simple, low-cost products.

Scale of entry affects how the product performs and how the market evolves. High levels of effort and resource commitment can stimulate market evolution and a critical factor in this is market exposure. The study by Green *et al.* (1995) of the wordprocessing software market found that:

> in markets similar to the word processing market explored here, in which basic features and evaluative criteria are quickly established, high levels of market exposure (particularly magazine coverage, but also advertising) during the entry period is associated with a product's long-term performance.

Getting prospective customers talking and thinking about the product is vital. This may mean the establishment of a strong market presence through press articles, advertising, participation at exhibitions and a highly visible presence in distribution channels.

Marketing research

Decisions about product strategy require a wealth of information and marketing research assists with the marketing-related issues. Approaches to this research can be descriptive, exploratory or causal. All three can use internal data sources, for example sales records, or external sources. The latter are usually considered to be primary if they involve original research, as in a survey, or secondary if they employ extant material, such as government statistics.

Descriptive research attempts to depict market characteristics. It could provide data on market size, market shares, consumer profiles and consumer evaluations of products and on topics related to marketing operations, such as audiences for advertising media or matters related to distribution. The bulk of what people call market research falls into this category. It is typified by structured surveys, although it can in addition make use of qualitative data from small group discussions, and internal company data and published information.

Exploratory research seeks to define problems or issues. There are no standardised procedures. It might look at symptoms or reveal them and it could employ some original research or review existing knowledge. The aim is to obtain a better insight, or a new insight, which could lead to a fuller definition of a problem.

Causal research tries to explain relationships. Which cause led to which effect? In marketing cause/effect relationships are not always obvious. Was a new product a success (or a failure) because of its intrinsic qualities, its positioning, its price, its promotion, its availability or its timing? Or was it because of the weak (or strong) competition, because of the economic situation, or did the weather have an impact? Econometric models, using input from descriptive research, are increasingly being used in an attempt to untangle these problems. Experiments can also be tried in a laboratory or in some limited field setting.

Marketing research attempts to answer questions and the questions posed in managing the product portfolio can relate to broad strategic issues or to narrower issues concerning just a part of the full product range. They could require a review of the present situation or necessitate speculation about the future. Table 4.1 sets out these possibilities and shows something of the issues that might be considered relevant.

In NPD the marketing questions are about the future, crucially about potential customer reactions. Research may provide views on this at several stages in the process: during concept development, at some time once prototypes are available and during market launch. The terms concept testing, product testing and market testing have been applied to these three. Generally, the earlier the testing the less realistic, and the less costly, it is likely to be.

Table 4.1 : Some research areas in managing the product portfolio

	Broad perspective	*Narrower perspective*
Present	Reviews of present portfolio to identify strategic issues	Market performance of existing products; customer and distributor acceptance and evaluation of those products
Future	Establishing the target shape of the overall product portfolio in the future	Investigations of future market requirements; assessments of possible future market acceptance of existing and new product(s)

Concept testing

Concept testing takes place during the concept-development or idea-generation phase. It is intended to glean something of customers' opinions about the product idea before very much investment has been committed. This is qualitative research and small group discussions (focus groups) are normal. In some markets the participants might be drawn from a user group, or they might be 'representative' in some other relevant way, for example for a product related to car maintenance the group would be of people who undertake their own car maintenance. It is a crude process because the concept might be quite abstract and participants might have little or nothing concrete to which to relate. Written statements about expected product performance characteristics, with the use of analogies or suggestions about positioning against existing brands or product categories, might form the stimulus to these discussions. Examples of use situations may be cited and there might also be some real or computer-simulated mock-up of the product, its packaging or advertising.

In industrial markets these discussions might be more informed because the intended technical characteristics of the product idea could be more fully conveyed, possibly with the aid of computer modelling. One or more groups of technical personnel from potential customer organisations might be brought together to talk about the concept, its possible usefulness and its possible problems. A spin-off could be that the interest of one or more respondents might be engaged sufficiently for them to offer collaboration in any subsequent development and to offer test sites for prototypes.

Research of this type is speculative, but it can be instructive. It could uncover clearly inappropriate product concepts. The discipline of having to explain to potential customers the nature of the concept, and its relevance to their needs, could reveal how hollow or limited it is. It may be that the explanation offered to consumers centres on the distinctiveness of the technology and that they find this difficult to understand, or that they find it difficult to see how the concept would result in a product that would be to their benefit. Discussions within the organisation until this time might have concentrated on the novelty of the technology. Bringing in a customer perspective at the earliest opportunity widens the viewpoint. It could have positive effects, revealing unexpected associations and unplanned applications that, with development, could lead to quite unanticipated new opportunities.

Discussion participants can be creative and offer ideas that could be stimulating, sparking enthusiasm, or frustrating because their naïveté shows a substantial communication gap. The discussions could begin to show something of the extent of the lack of understanding customers have of the innovation and the extent of the learning that they would need to acquire before they could utilise the idea. This could inform the marketing communication strategy and suggest the nature and the scale of the problem that it would need to address. This point is highlighted in the case study at the end of this chapter.

Blockages to customer acceptance may be uncovered. Customers may say that they are tied in to existing usage patterns and that to break those patterns might require them to undergo extensive change in associated products or systems that they use currently. The possible role of the new concept within this fuller customer context would then have to be investigated, and it could lead to revisions in the lead time to launch, or to revisions to the guesses made about the time required for the market to evolve.

In turn this could provoke more ideas about the extent and the timing of the marketing communication required.

Insights of this kind could be demoralising or they could be quite invigorating for the development team. In either of these cases, this first encounter with the market should underline the significance of opening and maintaining a communication flow to and from prospective customers.

As described above, the concept test is seen as essentially a diagnostic tool. It is not a sales prediction technique, although sometimes discussion participants may be asked some kind of purchase-intention question. The value of such data is questionable, although some might try to compare the results with previous new product developments.

Product testing

Product testing takes place when prototypes are available and in these tests a sample of consumers is given the product for evaluation. There is a range of variables in designing these tests and some of the choices are:

- *Consumer sample choice*: a judgement sample from the target market segment is often used, but because the consumer innovators might be unrepresented a qualifying questionnaire might be administered with questions about their relative innovativeness, to ensure some representation from the more innovative.

- *Single (monadic) or comparative tests*: comparative tests are useful because they provide a relative measure, but they may exaggerate differences because respondents may expect to find differences when they are asked to judge alternatives. Monadic tests require some benchmark for evaluation and an experienced company may feel that its bank of previous tests provides this.

- *Questions asked*: these usually seek scaled responses about overall disposition towards the product, which may include some intentions-to-buy questions and more detailed evaluation of product attributes; they may also cover usage and use situation questions and questions making comparisons with other products.

- *Test administration*: respondents may be asked to complete a questionnaire themselves or it may be completed by an interviewer. Observation of the product in use may also be a part of the test.

- *Test timing and location*: the test may be in-use (at the user's home or in the user's factory or office) or undertaken at some central location. In-use tests may be more realistic because they can be undertaken over an extended period of weeks or months, take place at the point of consumption and are within the particular application or usage context of the user. Central location testing (sometimes called hall tests) is expedient and many more tests can be concluded over a short time. There is another potentially useful adjunct to central testing related to computer simulation. Respondents may be shown product simulations as well as a physical prototype. They may scale their responses on product attributes at a computer screen and may introduce their own ideas on a restricted range of dimensions. These ideas may or may not be of direct use, but they could be indicative of customer connection with, and understanding of, the prototype.

Interpretation of the test results depends on knowledge of how the tests were designed and administered. Sometimes the results may be clear cut, but they can be indeterminate and management judgement often plays a major part in the interpretation. This stage is a step closer to the market than the concept test and so intentions-to-buy data may be sought from respondents; this should be a little better as an indicator taken at this stage than at the concept stage. Estimates of the market outlook, and views on the strategy being planned for the marketing effort at the launch, will be refined.

Market testing

Market testing occurs around the time of the market launch. Testing the market takes many forms and occurs at various times prior to a full-scale national or international launch. It can entail informal discussions with prospects and distributors or it can encompass more formal experiments, with or without sales being made. Depending on the definition of the geographic scope of the intended market, it can also include a local, regional or national launch of the product with full-scale marketing activity. Broadly, there are two types of market testing, referred to as limited testing and test marketing. Limited testing is early testing on a very limited scale, sometimes without a sale being offered. Test marketing has more of a tradition and the product is placed on sale in a relatively small area, often a region but sometimes just several towns.

Three broad purposes can be seen for market testing. They may all be present in a single test or the interest may centre on one of them. These purposes are noted below:

1 *Sales testing*: a major concern in NPD is the prospective level of sales. Throughout the development process guesses will have been made and changed successively about the expected sales level. A test market with the product on sale in a limited area is likely to give much better data for predictions.

2 *Refining marketing plans*: there may be great uncertainty about many marketing decisions. What should be the price level? What distribution system should be employed? How should the product be explained to buyers and which attributes or uses should be emphasised? Judgements will be made about these topics, but limited experiments might help clarify the position.

3 *Pilot run*: any system benefits from a rehearsal. Bringing out a new product, especially if it is important for the organisation, requires concerted effort across many diverse business functions. Co-ordinating all that activity in a timely fashion, ensuring that all the training needed within the organisation is completed, having sufficient product of the desired quality available, filling distribution chains and meeting deadlines for a collection of marketing communication tasks can be very demanding, and problems can be signalled for attention before full-scale launch.

Limited testing

Limited testing can occur before, or instead of, test marketing. Time pressure, cost, competitive reactions and IT developments have combined to increase its use. It may be a simulated experiment or a very limited commercial experiment using only a few sales outlets. For products that have an expected average repurchase cycle of weeks or months, a principal aim will be to generate an early sales forecast and this could concentrate on three key variables:

1 *Penetration rate*: the proportion of the buyers in the market that will make at least one purchase.
2 *Repeat rate*: the proportion of those who will make further purchases.
3 *Buying rate index*: the average purchase volume for those who repurchase.

Parfitt and Collins (1968) proposed the following model using these variables:

$$\text{Brand share} = \text{penetration rate} \times \text{repeat rate} \times \text{buying rate index}$$

If 50 per cent of those in a market buy a brand at least once (penetration) and repeat buys as a proportion of total purchases in a period settle to 20 per cent, that means that a half try it at least once and a fifth of those who try go on to buy more. A first estimate for brand share would be 10 per cent (20 per cent of 50 per cent), because a fifth of those who buy at all keep on buying. An adjustment would be made if repeat buys were at a different rate to all buys. Given an estimate of total market size, an estimate could be derived for the sales revenue.

Obtaining early indications on these variables has led to the development of a number of commercial market research services. Saunders (1985) comments on these. One service recruits a panel of 200 buyers in a product field who agree that an interviewer does their shopping for that product for a few months. They are shown the product in test together with competitive products and they make purchase choices from a catalogue. If the test item is chosen then it is delivered from a special stock, but otherwise the products come from local shops. Penetration and repeat rates are monitored.

Another service employs simulated shopping for a sample of 100. Respondents are interviewed to establish brand awareness and preferences and shown videos of a test item and competitors. They are given cash vouchers that can be exchanged for products from a simulated shop shelf. Later interviewers visit their homes and, prompted by a photographic display, offer respondents the opportunity to make purchases again. In another service several panels of 500 shoppers are visited weekly by a mobile self-service shop that has a conventional product range and includes a few test items.

For both these kinds of services there are experiments based on the technology of virtual reality, with people passing through simulated shops and making 'choices'.

More sophisticated procedures are evolving in scanner stores. A panel of several hundred regular shoppers in a store is recruited and the members complete a questionnaire giving demographic and attitudinal data. They are given some inducement to participate. Each time they visit the store they present a plastic card at the checkout for scanning. Recording all the purchases made by this group is then possible, including any purchases of test items that have been introduced in the store. Analyses of this data can provide measures of penetration, repeat and buying volume in aggregate or within demographic or attitudinal groupings as frequently as required. If several store tests are run simultaneously, variations could be made to prices, to elements of sales promotion and possibly to advertising. Comparisons of the effects might assist decisions in these areas. In the US, cable television enables panels of consumers in these experiments to receive particular advertising related to the test items.

These procedures can be useful for diagnostic as well as for predictive purposes. For example, high penetration followed by low repeat is problematic. Does that mean that the promotion was better than the product? Alternatively, low penetration with high repeat might suggest that the product was better than customers had been led to expect. Further research could be undertaken to investigate such situations.

Awareness, trial and repeat (sometimes referred to as ATR) models may be more appropriate in other markets and they require estimates of those three variables. It might be estimated that there are 1 million buyers in a product field, that 0.25 million try a new product once and that 0.1 million become regular repeat buyers. If these repeat buyers are estimated to buy two of the product a year on average, then an estimate can be made of annual sales volume (0.2 million). This might lead on to estimates about what kinds and what level of marketing effort would be required to induce the penetration and repeat rates. Clearly, the reliability of these estimates dictates the usefulness of this approach. For some products analogies can be used, such as data derived from another country where they have already been introduced. For products that are jointly consumed with other products, the sales of these other products may be indicative.

Test marketing

In traditional test marketing products are placed on sale in one or more representative areas for several months. For products which employ TV advertising these areas are often based on regional TV areas. However, there is now less of this regional activity for sales prediction purposes in fast-moving consumer goods, although a slow build-up from one or two areas to national distribution (national roll-out) could be seen as being related to the other reasons for market testing discussed earlier. Major multinationals might use country tests rather than regional tests within one country.

Reasons for this trend to less full-scale test marketing in some markets are speed to market and the perceived need not to disclose plans to competitors. Reactions of the main grocery chains are also influential. They might resist the special distribution arrangements that are required unless the launch is specific to them, but that could jeopardise the relationships with other retailers (*Management Today*, 1995). The development of limited testing as described above has also provided an alternative that takes place earlier and can be less costly.

Test markets are still conducted, not least because the reasons noted above are not apparent in many other markets. For example, companies in service industries can utilise test marketing. Thomas (1995, 208–19) gives the illustration of the Marriott hotel company's introduction of Courtyard in the mid-1980s. Following extensive concept development and testing, Marriott built a prototype room with several designs at one of its existing hotels for testing by several hundred customers. Based on knowledge from this test it built the first Courtyard to be used as a test market in Atlanta.

Launch and continuing improvement

From a business perspective the innovation is not a success until it has established and fixed its place in the market. That depends on how it is launched, its reception by customers and the continuing attention given to its improvement. The earlier discussion of market entry showed some key factors relevant to the launch strategy, but the act of putting the product on to the market is not an end: it is the beginning of a new phase. Close and constant monitoring of the reactions of customers, distributors and competitors is required to inform the proceeding strategy.

Having the product on the market allows the validation or rejection of important estimates or assumptions about customer attitudes and behaviour that would have been made during development. It could also reveal unanticipated problems or opportunities. What do customers now understand about the product and has comprehension of its benefits spread in the predicted way? Are there still difficulties? Are they using the product in the ways envisaged? Have customers found problems in using the product that had not come to light before? Do they use it as much as expected and as frequently as expected? Are any potential customers holding back because they see risk in adopting the product, perhaps delaying their acceptance in anticipation of further developments in the technology? Are there enough of those for it to be a problem? Do customers perceive the benefits that were promised and are these as important to them as originally hoped? Are the benefits now seen as interesting but irrelevant? And are there any problems with the product itself that customers have revealed? Unravelling these questions and dealing effectively with their implications will condition how the prospects for the product evolve.

Many assumptions will also have been built into the operations and marketing plans. Do they stand up? Was the desired positioning achieved and was that the right positioning decision? Is it now too narrowly defined on a relatively unimportant dimension? Was it conveyed appropriately to distributors and customers? Were the pricing and distribution plans appropriate? Are customer problems being handled efficiently and is the right level of customer service in place? On all these issues the organisation should be learning and responding, tracking and improving.

Thought given to how the product and the market will evolve from the launch might pay attention to three areas:

1 *Product platform evolution and brand extensions*: what is the next generation of the product? Can the basic product platform be enhanced and should this lead to brand extensions?

2 *Market evolution*: how rapidly will the innovation be diffused? Will there be a lengthy introductory period before any rapid growth? Will new market segments become apparent or can they be created? How should the geographic scope be widened?

3 *Competitive evolution*: how soon will competitors arrive? How predictable is their entry? What distinction, if any, will they bring? What kind of positioning and entry scale are they considering? What entry barriers are in place to deter rivals?

Inauguration is not enough. To be effective the innovation must be well founded in the market and receive customer acceptance, if not their acclaim, and plans need to be made to secure, deepen and widen its market position from the initial launch.

Withdrawing products

Pruning the product range can be an important part of managing the portfolio. Chronic poor sales performance would be a first indicator that consideration should be given to withdrawing products. Prior to that decision, careful assessments would be needed of the reasons for the poor performance, the possible future trends and the costs and benefits of continuing or withdrawing.

Investigations could first focus on how well the organisation had managed its efforts. It may have lost market share, in which case a series of questions could be posed. Is manufacturing cost out of line with others in the industry? Has there been any decline in quality relative to rivals? Has the product kept up with any evolution in the technology? Have marketing efforts tailed off? Fixing any problems that emerge from these analyses might give the product a new lease of life, and this may be associated with a repositioning exercise. However, if nothing significant is signalled then other possibilities would need to be examined.

If market share was constant but sales were nonetheless in chronic decline, this could indicate that the industry, or the particular product form, had passed maturity and was entering decline. Predictions about the future industry trend might confirm a pessimistic outlook and the firm would have to decide if it should withdraw quickly, more gradually or try to maintain a position in what may be a much smaller industry in the future.

Exit costs would feature strongly. There may be a complex manufacturing economy within the company with shared processes involving many products. The arbitrary removal of one may throw into jeopardy the economics of the remainder, and so it could be that the product is continued so long as it makes some contribution to overheads. The firm may also become an involuntary survivor in the industry because contractual obligations tie it in. These contracts may be with suppliers, customers, distributors or other partners in the network. An inflexible manufacturing plant could also hamper it. Reputation could be another issue: the company may not wish to undermine the confidence placed in it by customers or distributors. For example, customers may face high switching costs if they have to buy alternative products and may become resentful if they drop the product. If the product is part of a wide portfolio then the whole range may suffer if the organisation's reputation is damaged.

Alternatively, the firm may decide to make an active commitment to stay in the declining industry in anticipation of increasing market share.

The role of design in the development of a wheelchair for cerebral palsy sufferers[1]

Introduction

Having a new idea and creating a potentially new product is a rewarding experience in itself. This is even more so when the product you have designed and developed can relieve suffering for disabled children. However, even in these instances many product and business decisions still have to be taken. The impact of manufacturing costs on eventual profits can considerably affect the decision about whether the product, despite its apparent benefits, is produced. The commercial viability of any project has to be carefully considered and this is the subject of this case study, based on the film *Designing for Market* produced by TV Choice (1995).

Cerebral palsy

Cerebral palsy is a broad term used to describe injuries to the brain which usually occur at or prior to birth. The effect of the condition is a lack of physical control of limbs and difficulty in speaking. Sufferers of the condition were previously referred to as spastics. The term spastic was related to the muscle spasms that characterise the condition. It is estimated that about 20 000 children suffer from cerebral palsy.

For cerebral palsy sufferers the muscles within the body do not support the bones. In childhood this results in uncontrollable limbs, but later in life the bones themselves often become deformed. These deformities become fixed around puberty and buckled and twisted spines are not uncommon in adults with cerebral palsy. Keeping the spine straight as the child grows can help to prevent deformity in the future. It is this theory, together with many years of work as a physiotherapist with children suffering from cerebral palsy, that helped Pauline Pope develop a wheelchair that assisted in keeping the spine straight. Conventional chairs do not provide sufficient support for the body and can contribute to deformed spines as children grow older. Pope's design was based around the motorcycle seating position, whereby the seat forces the person to lean forward on to the petrol tank. A similar position is achieved when one sits on a chair with legs astride the back support and the chin on the back of the chair (*see* Figure 4.2).

Following many years of experiment and help from an engineer, a successful wheelchair was produced that contained a moulded seat and chest support. This enabled children to learn to move their arms, legs and head. Pauline decided to call her chair Seating and Mobility (SAM). She was pleased with the final design, which provided the necessary support to the child's spine. Unfortunately only six could be manufactured every year on a one-off basis, each tailored to fit a particular child. ▶

---

[1] This case has been written as a basis for class discussion rather than to illustrate effective or ineffective managerial or administrative behaviour. It has been prepared from a variety of published sources, as indicated, and from observations.

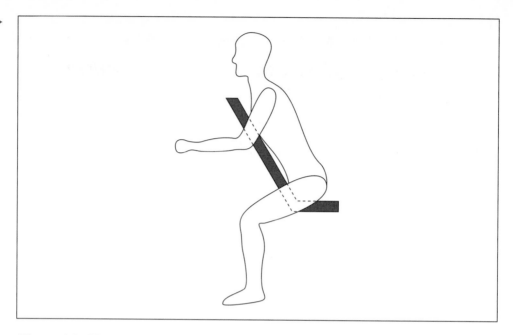

Figure 4.2 : The concept upon which SAM is based centres on the motorcycle seating position which helps to keep the spine straight

From tailor-made to mass-produced product

Armed with a firm belief in the idea as well as the physical product, Pauline decided to approach wheelchair manufacturers to see whether they would be interested in large-scale manufacture of the product. Sunrise Medical, one of the largest power wheelchair manufacturers in the UK, soon expressed interest in the design and signed an agreement with Pauline to explore the possibility of manufacturing the product.

The company was a natural partner for this product as it was already operating in the wheelchair market and could use its present product platform to develop SAM. One of the first difficulties faced by the company was how to convert a tailor-made product to a mass-produced product which, by definition, is not tailored to individual needs. With the help of computer-aided design technology, designers at the company eventually developed a proto-type product incorporating an adjustable seat that could be altered to fit different sizes. The design had several basic components that could be assembled to the required size; in this case foam wedges were used to provide the necessary support.

Commercial viability

Concurrent with the development of the prototype wheelchair, the marketing manager began to devise a market research study to explore the viability of the product for the company. It was clear to all those who had seen the wheelchair in use that it brought help to some of the most needy in society. However, it was also clear to everyone involved in the development of the product that the decision about manufacture of the product would depend largely on whether sufficient revenue could be generated to produce a profit for the company. The costs involved in manufacturing suggested a break-even price of approximately £1500. Revenue generation would depend on two variables: volume and profit margin. Two questions needed to be answered:

■ What volume was possible?
■ What profit margin was possible on such a product?

There was one additional factor that needed to be considered, the views of several key individuals within the company. As with all new ideas, not necessarily new product ideas, there will usually be resistance from some quarters to any form of change. In this case some of the engineers and designers had come across similar product ideas in the past and, following lengthy explorations, these had been abandoned due to poor revenue projections. Also, the eventual decision regarding manufacture would rest with the managing director; initial reactions suggested he was sceptical that the project would be successful.

Product testing

After approximately nine months of further trials and testing, the company produced a full-scale prototype product. Pauline, who had been involved closely with the development of the prototype, was pleased with the new SAM. A test run was set up with a nine-year-old girl who was suffering from cerebral palsy. SAM had an electrical power base that propelled the chair and was controlled by a hand-operated joystick. The new design contained an improved contoured seat and extra chest support. After a few minutes of practising with the chair and the controls, SAM was given a ringing endorsement by this young cerebral palsy sufferer. The product was clearly a technical success, but whether the company would be able to generate any revenue from it was still to be established.

Market testing

As the months passed the team were coming under increasing pressure to submit their findings on whether Sunrise Medical should continue with the project. The managing director would soon have to make a decision about the release of further funds. The team decided to undertake some market research to gather feedback from potential customers. Ten specialist cerebral palsy centres were identified across the UK. SAM was taken to each of these centres to collect information on three key areas:

■ interest in the product
■ likelihood of purchase
■ amount willing to pay.

This information would enable the team to decide whether the product could generate sufficient revenue. Unfortunately, the results were not encouraging. There was enormous interest in the product; many people including physiotherapists and parents of cerebral palsy sufferers had not seen a product like this before. Many, especially the specialist centres, said they would probably purchase one and would be willing to pay between £1500 and £2000. The final figure, however, was disappointing. Sales estimates for the whole market were 150 units. This figure was much smaller than had been expected. The company needed sufficient profit margin to ensure it was able to recover design costs, tooling costs and packaging and distribution costs. ▶

Discussion

Many readers may find this story disturbing. The fact that through profit considerations a product that can help disabled children was not manufactured on a large scale is sad indeed. This, however, is not a unique case. In the pharmaceutical industry profit considerations lie at the heart of any decision to proceed from research to expensive clinical trials. Moreover, the decision to conduct expensive research into cures for certain diseases such as malaria will be heavily influenced by whether and what the intended recipient is able to pay. Many pharmaceutical companies are currently investing large sums of money into research into AIDS, not least because many of the intended recipients are in the affluent developed world.

In many ways this case study tells a simple story. That is, it matters little whether the new product is technically advanced or offers significant improvement over existing products, what is important is market demand. The business has a responsibility to its investors not to take unnecessary risks. Without any evidence of demand, the business decided that SAM was an unnecessary risk.

Everett Roger's adoption theory can be used to explain why the market research revealed low expected sales. Rogers argued that first-time purchasers of new products could be classified according to the innovativeness of their adoption behaviour. He presented the adoption behaviour of purchasers of a new product as a time-dependent phenomenon that could be plotted within a normal distribution curve. He labelled the first two segments innovators and early adopters respectively. In this case study these groups did not adopt the product. There was some resistance from experts and physiotherapists working in the field. This was due to lack of knowledge of the product and the benefits that it could bring. Also the product lacked any explicit support from the professional bodies in the field, such as the British Medical Council (BMC), the Royal College of Nursing (RCN) or the Chartered Society of Physiotherapists.

Furthermore, there was limited, if any, promotion of the product. This contributed to the low expected sales. The market, in this case the cerebral palsy centres, did not appreciate fully the benefits of SAM and probably needed education. Clinical support from research papers or health bodies would have helped to assuage some of the scepticism in the market. The pharmaceutical industry has realised this and is fully aware that in order to persuade general practitioners to recommend its products it has to point to clinical trials and research results.

Source: Reproduced with permission of TV Choice Ltd. Copies of the film on which this case study is based are available from TV Choice Ltd, 22 Charing Cross Road, London, WC2H 0HR, UK. Tel: 0171 379 0873.

Chapter summary

Deciding how and on what basis a company wishes to compete with its competitors is of central concern to all companies. Firms need to consider a wide range of factors in order to maximise their products' chance of success in competitive environments. This chapter has shown that a company has to identify the specific ways in which it can differentiate its products in order to gain competitive advantage.

First and foremost, it has to consider the market in which it is competing, the nature of the competition and how its capabilities will enable its products to be successful. The concept of platforms in new product development was introduced as a way of developing product groups for the future. The positioning of the product and the brand strategy selected were also shown to be of particular importance. Finally, marketing research offers extensive opportunities in terms of information provision. The effective use of this information often leads to the successful development of new products.

Questions for discussion

1 If there is a strategic alliance between competitors for the development of a new technology, what are the strategic issues for these firms once that technology becomes available?

2 Apply the notion of the product platform to service industries. How relevant is it to financial services or to hotels? What are the issues that would need to be investigated if an idea emerged in a firm in those industries for a novel platform that had no connection with what had been done before?

3 Would you agree that product portfolio analysis is too simplistic to be of much value?

4 Trace the connections between differentiation strategy, core capabilities and positioning strategy. How are they relevant to new product planning?

5 Are brand extensions as relevant in industrial markets as in consumer markets? Do they have a strategic role or are they short-term tactical exercises?

6 What measures would you apply in assessing the success of a new product?

7 What is the point in concept testing if it can only be a crude process with inconclusive results?

8 Are there any ethical issues in the employment of consumer panels in scanner store market tests?

9a Can you think of other examples, similar to the wheelchair in the case study, where a scientific advance and subsequent new product idea is not developed further and introduced to the marketplace because of commercial arguments?

9b How should companies and society deal with these situations?

10 In the case study, what market testing was carried out and what conclusions were drawn?

11 In the case study, why is the distribution problem so critical?

References

Buzzell, R.D. and Gale, B.T. (1987) *The PIMS Principles*, Free Press, New York.
Crawford, C.M. (1997) *New Products Management*, 4th edn, Irwin, Burr Ridge, Illinois.
Doyle, P. (1995) 'Marketing in the new millennium', *European Journal of Marketing*, 29 (13), 23–41.
The Economist (1996) Management Focus column, 'Why first may not last', March 16, 65.
Green, D.H., Barclay, D.W. and Ryans, A.B. (1995) 'Entry strategy and long-term performance: conceptualization and empirical examination', *Journal of Marketing*, October, 59 (4), 1–16.
Jones, T. (1997) *New Product Development*, Butterworth-Heinemann, Oxford.
Kay, J. (1993) *Foundations of Corporate Success*, OUP, Oxford.
Levitt, T. (1986) *The Marketing Imagination*, Free Press, New York.

Management Today (1995) 'Why products are bypassing the market test', October, 12.

Meyer, M. and Utterback, J. (1993) 'The product family and the dynamics of core capability', *Sloan Management Review*, 34 (3) 29–38.

Moore, L.M. and Pessemier, E.A. (1993) *Product Planning and Management*, McGraw-Hill, New York.

Parfitt, J. and Collins, B. (1968) 'Use of panels in brand-share prediciton', *Journal of Marketing Research*, 5.

Saunders, J. (1985) 'New product forecasting in the UK', *Quarterly Review of Marketing*, July.

Thomas, R.J. (1995) *New Product Success Stories*, Wiley & Sons, New York.

Urban, G.L. and Hauser, J.R. (1993) *Design and Marketing of New Products*, 2nd edn, Prentice-Hall, Englewood Cliffs, NJ.

Wind, Y. (1982) *Product Policy*, Addison-Wesley, Reading, MA.

Further reading

Baker, M. (1998) *Product Strategy Management*, Prentice-Hall, Englewood Cliffs, NJ.

5

New product development

Introduction

Few business activities are heralded for their promise and approached with more justified optimism than the development of new products. Successful new products also have the added benefit of revitalising the organisation. Small wonder then that the concept of new product development (NPD) has received enormous attention in the management literature over the past 20 years. The result is a diverse range of literature from practitioners, management consultants and academics. This chapter explores this literature and examines the various models of NPD that have been put forward. It also explains the importance of NPD as a means of achieving growth.

Learning objectives

When you have completed this chapter, you will be able to:

- Examine the relationship between new products and prosperity
- Recognise the range of product development opportunities that can exist
- Recognise that a new product is a multidimensional concept
- Identify the different types of models of NPD
- Provide an understanding of the importance of external linkages in the new product development process.

Innovation management and NPD

When one considers a variety of different industries, a decline in product innovations is matched only by a decline in market share (Ughanwa and Baker, 1989). For example, in 1995 the last remaining British mass manufacturer of motor cars, Rover, has seen its market share slowly fall 20 per cent to only 10 per cent over the past 20 years. Companies need to reach out to the future and develop new products that will enable them to compete over the coming decades. The chief executive of BP Chemicals acknowledged recently that 'cost reduction is a miserable job but conceptually it is easy' (Houlder, 1994). The message here is that cutting costs, while a necessary part of business management compared to generating new products, is relatively straightforward.

This chapter looks at the exciting process of developing new products. Part One of this book has highlighted the importance of innovation and how the effective management of that process can lead to corporate success. To many people new products are the outputs of the innovation process, where the new product development (NPD) process is a subprocess of innovation. Managing innovation concerns the conditions that have to be in place to ensure that the organisation as a whole is given the opportunity to develop new products. The actual development of new products is the process of transforming business opportunities into tangible products. Figure 5.1 helps to illustrate the link between innovation and new product development.

New product development concerns the management of the disciplines involved in the development of new products. These disciplines have developed their own perspectives on the subject of NPD. These are largely based on their experiences of involvement in the process. Hence, production management examines the development of new products from a manufacturing perspective, that is, how can we most effectively manufacture the product in question. Marketing, on the other hand,

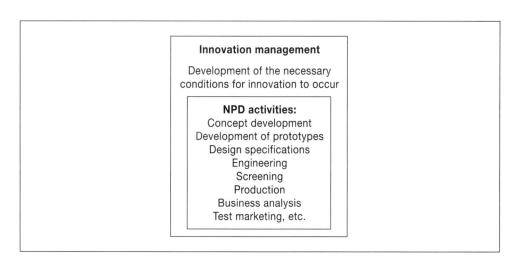

Figure 5.1 : A conceptual framework linking innovation management and NPD

would take a slightly different perspective and would be concerned with trying to understand the needs of the customer and how the business could best meet these needs. However, producing what the customer wants may or may not be either possible or profitable. The lack of a common approach to the development of new products is due to this multiple perspective. This is illustrated in Figure 5.2. The variety of views presented on the subject is not a weakness. Indeed, it should be viewed as a strength, for these different perspectives illuminate the areas that are left in the dark by other perspectives.

Usually, competition between companies is assessed using financial measures such as return on capital employed (ROCE), profits and market share. Non-financial measures such as design, innovativeness and technological supremacy may also be used.

Theoretically it is possible for a firm to survive without any significant developments to its products, but such firms are exceptions to the norm. Where long-term success is dependent on the ability to compete with others, this is almost always achieved by ensuring that your company's products are superior to the competition.

New products and prosperity

The potential rewards of NPD are enormous. One only has to consider the rapid success of companies such as Microsoft and Compaq in the rapidly growing home computer industry. Similar success was achieved by Apple and prior to this IBM, in the early development of the same industry. This example illustrates an important point, that success in one year does not ensure success in the next. Both Apple and IBM have experienced severe difficulties in the 1990s.

Research by Cooper and Kleinschmidt (1993) has suggested that, on average, new products (defined here as those less than five years old) are increasingly taking a larger slice of company sales. For 3M, for example, new products contributed to 33 per cent of sales in the 1970s. This increased to 40 per cent in the 1980s and accounts for over 50 per cent in the 1990s (*see* Figure 5.3). The life cycles of products are becoming increasingly shorter (*see* Chapter 1).

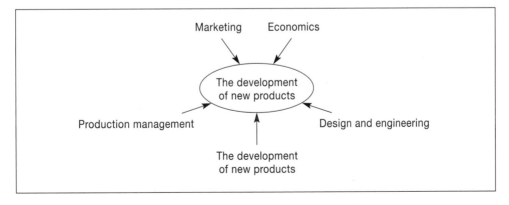

Figure 5.2 : A variety of perspectives from which to analyse the development of new products

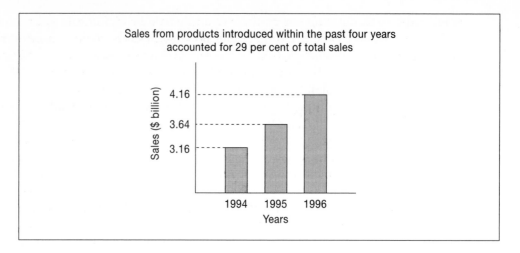

Figure 5.3 : 3M new product sales

Source: 3M Company Report (1996)

Considerations when developing a NPD strategy

Chapter 3 outlined many of the activities and factors that organisations need to consider in managing a business in the short and long term. In addition, Chapter 4 highlighted many of the factors that a business needs to consider if it is successfully to manage its products. It should be clear that establishing a direction for a business and the selection of strategies to achieve its goals form an on-going, evolving process that is frequently subject to change. This is particularly evident at the product strategy

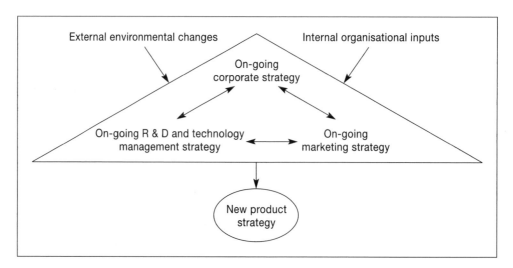

Figure 5.4 : Key inputs into new product strategy

level (Figure 5.3 illustrates the main inputs into the decision-making process). The process of product strategy was highlighted in Chapter 3 and is the creative process of recognising genuine business opportunities that the business might be able to exploit. It is commonly referred to as 'opportunity identification' (Crawford, 1997).

On-going corporate planning

In large organisations this can be a very formal activity involving strategic planners and senior managers with responsibility for setting the future direction of the business. In smaller organisations this activity may be undertaken by the owner of the business in an informal, even *ad hoc* way. For many businesses it is somewhere in the middle of these two extremes. The effects of any corporate planning may be important and long term. For example, the decision by a sports footwear manufacturer to exit the tennis market and concentrate on the basketball market due to changing social trends will have a significant impact on the business.

On-going market planning

Decisions by market planners may have equally significant effects. For example, the realisation that a competitor is about to launch an improved tennis shoe that offers additional benefits may force the business to establish five new product development projects. Two of these projects may be established to investigate the use of new materials for the sole, one could be used to develop a series of new designs, one could look at alternative fastenings and one could be used to reduce production costs.

On-going technology management

In most science- and technology-intensive industries such as the pharmaceutical and computer software industries, this activity is probably more significant than on-going market planning. Technology awareness is very high. The continual analysis of internal R&D projects and external technology trawling will lead to numerous technical opportunities that need to be considered by the business. Say that a recent review of the patent literature has identified a patent application by one of the company's main competitors. This forces the business to establish a new project to investigate this area to ensure that it is aware of any future developments that may affect its position. This area is explored in more detail in Chapter 8.

Opportunity analysis/serendipity

In addition to the inputs that have been classified above, there are other inputs and opportunities that are often labelled miscellaneous or put down to serendipity (*see* Chapter 1). The vice-president of 3M recently remarked that 'chaos is a necessary part of an innovative culture. It's been said that 3M's competitors never know what we are going to come up with next. The fact is neither do we' (*see* the case study at the end of this chapter).

NPD as a strategy for growth

The interest expressed by many companies in the subject of developing new products is hardly surprising given that the majority of businesses are intent on growth. Although, as was discussed in Chapter 3, this does not apply to all companies, nonetheless the development of new products provides an opportunity for growing the business. (It is worth reminding ourselves that new product development is only one of many options available to a business keen on growth.)

One of clearest ways of identifying the variety of growth options available to a business is using Ansoff's (1957) directional policy matrix. This well-known matrix, shown in Figure 5.5, combines two of the key variables that enable a business to grow: an increase in market opportunities and an increase in product opportunities. Within this matrix new product development is seen as one of four available options. Each of the four cells considers various combinations of product-market options. Growth can be achieved organically (internal development) or through external acquisition. A criticism of this matrix is that it adopts an environmental perspective that assumes that opportunities for growth exist – they may not. Indeed, often consolidation and retrenchment need to be considered, especially in times of economic downturn. Each of the cells in the matrix is briefly discussed below.

Market penetration

Opportunities are said to exist within a business's existing markets through increasing the volume of sales. Increasing the market share of a business's existing products by exploiting the full range of marketing mix activities is the common approach adopted by many companies. This may include branding decisions. For example, the cereal manufacturer Kellogg has increased the usage of its cornflakes product by promoting it as a snack to be consumed at times other than at breakfast.

	Current products	New products
Current markets	1 Market penetration strategy	3 Product development strategy
New markets	2 Market development strategy	4 Diversification strategy

Figure 5.5 : Ansoff Matrix

Source: Adapted from Ansoff (1968)

Market development

Growth opportunities are said to exist for a business's existing products through making them available to new markets. In this instance the company maintains the security of its existing products but opts to develop and enter new markets. Market development can be achieved by opening up new segments. For example, Mercedes has decided to enter the small car market (previously the company had always concentrated on the executive or luxury segment). Similarly, companies may decide to enter new geographic areas through exporting.

Product development

Ansoff proposes that growth opportunities exist through offering new or improved products to existing markets. This is the subject of this chapter and, as will become clear, trying to establish when a product is new is sometimes difficult. Nonetheless, virtually all companies try to ensure that their products are able to compete with the competition by regularly improving and updating their existing products. This is an on-going activity for most companies.

Diversification

It hardly needs to be said that opportunities for growth exist beyond a business's existing products and markets. The selection of this option, however, would be significant in that the business would move into product areas and markets in which it currently does not operate. The development of the self-adhesive note pads (Post-It) by 3M provided an opportunity for the company to enter the stationery market, a market of which it had little knowledge, with a product that was new to the company and the market.

Many companies try to utilise either their existing technical or commercial knowledge base. For example, Flymo's knowledge of the electric lawnmower market enabled it to diversify into a totally new market. Indeed, the introduction of its Garden-vac product led to the creation of the 'garden-tidy' product market. While this is an example of organic growth, many companies identify diversification opportunities through acquisition. For example, in the UK some of the privatised electricity companies have purchased significant holdings in privatised water companies. The knowledge base being utilised here is the commercial knowhow of the provision of a utility service (former public service).

Additional opportunities for diversified growth exist through forward backward and horizontal diversification. A manufacturer opening retail outlets is an example of forward integration. Backward integration is involvement in activities which are inputs to the business, for example a manufacturer starting to produce components. Horizontal diversification is buying up competitors (*see* Johnson and Scholes (1997) for a more detailed discussion of diversification).

A range of product development opportunities

A development of Ansoff's directional policy matrix was Johnson and Jones's (1957) matrix for product development strategies (*see* Figure 5.6). This matrix replaces Ansoff's product variable with technology. It builds on Ansoff's matrix by offering further clarification of the range of options open to a company contemplating product decisions. In particular, the use of technology as a variable better illustrates the decisions a company needs to consider. For example, Johnson and Jones distinguish between improving existing technology and acquiring new technology, the latter being far more resource intensive with higher degrees of risk. Ansoff's directional policy

	Increasing technology newness ⟶		
Products objectives	No technological change	Improved technolgy	New technology To acquire scientific knowledge and production skills new to the company
No martket change	Sustain	Reformulation To maintain an optimum balance of cost, quality and availability in the formulae of present products	Replacement To seek new and better ingredients of formulation for present company products in technology not now employed
Strengthened market To exploit more fully the existing markets for the present company's products	Remerchandising To increase sales to consumers of types now served by the company	Improved product To improve present products for greater utility and merchandisibility to consumers	Product line extension To broaden the line of products offered to present consumers through new technology
New market To increase the number of types of consumer served by the company	New use To find new classes of consumer that can utilise present company products	Market extension To reach new classes of consumer by modifying present products	Diversification To add to the classes of consumer served by developing new technology knowledge

(Left vertical axis: Increasing market newness ⟶)

Figure 5.6 : New product development strategies

Source: Johnson and Jones (1957)

matrix made no such distinction. Similarly, the market newness scale offers a more realistic range of alternatives. Many other matrices have since been developed to try to help firms identify the range of options available (*see* Dolan, 1993).

The range of product development strategies that are open to a company introduces the notion that a new product can take many forms. This is the subject of the next section.

What is a new product?

Attempting to define what is and what is not a new product is not a trivial task, although many students of business management have had much fun arguing over whether the Sony Walkman was indeed a new product or merely existing technology repackaged. Another example that illustrates this point is the product long-life milk, known in the US as aspectic milk (sold without refrigeration). This product has been consumed for many years in Europe but it is a relatively new concept for most consumers in the US. Consumers who drink refrigerated milk may be extremely wary of milk sold from a non-refrigerated shelf (Thomas, 1993). Once again, while clearly this product is not absolutely new, it can be seen that it is more useful from a product manager's perspective to adopt a relativistic view.

It is important to note, as was explained in Chapter 4, that a product is a multidimensional concept. It can be defined differently and can take many forms. Some dimensions will be tangible product features and others intangible. Does the provision of different packaging for a product constitute a new product? Surely the answer is no – or is it? New packaging coupled with additional marketing effort, especially in terms of marketing communications, can help to reposition a product. This was successfully achieved by SmithKline Beecham with its beverage product Lucozade. Today this product is known as a sports drink, yet older readers will recall that the product was originally packaged in a distinctive bottle wrapped in yellow cellophane and commonly purchased at pharmacists for sick children. This example illustrates the difficulty of attempting to offer a single definition for a new product.

The repositioning of Lucozade

The repositioning of Lucozade is one of the most famous of recent times. Lucozade was first launched on to the UK market nearly 60 years ago. The product is a carbonated beverage with a high level of glucose. The brand was originally associated with illness and convalescence. In the 1960s and 1970s bottles of Lucozade were a common sight by the side of a hospital bed. Some 20 per cent of sales came from pharmacists. Promotion of the brand focused on slice-of-life situations showing Lucozade as a source of energy when family members, especially children, were recovering from illness. The result was that few brands could claim to have such a strong association with sickness.

SmithKline Beecham was aware that many consumers purchased the product as a pick-me-up drink as well as for sickness. Following further studies in this area, the company decided to move the product from a sickness product to an in-health product. The end result of this was ▶

▶ one of the most recognisable television campaigns of the 1970s. It features a wavy line that went up and down, reflecting different times of the day. Lucozade was promoted as a drink that should be consumed during troughs to help one get through the day. The strap line was: 'Lucozade refreshes you through the ups and downs of the day'. Volume sales increased by 13 per cent in the first year.

This was not the end of Lucozade's repositioning. The move from a sickness drink to an in-health drink was further reinforced when the product was completely redeveloped as a sports drink in the 1980s. Top sports stars were used to promote the product as an energy product to be consumed after and during strenuous exercise.

If we accept that a product has many dimensions, then it must follow that it is theoretically possible to label a product 'new' by merely altering one of these dimensions, for example packaging. Figure 5.7 illustrates this point. Each dimension is capable of being altered. These alterations create a new dimension and in theory a new product, even if the change is very small. Indeed, Johne and Snelson (1988) suggest that the options for both new and existing product lines centre around altering the variables in the figure. Table 5.1 shows what this means in practice.

Defining a new product

Chapter 1 established a number of definitions to help with the study of this subject and provided a definition of innovation. In addition, it highlighted a quotation by Rogers and Shoemaker (1971) concerning whether or not something is new. It is useful at this juncture to revisit their argument. They stated that while it may be difficult to establish whether a product is actually new as regards the passage of time, so long as it is perceived to be new it *is* new. This is significant because it illustrates that newness is a relative term. In the case of a new product it is relative to what proceeded the product. Moreover, the overwhelming majority of so-called new products are developments or variations on existing formats. Research in this area suggests that only 10 per cent of new products introduced are new to both the market and the company (Booz, Allen and Hamilton, 1982). New to the company (in this case) means that the firm has not sold this type of product before, but other firms could have.

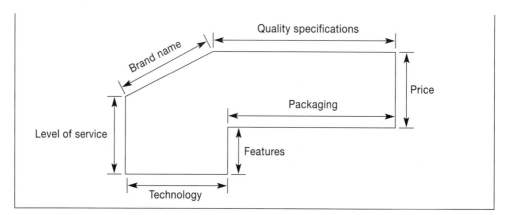

Figure 5.7 : A product is multidimensional

Table 5.1 : Different examples of 'newness'

1 Changing the performance capabilities of the product
   (for example, a new improved washing detergent)
2 Changing the application advice for the product
   (for example, the use of the Persil ball in washing machines)
3 Changing the after-sales service for the product
   (for example, frequency of service for a motor car)
4 Changing the promoted image of the product
   (for example, the use of 'green'-image refill packs)
5 Changing the availability of the product
   (for example, the use of chocolate-vending machines)
6 Changing the price of the product
   (for example, the newspaper industry has experienced severe price wars)

Source: Johne and Snelson (1988)

Table 5.2 : A new product has different interpretations of new

New product A

A snack manufacturer introduces a new, larger pack size for its bestselling savoury snack. Consumer research for the company revealed that a family-size pack would generate additional sales without cannibalising existing sales of the standard-size pack.

New product B

An electronics company introduces a new miniature compact disc player. The company has further developed its existing compact disc product and is now able to offer a much lighter and smaller version.

New product C

A pharmaceutical company introduces a new prescription drug for ulcer treatment. Following eight years of laboratory research and three years of clinical trials, the company has recently received approval from the government's medical authorities to launch its new ulcer drug.

New to the market means that the product has not appeared before in the market. However, the examples in Table 5.2 illustrate the confusion that exists in this area.

The three products in the table are all new in that they did not exist before. However, many would argue, especially technologists, that Product A does not contain any new technology. Similarly, Product B does not contain any new technology although its configuration may be new. Product C contains a new patented chemical formulation, hence this is the only truly new product. Marketers would, however, contend that all three products are new simply because they did not previously exist. Moreover, meeting the needs of the customer and offering products that are wanted is more important than whether a product represents a scientific breakthrough. Such arguments are common to many companies, especially those that have both a strong commercial and technological presence and expertise.

For the student of innovation and new product development, awareness of the debate and the strong feelings that are associated with it is more important than trying to resolve the polemics. Indeed, the long-term commercial success of the company should be the guiding principle on which product decisions are made. However, in some industries, the advancement of knowledge and subsequent scientific breakthroughs can lead to possible product offerings that would help certain sections of the population. Commercial pressures alone would, however, prevent these new products from being offered, as we saw in the case study in Chapter 4. The science and technology perspective should therefore not be dismissed.

Classification of new products

There have been many attempts to classify new products into certain categories. Very often the distinction between one category and another is one of degree and attempting to classify products is subject to judgement. It is worthy of note, however, that only 10 per cent of all new products are truly innovative. These products involve the greatest risk because they are new to both the company and the marketplace. Most new product activity is devoted to improving existing products. At Sony 80 per cent of new product activity is undertaken to modify and improve the company's existing products. The following classification (Booz, Allen and Hamilton, 1982) identifies the commonly accepted categories of new product developments.

New to the world products

These represent a small proportion of all new products introduced. They are the first of their kind and create a new market. They are inventions that usually contain a significant development in technology, such as a new discovery, or manipulate existing technology in a very different way, leading to revolutionary new designs such as the Sony Walkman. Other examples include Polaroid's Instamatic camera, 3M's Post-It notes and Guinness's 'In-can' system.

New product lines (new to the firm)

Although not new to the marketplace, these products are new to the particular company. They provide an opportunity for the company to enter an established market for the first time. For example, Canon was able to enter the paper copying market when it launched its own range of copiers to compete with Xerox, the originators of the product.

Additions to existing lines

This category is a subset of new product lines above. The distinction is that while the company already has a line of products in this market, the product is significantly different to the present product offering but not so different that it is a new line. The distinction between this category and the former is one of degree. For example, Hewlett-Packard's colour ink-jet printer was an addition to its established line of ink-jet printers.

Improvements and revisions to existing products

These new products are replacements of existing products in a firm's product line. For example, Hewlett-Packard's ink-jet printer has received numerous modifications over time and, with each revision, performance and reliability have been improved. Also manufacturing cost reductions can be introduced, providing increased added value. This classification represents a significant proportion of all new product introductions.

Cost reductions

This category of products may not be viewed as new from a marketing perspective, largely because they offer no new benefits to the consumer other than possibly reduced costs. From the firm's perspective, however, they may be very significant. The ability to offer similar performance while reducing production costs provides enormous added-value potential. Indeed, frequently it is this category of new product that can produce the greatest financial rewards for the firm. Improved manufacturing processes and the use of different materials are key contributing factors. The difference between this category and the improvement category is simply that a cost reduction may not result in a product improvement.

Repositionings

These new products are essentially the discovery of new applications for existing products. This has more to do with consumer perception and branding than technical development. This is nonetheless an important category. Following the medical science discovery that aspirin thins blood, for example, the product has been repositioned from an analgesic to an over-the-counter remedy for blood clots and one that may help to prevent strokes and heart attacks.

New product development as an industry innovation cycle

Abernathy and Utterback (1978) suggested that product innovations are soon followed by process innovations in what they described as an industry innovation cycle (*see* Chapter 1). A similar notion can be applied to the categories of new products. The cycle can be identified in a wide variety of industries. New to the world products (Category 1) are launched by large companies with substantial resources, especially technical or marketing resources. Other large firms react swiftly to the launch of such a product by developing their own versions (Categories 2 and 3). Many small and medium-sized companies participate by developing their own new products to compete with the originating firm's product (Category 4). Substantial success and growth can come to small companies that adopt this strategy. Compaq has grown into one of the most successful personal computer manufacturers even though it was not, unlike Apple and IBM, at the forefront of the development of the personal computer. As competition intensifies, companies will compete in the market for profits. The result is determined efforts to reduce costs in order to improve these profits, hence there are many cost reductions (Category 5).

Overview of NPD theories

The early stages of the new product development process are most usually defined as idea generation, idea screening, concept development and concept testing. They represent the formation and development of an idea prior to its taking any physical form. In most industries it is from this point onwards that costs will rise significantly. It is clearly far easier to change a concept than a physical product. The subsequent stages involve adding to the concept as those involved with the development (manufacturing engineers, product designers and marketers) begin to make decisions regarding how best to manufacture the product, what materials to use, possible designs and the potential market's evaluations.

The organisational activities undertaken by the company as it embarks on the actual process of new product development have been represented by numerous different models. These have attempted to capture the key activities involved in the process, from idea to commercialisation of the product. The representation of these tasks has changed significantly over the past 30 years. For example, the pharmaceutical industry is dominated by scientific and technological developments that lead to new drugs; whereas the food industry is dominated by consumer research that leads to many minor product changes. And yet the vast majority of textbooks that tackle this subject present the NPD process as an eight-stage linear model regardless of these major differences (Figure 5.8 shows how the process is frequently presented). Consequently this simple linear model is ingrained in the minds of many people. This is largely because new product development is viewed from a financial perspective where cash outflows

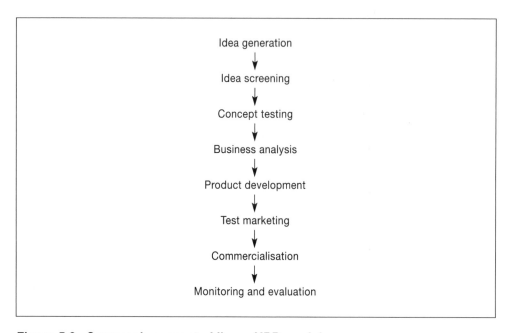

Figure 5.8 : Commonly presented linear NPD model

precede cash inflows (*see* Figure 5.9). This graph shows the cumulative effect on cash flow through the development phases, to the build-up of stock and work in progress in the early stages of production, when there is no balancing in-flow of cash from sales, to the phase of profitable sales which brings the cash in-flow.

Virtually all those actually involved with the development of new products dismiss such simple linear models as not being a true representation of reality. More recent research suggests that the process needs to be viewed as a simultaneous and concurrent process with cross-functional interaction (Hart, 1993).

For the reasons outlined above, the different perspectives on NPD have produced a wealth of literature on the subject (Brown and Eisenhardt, 1995; Craig and Hart, 1992). In addition, the subject has attracted the attention of many business schools and business consultants, all interested in uncovering the secrets of successful product development. Numerous research projects have been undertaken including in-depth case studies across many industries and single companies and broad surveys of industries (e.g. Ancona and Caldwell, 1992; Clark and Fujimoto, 1991; Dougherty, 1990; Zirger and Maidique, 1990).

As a result, research on new product development is varied and fragmented, making it extremely difficult to organise for analysis. Brown and Eisenhardt (1995) have tackled this particular problem head on and have produced an excellent review of the literature. In their analysis they identify three main streams of literature, each having its own particular strengths and limitations (*see* Table 5.3). These streams have evolved around key research findings and together they continue to throw light on many dark areas of new product development.

While this is an important development and a useful contribution to our understanding of the subject area, it offers little help for the practising manager on how he or she should organise and manage the new product development process. An analysis of the models that have been developed on the subject of new product development may help to identify some of the activities that need to be managed.

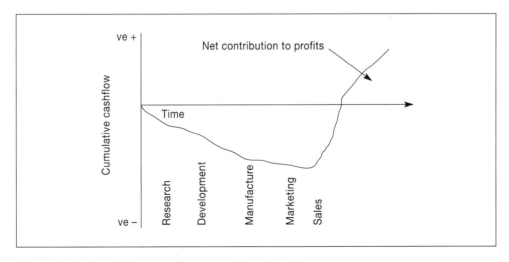

Figure 5.9 : Cash flows and new product development

Table 5.3 : The three main streams of research within the NPD literature

	Rational planning	Communication web	Disciplined problem solving
Aim/objective/title	Rational planning and management of the development of new products within organisations	The communication web studies the use of information and sources of information by product development teams	Disciplined problem solving focuses on how problems encountered during the NPD process were overcome
Focus of the research	The rational plan research focuses on business performance and financial performance of the product	The communication web looks at the effects of communication on project performance	The third stream tries to examine the process and the wide range of actors and activities involved
Seminal research	The work by Myers and Marquis (1969) and SAPPHO studies (Rothwell et al., 1974) was extremely influential in this field	Thomas Allen's (1969, 1977) research into communication patterns in large industrial laboratories dominates this perspective	The work by the Japanese scholars Imai et al. (1985) lies at the heart of this third stream of literature

Source: Brown and Eisenhardt, 1995

Models of new product development

Among the burgeoning management literature on the subject it is possible to classify the numerous models into seven distinct categories (Saren, 1984):

1 Departmental-stage models
2 Activity-stage models and concurrent engineering
3 Cross-functional models (teams)
4 Decision-stage models
5 Conversion-process models
6 Response models
7 Network models.

Within this taxonomy decision-stage models and activity-stage models are the most commonly discussed and presented in textbooks. Figure 5.8 is an example of an activity-stage model (*see also* Crawford, 1997, and Kotler, 1997, for examples of a decision-stage model).

It is worthy of note that there are many companies, especially small specialist manufacturing companies, that continue to operate a craftsman-style approach to product development. This has been the traditional method of product manufacture for the past 500 years. For example, in every part of Europe there are joinery companies manufacturing products to the specific requirements of the user. Many of these products will be single one-off products manufactured to dimensions given on a drawing. All the activities, including the creation of drawings, collection of raw materials, manufacture and delivery, may be undertaken by one person. Today, when we are surrounded by technology that is sometimes difficult to use never mind understand, it is possible to forget that the traditional approach to product development is still prevalent. Many activities, moreover, remain the same as they have always been.

Departmental-stage models

Departmental-stage models represent the early form of NPD models. These can be shown to be based around the linear model of innovation, where each department is responsible for certain tasks. They are usually represented in the following way: R&D provides the interesting technical ideas; the engineering department will then take the ideas and develop possible prototypes; the manufacturing department will explore possible ways to produce a viable product capable of mass manufacture; the marketing department will then be brought in to plan and conduct the launch. Such models are also referred to as 'over-the-wall' models, so called because departments would carry out their tasks before throwing the project over the wall to the next department (*see* Figure 5.10).

It is now widely accepted that this insular departmental view of the process hinders the development of new products. The process is usually characterised by a great deal of reworking and consultation between functions. In addition, market research provides continual inputs to the process. Furthermore, control of the project changes on a departmental basis depending on which department is currently engaged in it. The consequence of this approach has been captured by Mike Smith's (1981) humorous tale of 'How not to design a swing, or the perils of poor communication' (*see* Figure 5.11).

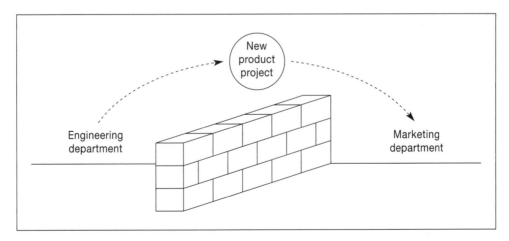

Figure 5.10 : Over the wall model

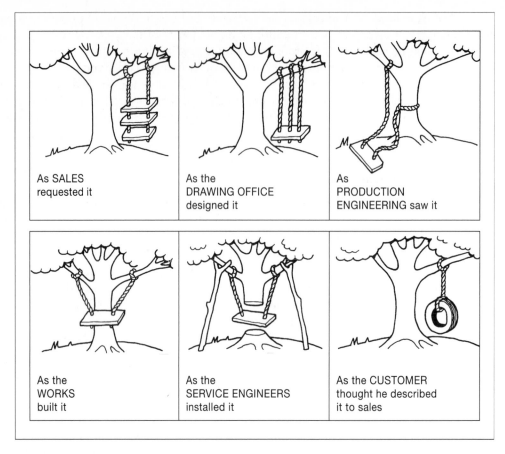

As SALES requested it

As the DRAWING OFFICE designed it

As PRODUCTION ENGINEERING saw it

As the WORKS built it

As the SERVICE ENGINEERS installed it

As the CUSTOMER thought he described it to sales

Figure 5.11 : Mike Smith's secret weapon: the salutary tale of 'How not to design a swing, or the perils of poor coordination'

Activity-stage models and concurrent engineering

These are similar to department-stage models but because they emphasise activities conducted they provide a better representation of reality. They also facilitate iteration of the activities through the use of feedback loops, something that the departmental-stage models do not. Activity-stage models, however, have also received fierce criticism for perpetuating the 'over-the-wall' phenomenon. More recent activity-stage models (Crawford, 1997) have highlighted the simultaneous nature of the activities within the NPD process, hence emphasising the need for a cross-functional approach. Figure 5.12 shows an activity-stage model where the activities occur at the same time but vary in their intensity.

In the late 1980s in an attempt to address some of these problems, many manufacturing companies adopted a concurrent engineering or simultaneous engineering approach. The term was first coined by the Institute for the Defense Analyses (IDA) in 1986 (IDA, 1986) to explain the systematic method of concurrently designing both the product and its downstream production and support processes. The idea is to focus attention on the project as a whole rather than the individual stages, primarily

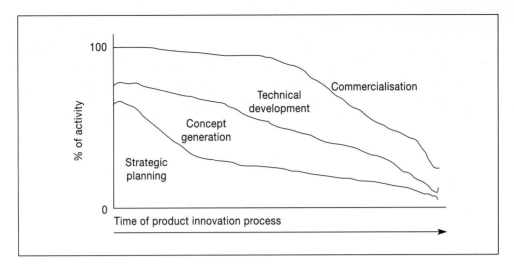

Figure 5.12 : An activity-stage model
Source: reproduced with permission from Crawford (1997)

by involving all functions from the outset of the project. This requires a major change in philosophy from functional orientation to project orientation. Furthermore, technology-intensive businesses with very specialist knowledge inputs are more difficult to manage (the case study at the end of Chapter 6 explores some of these problems). Such an approach introduces the need for project teams.

Cross-functional models (teams)

Common problems that occur within the product development process centre around communications between different departments. This problem, specifically with regard to the marketing and the R&D departments, is explored more fully in Chapter 6. In addition, projects would frequently be passed back and forth between functions. Moreover, at each interface the project would undergo increased changes, hence lengthening the product development process. The cross-functional teams (CFT) approach removes many of these limitations by having a dedicated project team representing people from a variety of functions. The use of cross-functional teams requires a fundamental modification to an organisation's structure. In particular, it places emphasis on the use of project management and inter-disciplinary teams.

Decision-stage models

Decision-stage models represent the new product development process as a series of decisions that need to be taken in order to progress the project (Cooper and Kleinschmidt, 1993; Kotler, 1997). Like the activity-stage models, many of these models also facilitate iteration through the use of feedback loops. However, a criticism of these models is that such feedback is implicit rather than explicit. The importance of the interaction between functions cannot be stressed enough – the use of feedback loops helps to emphasise this.

Conversion-process models

As the name suggests, conversion-process models view new product development as numerous inputs into a 'black box' where they are converted into an output (Schon, 1967). For example, the inputs could be customer requirements, technical ideas and manufacturing capability and the output would be the product. The concept of a variety of information inputs leading to a new product is difficult to criticise, but the lack of detail elsewhere is the biggest limitation of such models.

Response models

Response models are based on the work of Becker and Whistler (1967) who used a behaviourist approach to analyse change. In particular, these models focus on the individual's or organisation's response to a new project proposal or new idea. This approach has revealed additional factors that influence the decision to accept or reject new product proposals, especially at the screening stage.

Network models

This final classification of new product development models represents the most recent thinking on the subject. The case studies in Chapters 3 and 5 highlight the

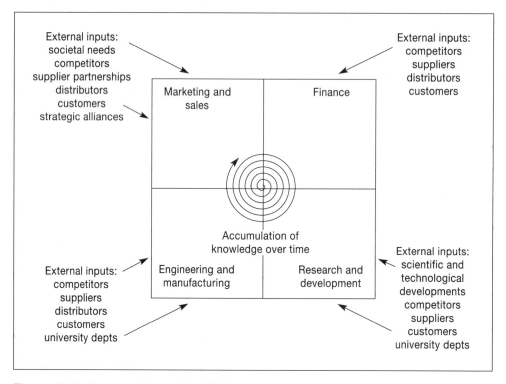

Figure 5.13 : A network model of NPD

process of accumulation of knowledge from a variety of different inputs, such as marketing, R&D and manufacturing. This knowledge is built up gradually over time as the project progresses from initial idea (technical breakthrough or market opportunity) through development. It is this process that forms the basis of the network models (these models are explored more fully in Takeuchi and Nonaka, 1986; Nonaka, 1991; Hagedoorn, 1990; Trott, 1993; Nonaka and Takeuchi, 1995).

Essentially, network models emphasise the external linkages coupled with the internal activities that have been shown to contribute to successful product development. There is substantial evidence to suggest that external linkages can facilitate additional knowledge flows into the organisation, thereby enhancing the product development process (Liker *et al.*, 1995; Kamath and Liker, 1994; Cusumano and Takeishi, 1991). These models suggest that NPD should be viewed as a knowledge-accumulation process that requires inputs from a wide variety of sources. The model in Figure 5.13 helps to highlight the accumulation of knowledge over time. This may be thought of as a snowball gaining in size as it rolls down a snow-covered mountain.

CASE STUDY

An analysis of 3M, the innovation company[1]

Introduction

Any review of the literature on new product development and innovation management will uncover numerous references to 3M. The organisation is synonymous with innovation and has been described as 'a smooth running innovation machine' (Mitchell, 1989). Year after year 3M is celebrated in the *Fortune* 500 rankings as the 'most respected company' and the 'most innovative company'. Management gurus from Peter Drucker to Tom Peters continually refer to the company as a shining example of an innovative company. This case study takes a look at the company behind some of the most famous brands in the marketplace, such as Scotch videocassettes and Post-It notes. It examines the company's heritage and shows how it has arrived at this enviable position. Furthermore, the case study attempts to clarify what it is that makes 3M stand out from other organisations.

Background

Originally known as the Minnesota Mining and Manufacturing Company, with its headquarters in St Paul, Minnesota, 3M was established in 1902 to mine abrasive minerals for the production of a single product, sandpaper. From these inauspicious beginnings, the company has grown organically, concentrating on the internal development of new products in a variety of different industries. The latest review of the company's position reveals that it manufactures over 60 000 products, has operations in 61 countries, employs 70 000 people and has achieved an average year-on-year growth in sales of 10 per cent (see Figure 5.14). Its products include Scotch adhesive tapes, fibreoptic connectors, abrasives, adhesives, floppy discs, aerosol inhalers, medical diagnostic products and Post-It notes.

[1] This case has been written as a basis for class discussion rather than to illustrate effective or ineffective managerial or administrative behaviour. It has been prepared from a variety of published sources, as indicated, and from observations.

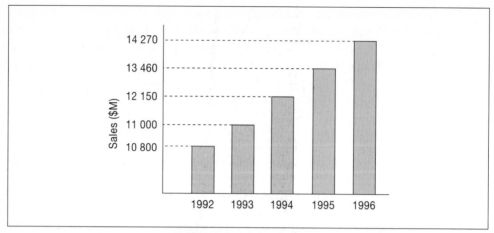

Figure 5.14 : Sales over the past five years
Source: 3M Corp (1998)

3M gave the world 'wet or dry' abrasives, which did so much to reduce the incidence of respiratory disease in the 1920s. It invented self-adhesive tape in 1925, light-reflective materials in the 1940s and pioneered magnetic recording and photocopying. This heritage established the technology from which many of its products are still derived. To reinforce this impressive performance, 3M is consistently ranked among the top 10 of America's most admired companies in the US journal *Fortune*, in its annual review of the top 500 companies in the US. 3M is a large and unusually diverse company. The company is currently restructuring, the spin-off of its data storage and imaging businesses forming a new company.

The 3M approach to innovation

Many writers, academics and business leaders have argued that the key to successful innovation is good management (Henderson, 1994). Arguably, this is precisely what 3M has mastered. A closer inspection, however, will reveal that the company has combined a variety of management techniques, such as good communications and the setting of clear objectives with a company culture built on more than 90 years of nurturing ideas and fostering creativity. It uses a combination of structured research and individual freedom to explore ideas by allowing research scientists to spend 15 per cent of their time conducting projects of their own choosing. It is a unique combination of activities that is, by definition, difficult to replicate. They are described in this case study under the following headings:

1 Company heritage and culture

2 The demand for innovation (the 30 per cent rule)

3 Freedom for creativity

4 Tolerating failure

5 Autonomy and small businesses

6 High profile for science and technology

7 Internal technology transfer

Company heritage and culture

Through a combination of formal and informal processes, the company has developed a culture devoted to creating new products and building new businesses. This is partly based on the simple idea of hiring good people and trusting them. Indeed, this is the first goal that is stated in 3M's formal principles of management: 'the promotion of entrepreneurship and the insistence upon freedom in the workplace to pursue innovative ideas' (Osborn, 1988).

The demand for innovation (the 30 per cent rule)

While the sales performance in Figure 5.14 is impressive, it conceals an important statistic; that is, 30 per cent of the company's sales come from products that are less than four years old. Indeed, this is a business objective that every 3M business manager has to try to achieve. What this means is that these business managers are under pressure to ensure that not only do they develop new products but that these new products will eventually represent 30 per cent of the business's sales. This objective has been effectively communicated throughout the organisation and is now ingrained within the management style and part of the culture of the company. Hence, the search for new ideas is part of daily activities.

Senior managers from other large manufacturing companies would rightly argue that a similar percentage of sales within their own companies comes from products less than four years old. However, the difference between 3M and other organisations is that 3M has developed this approach over many years and has worked hard to ensure that developing new products is much higher on the agenda in management meetings than at other companies. Moreover, the success of the approach is due to the continual reinforcement of the objective. Indeed, the performance of individual business managers is partly judged on whether they are able to achieve the objective.

The 30 per cent objective was first introduced in the 1980s when 25 per cent of sales had to come from products less than four years old. This was altered in 1992 to 30 per cent. 3M has recently added another goal, which is to ensure that 10 per cent of sales come from products that have been in the market for only one year.

Freedom for creativity

Scientists and engineers are given time to work on projects and ideas that they consider to be of potential interest to the company and 15 per cent of an individual's work week time may be dedicated to such activities. This is not exclusive to 3M and is common practice in most large R&D laboratories. Nonetheless, it is an effective method of providing room for creativity and another way of showing that the organisation encourages innovative effort. Indeed, it is a method of providing resources to entrepreneurs, allowing them to work on ideas without having to seek out approval from the organisation. Another way of allocating resources is the use of grants. Known as 'genesis grants', these give researchers up to $75 000 to develop their ideas into potential product opportunities.

One of 3M's most famous new products was the result of this practice, the Post-It note. Spencer Silver and Arthur Fry both invoked the 15 per cent rule to allow them to work on the project that eventually led to its development.

> Spencer Silver was a 3M research chemist working on adhesive technology. His brief was to produce the strongest adhesive on the market. By some extraordinary mischance he developed an adhesive that had none of the properties he was looking for, but which did have two interesting properties which he had never previously encountered: it could be reused and it left no residue on the material to which it was applied. Yet no one could find a use for it and the idea was shelved.

> Art Fry, one of Spencer Silver's colleagues, sang in a choir. Every Sunday he would carefully mark his hymnbook with slips of paper and every Sunday the slips fell out. Then he remembered Spencer Silver's useless adhesive. Applied to paper strips, Art Fry found that they made fine book markers that did not fall out when he opened the book. Post-It brand technology had been developed ten years before Art Fry discovered what to do with it!

In a recent lecture on the subject of innovation, the 3M vice-president for research and development (Coyne, 1996) reported that:

> The 15 per cent rule is meaningless. Some of our technical people use more than 15 per cent of their time on projects of their own choosing. Some use less than that; some none at all. The figure is not so important as the message, which is this: *the system has some slack in it. If you have a good idea, and the commitment to squirrel away time to work on it, and the raw nerve to skirt your manager's expressed desires, then fine.*

Tolerating failure

'It's easier to be critical than creative' is an adaptation of a famous quote from Benjamin Disraeli. It captures the essence of 3M's approach to tolerating failure. Most large companies with large R&D departments will have many on-going new product research projects. Many will consume large amounts of resources and will not result in a new product. This fact is all part of the new product game. Those close to the game are aware of this; at 3M it is argued that everyone is aware of the need to try new ideas. Its founder and early chief executive, W.L. Knight, stated over 60 years ago that:

> A management that is destructively critical when mistakes are made, kills initiative, and it is essential that we have people with initiative if we are to continue to grow.

Vasilash (1995) suggests that many of the senior managers within 3M are known to have made at least one mistake in their career while they tried to be innovative, thereby suggesting that W.L. Knight's philosophy continues.

3M has had its share of colossal failures. In the 1920s one of the company's top inventors had an incredible flash of brilliance: maybe people could use sandpaper as a replacement for razor blades. Instead of shaving your face or legs, you could just sand off the whiskers. Every man and woman would need it. The company would sell the product by the ton! Not surprisingly the idea was not realised in practice – but the inventor was not punished for following his idea. For every 1000 ideas only 100 are written up as formal proposals. Only a fraction of these become new product ventures and over half of the company's new product ventures fail (Coyne, 1996).

Autonomy and small businesses

Like many companies 3M realises that large organisations, with their inevitable corresponding structures and systems, can sometimes inhibit the creative dynamism often required to foster innovative effort. Hence, it has adopted an approach that enables individuals and groups within the organisation to establish small internal venture groups, with managers free to make their own decisions, develop their own product lines and take responsibility for the results, without continuous co-ordination across the company (Stewart, 1996). This approach attempts to offer an entrepreneurial environment under a corporate umbrella.

Provided that certain financial measures are met, such start-up venture groups follow a well-trodden path: a new business operation starts out as a project, if sales reach $1 million it becomes a fully fledged product. At $20 million, it becomes an independent product department separate from its parent department. If it continues to grow it will be spun off as a separate autonomous division. Currently, divisions characteristically have $200 million in sales. Experience has taught the company that in the early days of a business's life, many decisions are taken through informal discussions among the individuals involved. There are usually insufficient resources to allow for lengthy and detailed analysis, which is more common in more established businesses.

High profile for science and technology

Although the company was formed around a single technology sandpaper, today 3M makes use of more than 100 technologies such as membranes, biotechnology, artificial intelligence, high-vacuum thin films and superconductivity. These technologies underpin the products that the company develops and manufactures. To support these activities the company invests 6.5 per cent of its annual sales turnover in research and development. This is about twice that of the top 50 industrial companies in the US. The money is used to employ over 7500 scientists and technologists in developing new and interesting technology. It is this technological intensity that provides the company with the competitive advantage to compete with its rivals.

It is important to note that while the company is technology intensive, this does not imply a single-minded, technology-push approach to innovation. The role of the marketplace and users plays an important part in product development. For example, 3M's famous Scotch tape was once manufactured strictly as an industrial product, until a salesman got the idea of packaging it in clear plastic dispensers for home and office use.

Communication and technology transfer

The communication of ideas helps to ensure that a company can maximise the return on its substantial investments in the technology. Very often it is the combination of apparently diverse technologies through technology transfer that has led to major product innovations. For example, Microreplication technology is the creation of precise microscopic, three-dimensional patterns on a variety of surfaces, including plastic film. When the surface is changed numerous product possibilities emerge. It was first developed for overhead projectors, its innovative feature being a lens made of a thin piece of plastic with thousands of tiny grooves on its surface. Microreplication helped the plastic lens to perform better than the conventional lens made of heavy glass. 3M became the world's leading producer of overhead projectors. It is this technology, which can be traced back to the 1960s, that has spread ▶

throughout 3M and led to a wide range of products, including better and brighter reflective material for traffic signs; 'floptical' disks for data storage; laptop computer screens; and films.

Discussion

While few would argue with 3M's successful record on innovation, there may be some who would argue that, compared to companies such as Microsoft, IBM and Glaxo-Wellcome, its achievements in terms of growth have not been as spectacular. However, the point here is not that 3M is the most successful company or even that it is the most innovative, although one could surely construct a strong case, merely that the company has a long and impressive performance when it comes to developing new products.

This case study has highlighted some of the key activities and principles that contribute to 3M's performance. Many of these are not new and are indeed used by other companies. In 3M's case they may be summarised as an effective company culture that nurtures innovation and a range of management techniques and strategies that together have delivered long-term success. Many companies pay lip service to the management principles and practice set out in this case study. There is evidence that 3M support these fine words with actions.

For further information about 3M and its business activities, visit the 3M international Web page at: http://www.mmm.com

Chapter summary

This chapter has considered the relationship between new products and prosperity and shown that new product development is one of the most common forms of organic growth strategies. The range of NPD strategies is wide indeed and can range from packaging alterations to new technological research. The chapter stressed the importance of viewing a product as a multidimensional concept.

The later part of the chapter focused on the various models of NPD that have emerged over the past 50 years. All of these have strengths and weaknesses. By their very nature, models attempt to capture and portray a complex notion and in so doing often over-simplify elements. This is the central argument of critics of the linear model of NPD, that it is too simplistic and does not provide for any feedback or concurrent activities. More recent models such as network models try to emphasis the importance of the external linkages in the NPD process.

Questions for discussion

1 Explain why the process of new product development is frequently represented as a linear process.

2 List the key activities of NPD.

3 Explain why screening should be viewed as a continual rather than a one-off activity.

4 Discuss how the various groups of NPD models have contributed to our understanding of the subject of NPD.

5 Discuss the wide range of product development opportunities that exist.

6 Examine the concept of a multidimensional product.

7 Explain Booz, Allen and Hamilton's (1982) classification of new products.

8 Why do some marketers and scientists often argue about whether a product is new or not?

9 Discuss some of the strengths of network models of NPD.

10 There are many examples of successful companies. To what extent is 3M justifiably highlighted as the 'innovating machine'?

11 In the 3M case study, what is meant by the statement: 'the message is more important than the figures'?

References

3M Company Report (1996) http://www.mmm.com/profile/report2/chairman.html

3M Corp (1998) Financial results from 3M international Web page: 3M http://www.mmm.com

Abernathy, W.L. and Utterback, J. (1978) 'Patterns of industrial innovation', in Tushman, M.L. and Moore, W.L., *Readings in Management of Innovation*, 97–108, HarperCollins, New York.

Allen, T.J. (1969) 'Communication networks in R&D laboratories', *R&D Management*, 1, 14–21.

Allen, T.J. (1977) *Managing the Flow of Technology*, MIT Press, Cambridge, MA.

Ancona, D.G. and Caldwell, D.F. (1992) 'Bridging the boundary: External processesa and performance in organisational teams', *Administrative Science Quarterly*, 37, 634–65.

Ansoff, I. (1968) *Corporate Strategy*, Penguin, Harmondsworth.

Becker, S. and Whistler, T.I. (1967) 'The innovative organisation: a selective view of current theory and research', *Journal of Business*, 40 (4), 462–69.

Booz, Allen and Hamilton (1982) *New Product Management for the 1980s*, Booz, Allen and Hamilton, New York.

Brown, S.L. and Eisenhardt, K.M. (1995) 'Product development: past research, present findings and future directions', *Academy of Management Review*, 20 (2), 343–78.

Clark, K. and Fujimoto, T. (1991) *Product Development Performance*, Harvard Business School Press, Boston, MA.

Cooper, R.G. and Kleinschmidt, E.J. (1993) 'Major new products: what distinguishes the winners in the chemical industry?' *Journal of Product Innovation Management*, 10, 2, 90–111.

Coyne, W.E. (1996) Innovation lecture given at the Royal Society, March 5.

Craig, A. and Hart, S. (1992) 'Where to now in new product development', *European Journal of Marketing*, 26, 11.

Crawford, C.M. (1997) *New Products Management*, 5th edn, Irwin, Chicago.

Cusumano, M.A. and Takeishi, A. (1991) 'Supplier relations and management: a survey of Japanese, Japanese transplant, and US auto plants', *Strategic Management Journal*, 12 (November), 563–88.

Dolan, R.J. (1993) *Managing the New Product Development Process*, Addison-Wesley, Reading, Mass.

Dougherty, D. (1990) 'Understanding new markets for new products', *Strategic Management Journal*, 11, 59–78.

Hagedoorn, J. (1990) 'Organisational modes of inter-firm co-operation and technology transfer', *Technovation*, 10 (1), 17–30.

Hart, S. (1993) 'Dimensions of success in new product development: an exploratory investigation', *Journal of Marketing Management*, 9 (9) 23–41.

Henderson, R. (1994) 'Managing innovation in the information age', *Harvard Business Review*, January–February, 100–5.

Houlder, V. (1994) 'Rewards for bright ideas', *Financial Times*, December, 18.

Imai, K., Ikujiro, N. and Takeuchi, H. (1985) 'Managing the new product development process: how Japanese companies learn and unlearn', in Hayes, R.H., Clark, K. and Lorenz (eds) *The Uneasy Alliance: Managing the Productivity-Technology Dilemma*, Harvard Business School Press, Boston, MA, 337–75.

IDA (1986) *The Role of Concurrent Engineering in Weapons Systems Acquisition*, report R–338, IDA Washington, DC.

Johne, F.A. and Snelson, P.A. (1988) 'The role of marketing specialists in product development', proceedings of the 21st Annual Conference of the Marketing Education Group, Huddersfield, 3, 176–91.

Johnson, G. and Scholes, K. (1997) *Exploring Corporate Strategy*, 4th edn, Prentice Hall, Hemel Hempstead.

Johnson, S.C. and Jones, C. (1957) 'How to organise for new products', *Harvard Business Review*, May–June, 35, 49–62.

Kamath, R. and Liker, J.K. (1994) 'A second look at Japanese product development', *Harvard Business Review*, November–December (74) 154–70.

Kotler, P. (1997) *Marketing Management*, Prentice-Hall, Englewood Cliffs, NJ.

Liker, J.K., Sobek, A.C., Ward, and Cristiano, J.J. (1996) 'Involving suppliers in product development in the United States and Japan: evidence for set-based concurrent engineering', *IEE Transactions on Engineering Management*, 43 (2), May.

Liker, J.K., Kamath, R., Wasti, N. and Nagamachi, M. (1995) 'Integrating suppliers into fast-cycle product development', in Liker, J.K., Ettlie, J.E. and Campbell, J.C. (eds), Oxford University Press, *Engineering in Japan: Japanese Technology Management Practices*, New York.

Mitchell, R. (1989) 'Masters of innovation: how 3M keeps its new products coming', *Business Week*, April, 58–63.

Myers, S. and Marquis, D.G. (1969) 'Successful industrial innovation: a study of factors underlying innovation and selected firms', National Science Foundation, NSF 69–17, Washington.

Nonaka, I. (1991) 'The knowledge creating company', *Harvard Business Review*, November/December, 69 (6) 96–104.

Nonaka, I. and Takeuchi, H. (1995) *The Knowledge Creating Company*, Oxford University Press, Oxford.

Osborn, T. (1988) 'How 3M manages innovation', *Marketing Communications*, November/December, 17–22.

Rogers, E. and Shoemaker, R. (1972) *Communications of Innovations*, Free Press, New York.

Rothwell, R., Freeman, C., Horlsey, A., Jervis, V.T.P., Robertson, A.B. and Townsend, J. (1974) 'SAPPHO updated: Project SAPPHO phase II', *Research Policy*, 3, 258–91.

Saren, M. (1984) 'A classification of review models of the intra-firm innovation process', *R&D Management*, 14 (1) 11–24.

Schon, D. (1967) 'Champions for radical new inventions', *Harvard Business Review*, March–April, 77–86.

Smith, M.R.H. (1981), paper to *National Conference on Quality and Competitiveness*, London, November, reported in *Financial Times*, 25 November.

Stewart, T. (1996) '3M fights back', *Fortune*, 133 (2), February 5, 42–7.

Takeuchi, H. and Nonaka, I. (1986) 'The new product development game', *Harvard Business Review*, 64 (1), 137–46.

Thomas, R.J. (1993) *New Product Development*, John Wiley & Sons, New York.

Trott, P. (1993) 'Inward technology transfer as an interactive process: a case study of ICI', PhD thesis, Cranfield University.

Ughanwa, D.O. and Baker, M.J. (1989) *The Role of Design in International Competitiveness*, Routledge, London.

Vasilash, G.S. (1995) 'Heart and soul of 3M', *Production*, 107 (6) 38–9.

Zirger, B.J. and Maidique, M.A. (1990) 'A model of new product development: an emperical test', *Management Science*, 36, 876–88.

Further reading

Brown, S.L. and Eisenhardt (1995) 'Product development: past research, present findings and future directions', *Academy of Management Review*, 20 (2) 343–78.

Crawford, C.M. (1997) *New Product Development*, 5th edn, Irwin, Chicago.

Hart, S. (1996) *New Product Development, A Reader*, The Dryden Press, London.

Swink, M.L., Sandvig, J.C. and Mabert, V.A. (1996) 'Adding "zip" to product development: concurrent engineering methods and tools', *Business Horizons*, March–April, 39 (2) 41–50.

Takeuchi, H. and Vanaka, I. (1996) 'The new product development game', *Harvard Business Review*, 64 (1) 137–46.

6

Managing the new product development team

Introduction

The popular phrase 'action speaks louder than words' could be a subtitle for this chapter. While the previous two chapters helped to identify some of the key factors and activities involved in the new product development process, it is the execution of these activities that will inevitably lead to the development of a new product. The focus of this chapter is on the management of the project as it evolves from idea into a physical form. Many companies have become very good at effective NPD, demonstrating that they are able to balance the many factors involved.

Learning objectives

When you have completed this chapter, you will be able to:

● Examine the key activities of the NPD process
● Explain that a product concept differs significantly from a product idea or business opportunity
● Recognise that screening is a continuous rather than single activity
● Provide an understanding of the role of the knowledge base of an organisation in the new product development process
● Recognise that the technology intensity of the industry considerably affects the NPD process.

New products as projects

Over the past 50 years a large number of models and methods have been developed to help improve a company's performance in new product development (Craig and Hart, 1992). However, despite the positive influences these models may have on companies' efforts, Mahajan and Wind (1988) have shown low rates of usage in their study of *Fortune* 500 companies. More recently, Nijssen and Lieshout (1995) have shown in their study of companies in the Netherlands that the use of NPD models has a positive effect on profits.

The previous chapters have outlined some of the conditions that are necessary for innovation to occur and have shown various representations of the new product development process. However, while these conditions are necessary, they are insufficient in themselves to lead to the development of new products. This is because, as with any internal organisational process, it has to be managed by people. The concepts of strategy, marketing and technology all have to be co-ordinated and managed effectively. Inevitably, this raises issues in such areas as internal communications, procedures and systems. This is where the attention turns from theory and representation to operation and activities.

We have seen that a product idea may arise from a variety of sources. We have also seen that, unlike some internal operations, NPD is not the preserve of one single department. And it is because a variety of different functions and departments are involved that the process is said to be complicated and difficult to manage. Furthermore, while two separate new products may be similar generically, there will frequently be different product characteristics to be accommodated and different

Table 6.1 : NPD terminology

NPD terminology	Definition
Business opportunity	A possible technical or commercial idea that may be transformed into a revenue-generating product.
Product concept	A physical form or a technology plus a clear statement of benefit
Screening	A series of evaluations, including technical, commercial and business assessments of the concept
Specifications	Precise details about the product, including features, characteristics and standards
Prototype/pilot	A tentative physical product or system procedure, including features and benefits
Production	The product produced by the scale-up manufacturing process
Launch	The product actually marketed, in either market test or launch
Cojoint analysis	A method for deriving the utility values that consumers attach to varying levels of a product's attributes
Commercialisation	A more descriptive label would be market introduction, the phase when the product is launched and hopefully begins to generate sales revenue
Commercial success	The end product that meets the goals set for it, usually profit

market and technology factors to be addressed. To be successful new product development needs to occur with the participation of a variety of personnel drawn from across the organisation. This introduces the notion of a group of people working as a team to develop an idea or project proposal into a final product suitable for sale. The vast majority of large firms create new project teams to work through this process. From initial idea to launch, the project will usually flow and iterate between marketing, technical and manufacturing groups and specialists. The role of the new project team is at the heart of managing new products and is the focus of the case study at the end of this chapter.

The key activities that need to be managed

The network model of NPD shown in Figure 5.13 represents a generalised and theoretical view of the process. To the practising manager, however, this is of limited practical use. Business managers and the managers of project teams need to know what particular activities should be undertaken. From this practitioner standpoint it is more useful to view the new product development process as a series of linked activities.

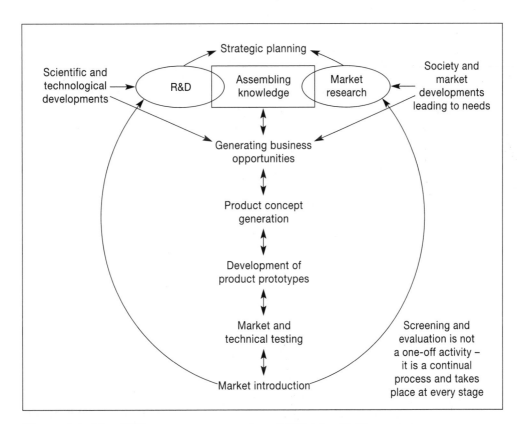

Figure 6.1 : The NPD process as a series of linked activities

Figure 6.1 attempts to identify and link together most of the activities that have been associated with the NPD process over the years. This diagram represents a generic process model of NPD. It is not intended to be an actual representation of the process as carried out in a particular industry. Rather, it attempts to convey to the practitioner how the key activities are linked together to form a process. Some of these labels differ between industries and a good example of this is in the pharmaceutical industry. Final testing of a product is referred to as the clinical trial, where the product is used by volunteers and the effects carefully monitored. In the automotive industry final testing may involve the use of consumers trying the product for the first time and offering their reflections on the design and ergonomics.

One of the most comprehensive studies on new product success and failure was undertaken by Cooper in 1979. In this study 12 activities were identified: initial screening; preliminary market assessment; preliminary technical assessment; detailed market study; financial analysis; product development; product testing (in-house); product testing (with customer); test marketing; trial production; full-scale production; and product launch. Since this a number of different studies have highlighted the importance of some of these activities over others. Other studies have shown that firms frequently omit some of these activities (Cooper, 1988; Sanchez and Elola, 1991). Students of new product development are left with an unclear picture of which activities are necessary and which are performed. The answer is context dependent and, in particular, industry dependent. Some industries no longer use test marketing, for example, whereas for others it is still a very important activity. This is explained below.

This section will examine the activities that need to be performed by businesses and NPD teams. The early activities are defined as the 'assembly of knowledge' and the 'generation of business opportunities'. These activities usually occur before a physical representation of the product has been developed. Up to this point costs have been relatively low, especially when compared to subsequent activities. These activities, defined here as product concept development and development of product prototypes, transform what was previously a concept, frequently represented by text and drawings, into a physical form. The product begins to acquire physical attributes such as size, shape, colour and mass. The final activities are market and technical testing and market introduction. It is worthy of note that these activities may occur at an earlier stage and that any of these activities can occur simultaneously.

Chapter 5 reviewed the wide range of models that have been developed to try to further our understanding of this complex area of management. Hopefully you will recognise the new product development process as a series of activities that transform an opportunity into a tangible product that is intended to produce profits for the company. In practice, the process is difficult to identify. Visitors who ask to see a company's NPD process won't see very much, because the process is intertwined with the on-going operation of the business. Furthermore, the process is fluid and iterations are often needed. Developments by competitors may force a new product idea due for impending launch back to the laboratory for further changes. The model in Figure 6.1 highlights many of the important features and also identifies the importance played by the external environment. From an idea or a concept the product evolves over time. This process involves extensive interaction and iteration, highlighted by the arrows in the diagram.

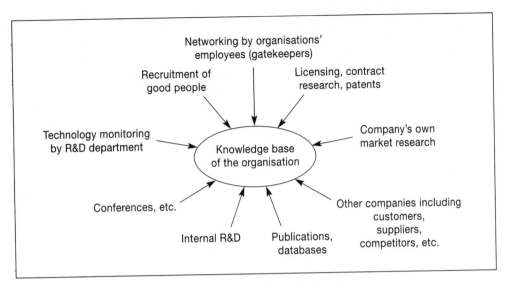

Figure 6.2 : Maintaining an organisation's knowledge base

Assembling knowledge

The vast majority of marketing textbooks fail to identify the first activity of the NPD process, the assembling of knowledge (Kotler, 1997; Brassington and Pettitt, 1997). It is from an organisation's knowledge base that creativity and ideas for new products will flow. Chapter 3 emphasised the importance of an organisation's knowledge base in underpinning its innovative ability. Without the continual accumulation of knowledge, an organisation will be hindered in its ability to create new product ideas. Figure 6.2 shows a wide range of activities that together help to maintain a company's knowledge base.

The generation of business opportunities

The generation of business opportunities is the next activity in the process of new product development. This was discussed in Chapters 3 and 5. You should therefore be aware of the concept, even if the process is not fully clear. This stage in the NPD process is also referred to as opportunity identification (OI). It is the process of collecting possible business opportunities that could realistically be developed by the business into successful products. This definition contains several caveats, which helps to explain the difficulty which faces businesses. New product ideas can emerge from many sources, as illustrated in Figure 6.3. Although this classification is not intended to be exhaustive, the figure identifies many of the key sources for product ideas which are explained below.

Existing products

Many new ideas will come from a company's existing range of products. Very often small changes to a product result in the development of new lines and brands. This

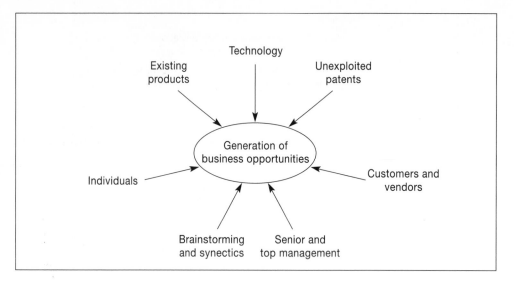

Figure 6.3 : Sources of business opportunity

was the case for Unilever, which since 1930 has added detergents to its original product line of bar soap. It has also developed new brands of detergent from its original detergent Persil, such as Surf.

Technology

The most obvious source of ideas is the company's own R&D department which is funded to research technology and develop new product ideas. It is also the responsibility of the R&D department to keep abreast of external technological developments of interest to the company. This is frequently referred to as technology assessment. Opportunities for the transfer of technology to the company need to be continually reviewed. This will be explored in further detail in Chapters 8 and 9.

Unexploited patents

For those companies that invest heavily in R&D, the development of patents is part of the day-to-day operation of a busy research and development laboratory. Many of these patents could be used in the eventual development of a new product; many, however, will not. Research and development laboratories continually scan patent databases, such as Derwent in the USA, for listings of interesting patents. In so doing, they can identify patents that have not yet been exploited and use them to develop new product ideas. This highlights and emphasises an earlier point made in Chapter 3 about the dual benefits of investment in R&D. In order to scan, search and identify interesting and potentially useful patents, a company needs to be knowledgeable in that area. Without this prior knowledge scanning patent databases would be akin to looking at a foreign language that one does not understand.

Customers and vendors

Eric von Hippel's (1988) famous study of medical equipment manufacturers and users identified that the highest percentage of new product ideas originated with customers (the users). It has, however, since been suggested that this was a particular trait of that industry. It is, nonetheless, an important contribution to the debate about the origin of new product ideas. Indeed, in many other industries, especially fast-moving consumer goods (FMCG) industries, consumers are carefully studied to try to identify possible product ideas. For example, Procter & Gamble and Unilever continually visit consumers in their homes to watch and analyse the way they clean their furniture and do the laundry. Such studies have produced numerous product ideas, as was highlighted in the case study at the end of Chapter 3. In addition, customer complaints about products are an excellent source of ideas. Many product packaging improvements have been the result of customer complaints. For example, many of the multiples have responded to complaints from customers about leaking liquid containers, such as those for milk and orange juice, and have developed improved packaging as a result.

Salesforce

Vendors (sales representatives) are a particularly good source of new product ideas. Gordon *et al.* (1962) have shown the important role played by this group in generating new business opportunities. They spend a large part of their time with customers discussing their own products and learning about competitors' products. Many companies insist that their sales representatives provide weekly reports on all the companies they have visited, noting any possible product development opportunities. For example, sales representatives from ICI frequently visit manufacturing companies which use chemicals in their manufacturing operations. It is during discussions with these manufacturers about the effectiveness of the chemicals that ideas for product modifications are generated. Several new chemicals have been developed for specific companies and later launched nationally or internationally as a new product.

This raises an important point about the role of sales representatives, especially in technology-intensive industries. They are expected to be qualified scientists or engineers who subsequently undergo extensive commercial training in marketing and sales. Such highly trained people are in stark contrast to the popular image of a sales representative often depicted as a smooth talking second-hand car salesman!

Senior and top management

Many company leaders have taken personal responsibility for technological innovation in their companies. As far back as the 1950s, Alistair Pilkington continued to push the float glass process in Pilkington Glass against severe opposition. His idea was eventually successful. Akio Morita adopted a similar approach at Sony with the development of the Walkman, even though initial market research suggested that there was limited demand for such a product. However, not all leaders are successful. Edwin Land, former CEO of Polaroid, pushed his idea of instantly developed movies against fierce opposition, but the product was a major failure.

Those companies that have developed a reputation for innovation and new product development, such as 3M, rely on their senior management to concentrate on providing an environment for innovation to flourish. This is emphasised in the case study at the end of Chapter 5.

Brainstorming and synectics

Brainstorming is a creativity exercise used with groups of about six to eight people. The idea is for people to use their own imagination and creativity and to build on the ideas of others in the group. There is usually a chairperson who asks for and records ideas relating to a specific problem. People within the group are encouraged to be liberal and uninhibited with their suggestions. A slightly more involved and subtle approach called synectics has been developed by Gordon *et al.* (1997), who suggest that if the problem under investigation remains a secret, more imaginative ideas will flow.

Individuals

In addition to the R&D department, sales representatives and marketers, product ideas can originate from areas not usually associated with product development. Accountancy departments, secretarial support staff and contract hire personnel have all been identified as originators of ideas for new products. Many inventors have remarked, after the event, that the original idea was conceived outside company time and far away from the company. Everyone has the ability to be creative.

Developing product concepts: turning business opportunities into product concepts

This activity involves transforming a list of ideas into potential product concepts. In some cases the identification of an opportunity is sufficient to reveal the product required. For example, a paint manufacturer may uncover a need for a new form of paint that will not drip on to carpets and clothes, is easy to apply, will wash off users' hands and clothes if spilt and is hard wearing like conventional paints. In other cases the concept is clear but the details need to be added. For example, a domestic appliance manufacturer may discover that some of its customers have expressed interest in a domestic water-cleaning device. In this case, the manufacturer is clear that the appliance will need to be fitted in the home but much more information is required. Sometimes it may not be clear at all what form the product will take. For example, a chemical manufacturer may uncover an opportunity in the treatment of water for industry. The eventual product could take many different forms and use many different technologies, chemical treatment, mechanical treatment etc. The idea is a long way from an actual product.

For a product idea to become a new product concept, Crawford (1997) argues that three inputs are required: form, technology and need.

Form: This is the physical thing to be created (or in the case of a service, the sequence of steps by which the service will be created). It may still be vague and not precisely defined.

Table 6.2 : A new product concept

Need	Form	Technology
A new low-fat yellow spread	A soft yellow spread that can be applied like margarine	An emulsion of fat droplets in water

Technology: In most cases there is one clear technology that is at the base of the innovation (for the 3M Post-It it was the adhesive; for the instamatic camera it was the chemical formulation which permitted partial development in light.

Need: The benefits gained by the customer give the product value.

The following example illustrates this point. A dairy food manufacturer may uncover an idea for a new type of yellow spread (butter or margarine). All the details for the product remain unknown. Once the details are known the product idea is said to be a product concept. In this case, the product concept could be an opportunity in the yellow spreads market for a low-fat spread that can be applied like soft margarine (an emulsion of fat droplets in water), which has a buttery taste (*see* Table 6.2).

It is important to remember that an idea is just that, an idea, whereas a concept is the conjunction of all the essential characteristics of the product idea. This usually incorporates form, technology and need but lacks detail. The underlying message here is that product ideas without details are often more like: an aircraft manufacturer may wish for a noise-free aircraft engine, or a pharmaceutical company may wish for a cure for AIDS.

The screening of business opportunities

Screening product ideas is essentially an evaluation process. It is important to note that it is not a single, one-off activity as portrayed in many textbooks. It occurs at every stage of the new product development process, and involves such questions as:

- Do we have the necessary commercial knowledge and experience?
- Do we have the technical knowhow to develop the idea further?
- Would such a product be suitable for our business?
- Are we sure there will be sufficient demand?

The main purpose of screening ideas is to select those that will be successful and drop those that will not – herein lies the difficulty. Trying to identify which ideas are going to be successful and which are not is extremely difficult. Many successful organisations have made serious errors at this point. The Research Corporation of America (RCA) identified the huge business opportunity of radio and television but failed to see the potential for videocassette recorders (VCR). Kodak and IBM failed to see the potential in photocopying but Xerox did not. The list grows each year and while the popular business press are quick to identify those companies which make a mistake they are not so quick to praise those companies which identify successful business opportunities. 3M, for example, recognised a business opportunity in self-adhesive notes. Even here, persistence was required on behalf of the individuals involved. This was because, initially, the company was not sure about the idea (*see* Chapter 5).

Distinguishing between dreams and reality

Recognising what is a possible product and what is fantasy is an important part of the screening process. There are many examples of businesses rejecting a new product idea (business opportunity) because they did not believe it would work. Some of these are so famous they are known outside the world of business: Xerox and the computer graphical interface; Dyson and the bagless vacuum cleaner; Whittle and the jet engine. There must be a distinction between those opportunities that the business could develop into a product and those which it could not, and recognition of those that are likely to generate revenue and those that will not.

Market research will clearly provide valuable market analysis input at this stage to help in the decision process. This is covered in Chapter 4 along with other activities often associated with the screening activity, such as concept testing, product testing, market testing and test marketing. Organisations use a variety of different labels for very similar activities. The following represents an overview of many of the activities associated with the screening process.

Initial screen, entry screen or preliminary screen

This represents the first formal evaluation of the idea. Each of the ideas that came from the pool of concepts has to be given an initial screen. This will involve a technical feasibility check and marketing feasibility test, plus a comparison with the strategic opportunity. This would include evaluating whether the particular product would fit with the business's existing activities. The advantage of early screening is that it can be done quickly and easily and prevents expenditure on product ideas that are clearly not appropriate.

Customer screen, concept testing

This can vary between informal discussions with potential customers and feedback on developed prototypes. Concept testing is extremely difficult and mistakes are very easy to make. People have difficulty reacting to an entirely new product concept without a learning period, as discussed below.

Technical screen, technical testing

This activity can vary from a few phone calls to technical experts to extensive analysis by an in-house R&D department or an analysis by a third party such as an independent consultant (often a university lab). Chapter 6 discusses the activity of technical testing during which evaluations are continually undertaken.

Final screen

This normally involves the use of scoring models and computer assessment programs. Various new product ideas are fed into the program and a series of questions and assessments, with different weightings, are made, resulting in a scoring for each. One of the most serious criticisms of scoring models is their use of weights, because these are necessarily judgemental.

Business analysis

This may involve the construction of preliminary marketing plans, technical plans, financial reviews and projected budgets. All of these may raise potential problems that were previously unforeseen. It is not uncommon for new products to reach the mass-production stage only to encounter significant manufacturing difficulties, often when production is switched from on-off prototypes to high-volume manufacture.

Development of product prototypes

This is the phase during which the item acquires finite form and becomes a tangible good. It is at this stage that product designers may develop several similar prototypes with different styling. Manufacturing issues will also be discussed such as what type of process to use. For example, in the case of a tennis racket, engineers will discuss whether to manufacture using an injection-moulding or compression-moulding process. During this activity numerous technical developments will occur. This will include all aspects of scientific research and development, engineering development and design, possible technology transfer, patent analysis and cost forecasts.

Technical testing

Closely linked to the development of product prototypes is the technical testing of a new product. It is sometimes difficult to distinguish between where prototype development finishes and testing begins. This is because in many industries it is frequently an on-going activity. Take the motor vehicle industry as an example. Engineers may be developing a new safety system for a vehicle. This might involve a new harness for the seat belt and a new airbag system. As the engineers begin designing the system they will be continually checking and testing that the materials for the belt are suitable, and that the sensors are not so sensitive that the airbag is inflated when the vehicle goes over a bump in the road. There will, of course, be final testing involving dummies and simulated crashes, but much of the technical testing is on-going.

Market testing and consumer research

These activities have been covered in Chapter 4, so they will only be dealt with briefly here. The traditional approach to NPD involved a significant stage devoted to market testing. Developed products were introduced to a representative sample of the population to assess the market's reaction. This was usually carried out prior to a full-scale national launch of the product. This was the commonly accepted approach, especially in fast-moving consumer goods industries such as confectionery, household products, food and drink. During the 1980s test marketing became synonymous with regional television channels such as Anglia or Tyne Tees. This was because manufacturers would select from these regions places in which to test their products. Much has since changed, not least the deregulation of the independent television industry (under which some independent channels control several former regions). More significantly, manufacturers have emphasised the need to be first into the market and have often skipped the test market. Linked to this is the fear that a test market may reveal a new product to competitors who may be able to react quickly and develop a similar product. Furthermore, the use of direct marketing and the Internet has seen many new products being introduced via these developing channels.

In today's fiercely competitive marketplace products tend to go straight from consumer research and product development to national launch:

> **Marketers claim that consumer research techniques are now so sophisticated that full-blown tests are no longer necessary. Besides, once they have invested in R&D plus new plant, and created an advertising campaign, they might as well go national immediately. The fixed costs are so high that you might as well get on with it, says Mark Sherrington of marketing consultancy Added Value.**

> *Management Today*

The debate about the benefits and limitations of consumer research has raged for many years. Put simply, critics associated with the consumerism movement claim that most new products are actually minor variations of existing products. They further argue that consumers are not able to peer into the future and articulate what products they want. They suggest that the major innovations of the twentieth century, such as electricity, frozen food, television, microcomputers and telecommunications, have been the result of sustained technological research uninhibited by the demands of consumers. Marketers, on the other hand, argue that without consumer research technologists will produce products that are not what the market wants. There are many examples to support both arguments. The Sony Walkman is often cited by those critical of consumer research, since the product was initially rejected on the basis of insufficient features such as the ability to record etc. Similarly, the Disk camera, developed by Eastman Kodak between 1980 and 1988, is used by supporters of consumer research to highlight the potential disaster of not seeking consumers' views. It was a very small instamatic camera designed to appeal to those seeking a simple-to-use machine. Unfortunately, it produced grainy photographs.

Research by Christensen and Bower (1995) and Daily (1996) suggests that listening to your customer may actually stifle technological innovation and be detrimental to long-term business success. Ironically, to be successful in industries characterised by technological change, firms may be required to pursue innovations that are not demanded by their current customers. Christensen and Bower distinguish between 'disruptive innovations' and 'sustaining innovations' (radical or incremental innovations). Sustaining innovations appealed to existing customers, since they provided improvements to established products. For example, the introduction of new computer software usually provides improvements for existing customers in terms of added features. Disruptive innovations tend to provide improvements greater than those demanded. For example, while the introduction of 3.5-inch disk drives to replace 5.25-inch drives provided an enormous improvement in performance, it also created problems for users who were familiar with the previous format. These disruptive innovations also tended to create new markets which eventually captured the existing market.

The results of this study suggest that managers may sometimes be wise to ignore the advice of their existing customers, who are primarily interested in incremental product improvements. This argument of not relying too heavily on the market derives further support from research conducted by Schmidt (1995). This revealed that for industrial products, technical activities are more important than marketing activities such as market assessment, detailed market study, product testing with customer and test marketing. Indeed, Schmidt argues that inadequate focus on the technical activities and excessive focus on marketing activities and the marketing concept are myopic.

Be wary of consumer research

If consumer research had been conducted at the turn of the century, the responses garnered from people as they walked along dusty dirt tracks meandering across the meadows of England would have halted research into the motor car. If asked whether they would like to have a noisy, dirty machine that would be responsible for thousands of deaths and cause enormous amounts of pollution, their answer would probably have been 'no thank you'.

Market introduction

Commercialisation is not necessarily the stage at which large sums of money are spent on advertising campaigns or multimillion-pound production plants, since a company can withdraw from a project following the results of test marketing.

It is important to remember that for some products, say in the pharmaceutical business, the decision to finance a project with 10 years of research is taken fairly early on in the development of the product and this is where most of the expense is incurred. With other fast-moving consumer goods, like foods, advertising is a large part of the cost, so the decision is taken towards the launch phase.

Launch

We must not lose sight of reality. Most new products are improvements or minor line extensions and may attract almost no attention. Other new products, e.g. a major cancer breakthrough or a potential AIDS cure, are so important that they will receive top TV news coverage.

James Dyson and the dual cyclone vacuum cleaner

James Dyson has become a household name. This development of a revolutionary vacuum cleaner had a dramatic impact on the domestic vacuum-cleaner market and brought enormous success to his company. The product is a vacuum cleaner without a bag for collecting dirt. It eliminates the main problems associated with conventional vacuum cleaners of burst bags and blocked air flow and provides virtually 100 per cent suction power. It is the first technological breakthrough in the industry since the invention of the vacuum cleaner in 1901.

The product took five years to develop and included over 5000 prototypes. It involved designers, engineers and scientists but, as is so often the case, the most difficult part of the project, according to Dyson, was trying to get retailers to stock the product. It was almost a 'Catch 22' situation, with retailers refusing to stock until convinced by sales figures. From the retailers' perspective, they saw this new product as very expensive – it was double the price of the best-selling units.

Eventually several electricity board retail chains and two big mail-order catalogues agreed to take the product. This provided publicity. It is now an enormous success and the market leader, overcoming resistance from three very big international brands. Technological innovation has provided differentiation and competitive advantage.

Source: Dyson Appliances Ltd and Miles (1995)

NPD across different industries

It has been stressed throughout this book that innovation and NPD in particular are context dependent. That is, the management of the process is dependent on the type of product being developed. A simple, but nonetheless useful, way of looking at this is to divide the wide range of activities involved in the development of a new product into technical and marketing activities. Figure 6.4 shows the NPD activities divided into the two categories. Against this are placed a variety of industries to illustrate the different balance of activities. It becomes clear that industrial products (products developed for use by other industries), such as a new gas-fired electricity generator, have many different considerations to those of a new soft drink. In the latter case there will be much more emphasis on promotion and packaging, whereas the electricity generator will have been designed and built following extensive technical meetings with the customer concentrating on the functional aspects of the product.

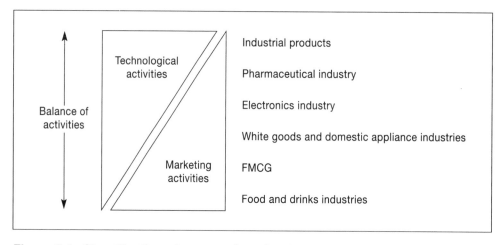

Figure 6.4 : Classification of new product development activities across different industries

Clearly, in between these two extremes the balance of activities is more equal. In a recent study of NPD involving 12 firms across a variety of industries, Olson *et al.* (1995) found that cross-functional teams helped shorten the development of times of truly innovative products. More bureaucratic structures may provide better outcomes for less innovative products.

Organisational structures and the use of teams

Industrialists and academics have for many years been interested in the subject of how organisations are structured and the relationships that occur between individuals and functions. The nature of the industry in general and the product being developed in particular will significantly influence the choice of structure. Moreover, the organisation structure will considerably affect the way its activities are managed. It is not possible to alter one without causing an effect on the other. For example, the introduction of concurrent engineering techniques means that companies will need to be less reliant on functional operations and adopt the use of project management and cross-functional teams. Organisational structures and teams will therefore be examined together in this section.

Teams and project management

The use of teams within organisations is certainly nothing new. In sport having between five and fifteen individuals all working together has been the foundation for games all over the world. Similarly, within organisations teams have been used for many years, especially on large projects. In industry, however, the concept of having teams of individuals from different functions with different knowledge bases is a recent development. Jones (1997) suggests that in the field of medicine the practice of having a group of experts from different functions working together on a project has been around for many years. In manufacturing industries the use of cross-functional teams has occurred in parallel with the introduction of concurrent engineering.

New product project teams in small to medium-sized organisations are usually comprised of staff from several different functions who operate on a 'part-time' basis. Membership of the project team may be just one of the many roles they perform. In larger organisations, where several projects are in progress at any one time, there may be sufficient resources to enable personnel to be wholly concerned with a project. Ideally, a project team will have a group of people with the necessary skills, who are able to work together, share ideas and reach compromises. This may include external consultants or key component suppliers.

Functional structures

Unlike the production, promotion and distribution of products, NPD is a cross-disciplinary process and suffers if it is segregated by function. The traditional

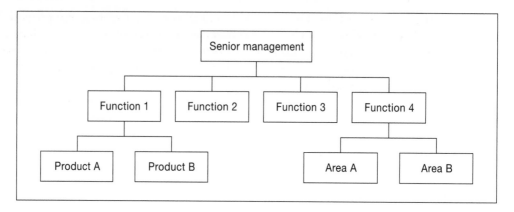

Figure 6.5 : Functional company organisation

functional company structure allows for a strong managerial layer with information flowing up and down the organisation. Each function would usually be responsible for one or more product groups or geographical areas (*see* Figure 6.5).

Another common approach used by many large manufacturing companies is to organise the company by product type. Each product has its own functional activities. Some functions, however, are centralised across the whole organisation. This is to improve efficiency or provide common features (*see* Figure 6.6). This type of structure supports the notion of product platforms (*see* Chapter 4) where a generic group of

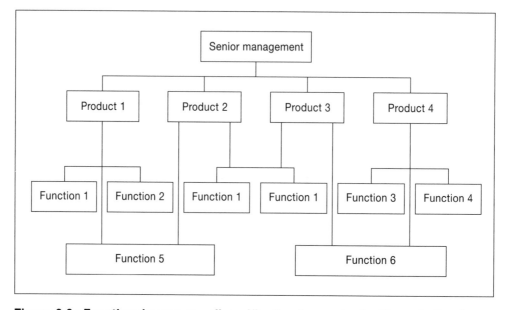

Figure 6.6 : Functional company: diversification by product with centralised functions

technologies are used in a variety of products. Sony, Phillips and ICI all have centralised R&D activities where the majority of products are developed allowing for a high degree of technology transfer between product groups. This is one of the key arguments in favour of a centralised R&D function, of which more later.

It is important to note that while many organisations have clearly defined company structures, closer inspection of the actual activities within these companies will invariably reveal an informal structure that sits on top of the formal structure. This is made up of formal and informal communication channels and networks that help to facilitate the flow of information within the organisation (*see* Figure 6.7).

Matrix structures

The use of a matrix structure requires a project-style approach to NPD. Each team will comprise a group of between four and eight people from different functions. A matrix structure is defined as any organisation that employs a multiple command system including not only a multiple command management structure but also related support mechanisms and associated organisational culture and behaviour patterns (Ford and Randolph, 1992).

Matrix structures are associated with dual lines of communication and authority (Tushman and Nadler, 1978; Lawrence *et al.*, 1988). They are seen as cross-functional

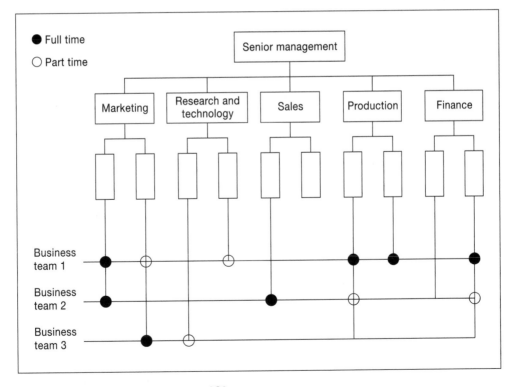

Figure 6.7 : Matrix structure at ICI

because they involve bringing people together from two or more separate organisational functional areas. This can be seen in Figure 6.7 that shows the matrix structure at ICI. The traditional hierarchy is functional, while the horizontal overlay consists of business areas known as business teams. Business team 1 comprises one full-time member from marketing, one full-time member from R&D, one full-time member from sales, one full-time member from production and one full and one part-time member from finance. Between them this group would manage a number of projects. There would be a team leader for each business team. However, this person would not necessarily be, and is often not, the most senior member of the group. The choice of business team leader is based on the type of project the team is undertaking. For example, a team looking at the introduction of new products is likely to be led by someone from the marketing function, even though there will almost certainly be someone more 'senior' from another function within the business team.

The following are some of the features and benefits of a matrix organisational structure that have been identified in the literature. However, for a full review of matrix organisation and project management see Ford and Randolph (1992).

- *Provision of additional channels of communication* – The combination of a matrix structure and business teams ensures that there is extensive lateral communication between functions. The diagram in Figure 6.7 shows how marketing personnel involved in business teams 1, 2 and 3 bring back to the marketing function knowledge of activities of the other functions. Communication skills are also developed as individual business team members learn the 'languages' of the other functions (Allen, 1984).

- *Increase in informal communication channels* – In addition to the increase in formal linkages, there is also an increase in informal networks between personnel from different functions. These develop from friendships and co-operation formed as a product of formal linkages.

- *Increase in information loads* – The increase in formal and informal channels of communication means that individuals collect more information. This information is brought back into the function and disseminated among colleagues in the group. There is support for this view in Joyce (1986).

- *Increase in diversity for individuals* – Some individuals may be involved in two or three business teams. Their role may be part time or full time. This enables them to work with a variety of people from different backgrounds and disciplines across the organisation. This type of working environment enlarges an individual's experience and outlook and provides them with an improved understanding of the organisation's entire activities (Kolodny, 1979).

Corporate venturing

The idea behind corporate venturing is that fledgling businesses should be given the freedom to grow outside the constraints of an existing large, established organisation. Conventional management thinking argues that new ventures should be sheltered from the normal planning and control systems, otherwise they will be strangled.

Ideally, they should be given high-level sponsorship from senior management, but must be able to manage their own relationships with other companies. Many large organisations such as DuPont, IBM and General Electric have a long experience of corporate venturing stretching back to the 1960s. However, following some high-profile failures, most notably by Shell in the mid-1980s, corporate venturing fell out of favour. More recent research suggests that the record of corporate venturing compared to external venture capitalists shows that the latter do no better than the corporations (Lorenz, 1993).

An internal corporate venture is a separate organisation or system designed to facilitate the needs of a new business. Companies usually adopt an internal corporate venture when the product involved is outside their existing activities. The case study at the end of Chapter 5 shows how 3M use internal corporate venturing to help transform business ideas into genuine businesses. For a more detailed discussion on the role of new ventures, *see* Tidd *et al.* (1997).

Project management

Whichever organisation structure is adopted, the project itself has to be well planned, managed and controlled. It is the setting of achievable targets and realistic objectives that helps to ensure a successful project. In addition, ensuring that resources are available at the appropriate time contributes to good project management.

Many organisations have tried and tested project management programmes and organisational systems to help ensure that projects are well managed. But even in these well run organisations there will often be individual project managers who build a reputation for delivering on time and for being able to turn a doubtful project into a successful project. This introduces the subject of managing people within organisations. This is not the place to explore these issues which are at the heart of theories of organisational behaviour. They are comprehensively examined by others such as Mullins (1997).

Reducing product development times through computer-aided design

When concurrent engineering is used in conjunction with other management tools the results can be very impressive. For example, the aerospace and automobile industries have been using computer-aided design (CAD) for more than 15 years. In both these industries product development times are relatively long, sometimes lasting 10 years. The ability to use CAD lies at the heart of broader efforts to compress product development times and share information across an organisation. This is even more important when there are several companies involved in the manufacture of a single product. The Airbus consortium of companies which manufactures aircraft has been using CAD to help with its very complicated product data management (PDM). This is particularly useful in helping speed up engineering and manufacturing processes. In addition, the Airbus Concurrent Engineering (ACE) project is helping to develop common product development processes across the consortium (Baxter, 1997).

The marketing/R&D interface

The case study at the end of this chapter highlights some of the difficulties of managing cross-functional teams in technology-intensive industries where the technology being used is complex and difficult to understand for those without scientific training. In such industries, scientists and engineers are often heard berating their commercial colleagues for failing to comprehend the technical aspects of the project. This introduces a common difficulty: the need to manage communication flows across the marketing and R&D boundaries. This problem was first recognised as important in the 1970s (Rubenstein *et al.*, 1976) and remains a critical issue in new product development (Souder and Sherman, 1993).

The main barriers to an effective R&D/marketing interface have been found to be related to perceptual, cultural, organisational and language factors (Wang, 1997). Marketing managers tend to focus on shorter time spans than R&D managers, who adopt much longer time frames for projects. In addition, the cultural difference results from the different training and backgrounds of the two groups. For example, scientists seek recognition from their peers in the form of published papers and ultimately Nobel prizes, as well as recognition from the company that employs them. Marketing managers, on the other hand, are able only to seek recognition from their employer, usually in the form of bonuses, promotions, etc. The organisational boundaries arise out of departmental structures and the different activities of the two groups. Finally, the language barrier is soon identified in discussions with the two groups, because while marketers talk about product benefits and market position, R&D managers talk the quantitative language of performance and specifications.

The extent of the integration required between marketing and R&D depends on the environment within which product development occurs. In many technology-intensive industries where the customer's level of sophistication is low, the extent of integration required may be less than that needed where the customer's level of sophistication is high and the technology intensity of the industry low. For example, in the pharmaceutical industry (high level of technological intensity) customers' sophistication is low because they are unable to communicate their needs. They may want a cure for cancer but have no idea how this can be achieved. On the other hand, in the food industry (low level of technological intensity) customers are able to articulate their needs. For example, they can explain that a particular food might taste better or look better if it contained certain ingredients. For a more detailed discussion on the difficulties of managing the relations between R&D and marketing, *see* Bruce and Cooper (1997).

High attrition rate of new products

As new product projects evolve and progress through each stage of development, many will be rightly cancelled or stopped for a wide variety of reasons. The failure of a product idea to be developed into a product is not necessarily a bad thing. Indeed, it may save the company enormous sums of money. This will be explored more fully in

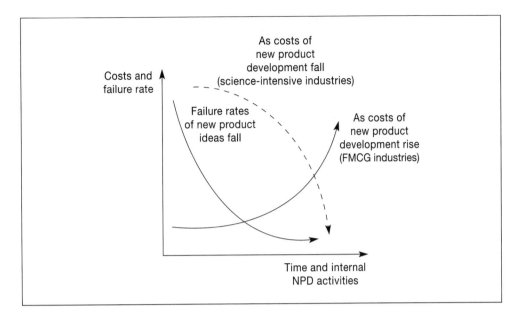

Figure 6.8 : Product failures

Chapter 7. More serious problems arise when, as often happens, new products are launched in the expectation of success, but then ultimately fail leaving high costs to be met by the company. Sometimes a product can cause harm and suffering, but these are rare; the example of the Thalidomide drug is a chilling reminder of a product failure.

Clearly, product ideas are rejected throughout the new product development process. Figure 6.8 shows the traditional view of the rising cost of new product development as it moves closer to launch. This is based on FMCG industries which involve high-cost promotional campaigns. Arguably, the cost curve for science-intensive industries is inverse, with high costs being associated with R&D activities and relatively low-cost promotional activities towards the end of the development.

Studies of why new products fail are difficult to undertake. This is partly due to an unwillingness by companies to let outsiders know that they have been unsuccessful. Also, it is difficult to untangle what happened and identify the cause of failure. With hindsight things often do not look the same. People are, in many cases, very defensive about their role in the development of a new product. There is always a reluctance to be associated with failure. Studies by Cooper (1984), Urban *et al.* (1987) and Crawford (1997) have identified many of the often cited reasons for failure. These are listed in Table 6.3.

There is much debate about the failure rates of new products, which vary widely. The collection of data on this issue is problematic, with a wide range of different definitions being used across industries and countries. Some companies now claim a maximum failure rate of 10 per cent. This is a long way from the failure rate, often quoted in the popular business press of 90 per cent. Products rarely fail in the marketplace: weak products are usually eliminated prior to entry to the market. Consequently any such failures command huge publicity, as the Daimler-Benz illustration shows.

Table 6.3 : Reasons for new product failure

1 Product offers nothing new or no improved performance

2 Inadequate budget to develop ideas or market the product

3 Poor market research, positioning, misunderstanding consumer needs

4 Lack of top management support

5 Did not involve customer

6 Exceptional factors such as government decision (e.g. new law on hand gun control may seriously affect the manufacturer of a new hand gun)

7 Market too small, either forecasting error with sales or insufficient demand

8 Poor match with company's capabilities, company has insufficient experience of the technology or market

9 Inadequate support from channel (a problem experienced by Dyson)

10 Competitive response was strong and competitors were able to move quickly to face the challenge of the new product (P&G highlighted weaknesses with Unilever's Persil Power)

11 Internal organisational problems, often associated with poor communication

12 Poor return on investment forcing company to abandon project

13 Unexpected changes in consumer tastes/fashion

Daimler halts A-Class car delivery to modify chassis

By Graham Bowley in Frankfurt

Daimler, Benz the German industrial group, yesterday temporarily halted delivery of its controversial Mercedes-Benz A-Class car model to give it a new chassis system in a fresh attempt to calm lingering concerns about its safety .

Daimler said deliveries would be stopped until February. It will install new stabilisers on front and rear axles, lower the car body and fit wider tyres. Daimler said the improvements and production delays would cost DM100m (£34.6m) this year and DM200m in 1998 – twice the original estimates.

Daimler faced embarrassment last month when stability of the A-Class – the company's first move into the smaller, economical car market – came under scrutiny just weeks after it went on sale. The car rolled over during the so-called "Moose test" driving manoeuvre which simulates swerving to avoid moose on Swedish road.

Daimler responded to the adverse publicity by calling in vehicles to change their tyres and fit electronic stabilisers.

But speculation about the car's safety refused to die down and Daimler said yesterday that intensive testing since then had shown that the chassis changes were necessary to overcome the problem. It said the modified car performed "marvellously", even in extreme situations.

Jügen Schrempp, chief executive, said: "That the A-Class has shown a weakness in extreme test situations is something nobody regrets more than we do. Our engineers have devoted all their energy, day and night, to the search for the optimal solution, and we have found it."

Analysts said they reserved judgement. "Their willingness to stand up and take this extraordinary action means that the betting must be that this puts it back on the right track," said John Lawson at Salomon Brothers in London.

However, some observers warned that Daimler was underestimating the marketing costs needed to rebuild consumer confidence as well as the damage to the Mercedes brand.

Daimler had planned to deliver 18,000 A-Class vehicles this year. It had expected to build about 180,000 in 1998, but said this figure had been reduced to about 160,000.

In spite of the extra costs, Daimler said it would not change its forecast for a group operating profit of about DM3.7bn this year, and group turnover of up to DM120bn.

Daimler said there had been about 3,000 cancellations since problems with the A-Class were made public but this had been outweighed by new orders.

Source: Financial Times, November 12 1997.

The article from the *Financial Times* shows that even multinational companies with an impressive history of introducing new products can make mistakes. For Daimler-Benz the technical difficulties encountered potentially highlight a poor match with its capabilities. This is the company's first attempt to enter the small car market. Investigations into the reasons behind this costly mistake may reveal that the company had insufficient experience of the particular technologies involved in the design and manufacture of small cars.

CASE STUDY

The use of cross-functional teams in new product development[1]

Part of this case study is presented as a discussion between the research and development manager and the production manager and reads like a short story. The names used are fictitious, but it is based on an original piece of research (Lothian, 1997) and explains some of the problems of managing cross-functional teams. It also highlights a common problem with business research, that practice very often differs from theory and rhetoric. The company in question is an internationally recognised manufacturer of computer hardware.

Background

In order to ensure that the time spent on new product development is kept to a minimum, companies are increasingly adopting concurrent engineering techniques and cross-functional teams (CFT). This case study explores the use of cross-functional teams in the development of new products. It analyses the effectiveness of cross-functional teams and identifies several limitations. Indeed, the case highlights how CFT can hinder NPD if used incorrectly.

The company, hereafter referred to as Xrend, is a leading manufacturer of advanced information technology products. It specialises in data capture, storage and delivery, via products ▶

---

[1] This case has been written as a basis for class discussion rather than to illustrate effective or ineffective managerial or administrative behaviour. It has been prepared from a variety of published sources, as indicated, and from observations.

▶ such as hard disk drives. The market in which the company operates is expanding rapidly and many opportunities exist for future developments. A closer inspection of the company's arrangements, however, revealed that it was heavily dependent on one customer which accounted for about 80 per cent of its turnover. This source of business was set to decline over the next five years and this had led to a realisation that the development of new products was urgently required. The company had embarked on an appraisal of its new product development operations and had decided that it needed to be overhauled. Cross-functional teams were to be at the centre of the company's new product development activities.

The introduction of cross-functional teams and concurrent engineering at Xrend

Prior to the implementation of CFT, the company structure was most akin to a matrix structure with functions such as accountancy, marketing and manufacturing lying across projects. The individual functions had their own hierarchies and line management structures. Such a structure is not uncommon in many technology-intensive manufacturing companies.

The introduction of CFT led to significant changes, particularly as the teams were not directly accountable to the functions, instead being accountable to project managers. This case focuses on the activities of one particular CFT. This team, called Centrus, was given the responsibility of developing small storage units for large computer machines. The team consisted of eight members, who were project team leader, test engineer, development engineer, manufacturing engineer and representatives from marketing, field support, materials and procurement. Each team member was expected to be actively involved in the project. In addition, they were required to represent their functional department and ensure their interests were considered by the team. This was fine in theory but practice, as will be seen, was very different.

When practice differs from theory

George Richardson placed both hands on top of his head and looked towards the sky.

'It's amazing', he said. 'How can it be that for the past year we have had a cross-functional team that is not a cross-functional team?'

Adam Wilson responded to the general manager's enquiry explaining that everyone had thought the Centris team was operating in a cross-functional way but it is only now emerging that the team had not actually been operating as it should.

Adam Wilson, production manager, had been called in to see the R&D manager following the publication of an internal report highlighting the weaknesses of the Centris new product team. Centris had been the first team to adopt the cross-functional approach to new product development. The report had not been full of praise. It had raised several issues, the most important of which was that the team had not been operating in a cross-functional manner. Adam Wilson offered a brief summary of the report's findings:

'The problem, George, is that the team has not yet been able to adapt to working in teams of people with diverse backgrounds. Some of the technical people feel the commercial people don't understand what is being said.'

'So what's new?' joked George.

'The point is,' replied Adam, ignoring George's facetiousness, 'that the Centris team has tried to overcome this difficulty by setting up so called "off-line" meetings'.

'What are off-line meetings?' snapped George.

Adam realised he would have to explain from the beginning. 'At first the Centris team used daily team meetings to discuss current issues as they arose. This gave each team member the opportunity to participate in the development of the project. As the project progressed a variety of difficulties and challenges would present themselves to the team. The issues raised ranged from financial and design requirements to manufacturing limitations. The point here is that many of the discussions involved detailed technical issues. Many of the team members felt that they were unable to contribute to these discussions because they felt they were outside their area of expertise. The team felt that already precious time was being used in an unproductive manner. In an attempt to reduce this unproductive time, the team decided that, as and when required, off-line meetings (OLMs) would be established to address those particular issues that required specialist input. OLMs would consist of members who could add value to the discussions. In effect, this meant those with prior knowledge and shared common knowledge – functional members.'

'This seems to be understandable and reasonable', interjected George.

'Indeed, at first this seemed to be an effective use of limited resources,' Adam continued. 'The Centris team would continue to meet daily and as and when particular difficulties arose an OLM was established to investigate. Unfortunately, the OLM began to cannibalise the cross-functional nature of the Centris team. For example, the marketing engineer has reported that decisions were occasionally made without his input. This reduces product integrity.'

'What does that mean?' demanded George.

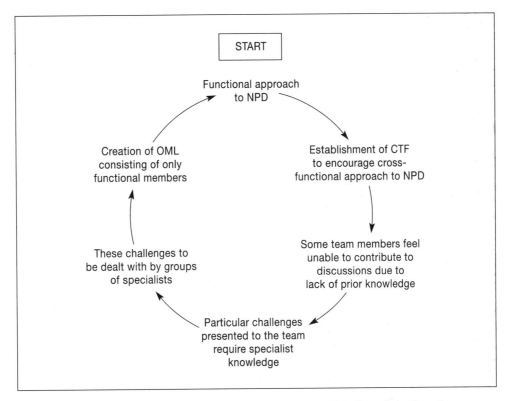

Figure 6.9 : Functional approach to cross-functional back to functional

▶ 'It's a marketing term. Essentially product integrity depends on a link between the customer's expectations and product performance. The marketing engineer should have been providing this link, but it seems that at times the link was not in place. Within six months from the start of the Centris team the OLM approach to difficulties has become the dominant means of problem resolution. Indeed, in many ways, it is the success of the OLM that has led to the downfall of the Centris team. The team's approach to problem solving had gone full circle.'

Adam reached for a marker pen and drew a diagram to emphasise the point (see Figure 6.9).

Adam continued, 'You see, the cross-functional nature of the team exists in name only. To all those outside the company, even to many inside the company, the Centris team is a cross-functional team. It consists of a variety of members from different functions and has regular meetings. It appears to operate in a cross-functional way. Indeed, even some of the members of the Centris team believe they are engaged in NPD using CFT. Individuals within the team, however, did wonder to themselves how their new method of working differed from their previous style of operating! The answer, of course, is not much.'

George sat upright, transfixed, nodding and agreeing with Adam's explanation. Adam continued in lecturer mode now that the attentive student was keen to learn more. 'What this means is that the excluded members of the OLM are no longer exposed to information flows in the team. Given the arguments for CFT – that they help to create new knowledge and facilitate the dissemination of it throughout the organisation – the effect of the use of OLM is to reduce cross-functionality; reduce knowledge-creating potential; and reduce 'product integrity.'

Adam scribbled these last three points on the whiteboard underneath his previous drawing. 'The overall effect has been to reduce the effectiveness of NPD by limiting interaction and the cross-fertilisation of ideas between different functions.'

Discussion

Scratching beneath the surface

This case study highlights a potential hurdle over which many stumble when studying aspects of business management. The popular business press and other publications for executives are full of prescriptions for business problems. Very often they recommend the adoption or implementation of a new management technique (cynics would refer to these as fads). On the face of it many businesses may be using this new technique. Had Xrend been approached regarding the use of CFT the response would surely have been affirmative. Scratch beneath the surface, however, and all is not as it first appears. Many studies of business management, especially those involving large surveys using postal questionnaires, suffer from this potential weakness. That is not to say that all such surveys are flawed, clearly, this is not so. It is, however, worthy of note, that it is healthy to enquire and to question the methodology used. The student of management should adopt a critical and inquisitive approach, especially when analysing the literature.

The reduction of knowledge-creating potential

The case study clearly shows that CFT by name is not necessarily cross-functional by nature. Indeed, at Xrend, decision making was dominated by the 'off-line' meetings, which occurred at a functional level, and the benefits of cross-functional teams were never realised. Regular meetings took place and team members engaged in detailed discussions, but problems that arose were dealt with in a functional manner. Hence, there was little cross-functional knowledge being created. Technical experts were reluctant or unable to engage in discussions with non-technical experts. It was as if they were operating as an exclusive group and restricting entry. Such behaviour can hinder organisational learning. Dougherty (1990) and Nonaka (1991) have identified that new knowledge is created through the frequent interaction of individuals who are able to combine their own knowledge and perspectives with others and that CFTs are an ideal mechanism to foster this activity.

The role of experts and professionalism

The notion of professionalism and the exclusion of non-experts have received a great deal of attention in the literature. Danziger and Kraemer (1985) refer to this notion as the 'skill bureaucracy', whereby groups of people create a bureaucracy around skills as well as jargon as a means to exclude, thereby making it very difficult for those without those skills or jargon to participate. They go on to argue that certain professions (medicine, law, education) use this approach as a means of exclusivity.

Managing teams

The membership of the Centris project team remained constant throughout the project's life. This facilitated continuity and fostered good working relationships among team members. It was, however, in contrast to the approach used by other organisations. For example, Deschamps and Nayak (1995) reported that Ford used an American football style approach to its projects, adding and discarding members as the project progressed.

Cultural issues and heritage of working practices

Many organisations have evolved from much smaller beginnings, yet many of their internal working practices have remained and they contribute to the organisation's heritage (*see* Chapter 1). Hence, any organisational change needs to consider these characteristics and peculiarities. In this case the functional method of working was heavily ingrained in the culture of the organisation. Thus the change to CFT was far more difficult than it might have been for other organisations.

Chapter summary

The main focus of this chapter has been an examination of the activities of the NPD process. Adopting a practitioner standpoint, the new product development process is viewed as a series of linked activities. Emphasis is placed on the iterative nature of the process and many of the activities occur concurrently. A new product needs to be viewed as a project that acquires knowledge gradually over time as an idea is transformed into a physical product. The knowledge base of the organisation will provide for a diverse range of contributions to a project. Furthermore, during this process there is continual evaluation of the project.

This chapter also offered a view of NPD across a variety of industries. The key point here is that the balance of technical and commercial activities will clearly vary depending on the nature of the industry and the product being developed.

Questions for discussion

1 Explain why there is not one best organisational structure for new product development.
2 Discuss the dilemma of trying to ensure that members of a team are, on the one hand, able to make meaningful contributions and, on the other hand, unable to make a contribution through a lack of prior knowledge.
3 Explain why the image of sales representatives as second-hand car dealers is at best misleading and at worst pejorative and incorrect.
4 Explain why screening in the development of a new product needs to be viewed as a continual process.
5 What are the differences between the way scientists view innovation and the way marketing people tend to view it?
6 'New products are a necessary evil'. From whose viewpoint are they necessary and whose viewpoint are they evil?
7 Why do so many new products fail?

References

Allen, T. (1984) *Managing the Flow of Technology*, MIT Press, MA.

Baxter, A. (1997) 'Designs for survival', *Financial Times*, November 20, 16.

Bruce, M. and Cooper, R.C. (1997) *Marketing and Design Management*, Thompson Business Press, London.

Brassington, F. and Pettitt, S. (1997) *Principles of Marketing*, Financial Times Pitman Publishing, London.

Christensen, C.M. and Bower, J.L. (1995) 'Customer power, strategic investment, and the failure of leading firms', *Strategic Management Journal*, 17, 197–218.

Cooper, R.G. (1979) 'The dimensions of industrial new product success and failure', *Journal of Marketing*, 43 (3), Summer, 93–103.

Cooper, R.G. (1988) 'Predevelopment activities determine new product success', *Industrial Marketing Management*, 17 (3), August, 237–47.

Craig, A. and Hart, S. (1992) 'Where to now in new product development', *European Journal of Marketing*, 26, 11.

Crawford, C.M. (1997) *New Products Management*, 5th edn, Irwin, Chicago.

Daily, C. (1996) 'Is the customer always right? (Effects of customers' influence on product development strategies)', *The Academy of Management Executive*, 10 (4), November, 105.

Danziger, J.N. and Kramer, K.L. (1985) 'Computerised data-based systems and productivity among professional workers – the case of detectives', *Public Administration Review*, 45 (1) 196–209.

Deschamps, J.P. and Nayak, P.R. (1995) *Product Juggernauts: How Companies Mobilize to Generate a Stream of Market Winners*, Harvard Business School Press, Boston, MA.

Dougherty, D. (1990) 'Understanding new markets for new products', *Strategic Management Journal*, 11, 59–78.

Ford, R.C. and Randolph, W.A. (1992) 'Cross functional structures: a review and integration of matrix organisations and project management', 18 (2) 269–94.

Gordon, W.J. (1962) 'Defining a creativeness in people', in Parnes, S.J. and Harding, H.F. (eds) *Source Book for Creative Thinking*, Scribners, New York.

Jones, T. (1997) *New Product Development: An Introduction to a Multifunctional Process*, Butterworth-Heinemann, Oxford.

Joyce, W.F. (1986) 'Matrix organisation: a social experiment', *Academy of Management Journal*, 29 (3) 536–61.

Kolodny, H.F. (1979) 'Evolution to a matrix organisation', *Academy of Management Review*, 4 (4) 543–53.

Kotler, P. (1997) *Marketing Management*, Prentice-Hall, Englewood Cliffs, NJ.

Lawrence, P.R., Kolodny, F.H. and Davis, S.M. (1982) 'The human side of the matrix', in Tushman, M.L. and Moore, W.L. (1988) *Readings in the Management of Innovation*, HarperCollins, New York.

Lorenz, C. (1993) 'The best way to rear corporate babies', *Financial Times*, 8 October, 23.

Lothian, I. (1997) 'New product development at Xyratex: a study of cross-functional teams', BA Business Studies dissertation, University of Portsmouth.

Mahajan, V. and Wind, Y. (1988) 'New product forecasting models: directions for research and implementation', *International Journal of Forecasting*, 14, 341–58.

Management Today (1995) 'Why new products are bypassing the market test', October, 12.

Miles, L. (1995) 'Mothers and fathers of invention', *Marketing*, June 1, 26.

Mullins, L.J. (1997) *Management and Organisational Behaviour*, 4th edn, Financial Times Pitman Publishing, London.

Nijssen, E.J. and Lieshout, K.F. (1995) 'Awareness, use and effectiveness of models for new product development', *European Journal of Marketing*, 29 (10) 27–39.

Nonaka, I. (1991) 'The knowledge creating company', *Harvard Business Review*, November–December, 69 (6) 96–104.

Olson, E.M., Orville, C.W. and Ruekert, R.W. (1995) 'Organising for effective new product development: the moderating role of product innovativeness', *Journal of Marketing*, 59, January, 48–62.

Rubenstein, A.H., Chakrabarti, A.K., O'Keefe, R.D., Souder, W.E. and Young, H.C. (1976) 'Factors influencing innovation success at the project level', *Research Management*, 19 (3), 15–20.

Sanchez, A.M. and Elola, L.N. (1991) 'Product innovation in Spain', *Journal of Product Innovation Management*, 11 (2), March, 105–18.

Schmidt, J.B. (1995) 'New product myopia', *Journal of Business and Industrial Marketing*, 10 (1), Winter, 23.

Souder, W.E. and Sherman, J.D. (1993) 'Organisational design and organisational development solutions to the problem of R&D marketing integration', *Research in Organisational Change and Development*, 7, 181–215.

Tidd, J., Bessant, J. and Pavitt, K. (1997) *Managing Innovation*, Wiley & Sons, Chichester.

Tushman, M.L. and Nadler, D. (1978) 'An information processing approach to organisational design', *Academy of Management Review*, 3, 613–24.

Urban, G.L., Hauser, J.R. and Dholaka, N. (1987) *Essentials of New Product Management*, Prentice-Hall, Englewood Cliffs, NJ.

von Hippel, E. (1988) *The Sources of Innovation*, Oxford University Press, New York.

Wang, Q. (1997) 'R&D/marketing interface in a firm's capability-building process: evidence from pharmaceutical firms', *International Journal of Innovation Management*, 1 (1), 23–52.

Further reading

Christensen, C.M. (1997) *The Innovator's Dilemma When New Technologies Cause Great Firms to Fail*, Harvard Business School Press, Boston, MA.

Crawford, C.M. (1997) *New Product Management*, 5th edn, Irwin, Chicago.

Deschamps, J. and Nayak, P.R. (1995) *Product Juggernauts: How Companies Mobilize to Generate a Stream of Market Winners*, Harvard Business School Press, Boston, MA.

Nonaka, I. (1991) 'The knowledge creating company', *Harvard Business Review*, 69 (6) 96–104.

PART THREE

Technology Management

The purpose of this part is to provide material, that it is hoped, will provoke you to think about the problems and challenges faced by managers of technology. Part Three examines the wide issue of technology management and in particular, how companies manage research and development (R&D). It details the main activities performed by R&D departments and how these can influence the development of new products. It also explores the strategic role of R&D. Important questions are raised concerning the extent to which resources should be directed towards defending existing businesses or developing new ones. The extent to which a company can acquire technology developed outside of the organisation is also studied.

The increasing use of strategic alliances is examined in Chapter Ten. It is not only large international companies that are using alliances to develop products and technology, small innovative companies also recognise the potential benefits of working with others. Closely linked to the subject of strategic alliances is the issue of intellectual property and who owns the output from any co-operation. Patents, trade-marks, copyright and registered designs are all discussed in this final chapter.

7

Management of research and development: an introduction

Introduction

The management of research and development (R&D) was, and in some cases still is, viewed as a form of insurance policy. Those companies that did not perform any R&D were regarded as either poor or irresponsible. The *raison d'être* of industrial R&D was to generate opportunities that the business could exploit through the application of science and technology. Today, however, R&D is viewed in the much wider context of technology acquisition. Indeed, it is debatable how far a company can acquire technology without any internal technological research and development.

Learning objectives

When you have completed this chapter, you will be able to:

- Recognise that R&D management is context dependent. The development of a new engine for an aircraft, for example, may take 10 years and involve many different component suppliers. The development of a new domestic cleaning product, however, may take only a few months
- Recognise that the R&D function incorporates several very different activities
- Explain that formal management techniques are an essential part of good R&D management
- Recognise that certain factors are necessary but their presence alone is not sufficient to achieve successful management of R&D projects.

What is research and development?

To many, especially academics, the term research will mean the systematic approach to the discovery of new knowledge. Universities do not usually develop products – unless one considers teaching material as the product of the research. In industry, however, research is a much more generic term and can involve both new science and the use of old science to produce a new product. It is sometimes difficult to determine when research ends and development begins. It is probably more realistic to view industrial R&D as a continuum with scientific knowledge and concepts at one end and physical products at the other. Along this continuum it is possible to place the various R&D activities (*see* Figure 7.1). Later in this chapter we discuss the variety of R&D activities usually found within a large R&D department.

Technology is a commonly used word and yet not fully understood by all those who use it. Hickman (1990) offers a comprehensive classification of technology, used to describe both products and processes. Roussel *et al.* (1991) define technology as the application of knowledge to achieve a practical result. More recently, the term knowhow has been used in the management literature to describe a company's knowledge base, which includes its R&D capability.

Research and development has traditionally been regarded by academics and industry alike as the management of scientific *research* and the *development* of new products; this was soon abbreviated to R&D. Twiss (1992) offers a widely accepted definition:

R&D is the purposeful and systematic use of scientific knowledge to improve man's lot even though some of its manifestations do not meet with universal approval.

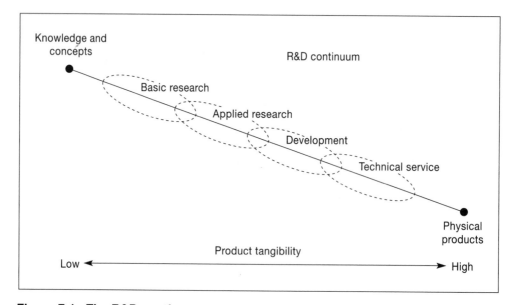

Figure 7.1 : The R&D continuum

The recent debates about scientific cloning of animal cells are a good example of what Twiss means by the results of R&D often delivering controversial outcomes. A more contemporary definition is offered by Roussel *et al.* (1991), who define the concept as:

> **To develop new knowledge and apply scientific or engineering knowledge to connect the knowledge in one field to that in others.**

This definition reflects the more recent view that scientific knowledge is expanding so rapidly that it is extremely difficult for one company to remain abreast of all the technologies that it needs for its products. Companies pull together scientific knowledge from a wide variety of sources. For example, the manufacture of a personal computer will require technology from several different streams including microprocessor technology, visual display technology and software technology. It would be almost impossible for a company to be a technology leader in all of these fields.

The traditional view of R&D

After World War II, research and development played an important role in providing firms with competitive advantage. Technical developments in industries such as chemicals, electronics, automotive and pharmaceuticals led to the development of many new products, which produced rapid growth. For a while it seemed that technology was capable of almost anything. The traditional view of R&D has therefore been overcoming genuine technological problems, which subsequently leads to business opportunities and a competitive advantage over one's competitors. The case study of the development of the smokeless cigarette highlights this traditional role of R&D which is still applied today.

President Kennedy's special address to the US congress in 1961, in which he spoke of 'putting a man on the moon before the decade was out', captured the popular opinion of that time. Many believed anything was possible through technology. This notion helps to explain one of the major areas of difficulty with R&D. Traditionally, it has been viewed as a linear process, moving from research to engineering and then manufacture. That R&D was viewed as an overhead item was reinforced by Kennedy who pledged to spend 'whatever it costs' and indeed enormous financial resources were directed towards the project. But this was a unique situation without the usual economic or market forces at play. Nevertheless, industry adopted a similar approach to that used by the space programme. Vast amounts of money were poured into R&D programmes in the belief that the interesting technology generated could then be incorporated into products. In many instances this is exactly what happened, but there were also many examples of exciting technology developed purely because it was interesting, without any consideration of the competitive market in which the business operated. Hence, many business leaders began to question the value of R&D.

The development of the smokeless cigarette

There are two big problems with cigarette smoking: it damages the smoker's health and it annoys those who dislike passive smoking. This presents companies involved in the manufacture of cigarettes with a genuine technological problem: how to produce a cigarette that overcomes these two key issues. For years now the big cigarette manufacturers, Philip Morris and R.J. Reynolds, have been thinking of ways to overcome the problem of passive smoking. The result has been the development of the smokeless cigarette.

There is enormous commercial logic in a cigarette that satisfies users without threatening their health or irritating others. It would have vast money-making potential. No wonder then that R.J. Reynolds has spent £325 million developing such a product.

Numerous prototype products have been developed and test marketed, but none has been commercially successful. The latest product, called Eclipse, launched by R.J. Reynolds in 1996, uses a smouldering carbon tip to heat moist tobacco creating a vapour instead of smoke. The vapour quickly evaporates after it has been exhaled.

Hot on the heels of R.J. Reynolds has been Philip Morris, which has launched an electronic smoking machine. The system comes in two parts, a low-tar cigarette and an electronic 'puff' activated lighter which fits permanently around the cigarette. The device is intended to make smoking more socially acceptable by eliminating the smoke given off by the burning end of the cigarette.

Previous products of this type have failed because smokers thought they lacked flavour. Many analysts also suggest that part of the allure of smoking is the smoke! However, pressure on smokers is mounting and it is increasingly outlawed in many public places.

Source: *Financial Times*, December 2, 1994 and October 24, 1997.

R&D management and the industrial context

As will become clear, there is no single best way to manage R&D. There is no prescription, no computer model that will ensure its success. Each company and every competitive environment is unique and in its own state of change. R&D needs to be managed according to the specific heritage and resources of the company in its competitive industry. While the management of R&D in the aircraft industry is very different to the textile industry, there are, nonetheless, certain factors and elements that are common to all aspects of R&D management, almost irrespective of the industry. This chapter will draw on examples from across several different industries. This will help to highlight differences as well as identify commonalties in the management of R&D. The following illustration taken from a 1919 visit to the occupied territories of Germany emphasises the very long history of industrial R&D.

Industrial R&D has a long history

Many of Europe's largest chemical companies have a long history of funding industrial research. After the end of World War I several reports were written examining the scope and nature of industrial research in German chemical companies. The following extract is taken from one of these reports:

> One of the most striking features in the works visited is the application in the broadest sense of science to chemical industry. This is naturally very prominent in the triumvirate of the Bayer, Farbwerke Hoechst and the BASF, but it is equally noticeable in many of the smaller undertakings. The lavish and apparently unstinted monetary outlay on laboratories, libraries and technical staff implies implicit confidence on the part of the leaders of the industry in the ability to repay with interest heavy initial expenditure.

Source: ABCM (1919)

At the beginning of this book we discussed one of the most fundamental dilemmas facing all companies, the need to provide an environment that fosters creativity and an inquisitive approach, while at the same time providing a stable environment that enables the business to be managed in an efficient and systematic way. Somehow businesses have to square this circle. Nowhere is this more apparent than in the management of research and development. For it is here that people need to question the accepted ways of working and challenge accepted wisdom.

One may be tempted to think that research, by definition, is uncertain, based around exploring things that are unknown. It cannot therefore be managed and organisations should not try to do so. There is, however, overwhelming evidence to suggest that industrial technological research can indeed be managed and that most of those organisations who spend large amounts of money on R&D, such as Microsoft, IBM, Sony, Siemens and Zeneca, do it extremely well (*see* Table 7.1). This table of Europe's leading firms in terms of R&D expenditure is part of the DTI's yearly *R&D Scoreboard*. It began in 1992 as a way of raising the profile of R&D in the UK and to try to give recognition to those companies who are investing in the future. The first *R&D Scoreboard* was sponsored by the *Independent* newspaper as a means of helping to promote the publication (Independent, 1992).

Large organisations with more resources can clearly afford to invest more in R&D than their smaller counterparts. Therefore, in order to present a more realistic comparison than that derived from raw sums invested, R&D expenditure is frequently expressed as:

R&D as % of sales = (R&D expenditure/total sales income × 100%)

This not only allows comparisons to be made between small and large firms, but also gives a more realistic picture of R&D intensity within the organisation. Across industry sectors there are great differences in expenditure. Table 7.2 shows typical levels of

Table 7.1 : Europe's R&D expenditure league (1996)

Rank	Company	R&D spend (000)	R&D as a % of sales	Rank as a % of sales	Industrial sector
1	Siemens Germany	2 766 466	7.7	85	Electronic and electrical equipment
2	Daimler-Benz Germany	2 115 421	5.2	143	Engineering, vehicles
3	Novartis Switzerland	1 591 087	10.1	55	Chemicals
4	Aesa Brown Boveri Switzerland	1 541 518	7.6	66	Engineering
5	Volkswagen	1 516 703	4.0	182	Engineering, vehicles
6	Ericsson Telefon Sweden	1 494 848	14.1	29	Telecommunications
7	Hoechst Germany	1 471 202	7.6	88	Chemicals
8	Phillips Netherlands	1 368 197	5.9	121	Electronic and electrical equipment
9	Bayer Germany	1 368 066	7.4	91	Chemicals
10	Alcatel Alsthom France	1 244 296	6.9	101	Telecommunications
11	Glaxo-Wellcome UK	1 161 000	13.9	31	Pharmaceuticals
12	Robert Bosch Germany	1 094 680	7.0	99	Electronic and electrical equipment
13	Roche Switzerland	1 064 496	15.3	19	Pharmaceuticals
14	Renault France	1 025 462	5.0	156	Engineering and vehicles
15	Rhone-Poulenc France	905 177	9.4	65	Chemicals
16	BASF Germany	866 720	4.7	165	Chemicals
17	Fiat Italy	802 835	3.0	218	Engineering and vehicles
18	Volvo Sweden	707 843	5.3	139	Engineering and vehicles
19	Peugeot France	664 636	3.6	197	Engineering and vehicles
20	Société Nationale Elf Aquitaine France	661 039	2.5	233	Chemicals

Source: UK R&D Scoreboard 1996, DTI (1997)

Table 7.2 : R&D expenditure across industry sectors

Industry sector	R&D expenditure as % of sales
Pharmaceuticals	14
Aerospace	5
Automotive	5
Chemicals	8
Electrical and electronics	7
Food	1.5
General manufacturing	6
Computers	10

Source: *UK R&D Scoreboard 1996*, DTI (1997)

R&D expenditure across different industry sectors. Some industries are technology intensive with relatively high levels of R&D expenditure. The case study at the end of this chapter shows that even in those industries not normally associated with R&D, the benefits of successful R&D can be large indeed.

The fact that some of the largest and most successful companies in the world spend enormous sums of money on R&D should not be taken as a sign that they have mastered the process. It is important to acknowledge that R&D management, like innovation itself, is part art and part science. Industry may not be able to identify and hire technological geniuses like Faraday, Pasteur or Bell, but many companies would argue that they already employ geniuses who, year after year, develop new patents and new products that will contribute to the future prosperity of the organisation. These same companies would also argue that they cannot justify spending several millions of dollars, pounds or deutschmarks purely on the basis of chance and good fortune. This would clearly be unacceptable, not least to shareholders. So while companies appreciate that there is a certain amount of serendipity, there are also formal management techniques that over the years have been learnt, refined and practised and which are now a necessary part of good R&D management.

R&D investment and company growth

On a global scale, R&D investment increased by an average of 23 per cent from 1991–6. R&D expenditure now consumes a significant proportion of a firm's funds across all industry sectors. This is principally because companies realise that new products can provide a huge competitive advantage. Table 7.3 shows the leading international increases in R&D expenditure between 1991 and 1996. Yet comparing national strengths in science and technology is a hazardous exercise, bedevilled by incompatible definitions. While it is relatively easy to measure inputs, it is far harder to measure outputs in terms of quality. Nonetheless, there is serious cause for con-

Table 7.3 : Leading international increases in R&D expenditure between 1991 and 1996

No.	Country	% increase	No.	Country	% increase
1	Sweden	104	6	Germany	25
2	Denmark	45	7	Belgium	21
3	France	35	8	Switzerland	11
4	USA	31	9	Italy	7
5	UK	27	10	Japan	6

Source: *UK R&D Scoreboard 1996*, DTI (1997)

cern. Statistics from the OECD suggest that the gap in investment in R&D is widening between Europe and the US and Japan. In 1991 the 12 EU countries devoted 1.96 per cent of GDP to R&D, compared with 2.74 per cent in the US and 2.87 per cent in Japan. Only Germany came close to the US and Japanese levels with 2.66 per cent (Lorenz, 1994).

It is now widely recognised that competition can appear from virtually anywhere in the world. Countries formerly viewed as receptacles for the outputs of factories across Europe are now supplying products themselves. Mexico, Brazil, Malaysia, China and India now supply a wide range of products to Europe, including car components, computer hardware and clothing. Globalisation provides opportunities for companies but it also brings increased competition. The introduction of new products provides a clear basis on which to compete, with those companies that are able to develop and introduce new and improved products having a distinct advantage.

Firms are also uneasy about R&D, or to be more accurate a lack of R&D. Ever since 1982 when ICI completed a study into the effects of stopping product innovation, companies have viewed innovation and R&D investment with some anxiety. They fear that should they stop investment in R&D, and product innovation in particular, the consequences would be severe. The results of the study showed that profits would decline very slowly for around 15 years, before falling very sharply. It is worthy of note that if a similar study were to be undertaken today it is almost certain that the 15 year figure would be halved to approximately eight. The ICI study also posed another important question. How long, it wondered, would it take for profits to recover, if after the 15 years the company magically resumed its product innovation at three times its previous rate? The study revealed that it would take another 25 years for profit to recover to the level achieved before the product innovation programme was stopped (Weild, 1986).

These findings reflect the conventional wisdom that has dominated thinking in this field for most of the twentieth century. That is, most companies assume that R&D investment is a good thing; like education, in general, it is surely a worthy investment. In the 1980s there was great interest in the concept of technology transfer and the belief that companies could buy in any technological expertise they required. More recent research has highlighted the folly of such arguments (Cohen and Levinthal, 1990; Quintas *et al.*, 1992) and the business community has returned to a view that fundamentally R&D investment is beneficial. The difficulty lies in where precisely to invest; which projects and technology to invest in; and when to stop pouring money into a project that looks likely to fail but could yet deliver enormous profits. The case study at the end of this chapter explores this point. It also shows how a major technological innovation led to substantial growth for the individual company in particular and the drinks industry in general.

Many international companies, including Unilever, ICI and British Aerospace (Lancaster, 1997), have conducted numerous studies attempting to justify R&D expenditure. This has not been easy because there is no satisfactory method for measuring R&D output. Many studies have used the number of patents published as a guide. This is mainly because it is quantifiable rather than being a valid measure. It is, however, quality not quantity of output that is clearly important. It is worthy of note that most companies would like to be able to correlate R&D expenditure with profitability. At present there is a lack of conclusive evidence to connect the two. Edwin Mansfield (1991) has undertaken many studies concerning the relationship between R&D expenditure and economic growth and productivity. He concludes that:

> although the results are subject to considerable error, they establish certain broad conclusions. In particular, existing econometric studies do provide reasonably conclusive evidence that R&D has a significant effect on the rate of productivity increase in the industries and time periods studied.

Furthermore, a study by Geroski, *et al.* (1993) did reveal a positive relationship between R&D expenditure and *long-term* growth. This raises an important point. R&D expenditure should be viewed as a long-term investment. It may even reduce short-term profitability. Company accountants increasingly question the need for large sums to be invested in an activity that shows no obvious and certainly no rapid return. Many argue that public money should be used for 'pure research' where there is no clear application. Its outputs could then be taken and used by industry to generate wealth. However, the UK government's recent initiatives to couple science to the creation of wealth, through such programmes as Technology Foresight, seems to suggest that even public money is being directed towards applied research.

This raises the issue of evaluating R&D. While few, if any, of the companies listed in Table 7.1 would question the value of R&D, this does not preclude the need for evaluation. How much money should companies invest in R&D? How much should be used for applied research and how much for pure research? These questions will be addressed later in this chapter and in Chapter 8.

Classifying R&D

Traditionally industrial research has focused on a variety of research activities performed *within* the organisation. This practice was modelled on the research undertaken within universities during the early part of the twentieth century. This was seen as public research financed by public money for the public good. In other words, research undertaken within universities was performed in the pursuit of new knowledge. Its results were publicly available and the commercial exploitation of this knowledge was largely disregarded. For example, Fleming's discovery of penicillin was initially not patented. Industrial research, on the other hand, was specifically intended for the benefit of the company funding the research. Industry's purpose was to grow and make profits and this was to be achieved through the development of new products and new businesses. Hence, industry's expectations of its own research expanded to include the development of knowledge into products (*see* Figure 7.2).

Over the years industrial research and development (R&D) has increasingly been guided by the aims of its financiers via its business strategy, and to a lesser extent by the pursuit of knowledge. The main activities of industrial R&D have included the following:

- discovering and developing new technologies
- improving understanding of the technology in existing products
- improving and strengthening understanding of technologies used in manufacturing
- understanding research results from universities and other research institutions.

The management of R&D can be viewed as two sides of the same coin. On the one side there are research activities, often referred to as fundamental or basic research, and on the other development, usually the development of products. Many industries make a clear distinction between research and development and some companies even suggest that they leave all research to universities, engaging only in development. Figure 7.2 shows the areas of research emphasis in industry and universities. In between the discovery of new knowledge and new scientific principles (so-called fundamental research) and the development of products for commercial gain (so-called development) is the significant activity of transforming scientific principles into technologies that can be applied to products. This activity is called applied research. The development of the videocasette recorder (VCR) shows how over a period of almost 30 years industry worked with existing scientific principles to develop a product with commercial potential.

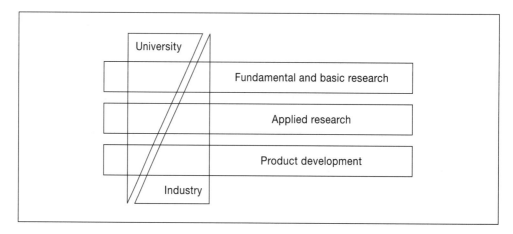

Figure 7.2 : Classification of areas of research emphasis in industry and university

Manipulating known scientific principles through technological development

At the heart of virtually all technologically innovative products lies good fundamental science. The ability to manipulate known scientific principles through technological development is the main research activity of most companies. A good example of this is the VCR industry.

Although videocassette recorders (VCRs) were first introduced in the early 1970s, the story begins long before this date. It was during the 1950s that firms (already in the broadcast industry) began experimenting with existing broadcasting technology to develop a videotape recorder. The front runners were RCA and Ampex in the USA and Toshiba in Japan, all of which had knowledge and experience of television broadcasting technology. In the early 1950s, the RCA team developed a machine that moved a narrow tape at very high speeds past fixed magnetic heads. Meanwhile Toshiba developed a different approach, in which the recording head rotated at high speed while the tape moved past relatively slowly. Toshiba's breakthrough was patented in 1954. Ampex developed a transverse scanner in which four recording heads on a rapidly rotating drum scanned across a two-inch-wide tape.

Ampex was the first to succeed commercially and its videotape recording machine made a huge impact on the broadcasting industry, despite a price of $50 000. Within a few years Ampex had licensed the technology to RCA and Toshiba.

None of the original technology pioneers viewed the idea of producing a product for the mass market as a business opportunity. This baton was to be taken up by three other Japanese firms: JVC, Sony and Matsushita. Spurred on by the success of the other companies, independently they began numerous technical development projects to try to exploit the commercial opportunity of a mass market videotape recorder.

It was only after many failed projects and learning from the mistakes of others that a design emerged in the late 1960s. It was Sony who in 1969 announced the development of a 'magazine-loaded' videotape recorder. JVC soon announced its own slightly different magazine-loaded recorder using half-inch tape as opposed to Sony's one-inch tape. The first Betamax model was offered to the market in April 1975. JVC revealed its VHS technology to its parent company Matsushita and this was launched at the end of 1976.

The war of the formats is now folklore, especially in business schools around the world. It may be useful to highlight some of the key issues.

The key point is the recording time of the two formats. VHS had a recording time of two hours while Betamax had a recording time of only one hour. Industry experts suggest that technologically the formats were equal. That is, on home commercial television sets the difference in picture quality was nil. In the early years it was Sony and Betamax who pioneered most of the technical developments, but in less than a year the VHS manufacturers had caught up. Another common misconception is that Sony refused to license its Betamax technology. This is not true. It tried from the very beginning to license the technology and have it accepted as standard.

Source: Rosenbloom and Cusumano (1988) and *Video Magazine* (1988)

The operations that make up R&D

Figure 7.1 illustrated the R&D operations commonly found in almost every major research and development department. They may have different labels, but within ICI, Unilever, BP, 3M and Shell such operations are well documented. In smaller organisations the activities are less diverse and may include only a few of these operations. This section explains what activities one would expect to find within each type of R&D operation.

Basic research

This activity involves work of a general nature intended to apply to a broad range of uses or to new knowledge about an area. It is also referred to as fundamental science and is usually only conducted in the laboratories of universities and large organisations. Outputs from this activity will result in scientific papers for journals. Some findings will be developed further to produce new technologies. New scientific discoveries such as antibiotics in the 1940s belong to this research category.

Applied research

This activity involves the use of existing scientific principles for the solution of a particular problem. It is sometimes referred to as the application of science. It may lead to new technologies and include the development of patents. It is from this activity that many new products emerge. This form of research is typically conducted by large companies and university departments. The development of the Dyson vacuum cleaner involved applying the science of centrifugal forces first explained by Newton. Centrifugal forces spin dirt out of the air stream in two stages (or cyclones), with air speeds of up to 924 miles an hour. This technology led to the development of several patents.

Development

This activity is similar to applied research in that it involves the use of known scientific principles, but differs in that the activities centre on products. Usually the activity will involve overcoming a technical problem associated with a new product. It may also involve various exploratory studies to try to improve a product's performance. To continue with the Dyson vacuum cleaner example, the prototype product underwent many modifications and enhancements before a commercial product was finally developed. For example, the company has recently launched a cylinder model to complement its upright model.

Technical service

This activity, as its title suggests, focuses on providing a service to existing products and processes. This frequently involves cost and performance improvements to existing products, processes or systems. For example, in the bulk chemical industry it means ensuring that production processes are functioning effectively and efficiently. This category of R&D activity would also include design changes to products to lower the manufacturing costs. For Dyson Appliances extensive efforts will be employed in this area to reduce the cost of manufacturing its vacuum cleaner, leading to increased profit margins for the company.

R&D management and its link with business strategy

Planning decisions are directed towards the future, which is why strategy is often considered to be as much an art as a science. Predicting the future is extremely difficult and there are many factors to consider: economic, social, political, technological, natural disasters etc. The strategic planning process in Chapter 2 illustrated many of these factors. The R&D function also has to make some assessment of the future in order to perform effectively. Thus senior R&D managers have to build into their planning process a conscious view of the future. However imprecise, this will include:

- environmental forecasts
- comparative technological cost-effectiveness
- risk
- capability analysis.

Environmental forecasts

These are primarily concerned with changes in technology that will occur in the future. But this cannot be considered in isolation and other factors such as economic, social and political factors also have to be considered:

- Who will be our competitors in five or ten years' time?
- What technologies do we need to understand to avoid technological surprises?
- What will be the new competitive technologies and businesses?

Comparative technological cost-effectiveness

It is argued that technologies have life cycles and that after a period further research produces negligible benefit. When this stage is reached a new branch of technology is likely to offer far more promising rewards. This may require a significant shift in resources. Today, for example, many car manufacturers are increasing their research efforts in electrical power technology.

Risk

The culture of the organisation and its attitude to risk will influence decision making. Usually risk is spread over a portfolio of projects and will include some exploratory high-risk projects and some developmental low-risk ones. Planning cannot remove risk but it can help to ensure that decisions are reached using a process of rational analysis.

Capability analysis

It is fairly obvious to state, but companies have to consider their own strengths and weaknesses. This analysis should help them ensure that they have the necessary capabilities for the future.

Integration of R&D

The management of research and development needs to be fully integrated with the strategic management process of the business. This will enhance and support the products that marketing and sales offer and provide the company with a technical body of knowledge that can be used for future development. Too many businesses fail to integrate the management of research and technology fully into the overall business strategy process (Adler *et al.* (1992)). A report by the European Industrial Management Association (EIRMA, 1985) recognises R&D as having three distinct areas, each requiring investment: R&D for existing businesses, R&D for new businesses and R&D for exploratory research (*see* Figure 7.3)

These three strategic areas can be broken down into operational activities.

Defend, support and expand existing businesses

The defence of existing businesses essentially means maintaining a business's current position, that is, keeping up with the competition and ensuring that products do not become outdated and ensuring that existing products can compete. For example, the newspaper industry has seen numerous technological changes dramatically alter the way it produces newspapers. In particular, the introduction of desktop publishing and other related computer software has provided increased flexibility in manufacturing operations as well as reducing production costs.

Drive new businesses

Either through identification of market opportunities or development of technology, new business opportunities will continually be presented to managers. Sometimes the best decision is to continue with current activities. However, there will be times when a business takes the decision to start a new business. This may be an extension of existing business activities, but sometimes it may be for a totally new product. For example, 3M's unexpected discovery of temporary adhesive technology to the creation of a completely new business – the Post-It notes.

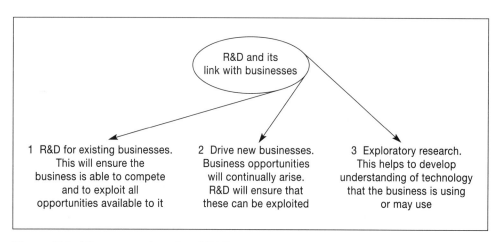

Figure 7.3 : The strategic role of R&D as viewed by the business
Source: EIRMA (1985); Roussel *et al.* (1991)

Broaden and deepen technological capability

The third area is more medium- to long-term strategy. It involves the continual accumulation of knowledge, not only in highly specialised areas where the company is currently operating, but also in areas that may prove to be of importance to the business in the future. For example, Microsoft initially concentrated its efforts on computer programming technologies. The company now requires knowledge in a wide variety of technologies, including telecommunications, media (music, film and television), sound technology etc.

Strategic pressures on R&D

In technology-intensive industries much of the technological resources consumed by a particular business are in the form of engineering and development (often called technical service). These resources can be spread over a wide range of technical activities and technologies. In addition, a firm will have a number of specific areas of technology in which it concentrates resources and builds a technological competence. As one would expect, there is a significant difference between possessing general technical service skills and possessing scientific competence in a particular area. The building and development of technological knowledge competencies take time and demand a large amount of research activity.

Mitchell (1988) suggests there is a trade-off between concentrating resources in the pursuit of a strategic knowledge competence and spreading them over a wider area to allow for the building of a general knowledge base. Figure 7.4 shows the demands on technical resources. The growth of scientific and technological areas of interest to the firm (in particular the research department) pressurises research management to fund a wider number of areas, represented by the upward curve. The need for strategic positioning forces the decision to focus resources and build strategic knowledge com-

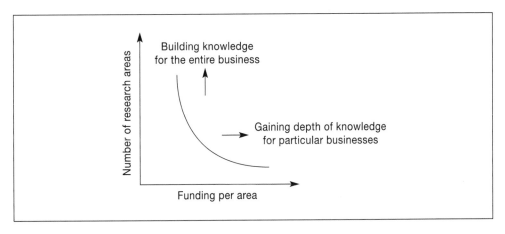

Figure 7.4 : Strategic pressures on R&D
Source: Mitchell (1988)

185

petencies, represented by the downward curve. In practice, most businesses settle for an uneasy balance between the two sets of pressures.

The technology portfolio

From an R&D perspective the company's technology base can be categorised as follows:

- core technologies
- complementary technologies
- peripheral technologies
- emerging technologies.

Core technologies

The core technology is usually central to all or most of the company's products. Expertise in this area may also dominate the laboratories of the R&D department as well as strategic thinking. For example, in the photocopying industry photographic technologies are core.

Complementary technologies

Complementary technologies are additional technology that is essential in product development. For example, microprocessors are becoming essential in many products and industries. For the photocopying industry there are several complementary technologies, including microprocessor technology and paper-handling technology, which enables the lifting, turning, folding and stapling of paper.

Peripheral technologies

Peripheral technology is defined as technology that is not necessarily incorporated into the product but whose application contributes to the business. Computer software is often in this category. The photocopying industry is increasingly using software to add features and benefits to its products, such as security.

Emerging technologies

These are new to the company but may have a long-term significance for its products. In the photocopying industry, telecommunications technologies may soon be incorporated as standard features of the product.

The difficulty of managing capital-intensive production plants in a dynamic environment

Many manufacturing operations involve the careful management of multimillion-pound production plants. Such businesses have a slightly different set of factors to consider than a company operating the manufacturing plant for say, shoes, which is labour rather than technology intensive. Hundreds of millions of pounds are invested in a new chemical plant and options open to it in terms of changes in products are limited. This is because a production plant is built to produce one chemical product. Moreover, the scrapping of an existing plant and the building of a new one may cost in excess of £300 million. There are few companies in the world who could continually build, scrap and rebuild chemical plants in response to the demands of the market and make a profit from such actions. Hence companies operating process plants cannot respond *completely* to market needs.

This particular dilemma faced by companies with large investments in production technology is frequently overlooked by those far removed from the production floor. Young marketing graduates may feel that a company should be able to halt production of one product in order to switch to the production of another offering better prospects. The effect of such a decision may be to bankrupt the company! The chemical industry is increasingly developing smaller, more flexible plants rather than the large, single-purpose plants that have been common since the turn of the century.

In some industries where investment lies less in the technology and more in the human resources, changes to a production plant are possible. Toshiba UK recently completely switched one of its production plants from producing microwave ovens to industrial air conditioners. It had been making microwave ovens in its Plymouth factory since 1985, but unfortunately due to low-cost competition from Korea production was halted in 1990. The new product was far more complex and cost up to 20 times more. This involved substantial changes to production methods and training of staff. Following £20 million investment and six years of development, the plant is seen as extremely successful with output valued at £30 million a year (*Financial Times*, November 19, 1997).

Which businesses to support and how?

It is well understood that technological developments can lead to improved products and processes, reduced costs and ultimately better commercial performance and competitive advantage. The ability to capitalise on technological developments and profit from the business opportunities that may subsequently arise requires a business to be in an appropriate strategic position. That is, it must possess the capability to understand and use the technological developments to its own advantage. This requires some form of anticipation of future technological developments and also strategic business planning. Technological forecasting and planning are fraught with uncertainty. Figure 7.5 illustrates the iterative and continual process involved in the management of research and technology.

The effect of corporate strategy is usually most noticeable in the selection of R&D projects. For example, a corporate decision by Unilever to strengthen its position in the luxury perfume business may lead to the cancellation of several research projects, with more emphasis being placed on buying brands like Calvin Klein. Ideally, a system is required that links R&D decision making with corporate strategy decision making. However, it is common in R&D departments to make decisions on a project-by-project basis in which individual projects are assessed on their own merits, independent of the organisation. This is partly because the expertise required is concentrated in the R&D

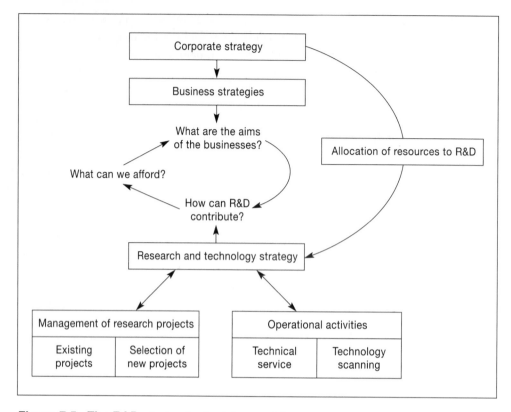

Figure 7.5 : The R&D strategic decision-making process

department and partly due to scientists' fascination with science itself. This used to be the case in many large organisations with centralised laboratories. Such a decision-making process, however, is only valid when funds are unlimited and this is rarely the case. In practice, funds are restricted and projects compete with each other for continued funding for future years. Not all projects can receive funding and in industrial R&D laboratories projects are cancelled week after week, frequently to the annoyance of those involved.

The flow diagram in Figure 7.5 highlights the need for integration of corporate and R&D strategy. The corporate strategy will have numerous inputs, many of which are discussed in Chapter 3. The process of corporate planning involves the systematic examination of a wide variety of factors. The aim is to produce a statement of company objectives and how they are to be achieved. Essentially, a number of questions need to be considered:

- What might the company do?
- What can the company do?
- What should the company do?

This leads to the development of business strategies. At the base of the diagram are the inputs from R&D activities, in particular existing R&D projects and potential projects that may be selected for funding. The organisation must repeatedly ask itself: What are the needs of the businesses? What should R&D be doing? What can R&D do? This process is neither a bottom-up nor a top-down process. What is required is continual dialogue between senior management and R&D management.

While it is tempting to say that technology influences the competitive performance of all businesses, in reality some businesses are more heavily influenced than others. In many mature and established industries, the cost of raw materials is much more of an influence on the competitive performance of the business than are technology developments. For example, the price paid for commodities like coffee, cocoa and sugar can dramatically influence profits in many food industries. Similarly, in the chemical industry the competitive position of petroleum-based plastics is determined by the price paid for the raw material, oil. Consequently, some businesses, especially those operating in mature industries, would be unable to influence their competitive position through technology alone. Even if the business was to substantially increase the level of R&D investment, its competitive position would still be determined by raw material prices.

Several attempts have been made by industry to quantify this factor when considering the level of R&D investment required. Scholefield (1993) developed a model using the concept of technology leverage. This is the extent of influence that a business's technology and technology base have on its competitive position. In general, technology leverage will be low when the influence of raw material and distribution costs and economic growth is high. High-volume, bulk commodity products would fall within this scenario.

Technology leverage and R&D strategies

The state of a business in terms of its markets, products and capabilities will largely determine the amount of research effort to be undertaken. Research by Scholefield (1993) suggests that there are essentially two forms of activity for a R&D department, growth and maintenance. Within these two groups it is possible to conduct significantly different types of activities. Hence, these categories can be subdivided into the four groups depicted in Figure 7.6.

Survival

This type of activity is conducted if the decision has been made to exit the business. In such circumstances the role of the R&D department is to ensure its interim survival against technological mishaps to process or product. This would be a reactive problem-solving role and may be termed 'survival research'.

Competitive

If the intention is to sustain the business, then the role of research is to maintain the relative competitive technological position by making improvements to both product and process. For example, in the automotive industry most manufacturers have invested heavily in their own processes and vehicle build-qualities have improved dramatically; so much so that reliability, although still improving, is almost taken for

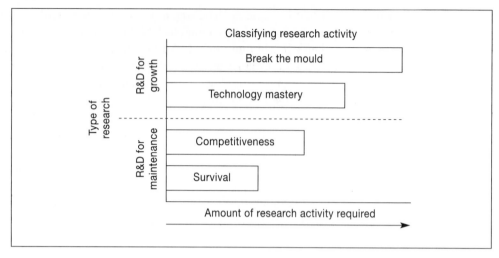

Figure 7.6 : Classifying the level of research using technology leverage

granted by car buyers. The process technologies involved have become widely accepted and used. However, if any one manufacturer allowed its process technologies to fall behind those of its competitors, it would almost certainly provide an advantage to them. The amount of research activity required to maintain a high-technology leverage position, however, will be significantly greater than that required to maintain a low-technology leverage position. Thus it seems reasonable to split this category in two: competitive (low-technology leverage) and competitive (high-technology leverage).

Technology mastery

Incremental growth of a business in a strong position involves improving the product and process relative to the competition. This will clearly involve a level of research activity greater than the competitive position outlined above. It will involve keeping abreast of all technological developments that may affect the business's products or processes. Hence, a much higher level of R&D expenditure will be required.

Break the mould

If the aim is to create a technological advantage then a much higher order of novelty and creativity is required. Following such a strategy will involve developing new patentable technology and may involve a higher level of basic scientific research.

Using the model

A business's expenditure on research activity would normally be reviewed annually or quarterly. The model is used as a guide to establish whether a business's research activity is appropriate for its position. Experience has shown that without such a guide research activity can drift over time, resulting in too much or too little activity appropriate for the business. The model provides the facility for business and research managers to monitor research activity. In practice this involves continual analysis, adjustment and realignment. For example, each quarter a business's executive would meet and discuss quarterly results. During these meetings, its strategic position could be reclassified according to performance and external environmental factors. That is, a business's category may change from, say, 3 to 4 or from 2 to 1.

Strengths and limitations of this approach

The model attempts to introduce some theory into what is often an arbitrary competition for research activity. It provides a framework within which discussions may take place. In practice, the model is used to check decisions made by research and business managers, as opposed to being used for dictating decisions. In addition, it includes a technological perspective for classifying a business's strategic position. Many strategic management tools, while paying lip service to the importance of technology, fail to accommodate a technological perspective in the decision-making process. There is an over-emphasis on the financial or marketing perspective (Ansoff, 1968; BCG, 1972; Porter, 1985).

It also shows how the role of strategic technology management and a business's selected growth strategy can influence the business climate within which managers operate. For example, if a strategic decision is taken to exit a business, this will clearly have a profound influence on the nature of activities. One would expect the activities of a business operating in a climate of growth to be different from those of one operating in a climate of decline.

CASE STUDY

Developing corporate success through successful R&D at Guinness plc[1]

Introduction

Guinness plc is one of the world's leading drinks companies, producing and managing an impressive portfolio of international brands such as Johnnie Walker, Bell's, Gordon's and the world's most distinctive beer. The merger of Guinness and Grand Metropolitan to form Diageo, has created one of the largest drinks groups in the world (*Financial Times*, 1997). Furthermore, the immediate future for the product that bears the company's name looks particularly bright. This is largely due to a major technological breakthrough which brought Guinness the Queen's Award for Technological Achievement, the first time that a drinks company has been presented with the award. This case study examines how this new product revolutionised the beer and lager industry. The Guinness 'In-can system', now referred to generically as 'widget technology' following heavy promotion by Courage, forces pressurised beer through a small aperture in the widget and into the beer when the can is opened. The effect is a foamy head.

▶

---

[1] This case has been written as a basis for class discussion rather than to illustrate effective or ineffective managerial or administrative behaviour. It has been prepared from a variety of published sources, as indicated, and from observations.

▶ *Background*

The Guinness company has a long history stretching back more than 230 years. Arthur Guinness began brewing ale for the people of Dublin. In those days ale was brewed using a blend of several barrels. In the 1770s a new beer appeared in Dublin that was imported from London. It was known as Entire and contained roasted barley, which gave it a characteristically dark colour. In addition, unlike the traditional Dublin ale, it was served from a single barrel. As the popularity of this imported beer grew, Arthur Guinness, along with many other Dublin brewers, decided to tackle the English at their own game. Not all the brewers were successful in developing this new ale. However, Arthur Guinness soon had to choose between producing the traditional Dublin ale and this new brew. It would appear that he made the correct decision.

Labels are used by companies to help identify the contents of their products and promote particular brands. The famous Guinness trademark with its Irish harp emblem first appeared in Britain in 1862 and was registered as a trademark in 1876. Guinness supplied its labels to bottlers, but only to those bottlers which sold no other bottled stout except Guinness. Bottlers which sold their own stouts as well as Guinness had to provide their own labels which Guinness insisted on approving.

Over the years the label has changed, sometimes because of legislation and the need to provide information to the consumer, but mainly to give it a more contemporary feel. The trademark remains much the same as in 1862.

By 1920 production of Guinness was three million barrels a week, and in 1936 the Park Royal brewery opened in London to cope with the extra demand.

In these early days beer was sold in wooden casks. Glass was not used until after the tax on glass bottles was repealed in 1845. Guinness did not undertake the bottling itself. Instead, the beer was sold to a multitude of independent bottlers, ranging from small pubs to major wholesale bottlers and even other brewers. Guinness still uses a small number of contract bottlers, but other more recently developed products such as Guinness draught bitter and Kaliber are packaged by the company's own packaging division based at Runcorn in Cheshire.

Market changes and threats from competition

While Guinness enjoyed long-term growth and continued success through much of the twentieth century, a rosy future for the company was not always so identifiable. During the 1980s the beer industry in the UK came under severe attack from international lager brands such as Castlemaine XXXX, Fosters, Miller Lite and others. At one point many industry analysts suggested that the UK beer industry might be so badly damaged that it would struggle to compete. There were additional threats on the horizon. The growing concern about drink-driving was beginning to have an impact on beer sales in pubs across the country. Projecting their research results forward, the beer industry predicted that the volume of draught sales was sure to fall, with the take-home market one of the few beneficiaries, along with soft-drinks manufacturers such as Schweppes and Britvic! More worrying still was the realisation that any growth in the take-home market was likely to be enjoyed by the lager producers as opposed to the beer producers. This was because lager from a can or bottle tasted much the same as lager on draught. The same could not be said for beer from a can. The future looked bleak.

The response: a focused R&D programme

Draught Guinness has a unique appearance which results from the initiation and surging of bubbles of nitrogen and carbon dioxide gas as the beer passes through a special dispensing tap called a font to form a smooth, white creamy head. This creamy top to a pint of Guinness as delivered in the pub is a major factor which creates the flavour differences between draught Guinness and Guinness Original (canned or bottled Guinness).

There was clearly a need to try to improve the taste and appearance of canned or bottled Guinness for the increasing take-home market. The problem was that the thick, creamy head associated with Guinness requires a high shearing force to initiate the break-out of mixed nitrogen and carbon dioxide. This is in contrast to carbonated drinks where the gas comes freely out of the solution (carbon dioxide readily comes out of a glass of lemonade, for example). The task therefore was to find a way of forcing the gas out of the solution. A shearing force similar to that used in the font was required.

Many research projects were started that considered new types of containers that replicated the font used in draught Guinness. The R&D department had been working on this particular problem as far back as the 1960s. In the early 1980s Guinness developed a packaging system that included a small syringe with which the consumer was to inject air into the stout after pouring it. This system was not commercially successful. Other projects looked at methods requiring the consumer to shake the container before pouring. In total over 100 research projects and ideas were tested. Some were very good but prohibitively expensive, making the final product uncompetitive. Others were too complicated, requiring the consumer to carry out several operations before serving.

After four years the research teams had been cut back and morale was low. The problems looked insurmountable. Over £5 million had been spent and research directors and senior managers were beginning to question whether the money should be directed into other projects. The perennial decision of whether to kill the project was discussed. Eventually in late 1987 Alan Forage and his team presented a system to senior management that has become known as the 'in-can system' (ICS). Forage explained:

> The 'ICS' itself is a plastic chamber insert with a minute hole which is placed in the bottom of a 500ml can. However, only 440ml of beer is dispensed into the can. This is to allow for head expansion when the can is opened. Beer containing dissolved gas is filled *under pressure* into the can and the can is sealed. Once the lid has been put on, the pressures in the can and inside the chamber equilibrate and beer is *forced* into the chamber which becomes partially filled. When a consumer opens the can of beer by pulling the ring-pull, the higher pressure in the can is released to atmosphere. The drop in pressure causes an *imbalance* between the beer in the can and the beer in the chamber forcing beer out of the chamber through the small hole. It is this process which creates the *shearing force* and characteristic 'surge' in draught Guinness. As the beer is forced through this very small hole, nitrogen and carbon dioxide are broken out from their dissolved state.
>
> (Guinness, 1995)

ICS was developed with a specialist plastics company, McKechnie Plastic Components, that makes parts for the automobile industry. A peripheral structure holds the unit firmly in place when pushed to the bottom of the can. The new product was test marketed in the Midlands and North of England from April 1988. Results were very encouraging. A few minor changes were made but the concept remained the same. Draught Guinness with ICS was launched nationally in March 1989. The product has been a huge commercial success.

The 'In-can' system

The complete canning system using the ICS is complex. The original canning line had to be considerably altered and involves several operations, including:

▶

▶ ■ location of plastic chamber in can

■ nitrogen is used to remove all oxygen from the can and insert prior to filling can with beer

■ liquid nitrogen is added which evaporates after the can is seamed to produce a high internal pressure

■ filled cans are pasteurised at 60°C to give a microbiologically stable product.

The canning line at Runcorn, Cheshire can now deliver 1400 cans a minute or more than 23 cans a second (Brown, 1997).

The response of the competition and avoiding patent infringement

If imitation is the highest form of flattery, then Guinness should be pleased. Virtually all the major brewers have responded to Guinness's development by developing their own systems. Some of the best known are Whitbread Draughtflow, Courage Caskpour, Bass Mark II, plus many bottled systems.

There is clearly fierce commercial rivalry between the brewers, hence they try to keep secret the names of the companies which supply their plastic inserts. It is true that the plastic inserts are described in published patents, but as with virtually all production lines there is a huge difference between patent technology and a fully operational canning production line. It is important to note that the ICS as developed by Guinness is not simply the plastic can insert, there is also a great deal of associated technology including filling the can under pressure; use of an inerting tunnel; application of high pressure nitrogen; seaming of the can; and the pasteuriser, all of which contribute to the technology.

Guinness's original patent was comprehensive and covered the plastic insert and most of the associated technology. *See* Appendix 1 for details of Guinness' original patent application. Those companies which followed were forced to become more ingenious and make their designs more complex to achieve the same result. Many of the technical difficulties have involved minimising the costs associated with canning.

Equipment suppliers have devised clever ways to overcome the patent. Each brewing company in association with insert suppliers has developed individual systems, some using more manual systems with lower equipment costs, others very sophisticated equipment without a large increase in the workforce. The developed cost of the Bass widget is claimed to be £10 million (Wainwright, 1995).

Many of the brewers claim that their widget technology is now superior to that originally developed by Guinness. Whitbread, for example, claims that its two-part injection-moulded widget enables the amount of gas in the can to be carefully preset, offering a more reliable force when the can is opened. Furthermore, because the Whitbread widget is sealed it minimises any air in the can.

Discussion

In many ways Guinness has revolutionised the concept of beer packaging. The can is no longer simply a container but performs a function and is itself an example of new technology. This was underlined when, in 1991, the ICS received the Queen's Award for Technological Achievement.

The product is now sold in more than 50 countries and in March 1993 it launched the sale of its 250 millionth can of draught Guinness. In 1994 it launched a £30 million investment programme in canning facilities at its Runcorn canning factory (*The Canner*, 1994). The wider brewing industry has also benefited from this technological development with higher margins now achievable; the new cans are 20 per cent above the price of the original packaged product.

The inclusion of plastic inserts in a metal can has generated much criticism from the recycling lobby. However, Bass has recently developed an aluminium widget. Also some consumer groups, particularly the Campaign for Real Ale (CAMRA), do not consider the use of widgets as a product improvement. They consider that the beer tastes blander.

Chapter summary

This chapter has introduced the substantial subject of R&D management and some of the challenges that it presents. Emphasis has been placed on highlighting the wide range of different activities undertaken by most R&D functions. Formal management techniques were shown to be an essential part of good R&D management. Companies are unable to justify spending millions of dollars purely on the basis of chance and good fortune. The issue of investment in R&D and industry comparisons was another area of discussion.

The link between R&D and the strategic management activities of the business was also discussed in some detail. This presents its own set of challenges in terms of deciding in which areas to invest and what type of R&D investment to follow. Most companies try to manage a balance of activities, but it is important to be aware of the nature of the pressures placed on management.

Questions for discussion

1 Show why R&D management is dependent on industrial context.

2 Discuss the range of operational R&D activities.

3 What was the traditional view of R&D?

4 What are the main strategic activities of R&D?

5 Discuss some of the strategic pressures on R&D.

6 What is meant by technology leverage?

7 Using the Guinness case, discuss the dilemma of having to decide whether or not to kill a project.

8 Show how the Guinness case study illustrates how the traditional view of R&D is still relevant today.

9 In the Guinness case study, to what extent did organisational knowledge and organisational heritage affect the development of the ICS?

References

ABCM (1919) *Report of the British Chemical Mission on Chemical Factories in the Occupied Area of Germany.*

Adler, P.S., McDonnald, D.W. and MacDonnald, F. (1992) 'Strategic management of technical functions'. *Sloan Management Review*, Winter, 19–37.

Ansoff, H.I. (1968) *Corporate Strategy*, Penguin, Harmondsworth.

BCG (1972) *Perspectives on Experience*, Boston Consulting Group, Boston, MA

Brown, D. (1997) 'Nitrogen and its foaming relationship with widgets', *The Brewer*, January, 25–32.

The Canner (1994) 'Widgets rule in UK beer market', March, 28–33.

Cohen, W.M. and Levinthal, D.A. (1990) 'A new perspective on learning and innovation', *Administrative Science Quarterly*, 35 (1) 128–52.

DTI (1997) *UK R&D Scoreboard 1996*, HMSO, Norwich.

EIRMA (1985) 'Evaluation of R&D output: working group report', 29, European Industrial Research Management Association, Paris.

Financial Times (1997) 'Philip Morris launches an electronic smoking machine', October 24, 7.

Geroski, P., Machin, S. and van Reenen, J. (1993) 'The profitability of innovating forms', *Rand Journal of Economics*, 24, 198–211.

Hickman, L.A. (1990) *Technology*, McGraw-Hill, Maidenhead.

Independent (1992) 'R&D Scoreboard;' June 10, 20.

Kennedy, J.F. (1961) Special address to Congress.

Lancaster, A. (1997) 'An investigation into the evaluation of an organisation's research and development performance', BA Business Studies undergraduate dissertation.

Lorenz, C. (1994) 'The real face of Japanese R&D in Europe', *Financial Times*, November 17, 22.

Mansfield, E. (1991) 'Social returns from R&D: findings, methods and limitations', *Research, Technology Management*, November/December, 24.

Mitchell, G.R. (1988) 'Options for the strategic management of technology', *UNESCO Technology Management*, Interscience Enterprises Ltd, Geneva.

Porter, M.E. (1985) *Competitive Advantage: Creating and Sustaining Competitive Advantage*, Free Press, New York.

Quintas, P., Weild, D. and Massey, M. (1992) 'Academic–industry links and innovation: questioning the science park model', *Technovation*, 12 (3) 161–75.

Rosenbloom, R.S. and Cusumano, M.A. (1988) 'Technological pioneering and competitive advantage: the birth of the VCR industry', in Tushman, M.L. and Moore, W.L., *Readings in the Management of Innovation*, HarperCollins, New York.

Roussel, P.A., Saad, K.N. and Erickson, T.S. (1991) *Third Generation R&D*, Harvard Business School Press, Boston, MA.

Scholefield, J.H. (1993) 'The development of a R&D planning model at ICI, *R&D Management*, 23, 4.

Twiss, B. (1992) *Managing Technological Innovation*, 4th edn, Financial Times Pitman Publishing, London.

Video Magazine (1988) 'The format war', April.

Wainwright, T. (1995) 'Canned beers get a head', *Beverage World International*, July/August, 39–46.

Weild, D. (1986) 'Organisational strategies and practices for innovation', in Roy, R. and Weild, D. (eds) *Product Design and Technological Innovation*, OU Press, Milton Keynes.

Further reading

Chiesa, V. and Masella, C. (1996) 'Searching for an effective measure of R&D performance', *Management Decision*, 34 (7) 49–58.

Roussel, P.A., Saad, KN. and Erickson, T.J. (1991) *Third Generation R&D*, Harvard Business School Press, Boston, MA.

Tushman, M.L. and Moore, W.L. (1988) *Readings in the Management of Innovation*, HarperCollins, New York.

Twiss, B. (1992) *Managing Technological Innovation*, 4th edn, Financial Times Pitman Publishing, London.

8

Effective research and development management

Introduction

The past 10 years have witnessed enormous changes in the way companies manage their technological resources and in particular research and development. Within industrial R&D the effect is a shift in emphasis from an internal to an external focus. Contract R&D, R&D consortia and strategic alliances and joint ventures now form a large part of R&D management activities.

The need to provide scientific freedom and still achieve an effective return from any R&D investment, however, remains one of the most fundamental areas of R&D management. The use of formal planning techniques for R&D is viewed by many as a paradox: the introduction of any planning mechanism would surely stifle creativity and innovation. And yet R&D departments do not have unlimited funds, so there has to be some planning and control.

Learning objectives

When you have completed this chapter, you will be able to:

- Examine the key activities of R&D management
- Recognise the changing nature of R&D management
- Recognise the factors that influence the decision whether to undertake internal or external R&D
- Recognise the value of providing scientific freedom
- Examine the link with the product innovation process
- Explore the various ways of funding R&D.

Successful technology management

Organisations that manage products and technologies and have been built on a strong research and development base are constantly looking for opportunities to diversify horizontally into new product markets. Their strategic management activities seek to mobilise complementary assets to successfully enter those markets. For example, Eastman Kodak's knowledge of manufacturing photographic film enabled it to move into the manufacture of computer floppy disks. Similarly, in production-based technologies, key opportunities lie in the technological advances that can be applied to products and production systems, enabling diversification vertically into a wider range of production inputs. The injection-moulding process has had many adaptations, enabling its use in an increasing range of manufacturing techniques. However, companies do not have a completely free choice about the way they manage their technologies (Pavitt, 1990):

> **In many areas it is not clear before the event who is in the innovation race, where the starting and finishing lines are, and what the race is all about. Even when all these things are clear, companies often start out wishing to be a leader and end up being a follower!**

This argument reveals the weaknesses in some of the commonly accepted views of technology strategy promoted by many business schools and management consultants. It is not helpful to the organisation to try to predetermine whether its technology strategy should be to lead or to follow, to develop a product or a process. Technology cannot be developed to order or acquired to fill a position in a matrix. It can only be successful if it is fully integrated into the company's business. This means that the company needs a range of complementary assets in other areas such as marketing and distribution, in order to exploit its technology successfully. Developing these skills and capabilities and integrating them into the company takes time. Often these characteristics will be determined by the company's size, its previous activities and its accumulated competences. However, it is these latter factors and not the company's strategy that will determine whether it will successfully exploit its technology.

As virtually all practitioners realise, there is no easy formula for success. In a review of the literature on technology management, Pavitt (1990) identified the following necessary ingredients for successful technology management:

- the capacity to orchestrate and integrate functional and specialist groups for the implementation of innovations
- continuous questioning of the appropriateness of existing divisional markets, missions and skills for the exploitation of technological opportunities
- a willingness to take a long-term view of technological accumulation within the firm.

The changing nature of R&D management

R&D activities have changed dramatically since 1950. The past 10 years have witnessed enormous changes in the way companies manage their technological resources and in particular their research and development. There are numerous factors that have contributed to these changes. Rothwell and Zegveld (1985) identify three important factors:

- *Technology explosion* – They estimate that 90 per cent of our present technical knowledge has been generated during the last 55 years.

- *Shortening of the technology cycle* – The technology cycle includes scientific and technological developments prior to the traditional product life cycle. These cycles have been slowly shortening, forcing companies to focus their efforts on product development. For example, the market life of production cars has decreased from approximately 10 years in the 1960s to approximately six years in the 1990s. In some cases a particular model may be restyled after only three years.

- *Globalisation of technology* – Countries on the Pacific Rim have demonstrated an ability to acquire and assimilate technology into new products. This has resulted in a substantial increase in technology transfer in the form of licensing and strategic alliances.

Figure 7.2 showed the traditional areas of research activity for universities and industry. University emphasis has been on discovering new knowledge, with industry exploiting these discoveries in the form of products. The last decade has seen a significant increase in collaborative research, with industry sponsoring science departments in universities and engaging in staff exchanges with university departments.

The effect of these macro factors is a shift in emphasis within industrial R&D from an internal to an external focus. In a study of firms in Sweden, Japan and the US, Granstrand *et al.* (1992) revealed that the external acquisition of technology was the most prominent technology management issue in multitechnology corporations. Traditionally, R&D management, particularly in Western technology-based companies, has been management of internal R&D. It could be argued that one of the most noticeable features of Japanese companies since World War II has been their ability successfully to acquire and utilise technology from other companies around the world. Granstrand *et al.* (1992) suggest that the external acquisition of technology exposes technology managers to new responsibilities. Although this implies that acquiring technology from outside the organisation is something new, this is clearly not the case, as the long history of licensing agreements will show. However, the importance now placed on technology acquisition by technology-based companies reveals a departure from a focus on internal R&D and an acknowledgement that internal R&D is now only one of many technology development options available. The technology base of a company is viewed as an asset; it represents the technological capability of that company. The different acquisition strategies available involve varying degrees of organisational and managerial integration. For example, internal R&D is viewed as the most integrated technology acquisition strategy with technology scanning the least integrated strategy. Technology scanning is rather narrowly defined by Granstrand *et al.* (1992) as both illegal and legal forms of acquiring technological knowhow from outside.

The classification of technology acquisition strategies offered by Granstrand *et al.* (1995) provides an illustration of the numerous ways of acquiring external technology (*see* Figure 8.2 later). Other classifications can be found in the technology transfer literature: Auster (1987); Chesnais (1988); Hagedoorn (1990); Lefever (1992). All these studies, however, offer classifications of only the formal methods of technology transfer. They ignore the many forms of informal linkages, alliances and industry associations that are known to exist and that often result in extensive transfer of knowledge and technology (Kreiner and Schultz, 1990; Rothwell and Dodgson 1991).

The wide range of activities now being expected from R&D departments and the demands being placed on them are becoming ever more complex. Particular emphasis is being placed on a company's linkages with other organisations. Networking is now regarded as an effective method of knowledge acquisition and learning (Trott and Cordey-Hayes, 1996; Albertini and Butler, 1995). It is argued that the ability to network in order to acquire and exploit external knowledge enables the firm to enter new areas of technological development. The following areas now explicitly require involvement from the R&D department:

- Industry has expanded its support of university research and established numerous collaborations with university departments (Abelson, 1995).

- Industry has increased the number of technological collaborations. R&D personnel are increasingly being involved in technology audits of potential collaborators.

- Research and development personnel are increasingly accompanying sales staff on visits to customers and component suppliers to discuss technical problems and possible product developments (Trott, 1993).

- The acquisition and divestment of technology-based businesses have led to a further expansion of the role of R&D. Input is increasingly required in the form of an assessment of the value of the technology to the business.

- The expansion of industrial agreements, usually in the form of licensing, contract work and consultancy, has resulted in a new area of work for R&D. The rapid growth in knowledge-intensive service firms is clear evidence of this (Kastrinos and Miles, 1995).

The focus of these new areas of work is on external knowledge acquisition and assimilation. This is forcing many companies to reassess the way they manage their R&D. In addition, this increased portfolio of activities requires a different range of skills from the individuals involved. The traditional role of a research scientist as a world expert in a particular field, who uses a convergent, narrow-focus approach to uncover new and cheaper ways of producing chemicals and products, is being replaced by researchers who have additional attributes. These include an ability to interact with a wide variety of external organisations, thereby increasing awareness of specific customer needs, market changes, the activities of competitors and the larger environment. Historically, R&D staff faced alternative definitions of career success and reward in career paths either involving increasing administrative responsibility and a path into managerial hierarchy or one involving increasing prestige as technical specialists. This dual-ladder career structure looks more and more out of place in today's varied and rapidly changing R&D environment.

Organising industrial R&D

The increasing emphasis on knowledge acquisition and assimilation is forcing companies to look for ways to improve their effectiveness in this area. Given the growing use of external sources of technology, the R&D manager now has to determine which form of R&D is most appropriate for the organisation. Figure 8.1 shows the many guises of R&D.

Centralised laboratories

The main advantage with centralised laboratories is critical mass. The idea is that far more can be achieved when scientists work together than when they work alone. Those firms trying to achieve technological leadership often centralise their R&D. There is also the possibility that synergy can result, with technologies from different businesses being employed in different unrelated businesses. When Zeneca was separated from ICI one of the limitations of the demerger was that R&D would suffer through a reduction in synergies.

Decentralised laboratories

The main advantage of decentralising the R&D function is to reinforce the link with the business, its products and its markets. It is argued that with a large, centralised R&D effort it is often too removed from where the technology is eventually applied. By providing each business or division with its own R&D effort, it is argued that this fosters improved communication and product development. However, the weakness of this closer link is that it can lead to an emphasis on short-term development only.

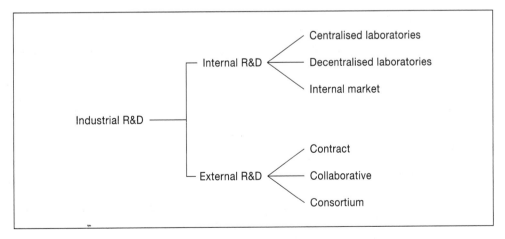

Figure 8.1 : Organising industrial R&D

Internal R&D market

An internal market structure for R&D essentially involves establishing a functional cost centre, where each business pays for any R&D services required. This raises the issue of whether a business is also able to use external R&D services, say from a university. The extent to which this erodes the knowledge base of the organisation, however, is debatable. The limitations of this approach are similar to those for decentralised R&D laboratories.

The acquisition of external technology

So far in this book, we have concentrated on viewing R&D as an activity performed internally by the business. It is necessary, however, to understand that R&D is not necessarily an internal organisational activity. R&D, like any other business function, say marketing or production, can be contracted out and performed by a third party. The previous section highlighted the increasing use of collaborations and strategic alliances to acquire technology (the role of strategic alliances will be discussed in detail in Chapter 10). The extent to which it is possible for an organisation to acquire externally developed technology is uncertain and is discussed in Chapters 3 and 9. Nonetheless, many businesses establish research contracts with organisations such as universities to undertake specific research projects.

There is a significant difference between acquiring externally developed technology and external R&D. This difference lies in the level of understanding of the technology involved, often referred to as prior knowledge. To illustrate, the purchase of new computer software will lead to the acquisition of new technology. This is an option available to virtually all businesses, irrespective of their prior knowledge of the technology. However, developing an R&D strategic alliance or an external R&D contract with a third party requires a high level of prior knowledge of the technology concerned. Similarly, the level of prior knowledge of the external third party also influences the choice of method to acquire the technology concerned.

The matrix in Figure 8.2 offers an insight into the issue of technology acquisition. While the matrix is an over-simplification of a complex subject, it does nonetheless help to classify the wide range of acquisition options available to companies, from purchasing technology 'off the shelf' to conducting internal R&D. The horizontal axis refers to the level of prior knowledge of the business acquiring the technology. The vertical axis refers to the level of prior knowledge of external third parties.

As was explained in Chapter 2, there are many companies that conduct little, if any, R&D, yet are associated with a wide variety of technology-intensive products. This is particularly the case for supplier-dominated and scale-intensive firms (Pavitt, 1984). Many such companies assemble component parts purchased from other manufacturers and sell the final product stamped with their own brand. Some companies do not even assemble, they simply place their own brand on the purchased product (often called re-badging). In these cases the company concerned usually has commercial and marketing strengths such as service quality and distribution skills. This is similar to own branding in the grocery market.

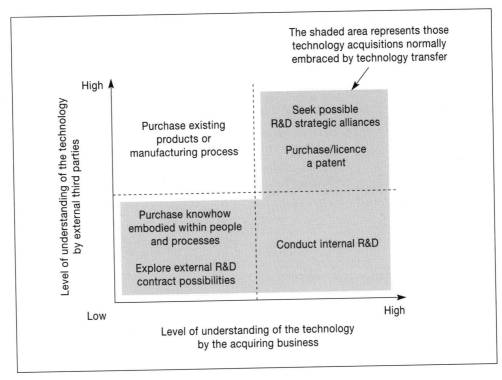

Figure 8.2 : Acquisition of external technology/knowledge matrix

The subject of technology transfer is discussed in detail in the next chapter. It is nonetheless worth pointing out here that technology transfer usually embraces the activities in the shaded area on the matrix. It is not normally used to describe, say, the purchase of new computer software. Technology transfer is defined as:

> The process of promoting technical innovation through the transfer of ideas, knowledge, devices and artefacts from leading edge companies, R&D organisations and academic research to more general and effective application in industry and commerce.　　　　　　　*Seaton and Cordey-Hayes (1993)*

Level of control of technology required

In acquiring externally developed technology, a business must also consider the extent of control over the technology that it requires. For example, if a research project shows promising results that could lead to the development of a new radical technology with many new product opportunities, it is likely that the business would want to keep such research under close control and thus internal. On the other hand, a project with specific technical problems requiring expertise in an area of technology beyond the scope of the business may be ideally suited to a research contract with a university department. Figure 8.3 shows a classification of technology acquisition methods. You will see that they are classified according to the degree of integration with the organisation.

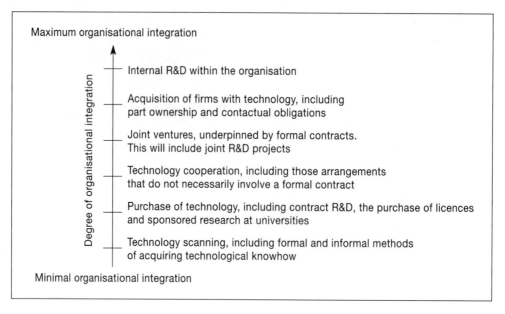

Figure 8.3 : Technology acquisition: How much control of the technology is required?

Source: Adapted from Granstrand *et al.* (1992)

The particular stage of development of the research, or its position in the technology life cycle, will heavily influence the level of control required. For example, is the research at an early stage without any particular product idea in mind (pre-competitive) or is it near completion and shortly to be incorporated in a new product launch (competitive)? Clearly, competitive research will require careful monitoring to ensure that maximum competitive advantage can be secured.

There may also be occasions when the company does not have the in-house expertise to undertake the research. In this case some form of external R&D will be necessary.

Forms of external R&D

Contract R&D

In those situations where the business has a low level of understanding of the technology (bottom left-hand corner of technology acquisition matrix), contracting the R&D out to a third party is often suitable. University research departments have a long history of operating in this area. However, the use of commercial research organisations is rapidly expanding, especially in the field of biotechnology. This method of R&D is also used in urgent situations, when setting up internal research teams would be too slow.

R&D strategic alliances and joint ventures

This area of management is explored in Chapter 10. At this point it is necessary only to be aware of the key advantages and disadvantages of using strategic alliances. This is a generic term for all forms of co-operation, both formal and informal, including joint ventures. With a joint venture, the costs and possible benefits from an R&D research project would be shared. They are usually established for a specific project and will cease on its completion. For example, Apple and IBM established an R&D joint venture in 1991 to develop a new computer operating system. The advantages are usually obvious. In this example, both companies were able to share their expertise and reduce the inevitable costs and risks associated with any R&D project. The disadvantages are that either company could inadvertently pass knowledge to the other and receive little in return. It is for this reason alone that many companies still refuse to enter into any form of strategic alliance. It can be usefully explained using game theory principles and in particular the prisoner's dilemma (*see* Chapter 10).

R&D consortia

In this context, R&D consortia are separate from the large-scale technology consortia often found in the Far East. In Japan *keiretsu* (literally meaning societies of business) consist of 20–50 companies, usually centred around a trading company and involving component suppliers, distributors and final product producers, all interwoven through shareholdings, trading arrangements. In South Korea, *chaebols* are similar to *keiretsus* except that they are financed by the government rather than by banks or a trading company and usually the company links are based on family ties (Powell, 1996). Such types of business groups are based on common membership and collaborate over a long period of time.

The use of R&D consortia has increased substantially over the past 10 years in both the US and Europe. Rhea (1991) claims that there have been in excess of 200 R&D consortia registered in the US since 1984. The EU offers a number of programmes to encourage R&D co-operation across the Union (*see* example below). One of the most successful, and certainly high-profile, cases is SEMTECH, a consortium of 14 US semiconductor manufacturers. In 1980 nine out of the top ten silicon chip makers were from the US. By 1990 five out of the top six were Japanese. SEMTECH was established to try to help the US chip manufacturers. It had substantial funding from the US Defense Department with the aim of creating a viable semiconductor manufacturing equipment and materials industry, thus ensuring that domestic chip producers would not be dependent on Japanese equipment sources. SEMTECH has played a major role in developing successive generations of chip-making technology. By 1995, the US semiconductor industry had experienced a dramatic increase in its share of the world market (Corey, 1997).

One of the potential weaknesses of this concept is the potential for reducing competition. The EU and the US government spend a great deal of time and money trying to detect those organisations operating a cartel. Harsh penalties are usually enforced on any offending organisation. R&D consortia are closely monitored and have to be registered.

The main advantages of this approach are the ability to reduce costs and risks, the ability to access technologies and to influence industry standards on new technology (the experience of the VCR industry and the computer operating system industry have shown the potential dangers in having competing industry standards). The main disadvantages are similar to those for joint ventures, in that one party may not be able to gain any technological benefit from the consortia. The development of IMAGE is a good example of an effective R&D consortium (*see* example below).

The development of IMAGE

This example shows how pre-competitive R&D collaboration led to the development of an exciting new multimedia product for Olivetti. This co-operation led to further agreements with other firms concerning the manufacturing and marketing of a range of products.

The Olivetti product, called IMAGE, is a software authoring environment for the development of interactive multimedia applications, which enables the user to manipulate graphics, animation, photographs and sound in an integrated manner. The product was eventually launched in 1991 and was one of the first in the field.

The idea for a new multimedia product emerged during the final phases of a research project called MULTOS, financed by the European Union's ESPRIT programme. This programme aims to encourage co-operation between member states in industrial R&D projects, specifically in the area of information technologies. It is managed by DG III, the Directorate General for Industry of the European Commission.

The objective of the project was to develop a basic software system that would store and retrieve multimedia documents. The original group comprised the Crete Research Centre, IEI, and Olivetti Pisa Research Laboratories. Each partner would carry out specific research tasks and researchers would meet on a monthly basis to discuss progress. Close contact facilitated the exchange of information and experience, and enabled friendships to develop.

Moreover, there was a common desire to overcome technical problems and develop scientific understanding. The university partners were primarily interested in the theoretical aspects of the MULTOS system, whereas the industrial partners were interested in how the technology could be further developed into products.

This particular project ran from 1985–91 and was very successful. There were two key benefits:

1 Basic R&D was not constrained by costs. This enabled the group to explore the subject rather than focusing on a specific business objective. This type of research (often referred to as 'blue-sky research') is limited in industry today.
2 Individuals received excellent training and experience. The postgraduate researchers involved in the project benefited from wonderful experience of scientific and technical research and the management of an international research project.

The research offered several exciting avenues to pursue, in the fields of software engineering, artificial intelligence, multimedia and office automation. Olivetti Research Labs eventually decided to explore the possibility of a multimedia product.

Source: ESPRIT, DG III, European Commission, Luxembourg

Effective R&D management

Managers of R&D have to try to develop systems and procedures which will enhance the probability of success. To outside observers the research and development process

Table 8.1 : Organisational characteristics that facilitate the innovation process and the management of R&D

R&D requirement	Characterised by
1 Growth orientation	A commitment to long-term growth rather than short-term profit
2 Vigilance	The ability of the organisation to be aware of its threats and opportunities
3 Commitment to technology	The willingness to invest in the long-term development of technology
4 Acceptance of risks	The willingness to include risky opportunities in a balanced portfolio
5 Cross-functional cooperation	Mutual respect among individuals and a willingness to work together across functions
6 Receptivity	The ability to be aware of, to identify and to take effective advantage of externally developed technology
7 'Slack'	An ability to manage the innovation dilemma and provide room for creativity
8 Awareness of business strategy	High degree of awareness of corporate objectives
9 Project management	Good project management skills and systems
10 Market orientation	An awareness of the needs and changing nature of the market
11 Diverse range of skills	A combination of specialisation and diversity of knowledge and skills

Source: (adapted from Table 2.4)

may seem like a random procedure in which inspired scientists, working around the clock, come on major breakthroughs late at night. It is true that R&D is a high-risk activity, but the process is much less random than it first appears. Over the past 40 years there has been extensive research in R&D management and there is an academic journal dedicated to the subject (*R&D Management*). This research has revealed the presence of certain factors in many successful R&D projects and their absence in many failed projects. Table 8.1 summarises these factors.

Effective R&D management can make a considerable impact on the performance of a company. The example of aspirin shows how over a period of 100 years R&D has led to many different applications of the drug.

The continued development of aspirin

Through continued research and development, new uses are continually being found for one of the oldest pharmaceutical products – aspirin. Aspirin was first introduced to the market more than 100 years ago in 1897. It was research into salicin, a compound that is found naturally on willow bark, by Bayer, a large German chemical manufacturer, that led to the development of aspirin as we know it today.

▶

▶ The drug was first used as a treatment for arthritis sufferers. Pharmacologist John Vane received the Nobel Prize for chemistry for uncovering how aspirin relieved arthritis. He showed that prostaglandins are released by the body when cells are injured, triggering the symptoms of inflammation, swelling and pain. Aspirin halts the production of these prostaglandins, hence its effectiveness in treating arthritis.

Aspirin has been shown to have a number of additional effects:

■ It acts as an analgesic to ease pain

■ It acts as an anti-inflammatory to control inflammation

■ It acts as an antipyretic to reduce fever

■ By thinning the blood it helps to reduce the danger of blood vessels clotting, thereby helping to prevent strokes and heart attacks

■ It has also been shown to help reduce colonic cancer

■ It is currently being used in the treatment of Alzheimer's disease.

Source: Dobson (1997)

Managing scientific freedom

The idea of applying formal planning techniques to R&D is viewed by many as a paradox. The popular view is that research, by definition, is concerned with uncovering new things and discovering something that previously was unknown. To try to introduce any form of planning would surely stifle creativity and innovation. This leads to one of the most fundamental management dilemmas facing senior managers: how to encourage creativity and at the same time improve efficiency. This dilemma was tackled at a generic level in Chapter 2, so to avoid repetition we will address the problem from an R&D perspective.

R&D managers will argue that the technologist's and scientist's spirit of enquiry must be given room and freedom to exercise. Without the freedom to work on projects that may not appear of immediate benefit to the company, the laboratory may become conservative and uncreative. Furthermore, it may be difficult to attract and retain the best scientists if they are not allowed to pursue those areas that are of interest to them. There are many disputes between research and technology managers and other senior functional managers concerning the extent of time that scientists and research teams should be able to allocate for personal research programmes.

However, R&D managers are realistic: they recognise that few companies, if any, are going to invest large sums of money solely as an act of faith. There are many formal management techniques that are employed to help to improve the effectiveness and productivity of R&D without necessarily destroying the possibility of serendipity.

Virtually all companies accept that a certain amount of time should be made available for scientific enquiry (after all, there are many examples of such research producing profitable outcomes, *see* the case study in Chapter 5). The issue is, *how much time*? One approach, adopted by many technology-intensive companies, such as 3M, ICI, Unilever and BP, is to consider that a company that invests heavily in R&D is, in reality, managing two types of R&D projects. This can best be shown schematically as in Figure 8.4. This diagram is an extension of Figure 7.5.

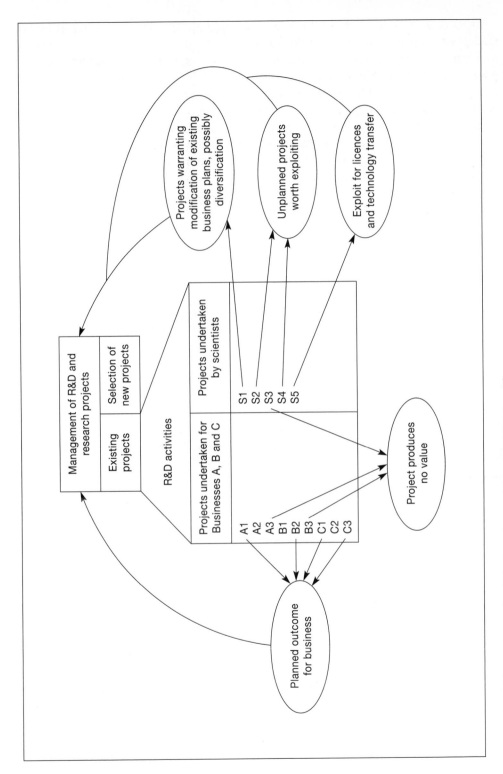

Figure 8.4 : Managing scientific freedom within an R&D function

The R&D projects are divided into two separate groups. The first group is by far the largest, usually accounting for 90 per cent of the R&D budget. It is established in response to requests from the various businesses and supports and maintains the corporate objectives. In Figure 8.4 these projects are labelled A, B and C. The second group of projects are those generated by the scientists themselves, usually as a result of personal interest in the technology. These are labelled S1 to S5. These projects will be generating technology of a commercial value but free from the constraints of corporate objectives. This latter group of research projects is financed by funds that are allocated at the discretion of the R&D manager or more usually an R&D committee or team. Very often these funds represent about 10 per cent of the total R&D budget. This group of research projects has a variety of labels in industry, including blue-sky research, special projects and personal research. Virtually all major technology-intensive companies accommodate a certain amount of time for individuals to pursue their own research projects. Typically, about 10 per cent of a scientist's time will be spent on autonomous research projects.

Twiss (1992) develops this idea of two types of research projects further by suggesting that R&D managers are in effect managing two business activities. The primary activity supports the various businesses and the corporate objectives and the other supports a technology business, involved in generating technology of a commercial value that is unrelated to the corporate objectives.

Skunk works

Technology-intensive companies recognise that if they are to attract and retain the best scientists they have to offer scientific freedom. Moreover, experience has shown that scientists will covertly undertake these projects if autonomy is not provided. There are many examples of exciting technology and successful products that were initiated by scientists operating in a covert manner. In the US such research projects are referred to as 'skunk works' (*see* the Lockheed example for an explanation of its origin).

The original skunk works

The name 'skunk works' can be traced back to US aircraft manufacturer Lockheed. It originally used by Al Capp's 'Li'l Abner' comic strip which featured the 'Skonk works' (sic) where Appalachian hillbillies ground up skunks, old shoes and other foul-smelling ingredients to brew fearsome drinks and other products. Lockheed engineers identified the secret jet aircraft assembly facility as the place where Clarence Johnson was stirring up some kind of 'potent brew'. The skunk works was created by Johnson to design and develop the XP-80 Shooting Star, the US's first production jet aircraft. The nickname stuck, although 'skonk' became 'skunk' in deference to the non-hillbillies working at the Lockheed facility and because Al Capp objected to anyone else using his unique spelling. Cartoonist Capp and the 'Li'l Abner' comic strip departed many years ago, but skunk works is now a registered service mark of Lockheed along with the familiar skunk logo.

Source: Lockheed Martin Corporation (1998)

Table 8.2 : Research project outcomes

Research project	Outcome	Action
A1, B2, C1 and C3	Planned outcome for the business	Research project produces desired results for business to incorporate into products
A3, B3 and S3	Project produces no immediate commercial value	Results of project will be examined by other research groups to see if the findings can be used; knowledge remains with R&D department
S1	Project warrants changing existing business strategy	In exceptional circumstances the findings from a research project can be so unusual and promising that they warrant a change in business strategy to accommodate possible new product ideas
S5	License technology to third party	When the research results produce interesting technology that is beyond exploitation by the business, it may be possible to generate income from licensing the technology to a third party
S2 and S4	Unplanned projects worth exploiting further	The findings from these personal research projects are so interesting that they require further funding and possible inclusion in business research
A2, B1 and C2	Projects lead to further research projects undertaken by scientists	The findings in themselves are of limited commercial value but stimulate further research projects

Figure 8.3 shows a variety of project outcomes. These are explained in Table 8.2.

The link with the product innovation process

Chapters 5 and 6 outlined the main factors to be considered in managing the development of new products. Many of the models of NPD emphasised the link to the R&D department. In particular, the network model of new product development shown in Figure 5.13 emphasises this continual interaction throughout the development of the product. Knowledge is accumulated over time as an idea for a product is transformed into a research project. The R&D function will be continually consulted on virtually all aspects of the product, including:

- design
- manufacturing
- choice of materials to be used
- required shelf life

- effects of transportation
- intellectual property rights
- product safety, etc.

It is important to bear in mind that an investment in R&D to develop an existing product further is not generally viewed by product managers as a high-risk activity. The following quote from the brand manager of the makers of one the leading washing detergents in Europe reflects a commonly held view:

> We know we can improve the product, our scientists can always improve the product. In fact the launch date for our new improved X has been set but the research is still on-going! The only doubt is the extent of the improvement that our scientists will make.

A similar example could be drawn from the software industry, which is synonymous with new, improved versions of its software. The key point here is the way R&D investment is viewed. For many firms with years of experience in the management of R&D, an output is expected from their investment in R&D; the only doubt is the detail. Given this perspective on R&D, the following section analyses the range of effects that R&D investment can have on a product's profitability.

The effect of R&D investment on products

Analysis of the products that a company manages will reveal that these contribute in different ways to the overall profit and growth of the company. It is important to recognise that R&D activities can influence this profit contribution in several ways.

Development of existing products

The life cycle of most products lasts for several years. There are some products, especially in the food industry, that seem to have an eternal life cycle. Cadbury's Milk Tray and Coca-Cola are two examples of products that have been on the market for over 100 years. In virtually all other industry sectors, however, a product's market share will slowly fall as competitors compete on price and product improvements (*see* Chapter 5). R&D's role is to extend the life of the product by continually searching for product improvements. The two most common approaches to extend the life of a product are capturing a larger market share and improving profit margins through lowering production costs. For example, the performance of Zinc-carbon batteries has improved greatly due to the threat of alkaline batteries like Duracell. This has helped to improve the market share for alkaline batteries. Similarly, personal computer manufacturers such as Dell, Apple, Compaq and IBM are continually lowering their production costs in order to ensure that their products compete successfully in the PC market.

Early introduction of a new product

Many companies strive to be technological leaders in their industry. Their aim is to introduce innovative products into the market before the competition to gain a competitive advantage. In some industries, such as pharmaceuticals, this approach is very successful. In other sectors being first to market does not always ensure success (*see* Chapter 4 on market entry).

Late introduction of a new product

Deliberately postponing entry into a new market until it has been shown by competitors to be valid reduces the risk and costs. This was the approach used by Amstrad in the UK consumer electronics market. Furthermore, by deliberately slowing down product launches into the market it is possible to maximise profits. For example, software companies have been very successful in launching improved versions and upgrades every six to nine months.

Long-term projects

Looking further in the future, R&D departments will also be developing products that the public do not yet realise they require. This area also includes starting new initiatives and new areas of research. Technology-intensive companies such as Siemens, Microsoft, Airbus and 3M will be working on products for 2010 and beyond.

Funding R&D projects

Unlike many other business activities, successful R&D cannot be managed on an annual budgetary basis. It requires a much longer-term approach enabling knowledge to be acquired and built up over time. This often leads to tensions with other functions that are planning activities. Nonetheless, as was explained in Chapter 7, R&D has to be linked to the business strategy.

It is unusual for unlimited funds to be available, hence business functions usually compete with other departments for funds. Marketing will no doubt present a very good case for why extra money should be spent on new marketing campaigns; the IT department will request more funds for more equipment and valuable training for everyone; and the sales department will almost certainly ask for more salespeople to boost sales. It is a difficult circle to square. A great deal depends on the culture of the organisation and the industry within which it is operating (*see* Chapters 2 and 7). Pilkington, for example, spends proportionally large sums on R&D, many say too much, especially when one considers its more recent performance (*Financial Times*, 1998). Other companies spend very little on R&D but huge amounts on sales and marketing. This is the case for the financial services industry. So one of the most difficult decisions facing senior management is how much to spend on R&D. Many companies now report R&D expenditure in their annual reports. However, the fact that it is now relatively easy to establish, for example, that Rubbermaid spent 14 per cent of sales on R&D in 1994, exactly how the company arrived at this figure is less clear.

Setting the R&D budget

In practice, establishing the R&D budget for a business is influenced by short-term performance fluctuations and availability of funds, which is, in turn, influenced by the setting of annual budgets. Additionally, budgets are also influenced by the long-term strategic technological needs of the business. It is extremely difficult to establish a basis for the allocation of funds that will be acceptable to all parties. A number of different approaches are used by different companies (*see* below). In practice, businesses use a combination of these methods. In addition, managerial judgement and negotiation will often play a significant role. The portfolio management approach, outlined in Chapter 7, enables profits from today's successful businesses to be invested into what the company hopes will become the profitable businesses of tomorrow. Many businesses also invest in basic research. This is research that is perceived to be of interest to the company as a whole and of benefit to the organisation in the long term.

There are several key factors that need to be considered when allocating funds to R&D:

- expenditure by competitors
- company's long-term growth objectives
- the need for stability
- distortions introduced by large projects.

Six approaches can be used for allocating funds to R&D.

Inter-firm comparisons

While R&D expenditure varies greatly between industries, within similar industries there is often some similarity. It is possible to establish reasonably accurately a competitor's R&D expenditure, the number of research personnel employed etc. By analysing the research expenditure of its competitors, a business is able to establish an appropriate figure for its own research effort. Table 8.3 would suggest that a company trying to establish its R&D budget should consider spending between 10 and 25 per cent of sales on R&D.

A fixed relationship to turnover

R&D expenditure can be based on a constant percentage. Turnover normally provides a reasonably stable figure that grows in line with the size of the company. As an exam-

Table 8.3 : Comparison of R&D expenditure within the European chemical industry

Company	R&D expenditure as % of sales
Novartis (Switzerland)	10
Hoechst (Germany)	18
Bayer (Germany)	19
Rhone-Poulenc (France)	14
BASF (Germany)	25

Source: DTI (1997)

ple of this method, a company has decided to spend 2 per cent of its annual turnover on R&D. If its turnover is £10 million then its annual R&D expenditure would be £200 000. A criticism of this method is that it uses past figures for future investments.

A fixed relationship to profits

Fixing R&D expenditure to profits is highly undesirable. It implies that R&D is a luxury which can only be afforded when the company generates profits. This method completely ignores the role of R&D as an investment and the likely future benefits that will follow. Often, in fact, poor profits can be turned around with new products.

Reference to previous levels of expenditure

In the absence of any criteria for measurement, a starting point for discussions is likely to be the previous year's expenditure plus an allowance for inflation. In spite of its crudeness, this method is often used in conjunction with one or more of the other methods, especially during negotiations with other functional managers.

Costing of an agreed programme

An R&D manager is concerned with managing research projects, so the allocation of funds for each individual project may seem attractive. This allows him or her to add together the requirements for certain projects and arrive at a figure. Invariably the total will exceed what the department is likely to receive. Negotiations are then likely to ensue, focusing on which projects to cut completely or on which to reduce expenditure.

Internal customer–contractor relationship

In some large multinational companies, the individual business units may pay for research carried out on their behalf by the R&D function. In addition, there is usually some provision for building the knowledge base of the whole organisation. For example, each business manager within ICI manages his or her own R&D budget but each business must also contribute 10–12 per cent for long-term research. Shell operates a similar programme.

Evaluating R&D

Lord Lever's famous quote about advertising expenditure could equally be applied to R&D investment: 'half the money I spend on advertising is wasted, the problem is I don't know which half'. Scientists and technologists would rightly argue that even if the return on investment is not a profitable product, the investment in knowledge is not wasted. Without getting drawn into a philosophical debate on the acquisition of knowledge, the point is that an evaluation of a financial investment in R&D should be subject to the same criteria as evaluations of other investments made by the organisation. However, herein lies the difficulty. There are many short-term returns from an R&D investment, as was made clear above, but there is also a longer-term return.

Often technological expertise is built up over many years through many consecutive short-term research projects. It is extremely difficult to apportion the profit to all contributing functions from a product developed over a period of several years. There is also considerable merit in the argument that without the R&D investment there would not have been a product at all. This subject has received a great deal of attention over the past four decades (Williams, 1969; Mansfield *et al.*, 1972; Meyer-Krahmer, 1984; Cordero, 1990; McGrath and Romeri, 1994).

The R&D manager is under the same pressures as the senior management team. They have to ensure that the business has opportunities to exploit for future growth. In reality a few successful projects are usually sufficient to justify the investment.

Virtually all R&D managers are responsible for a portfolio of projects. The aim is to try to select those that will be successful and drop those which will not. The Guinness case study in Chapter 7 highlighted the difficulty of project selection. Sometimes it is the project least likely to succeed that turns out to be the next Post-It notes business.

Financial forecasts made at the time of R&D project selection are subject to gross errors, either because the development costs turn out to be much higher (rather than lower) or the financial benefits derived from the project are higher or lower than was originally forecast (Twiss, 1992). Such forecasts are clearly of limited value. Nonetheless, some form of financial analysis cannot be avoided. It will certainly be demanded by senior management. Analyses which are unrealistic and have no credibility within the organisation are of limited value. This area of decision making is dominated by personal experience and historical case studies that the company has experienced.

A variety of quantitative and qualitative measurements have been developed to try to help business managers tackle the problem of project selection (Chiesa and Masella, 1996). It remains, however, a combination of uncertain science and black art.

CASE STUDY

The role of clinical research in the pharmaceutical industry[1]

Introduction

In August 1997, an advertisement appeared in the worldwide professional journal of the International Association of Physicians in Aids Care (IAPAC) asking more, perhaps, than medical research has ever asked before. It asked for healthy human volunteers who would be willing to test a new AIDS vaccine (Sarler, 1997).

HIV (Human Immunodeficiency Virus, that can lead to AIDS) was discovered in 1984; since then, enormous sums of money have been spent by governments, pharmaceutical companies and other interested parties in the search for a cure and a vaccine. The latest figures from the World Health Organisation show that, worldwide, there are 8500 new HIV infections a day, the

---

[1] This case study has been written as a basis for class discussion rather than to illustrate effective or uneffective managerial or administrative behaviour. It has been prepared from a variety of published sources, as indicated, and from observations.

majority of which are in the Developing World. What makes HIV so appalling is that it is an infection of the young rather than the old. The syndrome is wiping out people in the prime of life, so the benefits of developing a successful vaccine are clear.

Professor Desrosiers, a microbiologist from Harvard Medical School, has developed a live attenuated vaccine for the monkey equivalent of HIV. This has now been developed further and needs to be tested on humans. Within the pharmaceutical industry this particular stage of research is referred to as clinical trials. The monkey form of AIDS is caused by a slightly different virus to the human one. Past experiments on AIDS in monkeys have had disappointing results; nonetheless, like all other pharmaceutical drugs, this new attenuated vaccine must undergo clinical trials. These will establish whether or not the vaccine could be beneficial and if this approach could lead to further AIDS vaccines. As will be shown later, the first stage of any clinical trials requires healthy human volunteers.

This highlights an ethical dilemma frequently encountered within research in the pharmaceutical industry. Unlike drug research, which clearly has benefits to the individual recipient, vaccine research has a more altruistic benefit to society at large. This is because a successful vaccine can potentially rid the world of a disease. Like most successful vaccines, such as those for polio, smallpox, yellow fever, mumps and measles, this new vaccine is a live attenuated one. That is, it is a weakened version of the disease.

Pharmaceutical companies are less interested in vaccine research than in drug research. Vaccine production is more expensive than drug manufacture because you have to prove not only that it is safe but that it works. This takes more time and more money.

This very topical and emotive illustration introduces the area of pharmaceutical research, and in particular the area of clinical trials. In the pharmaceutical industry clinical trials form an important part of the research process for developing new products. New product development in the pharmaceutical industry is very different to that in many other industries. This particular case study explores the unique role of clinical research associates in the development of new drugs for the pharmaceutical industry.

Research and NPD in the pharmaceutical industry

The pharmaceutical industry is relatively young. While its origins can be traced to the turn of the century, the industry as it is known today is largely a post-war phenomenon. It grew out of the chemical industry. For example, betablocker drugs were developed by ICI and this laid the foundations for its pharmaceutical operations and eventually the formation of Zeneca. The anti-ulcer treatment drug Zantac was the basis for the foundation and growth of Glaxo; this one drug achieved sales in excess of $2 billion per annum. Moreoever, the development of the industry has been fuelled by technological innovation. Figure 8.5 is an overview of new product development in the pharmaceutical industry. The pharmaceutical industry is one of the few industries that follows the classical technology-push model of innovation (see Chapter 1). Put simply, scientific research is followed by product development and then marketing. This complete product development process will now be examined in more detail.

The first stage is referred to as pre-clinical scientific research. This involves chemistry, biology, pharmacology (the science of the properties of drugs and their effectiveness on the body) and toxicology (the degree to which a substance is poisonous). In addition, issues of intellectual property and, in particular, the application for patents are key activities. With R&D lasting up to 10 years, it is imperative that a company is able to protect its intellectual property so that it is able to generate some income from its investment. The rising cost of R&D is ▶

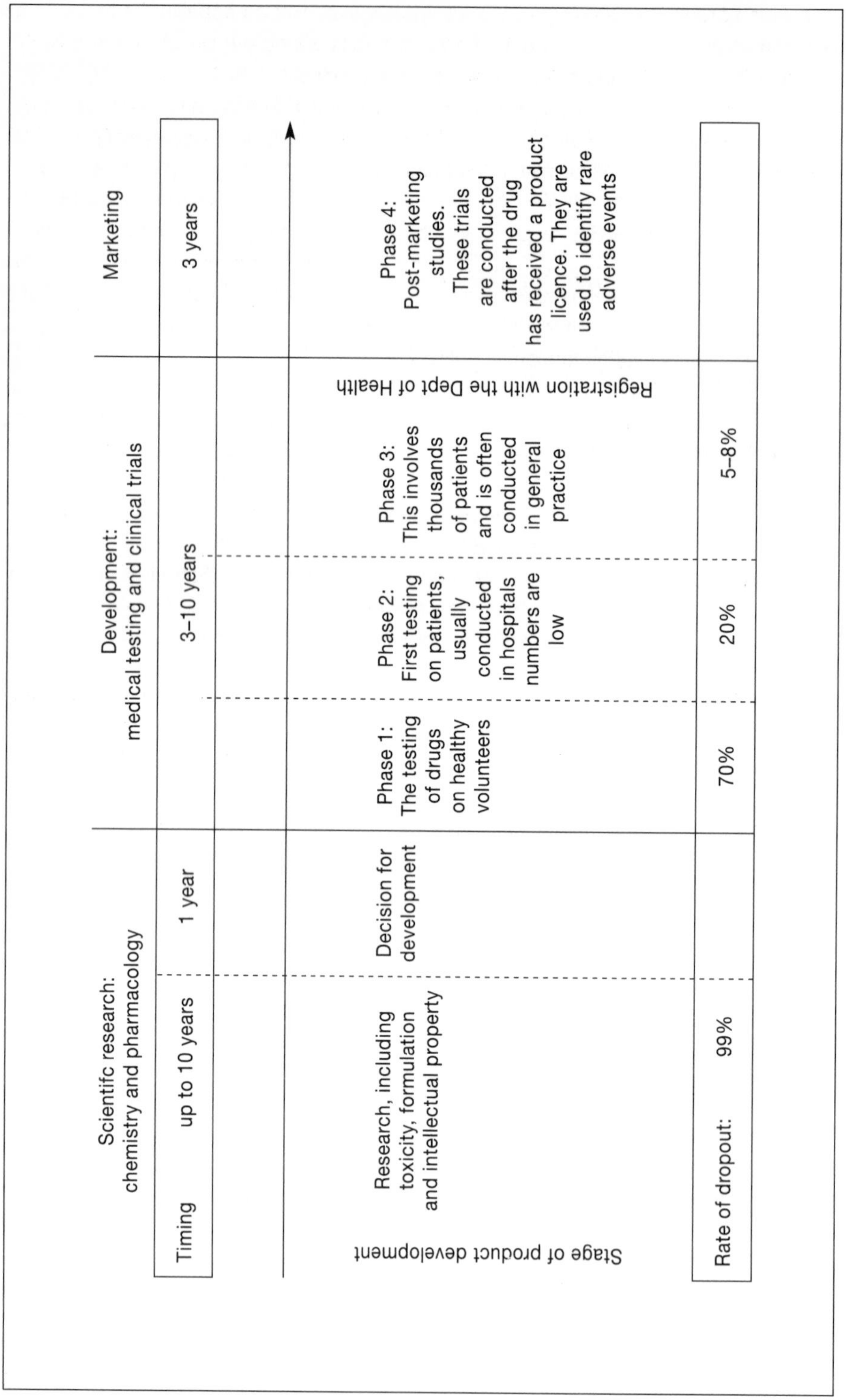

Figure 8.5 : The product development process in the pharmaceutical industry

Source: Jansen Cilag (1998)

making this activity even more important. The pie chart in Figure 8.6 shows a break-down of the main areas of R&D expenditure in the pharmaceutical industry. Experimental research, which includes clinical trials, consumes a large portion of the total funds. Those drug formulations that show promising results are put forward for development and clinical trials. The decision to undertake clinical trials on a potential drug is a critical one because of the high costs associated with these trials.

Clinical research

The testing of drug formulations on humans is referred to as clinical trials. Within the pharmaceutical industry this is the largest area of R&D expenditure, representing 41 per cent of the total (see Figure 8.6). This new product development activity is unique to the pharmaceutical industry. Clinical trials follow four distinct phases.

■ *Phase 1 clinical trials* – Phase 1 is the testing of developed drugs on healthy human volunteers. This attempts to establish how the human body handles the new drug and what toxic effects, if any, are experienced. These trials are invariably placebo controlled and involve small numbers of healthy volunteers. These trials are conducted within hospitals and volunteers are often young men, traditionally medical students.
■ *Phase 2 clinical trials* – In Phase 2 the drug is tested on patients for the first time. Once again, these trials will usually be conducted in hospitals but will possibly involve a few hundred patients. The objective here is to discover optimum dosage and effects on actual patients.
■ *Phase 3 clinical trials* – Phase 3 trials involve thousands of patients and are very expensive. Due to the number of patients required, many of these trials are conducted in general practice. These trials, and the administration of the drug in particular, will be conducted under the same conditions as would exist once the drug has been marketed.
■ *Phase 4 clinical trials* – Phase 4 trials are conducted after the drug has received a product licence and has been marketed. Such trials usually involve large post-marketing studies (PMS) to identify rare adverse events.

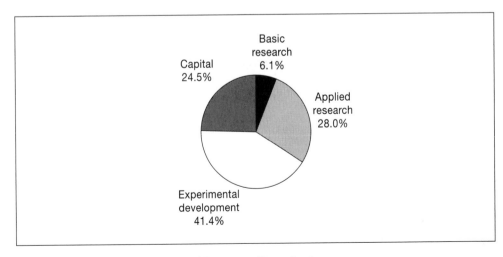

Figure 8.6 : Pharmaceutical R&D expenditure by type

Source: ABPI (1993)

▶ At the heart of clinical trials is either a general practitioner or a consultant in a hospital. These people are referred to as clinical research investigators and are responsible for the investigation of new treatments in patients. Early investigations are normally conducted in teaching hospitals. Later studies (Phases 2 and 3) involving larger numbers are frequently conducted in district or general hospitals. Pharmaceutical companies developing new drugs have to find investigators to conduct clinical trials on their behalf. Clinical research associates can identify possible investigators and set up clinical trials.

Clinical research associates

Clinical research associates (CRA), sometimes called clinical trial co-ordinators or scientists, are science graduates (usually in chemistry or pharmacology) often with a PhD and with several years of training within the pharmaceutical industry. Their role involves meeting senior doctors and research scientists. They need to have good interpersonal skills plus skills in analysing scientific results and statistics. A high proportion are female. In the pharmaceutical industry it is common to have senior CRAs managing a small team of CRAs, according to either geographic region or therapeutic group.

The *raison d'être* of the CRA is to co-ordinate the trial of new drugs. This involves designing the study and preparing the protocol (the design document for the research trial including methodology) and case record forms. CRAs usually select suitable investigators and organise trial supplies of the drug from the pharmaceutical company via the hospital pharmacist. They also negotiate payment for all aspects of the clinical trial. Once the trial is under way the CRA will regularly visit the investigator to discuss its development. Particular attention has to be given to the patients, because frequently it emerges later that patients had taken another drug during the trial (this is often an over-the-counter drug taken innocently at home). This, however, would clearly exclude them from the trial results.

Another major activity of the CRA is to ensure that the trial runs to schedule. Finding patients suitable for a trial is often problematic. Also many clinical research investigators fail to deliver on time, sometimes for justifiable reasons. And frequently the number of patients excluded from a trial, for example due to concomitant medication, will mean that the trial has to be repeated.

Once the clinical trial is complete and the case record forms (CRF) have been filled in, these then have to be analysed with all other trial documentation. This analysis should enable conclusions to be drawn about the drug under investigation. Examples would be: Drug A works better than Drug B, or Drug D and Drug F are equally effective but Drug H causes the following side effects, or Drug T is no better than a placebo or showed no benefit to the patients treated.

Almost all clinical investigators will be very keen to publish the results of any study with which they have been involved. Usually the pharmaceutical company would also be keen to publicise results. This may depend on intellectual property rights issues. Many large pharmaceutical companies favour the idea of a small conference to discuss the development of a new drug. The CRA will have a significant role to play in such an event.

Discussion

In order to perform the necessary clinical trials, the AIDS vaccine under development is clearly going to need healthy human volunteers. At first sight, this may seem like an impossible task. However, so many people have lost loved ones and so many families have been affected by this terrible disease that there are people willing to volunteer. Also further research may enable far safer trials to be established.

The rising cost of healthcare means that pharmaceutical companies are being forced to demonstrate that their new drugs are good value for money. It is therefore important for the results of the clinical trials to show not only that the drugs are not harmful, but also that they are significantly better than existing drugs.

Chapter summary

This chapter has focused on the key activities of R&D management. It has shown that these have changed significantly over the past few decades. Emphasis has traditionally been placed on internal R&D, but now there is an increase in the use of external R&D. This presents another set of challenges. In particular, when acquiring externally developed technology, a business must also consider the extent of control over the technology that it requires. The need to provide scientific freedom for R&D personnel and the benefits that this brings were also considered.

R&D plays a considerable role in the product innovation process. Indeed, there is often continual interaction with R&D throughout the development of the product. Finally, the chapter considered the various ways of funding the R&D activity. The approach adopted will significantly affect the way R&D is perceived within and outside the company.

Questions for discussion

1 Highlight the salient points in the ethical dilemma for pharmaceutical companies that are highlighted in the clinical trials case.

2 Explain why managing an R&D function in 1998 would be different from managing an R&D function in 1978.

3 Discuss the strengths and limitations of undertaking external R&D.

4 What is meant by scientific freedom and why is it important?

5 Explain why the degree of control needed over a firm's technology may vary depending on the technology concerned.

6 Discuss the variety of ways of funding R&D.

7 Explain why many product managers do not view an investment in R&D as a high-risk activity.

8 Discuss the unique nature of new product development in the pharmaceutical industry and the role played by the CRA.

References

Abelson, P.H. (1995) 'Science and technology policy', *Science*, 267 (27).

ABPI (1993) *Pharma Facts and Figures*, The Association of the British Pharmaceutical Industry, London.

Albertini, S. and Butler, J. (1995) 'R&D networking in a pharmaceuticals company', *R&D Management*, 25 (4), 377–93.

Auster, E.R. (1987) 'International corporate linkages: dynamic forms in changing environments', *Columbia Journal of World Business*, 22.

Chesnais, F. (1988) 'Multinational enterprises and the international diffusion of technology', in Dosi, G., Freeman, C., Nelson, R., Silverberg, G., and Soete, L. (eds), *Technical Change and Economic Theory*, Pinter, London.

Chiesa, V. and Masella, C. (1996) 'Searching for an effective measure of performance', *Management Decision*, 34 (7), December, 49–58.

Cordero, R. (1990) 'The measurement of innovation performance in the firm: an overview', *Research Policy*, 19 (2), April.

Corey, E.R. (1997) *Technology Fountainheads: The Management Challenge of R&D consortia*, Ziff-Davis/Harvard Business School Press, Boston, MA.

Dobson (1997) 'A little miracle', *Sunday Times* Magazine, October 16, 36.

DTI (1997) *UK R&D Scoreboard 1996*, HMSO, Norwich.

Financial Times (1998) 'Pilkington hit hard by restructuring', June 5.

Granstrand, O., Bohlin, E., Oskarsson, C. and Sjoberg, N. (1992) 'External technology acquisition in large multi-technology corporations', *R&D Management*, 22 (2), 111–33.

Hagedoorn, J. (1990) 'Organisational modes of inter-firm co-operation and technology transfer', *Technovation*, 10 (1), 17–30.

Jansen Cilag (1998) Discussions with CRA employed by Jansen Cilag.

Kastrinos. N. and Miles, I. (1995) 'Knowledge base, technology, strategy and innovation in environmental services firms', paper presented at R&D Management Conference, September 20–22, *Knowledge, Technololgy and Innovative Organisations*, Pisa, Italy.

Kreiner, K. and Schultz, M. (1990) 'Crossing the institutional divide: networking in biotechnology', paper for the tenth International Conference *Strategic Bridging to meet the Challenge of the 90s*, Strategic Management Society, Stockholm, September 24–27.

Lefever, D.B. (1992) 'Technology transfer and the role of intermediaries', PhD thesis, INTA, Cranfield Institute of Technology.

Lockheed Martin Corporation (1998) WWW page: (http://www.lmsw.external.lmco.com/lmsw/html/index.html).

Mansfield, E. *et al.* (1972) *Research and Innovation in the Modern Corporation*, Macmillan.

McGrath, M.E. and Romeri, M.N. (1994) 'The R&D effectiveness index', *Journal of Product Innovation Management*, 213–20.

Meyer-Krahmer, F. (1984) 'Recent results in measuring innovation output', *Research Policy*, 13 (3), June.

Pavitt, K. (1984) 'Sectoral patterns of technological change: towards a taxonomy and theory', *Research Policy*, 13, 343–73.

Pavitt, K. (1990) 'What we know about the strategic management of technology', *California Management Review*, Spring 17–26.

Powell, W.W. (1996) 'Trust based forms of governance', in Kramer, R.M. and Tyler, T.R., (eds) *Trust in Organisations*, Sage, London.

Rhea, J. (1991) 'New directions for industrial R&D consortia', *Research Technology Management*, September–October, 16–19.

Rothwell, R. and Dodgson, M. (1991) 'External linkages and innovation in small and medium-sized enterprises', *R&D Management*, 21 (2), 125–36.

Rothwell, R. and Zegveld, W. (1985) *Reindustrialisation and Technology*, Longman, London.

Sarler, F. (1997) 'Dance with death', *Sunday Times* magazine, December 11, 38–44.

Seaton, R.A.F. and Cordey-Hayes, M. (1993) 'The development and application of interactive models of technology transfer', *Technovation*, 13 (1), 45–53.

Trott, P. (1993) 'Inward technology transfer as an interactive process: a case study of ICI', PhD thesis, Innovation and Technology Assessment Centre, Cranfield University.

Trott, P. and Cordey-Hayes, M. (1996) 'Developing a "receptive" environment for inward technology transfer: a case study of the chemical industry', *R&D Management*, 26 (1), 83–92.

Twiss, B. (1992) *Managing Technological Innovation*, 4th edn, Financial Times Pitman Publishing, London.

Williams, D.J. (1969) 'A study of a decision model for R&D project selection', *Operational Research Quarterly*, 20, September.

Further reading

Pavitt, K. (1990) 'What we know about the strategic management of technology', *California Management Review*, Spring, 17–26.

Roussel, P.A., Saad, K.N. and Erickson, T.J. (1991) *Third Generation R&D*, Harvard Business School Press, Boston, MA.

Tidd, J., Bessant J. and Pavitt, K. (1997) *Managing Innovation*, John Wiley & Sons, Chichester.

Twiss, B. (1992) *Managing Technological Innovation*, 4th edn, Financial Times Pitman Publishing, London.

9

The role of technology transfer in innovation

Introduction

Information is central to the operation of firms. It is the stimulus for knowledge, knowhow, skills and expertise and is one of the key drivers of the innovation process. Most firms are involved with a two-way flow of technology. Those companies that spend the most on R&D are also some of the biggest licensors of technology; and dynamic, innovative firms are likely to buy in more technology than their static counterparts. This chapter examines the complex subject of technology transfer. It explores its role in the innovation process and its influence on organisational learning.

Learning objectives

When you have completed this chapter, you will be able to:

- Recognise the importance of the concept of technology transfer with respect to innovation management
- Provide a summary of the process of technology transfer
- Examine the various models of technology transfer
- Assess the importance of internal organisational factors and how they affect inward technology transfer
- Explain why a 'receptive' environment is necessary for technology transfer
- Identify the different barriers to technology transfer
- Recognise how tacit knowledge links technology transfer and innovation.

Background

The industrialised world has seen a shift from labour- and capital-intensive industries to knowledge- and technology-based economies. As competition has increased in markets throughout the world, technology has emerged as a significant business factor and a primary commodity. Knowledge transformed into knowhow or technology has become a major asset within companies. Technology is vital for a business to remain competitive. In rapidly evolving markets such as electronics and biotechnology, new products based on new technology are essential. Even in mature markets, new technology is necessary to remain competitive on cost and quality.

In the 1960s, 1970s and 1980s many businesses favoured the internal development of technology. But today, with the increasing technological content of many products, many organisations consider internal development too uncertain, too expensive and too slow for the rapid technological changes that are occurring in the market. These drawbacks can be traced to a more fundamental cause; that is, the increasing complexity of technologies and the increasing range of technologies found within products. This has led to a shortening of product life cycles with replacement technologies rapidly succeeding others. The rising costs of conducting R&D have forced many organisations to look for research partners. In addition, companies are finding it increasingly difficult to sustain R&D capability over all areas of their business as the complexity of these areas increases. Internal R&D is increasingly focused on core competencies (*see* Hamel and Prahalad, 1990). R&D in all other business activities is progressively covered by collaborations, partnerships and strategic alliances. While the activity is not new – Alfred Marshal noted the extensive linkages between firms in his work in 1919 (CEST, 1991) – the extent of collaboration appears to be on the increase. Hagedoorn (1990), for example, has shown a marked rise in the amount of collaboration between firms during the 1980s and 1990s.

Many large firms operate in several technology fields and are often referred to as multitechnology corporations (MTC). It is extremely difficult and expensive for such corporations to be technological leaders in every technology within their scope. More and more companies are looking for outside sources of either basic technology to shorten product development time, or applied technology to avoid the costs and delay of research and development. In addition, avoiding 're-inventing the wheel' appears to be high on the list of corporate objectives. Previously, there was one well-known exception to this and that was where a competitor was undertaking similar research. Under these circumstances duplication of research was regarded as inevitable and thus acceptable. However, numerous recent technological collaborations between known competitors, for example IBM and Apple, General Motors and BMW, would suggest that even this exception is becoming less acceptable to industry.

The search for, acquisition and exploitation of developed technology is clearly of interest to virtually all sectors of industry, but it is of particular interest to R&D-intensive or science-based industries. A recent US government study on technology transfer stated: 'Corporations trade in technology in world markets just as they do in other goods and services'.

The dominant economic perspective

It was in the 1980s that governments around the world began to recognise the potential opportunities that technology transfer could bring. This was based on a simple economic theory. Technology which has already been produced, and hence paid for by someone else, could be used and exploited by other companies to generate revenue and thereby economic growth for the economy (*see* Figure 9.1).

It was with this theory in mind that governments began encouraging companies to be involved in technology transfer. They set up a whole variety of programmes trying to utilise technology that had been developed for the defence or space industries (*see* the later section on models of technology transfer). They also encouraged companies to work together to see if they could share technology for the common good. An example of this was the establishment of Regional Technology Centres (RTC) in the late 1980s around the UK to serve the various regions. It was even suggested by some commentators that technology transfer could solve the serious problem of the US national debt. In response to this impetus, companies set up their own internal technology transfer departments to try to seek out technology that might be worth exploiting. There were many reports of companies visiting university laboratories and government research establishments in an effort to find useful technology. Moreover, the subject of technology transfer began to receive attention from many different quarters. If you were to get the chance to key in the words technology transfer into a database of management and science journal abstracts, you would be amazed at the high number of articles that contain these words in their title. Many of these articles were written in the late 1980s.

The alleged panacea for industry's problems did not materialise. Looking back, some still argue that it was a commendable theory, it just did not seem to work in practice. Others argue that the theory was flawed and would never work in practice (Seaton and Cordey-Hayes, 1993); this will be discussed later in the section on limitations of and barriers to technology transfer. There were, however, many benefits that emerged from the energetic interest in technology transfer. One of them was the realisation that successful collaboration and joint ventures could be achieved even with competitors.

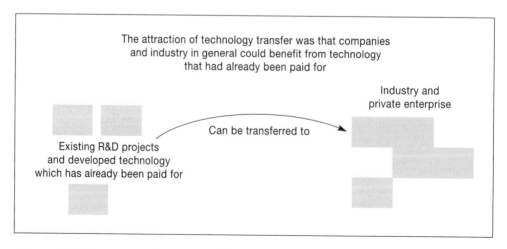

Figure 9.1: The economic perspective of technology transfer

Introduction to technology transfer

The concept of technology transfer is not new. In the thirteenth century Marco Polo helped introduce to the Western world Chinese inventions such as the compass, papermaking, printing and the use of coal for fuel. In more recent years, the concept has generated an enormous amount of debate. Many argue that it was a change in US law which led to the surge of interest in the subject. The passage of the landmark National Co-operative Research Act (NCRA) of 1984 officially made co-operation on pre-competitive research legal. This certainly helped raise the profile of the concept of technology transfer (Werner, 1991).

> **Technology Transfer is the application of technology to a new use or user. It is the process by which technology developed for one purpose is employed either in a different application or by a new user. The activity principally involves the increased utilisation of the existing science/technology base in new areas of application as opposed to its expansion by means of further research and development.** *Langrish et al. (1982)*

One of the main problems of research into technology transfer is that over the years the term has been used to describe almost any movement of technology from one place to another, to the ridiculous point where the purchase of a car could be classified as an example of technology transfer. It is true that the technology in question may take a variety of forms – it may be a product, a process, a piece of equipment, technical knowledge or expertise or merely a way of doing things. Further, technology transfer involves the movement of ideas, knowledge and information from one context to another. However, it is in the context of innovation that technology transfer is most appropriate and needs to be considered. Hence, technology transfer is defined as:

> **The process of promoting technical innovation through the transfer of ideas, knowledge, devices and artefacts from leading edge companies, R&D organisations and academic research to more general and effective application in industry and commerce.** *Seaton and Cordey-Hayes (1993)*

Information transfer and technology transfer

It was suggested at the beginning of this chapter that information is central to the operation of firms and that it is the stimulus for knowledge, knowhow, skills and expertise. Figure 9.2 helps distinguish information from knowledge and knowhow according to its context. It is argued that it is the industrial context which transforms knowledge into action, in the form of projects and activities. It is only when information is used by individuals or organisations that it becomes knowledge, albeit tacit knowledge. The application of this knowledge then leads to actions and skills (projects, processes, products, etc.). Consider the example of Pilkington's float glass.

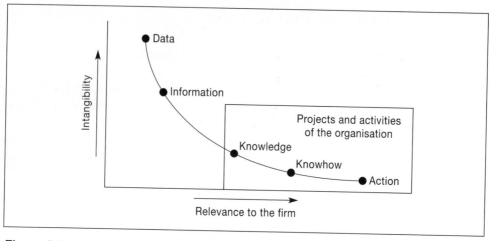

Figure 9.2 : The tangibility of knowledge

Source: adapted from Cooley (1987)

Pilkington, information and knowledge

Materials have different melting points; for example glass is molten at 1500°C whereas tin is molten at 180°C. On its own, this is information that can be found in most metallurgy books. Provide an industrial context and the information is transformed into knowledge, knowhow and expertise.

Pilkington pioneered the manufacturing process of 'float glass'. This essentially involves heating sand to 1500°C and forcing it out through rollers and over a pool of molten tin to cool prior to being cut to size. This patented process is now universally used by every glass manufacturer in the world. Pilkington developed the process in the 1950s and 1960s and then licensed it to every glass manufacturer in the world. For an entire year, however, the pilot plant had produced nothing but scrap glass. After many operating difficulties, production engineers eventually succeeded in getting the process to work. The company made so much money out of licensing the process that it was able to purchase what was at that time the largest glass manufacturer in the world.

Models of technology transfer

A wide variety of models of technology transfer have been used over the years, particularly in the past 20 years Dorf (1998). The following section examines some of these models and offers examples of their application.

Licensing

Essentially, licensing involves the technology owner receiving a licence fee in return for access to the technology. Very often the technology in question will be protected by patents. The details of each licensing agreement will vary considerably. Sometimes the licensor will help the licensee in all aspects of development and final use of the technology. In other cases, the amount of involvement is minimal.

Mutual self-interest is the common dominator behind most licensing contracts, as it is in other business contracts. Licensing is the act of granting another business permission to use your intellectual property. This could be a manufacturing process which is protected by patents or a product or service which is protected by a trademark or copyright. Licensing is the main income generator for BTG, a FTSE 100 listed company. It helps businesses and universities generate income from their intellectual property through the licensing of technology to third parties.

Licences to competitors constitute a high percentage of all licences extended; Microsoft's disc-operating system (MS-DOS) is a case in point. These normally arise out of a desire on the part of the competitor to be free of any patent infringement in its development product features or technology. They are also due to the owner of the patent seeking financial gain from the technology.

The licensee must be careful to evaluate the need for and the benefits likely to accrue from the technology before making the commitment to pay. Technology which is only marginally useful, or which may be quickly superseded by new developments in the field, may not be worth a multimillion-dollar licensing agreement. Many companies with sufficient R&D resources believe that patents can be legally breached through creative use of technology. This point is well made in the Guinness case study at the end of Chapter 6. All the other brewers were eventually able to develop their own in-can technology.

Other reasons for licensing are (Rothberg, 1976):

- to avoid or settle patent infringement issues
- to diversify and grow through the addition of new products
- to improve the design and quality of existing products
- to obtain improved production or processing technology
- to ensure freedom of action in the company's own R&D programme (patents held by other companies may inhibit R&D activities)
- to save R&D expense and delay
- to eliminate the uncertainty and risk involved in developing alternative processes and technology
- to accommodate customer needs or wishes
- to qualify for government and other desirable contracts.

Science park model

Science parks are a phenomenon that originated in the US. The idea is to develop an industrial area or district close to an established centre of excellence, often a university. The underlying rationale is that academic scientists will have the opportunity to take laboratory ideas and develop them into real products. In addition, technology- or science-based companies can set up close to the university so that they can utilise its knowledge base. In the US, where science parks have existed for 40 years, the achievements have been difficult to quantify. Examples are Silicon Valley, a collection of companies with research activities in electronics, and the 'research triangle' in North Carolina, which has several universities at its core. In the UK, one of the first science parks to be established was the Cambridge Science Park. Over the past 20 years, this has grown into a large industrial area and has attracted many successful science-based companies. Many other universities have also set up their own science parks, such as Southampton, Warwick and Cranfield. It is worth noting that the science park notion separates the innovation process: the R&D is conducted at the science park but manufacturing is done elsewhere (Dabinett, 1995).

Intermediary agency model

These come in a variety of forms and ranged from Regional Technology Centres (RTC) to university technology transfer managers. Their role, however, is the same: they act as the intermediary between companies seeking and companies offering technology.

Directory model

During the explosion of interest in technology transfer during the 1980s, many new companies sprang up in an attempt to exploit interest in the subject. Companies such as Derwent World Patents, Technology Exchange, NIMTECH and Technology Catalysts offered directories listing technology that was available for licence. Some universities in the US also produced directories of technology available from the university's own research laboratories. (For an example of the type and range of patents available, *see* Derwent World Patents: http://www.patentexplorer.com/). The case study at the end of this chapter explores the role of an intermediary (NIMTECH) in helping to provide technology for a small manufacturing company.

Teaching Company Scheme model

This UK Research Council funded programme aims to transfer technology between universities and small companies. This is achieved through postgraduate training. Students registering for a two-year MSc at a university are linked to a local company-based research project. The student studies part time for two years with the university, say two days a week, and the other three days are spent at the company working on the project. The university provides support to the student and offers other expertise to the company. These programmes continue to be very successful.

Ferret model

The Ferret model was first used by Defence Technology Enterprises (DTE). DTE resulted from a joint initiative between the UK Ministry of Defence (MOD) and a consortium of companies experienced in encouraging, exploiting and financing new technology. The *raison d'être* of DTE was to provide access to MOD technology and generate commercial revenue. This was achieved through the use of so called 'ferrets', qualified scientists and engineers who would ferret around for interesting defence technology that could have wider commercial opportunities. The company ceased trading in 1989.

Hiring skilled employees

One of the oldest methods of technology transfer, and one of the most effective according to many research managers, is hiring people with the necessary skills and knowledge. For R&D managers who wish to establish a range of research projects in an area of technology where the company has limited knowledge or experience, this is one of the fastest methods of gaining the necessary technology. People are either recruited from other organisations, including competitors, or from university research departments that have relevant expertise. These people will bring to the organisation their own knowledge, and the ways of working and methods used by their previous organisation – some of which may be replicable, others may not. The role of individual and organisational learning is explored towards the end of this chapter.

Technology transfer units

In the 1980s the US Federal Labs and other research-based organisations, including universities, established industrial liaison units and technology transfer units to bring in technology from outside and/or to find partners to help exploit in-house developments. In the US, academia has always been subject to financial pressures to generate funds. In Europe, however, universities have traditionally relied on government to fund their needs. With an ever-decreasing pool of resources, universities have recognised the potential benefits from exploiting in-house technology. This has also led to the growth in science parks. Technology transfer units use elements of the intermediary and licensing models.

One of the most successful examples of this approach is the British Technology Group (BTG), a state-owned corporation that was set up to commercialise as much state-funded research as possible, including that undertaken by universities. It was previously known as the National Research Development Corporation. It became so successful and profitable that in 1993 BTG was sold to private investors and it is now operating as a successful public limited company with a FTSE 100 listing. Its main activities are the licensing of new scientific and engineering products to industry and providing finance for the development of new technology (*see* www.btg.co.uk).

Research clubs

This is a UK Department of Trade and Industry (DTI) funded programme which tries to bring companies together with common interests in particular research areas. Some conduct collaborative research, others exchange information, knowledge and/or experience. This approach adopts the science park model of technology transfer. One of the most successful clubs is the M62 Sensors and Instrumentation Research Club, so called because it originated from a group of companies along the M62 motorway in the North West of England.

European Space Agency (ESA)

The ESA offers access to space research in virtually all fields of science and technology. This is achieved using a combination of three models: the intermediary agency model, the directory model and the Ferret model (*see Financial Times* article below).

Science brought down to earth

Miranda Eadie on a programme to promote terrestrial uses of innovations developed for space missions

For two decades, space technology has provided innovative technical solutions to everyday problems as well as making glamorous space exploration missions possible. The European Space Agency (ESA) has realised, however, that many more earth-based uses for space technology could be found in fields such as medicine, electronics, communications, energy and materials science.

Everyday examples of space technology transfer – the process of applying innovations developed for particular space missions for earth-based use – include the anti-scratch protective layer on plastic contact lenses, air-filled soles of high-tech running shoes, aluminium foil, digital clocks and microwave ovens.

Although technology transfer has occurred informally in space research for several years, many potential terrestrial applications remain unexploited. Lack of time and tunnel vision on the part of research engineers, are two of the main reasons for this.

ESA therefore initiated a technology transfer programme in October 1991, with the aim of identifying space technologies that might have civil or commercial applications, and encouraging their transfer.

The initiative is run by Spacelink Europe, a consortium of technology brokers from the UK (JRA Aerospace),

France (Novespace), Germany (MST Aerospace) and Italy (D'Appolonia).

Spacelink scouts ESA contractors for possible transfers, catalogues the ideas, contacts non-space companies which may be interested, and eventually negotiates a deal and takes care of inquiries.

The Spacelink catalogue, featuring the space technologies available for exploitation, is called Test (Transferable European Space Technologies) and is published annually. The latest edition, Test 3, contains 60 technologies in many fields, such as optics, sensors, communications, life sciences and robotics. Including the earlier catalogues, there are 170 technologies on offer.

Spacelink's objective is for non-space companies to sign a licensing agreement or form a joint venture with the "owner" of the technology. This is either the ESA contractor, ESA itself or shared between the two. The technology may be protected by a patent, but this is not always necessary to license the technology.

Although one of the original goals of the programme was for it to become self-financing, through licensing and technology transfer services, its main aim is not economic benefit but to show that space is not just for sending rockets but can have applications on earth.

Anna Marie Hieronimus-Leuba, head of ESA's space commercialisation office, say that it is "more concerned with showing that investment in space is paying dividends in terms of terrestrial applications, and that it is not just about sending beautiful objects into space."

The ESA also hopes the programme will increase each of the member states' financial return and share in the technology spin-off. It is an ESA policy that each accounting unit paid by a member state into the agency budget awarding industrial contracts should eventually flow back to that member state.

The direct terrestrial applications of space research (weather forecasting, communications via satellites, satellite television, etc.) are more evident than the indirect ones, or spin-offs, which do appear in nearly all fields of science and technology; lucid image processing software, developed for use in remote sensing, has applications in the security forces in number plate detection, face recognition and fingerprint analysis, Aerocoat fire protection materials, developed to protect equipment on the Ariane space rocket from very high local temperatures generated during the launch phase are now used to protect sensitive equipment in trains for the Channel tunnel link; human waste management systems, developed for use in space, are now being considered for hospital clean rooms, where hygiene is also a priority; Cream (Cosmic Radiation Effects and Activation Monitor), developed for the Nasa Space Shuttle has been adapted for high flying aircraft and fitted to Concorde; and Radfets, miniature real-time radiation dosimeters used to monitor background radiation on ESA spacecraft, are being developed to measure radiation doses during cancer treatment.

"Technology transfer is a very slow process and financial return cannot be expected in less than four years," says John Rootes, managing director of JRA

Aerospace. "There is a time delay of about a year and a half between the initial contact with a technology, the definition of the licensing agreement and the signing of a contract. A further two years is then needed for the adaptation, testing and fabrication of the technology."

Although the process is traditionally slow, the programme has advanced more rapidly than expected. When it began, the goal was to secure six transfers in the first three years.

The fact that nine have already been agreed (and that there are many more in the pipeline) indicates great prospects for the programme. The rapidity of these transfers can, in part, be explained by the fact that 40 per cent of them have occurred in the field of software engineering where transfer modifications are minimal.

ESA invested £2m in the programme at its conception. The majority of this is used to pay the members of Spacelink to run the programme but, occasionally, if a transfer looks interesting and there is a shortage of finance to carry it out, ESA may offer some financial support.

This was the case at the Brunel Institute of Bioengineering, where shape memory alloys, originally used to make linear actuators for a space bioprocessing facility, showed prospects in medicine as "staples" to mend broken bones.

The institute received £12,000 from ESA to develop these staples, and general advice was given with regard to the technology transfer. Financial support was also gained by AEA Technology after the huge interest shown in its solid lubricants which appeared in Test 1: £5,600 was donated to help pay for a short study into possible terrestrial applications.

Tony Anson, the research engineer at Brunel, is an "enthusiast" of the programme. He says that besides the

▶

233

programme being an encouraging initiative, the financial support is "extremely welcome in a country like the UK where the government does not have a particularly philanthropic approach towards research and where there is a dire shortage of funding." He believes he has a dozen or so technologies which could realistically have a considerable impact in the medical field, if only he could find the money to exploit them.

One of these is the use of shape memory alloys as a prosthesis for hole in the heart. Other transfers which have taken place as a result of the programme include: high stiffness composites developed by Dornier to build space structures for the Rosat X-ray satellite, which are now used for ground-based telescope reflectors and for large screens needed for training systems; ESA's software standards, which have been adopted by many space and non-space companies and which are

about to be published by Prentice Hall for worldwide distribution; and image processing software, developed to analyse astronomical images, such as those from Hubble, licensed by Photek for possible application in an image intensification camera.

This camera, which contains a Swedish optical chip, again identified through the programme, could be used for research into arthritis and cancer. The latter examples demonstrate the range of applications for space technology and highlight how separate European initiatives can combine for common good.

ESA ultimately hopes that space industries themselves will strive to identify potential technology transfers as early as possible in the R&D stage. Such lateral thinking should lead to joint development schemes and more marketable products.

Source: *Financial Times*, March 15 1994

Consultancy

This area has experienced rapid growth from a non-existent base in the early 1980s to a multibillion-dollar industry in the 1990s. Although it is management consultancy groups who receive a great deal of attention from the business sections of the quality press, it is the lesser-known technology consultants that have been used and continue to be used by many science-based organisations. Very often they were formerly employed in a research capacity within a large organisation. After developing their knowledge and skills in a particular area of science, they offer their unique skills to the wider industry. R&D research groups within large organisations will often contact several consultants prior to establishing a research project in a particular field related to the consultant's area of expertise. Consultants are able to offer help, advice and useful contacts to get the research project off to a flying start. Frequently they will remain part of the research group during the early years of the project. This is a very popular method of technology transfer and essentially adopts the hiring skilled employees model.

Limitations and barriers to technology transfer

The management of technology transfer has not been entirely straightforward, as is demonstrated in the range of technology transfer mechanisms that have been developed over the last 20 years or so. Research into technology transfer suggests that this is because emphasis has been on providing information about access to technology (Seaton and Cordey-Hayes, 1993). While the provision of technical ideas is a necessary part of technology transfer, it is only one component of a more complex process. Research at the Innovation and Technology Assessment Unit, Cranfield University, over the past 10 years has led to the development of a comprehensive conceptual framework that has helped develop understanding of the complex nature of inward technology transfer and knowledge accumulation.

The conceptual framework, shown in Figure 9.3, views technology transfer and inward technology transfer as a series of complex interactive processes as opposed to a simple decision process. It breaks down the transfer process into a series of sub-processes. The initial framework was developed following a study of the role of intermediaries in the technology transfer process. A mismatch was identified between the needs of potential innovators and the activities of information-centred technology transfer intermediaries (Lefever, 1992). This deficiency was illuminated through the use of the conceptual framework: Accessibility–Mobility–Receptivity (AMR). The research revealed that while much effort appeared to have been directed at providing access to technology, little effort had been aimed at understanding the needs of organisations acquiring technology developed outside the organisation. An organisation's overall ability to be aware of, to identify and to take effective advantage of technology is referred to as 'receptivity'.

The original framework has since been developed further to show the elements which constitute the inward transfer of technology from the viewpoint of the receiving organisation. Figure 9.3 breaks down the receptivity element into four further components. This has provided a useful theoretical framework from which to analyse the notion of technology and knowledge transfer. It is important, however, to understand that this overarching conceptual framework, has limitations as a concept. These limitations are a consequence of the fact that, while it expresses the nature of the

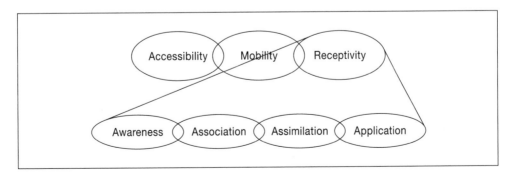

Figure 9.3 : Conceptual framework of technology transfer and inward technology transfer

internal organisational processes and identifies a number of key areas that constitute such processes, it does not itself operationalise these processes. Hence, it functions as a vantage point from which to explore the issues involved.

Subsequent research has uncovered the nature of some of the internal processes of inward technology transfer and has provided an insight into how they affect an organisation's ability to capture, assimilate and apply technology to commercial ends (Trott and Cordey-Hayes, 1996). Research by Macdonald (1992) identified the difficulty of applying other people's technology and the need for this technology to be in such a form that the organisation can reap some benefit. This highlights the importance of viewing technology development as a combination of knowledge, skills and organisations (all embodied in 'organisational knowhow') rather than the economist's view of technology as an artefact to be bought and sold. Chapter 3 portrayed the notion of assimilation as an internal knowledge accumulation process, which offers an explanation of how organisations are able to use, manipulate and retain knowledge.

NIH syndrome

One of the best-known barriers to technology transfer is the not-invented-here (NIH) syndrome. This is defined as the tendency of a project group of stable composition to believe that it possesses the monopoly of knowledge in its field, leading it to reject new ideas from outsiders to the likely detriment of its performance (Katz and Allen, 1988). It is general folklore among R&D professionals that groups of scientists and engineers who have worked together for many years will begin to believe that no one else can know or understand the area in which they are working better than they do. In some cases this attitude can spread across the whole R&D function, so that the effect is a refusal to accept any new ideas from outside. This syndrome has been so widely discussed since it was first uncovered that, like many diseases, it has been virtually wiped out. R&D managers still need to be vigilant to ensure that it does not re-occur.

The next section addresses the issue of receptivity and, in particular, how an organisation's own internal activities affect its ability to transfer technology successfully.

Internal organisational factors and inward technology transfer

Danhof (1949) may be described as one of the first attempts to explore the inward technology transfer process. In his study of the adoption of innovations by industrial companies he identified four different types of company:

- Innovators: the first firm to adopt a new idea
- Initiators: the firms who adopted the idea soon after the innovators
- Fabians: the firms who adopted the idea only after its utility was widely acknowledged in the industry
- Drones: the last firms to adopt new ideas.

This study revealed that there was considerable difference in the responsiveness of organisations to take up externally developed technology. A similar conclusion was drawn by Kroonenberg (1989) following a study of 3000 firms in the Netherlands. He suggests that small and medium enterprises can be classified into one of three groups:

1 technology-driven SME

2 technology-following SME

3 technology-indifferent SME.

Both of these studies reveal clear distinctions between firms in either their ability or their willingness to adopt new technology. Establishing the precise nature of the activities that are required to ensure that organisations can either remain as innovators or become innovators has been the subject of numerous studies. Carter and Williams' (1959) study of technically progressive firms uncovered a number of shared characteristics within organisations that facilitate innovation. In a comprehensive review of the technology transfer literature, Godkin (1988) suggests that these same factors would foster technology transfer. The factors are shown below:

- High quality of incoming communication
- A readiness to look outside the firm
- A willingness to share knowledge
- A willingness to take on new knowledge, to license and to enter joint ventures
- Effective internal communication and co-ordination mechanisms
- A deliberate survey of potential ideas
- Use of management techniques
- An awareness of costs and profits in R&D departments
- Identification of the outcomes of investment decisions
- Good-quality intermediate management
- High status of science and technology on the board of directors
- High-quality chief executives
- A high rate of expansion.

Godkin's classification is one of the earliest studies, specifically on technology transfer, to recognise that the existence of certain activities within the recipient organisation is necessary for successful technology transfer. This point will be explored in detail in the following two sections.

Developing a receptive environment for technology transfer

As was shown above many of the traditional technology transfer mechanisms concentrate on providing access to technology, with little effort directed towards understanding the needs of organisations acquiring externally developed technology

(Seaton and Cordey-Hayes, 1993). The early literature on inward technology transfer centred on the ability of organisations to access technological knowledge (Gruber and Marquis, 1969) and their subsequent ability to disseminate this information effectively. Allen's work in the 1960s on the role of gatekeepers within organisations exemplifies this (*see* Allen 1966, 1977; Allen and Cohen, 1969). Seaton and Cordey-Hayes (1993) argue that there has been little thought and research aimed at the difficulties of exploiting externally developed technology. They suggest that this is because technology transfer has largely been seen in terms of providing access to technology. They emphasise the need to view technology transfer as a process.

An organisation's ability to develop new products that meet current market needs, to manufacture these products using the appropriate methods and to respond promptly to technology developments clearly involves more than technical capabilities. However, discussions concerning how organisations utilise their technological base tend to focus on R&D activities and other technical activities alone. Nelson (1991) argues that in industries where technological innovation is important, firms need more than a set of core capabilities in R&D. This point is discussed in detail in Chapter 3.

The notion of receptivity advocated by Seaton and Cordey-Hayes (1993) suggests that there are certain characteristics whose presence is necessary for inward technology transfer to occur. In a similar vein, but within an R&D context, Cohen and Levinthal (1990) put forward the notion of 'absorptive capacity'. In their study of the US manufacturing sector they reconceptualise the traditional role of R&D investment as merely a factor aimed at creating specific innovations. They see R&D expenditure as an investment in an organisation's absorptive capacity and argue that an organisation's ability to evaluate and utilise external knowledge is related to its prior knowledge and expertise and that this prior knowledge is, in turn, driven by prior R&D investment.

Seaton and Cordey-Hayes (1993) argue that inward technology transfer will only be successful if an organisation has not only the ability to acquire but also the ability effectively to assimilate and apply ideas, knowledge, devices and artefacts. Organisations will only respond to technological opportunity in terms of their own perceptions of its benefits and costs and in relation to their own needs and technical, organisational and human resources. The process view of inward technology transfer, therefore, is concerned with creating or raising the capability for innovation. This requires an organisation and the individuals within it to have the capability to:

- search and scan for information which is new to the organisation (awareness)
- recognise the potential benefit of this information by associating it with internal organisational needs and capabilities
- communicate these business opportunities to and assimilate them within the organisation
- apply them for competitive advantage.

These processes are captured in the following stages: Awareness, Association, Assimilation and Application. This four-stage conceptual framework (4A) is used to explore the processes involved in inward technology transfer (*see* Table 9.1).

Table 9.1 : 4A conceptual framework of technology transfer

Activity	Process
Awareness	Describes the processes by which an organisation scans for and discovers what information on technology is available
Association	Describes the processes by which an organisation recognises the value of this technology (ideas) for the organisation
Assimilation	Describes the processes by which the organisation communicates these ideas within the organisation and creates genuine business opportunities
Application	Describes the processes by which the organisation applies this technology for competitive advantage

Identifying external technology: the importance of scanning and networking

Scanning by individuals on behalf of the organisation is often regarded as an informal and unassigned activity. But in order for individuals to practise the process effectively, organisations must recognise its value (Trott, 1993). However, it is because organisations are unaware of its value that they do not provide support for the process. Research by Oakley *et al.* (1988) on the subject of the search for technical knowledge argues that small firms in particular do not recognise the importance of external technical contacts, suggesting that they do little if any technology scanning.

It has long been recognised that a key characteristic of technically progressive firms is the high quality of their incoming information. In 1959 Carter and Williams reported this in almost 200 firms over a wide range of industries. Many other studies have since demonstrated the importance of external information for successful innovation. For example, SPRU's Project SAPPHO confirmed the need for high-quality external linkages (Rothwell *et al.*, 1974); Peters and Waterman (1982); CEST (1991).

The process of searching for and acquiring technical information is a necessary activity for organisations in order to maintain their knowledge base (*see* Johnson and Jones, 1957). This can be effectively achieved by scanning the technological environment, either through the scientific literature or through interactions with other people (often called networking). Thus, innovation within firms is a process of knowhow accumulation based on a complementary mix of in-house R&D and R&D performed elsewhere, obtained via the process of technology scanning.

Each organisational research effort or technological activity represents a fraction of the world's total scientific and technological activity. Organisations are constantly surprised by the amount of technology around that they do not know about. Hence they must somehow ensure that their personnel are aware of technological developments performed elsewhere. During the 1960s and 1970s the question of how to keep personnel aware of technological developments was the subject of intense study (*see* Allen, 1966; Allen and Cohen, 1969; Allen, 1977; Tushman, 1977). Some interesting and useful concepts were developed that helped improve our understanding of the complex nature of how individuals within organisations acquire technological information. One of the most effective ways to capture this knowhow is through personal interaction (networking).

Figure 9.4 shows the wide variety of sources of information used by firms to help maintain their awareness of technological developments. Different industry sectors have different information requirements. It is self-evident that they produce different products using different technologies and face different market structures. Consequently, research by Bosworth and Stoneman (1996) have revealed that some sectors are extremely reliant on certain external sources of information. The chemical industry, for example, is a high user of scientific and academic journals.

Research at Aston University has also shown that organisations that do not possess boundary-spanning individuals (scanning) will be restricted in the degree to which the organisation becomes aware of and assess the relevance of innovations in the first place (Newell and Clark, 1990).

Given the importance of an awareness of external information and the role of technological scanning and networking, awareness is seen as the necessary first stage in the inward technology transfer process.

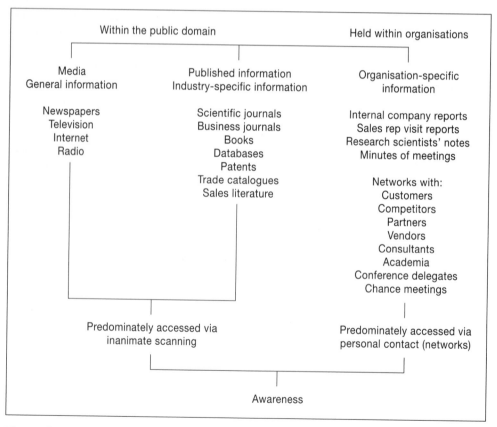

Figure 9.4 : Sources of information from scanning and networking

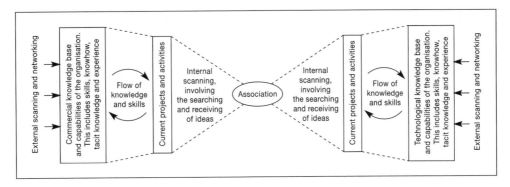

Figure 9.5 : Creating business opportunities through association: a conceptual framework for the development of genuine business opportunities

In order for an organisation to search and scan effectively for technology that will match its business opportunities, it needs to have a thorough understanding of its internal organisational capabilities. This can be effectively achieved via internal scanning and networking, which will enable it to become familiar with its internal activities. The coupling of internal technology scanning with external technology scanning activities can be seen in Figure 9.5. (*See* Trott (1998) for a more detailed explanation of the development of this model.)

Linking external technology to internal capabilities

External scanning without a full understanding of the organisation's capabilities and future requirements is likely to produce much 'noise' along with the 'signal'. 'Tuned scanning', achieved through the internal assimilation of an organisation's activities, as opposed to 'untuned scanning', will produce a higher 'signal-to-noise' ratio (Trott and Cordey-Hayes, 1996).

Inward technology transfer, however, involves more than identifying interesting technology; it is necessary to match technology with a market need in order to produce a potential opportunity for the business. The scanning process needs to incorporate commercial scanning as well as technology scanning so that technological opportunities may be matched with market needs (*see* Figure 9.5).

Such levels of awareness increase the probability of individuals being able to develop and create associations on behalf of the organisation between an internal opportunity and an external opportunity. This process of association is the second stage in inward technology transfer.

Chapter 3 emphasised the importance of recognising that the knowledge base of an organisation is not simply the sum of the individual knowledge bases. Nelson and Winter (1982) argue that such learning by doing is captured in organisational routines. It is these internal activities undertaken by an organisation that form the third stage in the process, assimilation.

Managing the inward transfer of technology

The final stage in the inward technology transfer process is the application of the business opportunity for competitive advantage. This is the stage where the organisation brings about commercial benefit from the launch of a new product or an improved product or manufacturing process. In science-based organisations a combination of credibility and respect, coupled with extensive informal and formal communications among individuals within the organisation, facilitates this process (referred to as an internal knowledge accumulation process). This is not to disregard totally the presence of external influences.

Even in science-based industries few companies are able to offer their researchers total scientific freedom, untouched by the demands of the market. R&D programmes are therefore focused on the business aspirations of the company and its future markets. These are usually set out using the most applicable technology. There is not a constant need for new ideas in technologies beyond these programmes – there are clearly resource limits on R&D departments (*see* Figure 9.6). Inevitably there will be crisis points, where the competition brings out something involving new technology. At these times, there is usually full management commitment and money is invariably made available to bring in new technology quickly to respond to the competition. Here the inward technology transfer processes (as illustrated in Figure 9.6) generally works well due to total commitment from all levels within the organisation.

Where technology is introduced on a more routine basis, a decision has to be made about spending money on a prototype or a demonstrator. The assimilation phase is usually dominated by who will put up the money to try out the new technology. This raises the question: what is the business need and who has the budget to address it and, moreover, do they have any money that can be diverted from something they are already doing to implement this new technology?

There is also an important distinction to be made here between science-based industries and other less capital-intensive industries. The vast majority of the businesses in the chemical industry, for example, operate and manage manufacturing processes which are highly capital intensive and the plant, when built, is designed to have a life of many years. The building of a new plant is future market dependent, it sets the need for inward technology transfer and is the catalyst to bringing in new technology. At these times, the businesses tend to be very receptive to new technology, particularly in the concept and design phase of new plant. There exists a window of opportunity for bringing in new, proven process technology. Internal R&D programmes are generally slightly in advance of this and are engaged in proving the technologies which will be applied in the plant. Without this proof and qualification they would not reach the final application stage. In other less capital intensive industries these circumscribed windows of opportunity are not so apparent; and opportunities may be more consistent.

Thus in addition to the internal processes illustrated in Figure 9.6, there are the inescapable external issues which, have been grouped together under the heading of 'external operating climate'. This model explains how internal processes affect an organisation's ability to engage in inward technology transfer and contribute to the development of a receptive environment.

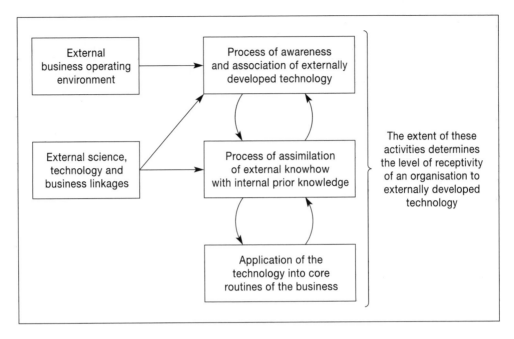

Figure 9.6 : The inward technology transfer process

Technology transfer and organisational learning

Several different pieces of research have identified a number of stages that form an inherent part of the knowledge transfer process (Trott and Cordey-Hayes 1996; Gilbert, 1996; Cordey-Hayes *et al.*, 1996). These must occur if the process of knowledge transfer and thus organisational learning is to be complete. While each organisation conducts its activities in different ways, members of that organisation soon adopt the company's way of operating. Organisational knowhow is captured in routines, such as particular ways of working. The relationship between knowledge transfer between individuals and groups and the whole organisation may be expressed as two interlinked systems, as in Figure 9.7.

In order for inward technology transfer to take place, members of the organisation must show an awareness of and a receptivity towards knowledge acquisition. Individual learning involves the continual search for new information of potential benefit to the organisation. This frequently challenges existing procedures. Individuals must be continually scanning the internal and external environments for relevant information that can be used to develop associations with internal knowledge. Over time these associations, coupled with additional internal knowledge, can lead to the creation of genuine business opportunities. Having created these opportunities the knowledge can be said to be assimilated at the individual and work group level (referred to in Figure 9.7 as the internal knowledge accumulation process). At this point the organisation has not accepted the change nor has it learnt: knowledge has not been transferred, it remains within the work group. However, the idea is implicitly accepted in its adoption by the individual/group.

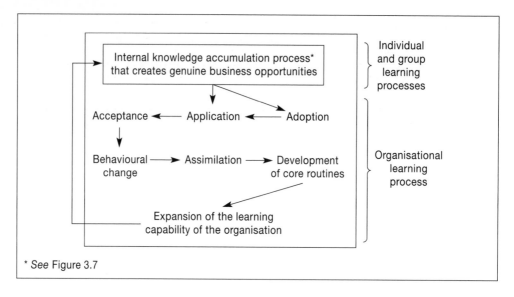

Figure 9.7 : Individual and organisational learning: integrated model of knowledge
* see Figure 3.7

In order for the organisation to learn, the knowledge must be assimilated into the core routines of the organisation. That is, the knowledge becomes embedded in skills and knowhow. It is during application by the work group that knowledge transfers from the individual to the organisation. However, before this knowledge can be assimilated into the core routines of the organisation, there needs to be explicit acceptance by the organisation. There are many examples of individuals bringing technology into an organisation that they believe to be beneficial and yet it does not become accepted by all or part of the organisation. A simple but useful example is that of different versions of software. Several people may have a preference for a certain spreadsheet package, but usually only one version is adopted.

Technological and organisational change can be achieved at the acceptance stage, yet the organisation has not gone through the full learning cycle so this knowledge is not completely transferred into the core routines. Examples of this frequently occur during the implementation of new enterprise resource planning (ERP) systems. There will be some individuals who, because they are closely involved with the new system, will be able to generate enormous amounts of information from it. Others, however, will still be using the previous system and will not be familiar with the new one. It will take several weeks before everyone in the organisation is familiar with the new system and it becomes a 'taken for granted' way of working. The point at which the knowledge becomes embedded in the organisation has recently been referred to as 'tacit knowhow' (Howells, 1996).

The way in which the learning cycles link together is illustrated in Figure 9.7. In the manner of double-loop, learning the individual and organisational cycles are inter-related and inter-dependent (Argyris and Schon 1978). The learning process forms a loop, transferring knowledge from individual into the group. The process of assimilation and adoption of this new knowledge within the inner cycle moves the knowledge into the wider environment and thus into the loop of organisational learning. The role of assimilation has a slightly different emphasis within the individual loops. Assimilation in the individual and group learning cycle refers to assimilation of knowledge from an external source, which may then be applied within the company. Assimilation in the wider cycle relates to assimilation of technology into the core routines of the organisation which, is evidenced by a behavioural change within the organisation. It is only when assimilation in the wider cycle has occurred that learning has truly taken place.

CASE STUDY

How technology transfer can help businesses to grow[1]

This case study shows how technology transfer not only contributed to the growth of a small business, but also helped to improve the quality of life for the blind community in a small town in the North West of England.

Introduction

Traverse Engineering is a small business specialising in metal fabrication. The company has thirty employees and a turnover of £1 800 000. It is a family-run organisation that was started in 1965 by two brothers, both of whom studied mechanical engineering at university. Peter and Thomas Walker continue to be involved with the business and still relish the challenge of a technical or manufacturing problem. The business manufactures a range of specialist metal products for the aircraft industry, many of which involve fabricating aluminium alloys. This case, however, focuses on one of the business's simplest, yet highly profitable, product lines.

Five years ago Traverse Engineering signed a contract with a local chain of nursing homes to manufacture, supply and fit high-quality brass nameplates for all its properties. During this time the product line has grown quickly and now contributes in excess of £100 000 per annum to the business. Many business premises and large private properties have placed orders with Traverse Engineering for nameplates. Traverse is able to produce virtually any design and style required. Typically the name and address of the property are stamped into a brass plate, which is then mounted on a hardwood frame. The price for the plate includes fitting, which is undertaken by one of Traverse's fitters. Peter and Thomas were initially amazed at the profit margins that could be achieved on what to them was a very simple product involving limited engineering skills. It is largely because of the margins that the brothers have continued to manufacture the product. Ideally, the brothers would prefer to focus on technology-intensive products. This case shows how a simple product idea benefited from computer programming technology transferred from the local university.

The difficulty of identifying shops

The story begins during the fitting of a plaque to a large retail outlet in Preston town centre. As the fitter, Steve Jones, was securing the plaque to the entrance to the shop, he noticed a blind lady stop and ask a man whether the shop she was about to enter was a pharmacy. Steve explained that the shop she wanted was the next one. Driving back to the factory he ▶

▶ began to ask himself about the possibility of etching into the plaque the name of the shop in Braille – surely technically this would not be a problem. Also, the retail outlets in the town would no doubt want to help the blind community.

Back at the factory Steve discussed the idea with Thomas who also thought it would be worth exploring, although he was doubtful that the small retail outlets would part with their money. During lunch the same day Thomas mentioned it to Peter, who was much more enthusiastic. The three of them discussed the idea further and began to consider the possibility of supplying every retail outlet in the county or even the country. Just how big was this business idea, they wondered.

Peter contacted several of the retail outlets to gauge their interest in the name plates. A few expressed interest but would not be prepared to spend more than £40. Others argued that they had few blind people enter their shop. Peter refrained from suggesting that this might be because they could not find the shop in the first place!

He decided to contact the local authority to see if it would be interested in providing financial help to ensure that all retail outlets in the town had Braille signs to help the blind. The local borough council was enthusiastic and said it might be able to subsidise the cost of the Braille sign. It seemed that much still depended on what the manufacturing cost and the profit margin, if any. Within the space of an hour the business idea had spiralled from a multi-million-pound business into a possible 'non-starter'.

Producing Braille characters

Peter Walker spent the next few days speaking to colleagues in the business about printing and embossing Braille characters. He went to the local library to read about writing in Braille and the Braille alphabet. He also contacted the Royal Institute for the Blind for help and advice. It seemed that this was not going to be as straightforward as he had imagined. Thomas and Peter began to investigate the possibility of generating Braille themselves. It seemed that a whole series of tools would have to be made which would add to the cost. It was also a very labour-intensive operation. The project began to look very expensive.

Braille, as Thomas and Peter discovered, is a complex subject. The representation of letters, common punctuation marks and a few other symbols as raised dot patterns readable by blind people was developed by Louis Braille in the early part of the nineteenth century.

The Braille alphabet, the method for representing numbers and most punctuation marks are used in all languages that share the Roman alphabet, although there are some language-

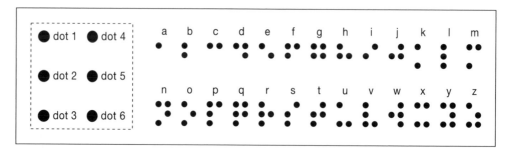

Figure 9.8 : The Braille dot cell and the Braille alphabet

Source: Oregon State University (1998)

to-language variations. Common Braille characters are based on a six-dot cell which has two columns of three dots. Each letter of the alphabet has a code. For example, a=[1]; b=[1,2]. If the empty cell is counted, 64 unique dot combinations are possible with a six-dot cell. Figure 9.8 shows the labelling of the dots.

Dot height is approximately 0.5 mm; the horizontal and vertical spacing between dot centres within a cell is approximately 2.5 mm; the blank space between dots on adjacent cells is approximately 3.75 mm horizontally and 5.0 mm vertically. A standard Braille page typically has a maximum of 40 to 42 Braille cells per line and 25 lines per page.

While Thomas and Peter were in little doubt that they could produce Braille-embossed brass plates, the cost of so doing would not make it a viable project to pursue. They decided to put it to one side; a big order from one of their regular customers had just arrived. It was time to concentrate on the present.

The role played by NIMTECH

Several weeks passed and the Braille project remained under consideration. Steve Jones accepted that the high cost of manufacture made it difficult to justify the project. A few more meetings took place among the three men. Finally, three months after the idea was first floated, the group decided it would not be financially viable for Traverse Engineering to manufacture the product. At the meeting Thomas suggested seeking outside help. Earlier that week he had received a letter and mail shot which offered to 'solve your technical problems'. The source was a technology transfer company that aimed to link technology solutions to technology problems. The company's name was NIMTECH (New and IMproved TECHnology) based in the North West of England to help smaller firms make use of new and improved technologies (NIMTECH, 1998). Somewhat sceptical, the three agreed that Thomas should contact NIMTECH to see if the company could offer any help or advice.

Thomas explained that his problem was a manufacturing one. He needed somehow to develop a low-cost process to produce Braille-embossed characters in brass plate. Using a directory and database of local firms offering technical expertise, NIMTECH began to search for help and possible solutions. Eventually Traverse Engineering was put in contact with the computing department of Lancashire University which had experience of writing programs for the operation of robotic spot-welding machinery for the automotive industry. Following an initial meeting with Thomas, the computing department were confident that a computer program could be developed that would enable the robot arm to emboss brass plates with the necessary Braille markings. Moreover, the university library had several librarians who had specialist knowledge of Braille and working with the blind. Together they would be able to develop a program that would meet the needs of Traverse Engineering.

After only two months of working together they arrived at the finished product. A standard keyboard and wordprocessor were used to enter the letters and words required. The robot arm would then recreate this on-screen version using a special embossing attachment, provided by Traverse Engineering. This user-friendly manufacturing process was able to produce a Braille-embossed brass plate in a matter of minutes.

Discussion

This case illustrates the role played by technology transfer and, in particular, a technology transfer intermediary company. It also demonstrates the role played by internal and external ▶

▶ technical and commercial knowledge in developing a genuine business opportunity. Indeed, without the external knowledge the business idea would not have been developed by Traverse Engineering.

In many ways this case study tells a simple story; how technology transfer can contribute to business growth. In particular, however, it helps explain the technology transfer process. The AMR framework put forward in this chapter can be used as a vantage point to identify the key components of the process. The university was keen to make its technology accessible in return for a small financial reward. The intermediary company provided the mobility and Traverse Engineering was receptive because it had a technical problem. Arguably, Traverse Engineering had an initial low level of receptivity, because it was about to abandon the project. The 4A model can also be applied here to analyse the receptivity of Traverse Engineering. It was left to the intermediary company to provide the awareness and make the association with the university's computer department. The assimilation and application of the technology occurred as the computer department worked with Traverse Engineering to develop the necessary equipment.

Chapter summary

Technology transfer has a significant impact on the management of innovation. The process is concerned with facilitating and promoting innovation. The increasing use of strategic alliances means that its importance is set to increase. This chapter has introduced the subject of technology transfer and examined various models of the process. Most models of technology transfer emphasise access to technology rather than trying to understand the receptivity issues of the receiving organisation. The case study showed how meaningful co-operation with the recipient organisation can facilitate successful technology transfer.

Questions for discussion

1 What was the technology being transferred to Traverse Engineering in the case study?

2 Why was technology transfer considered to be a solution for budget deficits?

3 Explain the limitations of many of the models of technology transfer.

4 Explain how a firm's internal activities affect its ability to acquire external technology.

5 Explain the importance of tacit knowledge to the technology transfer process.

6 Explain why any technology transfered to an organisation needs to be embedded into its core routines.

References

Agryis, C. and Schon, D.A. (1978) *Organisational Learning*, Addison-Wesley, Reading, MA.

Allen, T.J. (1966) 'Performance of communication channels in the transfer of technology', *Industrial Management Review*, 8 (Fall), 87–98.

Allen, T.J. (1977) *Managing the Flow of Technology*, MIT Press, Cambridge, MA.

Allen, T.J. & Cohen, W.M. (1969) 'Information flow in research and development laboratories', *Administrative Science Quarterly*, 14 (1), 12–19.

Bosworth, D. and Stoneman, P. (1996) *Technology Transfer, Information Flows and Collaboration: an Analysis of the CIS*, European Commission, DG XIII: The innovation Programme, EIMS Project No 93/53, Brussels.

Carter, C.F. and Williams, B.R. (1959) 'The characteristics of technically progressive firms', *Journal of Industrial Economics*, March, 87–104.

Centre for Exploitation of Science & Technology (CEST) (1991) *The management of technological collaboration*, March, Manchester.

Cohen, W.M. and Levinthal, D.A. (1990) 'A new perspective on learning and innovation', *Administrative Science Quarterly*, 35 (1) 128–52.

Cooley, M. (1987) *Architect or Bee? The Human Price of Technology*, Hogarth Press, London.

Cordey-Hayes, M., Trott, P. and Gilbert, M. (1996) 'Knowledge assimilation and learning organisations', in Butler, J. and Piccaluga, A. (eds), *Knowledge, Technology and Innovative Organisations*, Guerini E Associati, Italy.

Dabinett, G. (1995) 'The role of science parks and technology centres in technology transfer', *Industry and Higher Education*, February, 31–5.

Danhof, C. (1949) *Observations on Entrepreneurship in Agriculture: Change and the Entrepreneur*, Harvard Research Center on Entrepreneurship History, Harvard University Press, Cambridge, MA.

Dorf, R.C. (1988) 'Models for technology transfer from universities and research laboratories', in *Technology Management 1*, Interscience Enterprises Ltd, Geneva.

Gilbert, M. (1996) 'Technological change as a knowledge transfer process', PhD thesis, INTA, Cranfield University.

Godkin, L. (1988) 'Problems and practicalities of technology transfer: a survey of the literature', *International Journal of Technology Management*, 3 (5), 597–603.

Gruber, W.H. and Marquis, D.G. (1969) *Factors in the Transfer of Technology*, MIT Press, Cambridge, MA.

Hagedoorn, J. (1990) 'Organisational modes of inter-firm co-operation and technology transfer', *Technovation*, 10 (1), 17–30.

Howells, J. (1996) 'Tacit knowledge and innovation and technology transfer', *Technology Analysis and Strategic Management Journal*, 8, 91–106.

Johnson, S.C. and Jones, C. (1957) 'How to organise for new products', *Harvard Business Review*, May–June, 35, 49–62.

Katz, R. and Allen, T. (1988) 'Investigating the NIH syndrome: a look at the performance, tenure and communication patterns of 50 R&D project groups', in Tushman, W.L. and Moore, M.L. (eds), *Readings in the Management of Innovation*, HarperCollins, New York.

Kroonenberg, H.H. van den (1989) 'Getting a quicker pay-off from R&D', *Long Range Planning*, 4, 22, October.

Langrish, J., Evans, W.G. and Jerans, F.R. (1982) *Wealth from Knowledge*, Macmillan, London.

Lefever, D.B. (1992) 'Technology transfer and the role of intermediaries', PhD thesis, INTA, Cranfield Institute of Technology.

Lewis, J.D. (1990) *Partnerships for Profit*, Collier Macmillan, London.

Macdonald, S. (1992) 'Formal collaboration and informal information flow', *International Journal of Technology Management*, Special Issue on Strengthening Corporate and National Competitiveness through Technology, 7 (1/2/3), 49–60.

Nelson, R.R. (1991) 'Why do firms differ, and how does it matter?' *Strategic Management Journal*, 12 (1) 61–74.

Nelson, R.R. and Winter, S. (1982) *An Evolutionary Theory of Economic Change*, Harvard University Press, Boston, MA.

Newell, S. and Clark, P. (1990) 'The importance of extra-organisational networks in the diffusion and appropriation of new technologies', *Knowledge: Creation, Diffusion and Utilisation*, 12 (2), December, 199–212.

NIMTECH (1998) http://www.nimtech.co.uk.

Oakley, R.P., Rothwell, R. and Cooper, S.Y. (1988) *The Management of Innovation in High Technology Small Firms*, Frances Pinter, London.

Oregon State University (1998) http://dots.physics.orst.edu:80/gs_layout.html.

Peters, T. and Waterman, R.H. (1982) *In Search of Excellence: Lessons from America's Best Run Companies*, Harper & Row, New York.

Prahalad, G. and Hamel, C.K. (1990) 'The core competence of the corporation', *Harvard Business Review*, 68 (3) 79–91, May/June.

Rothberg, R. (1976) *Corporate Strategy and Product Innovation*, Free Press, New York.

Rothwell, R., Freeman, C., Horsley, A., Jervis, V.T.P., Robertson, A.B. and Townsend, J. (1974) 'SAPPHO updated: Project SAPPHO phase II', *Research Policy*, 3, 258–91.

Seaton, R.A.F. and Cordey-Hayes, M. (1993) 'The development and application of interactive models of technology transfer', *Technovation*, 13 (1), 45–53.

Trott, P. (1993) 'Inward technology transfer as an interactive process: a case study of ICI', PhD thesis, *Innovation and Technology Assessment Centre*, Cranfield University.

Trott, P. and Cordey-Hayes, M. (1996) 'Developing a "receptive" environment for inward technology transfer: a case study of the chemical industry', *R&D Management*, 26 (1), 83–92.

Trott, P. (1998) 'Growing businesses by generating genuine business opportunities: a review of recent thinking', *Journal of Applied Management*, 8, 2.

Tusham, M.L. (1977) 'Communication across organisational boundries: special boundary roles in the innovation process', *Administrative Science Quarterly*, 22, 587–605.

Werner, J. (1991) 'Can collaborative research work? Success could spawn "collateral benefits" for all industries', *Industry Week*, 240 (13), July 1, 47.

Further reading

Ford, D. and Saren, M. (1996) *Technology Strategy for Business*, International Thompson Business Press, London,

Howells, J. (1996 'Tacit knowledge and innovation and technology transfer', *Technology Analysis and Strategic Management Journal*, 8 (2) 91–106.

Lewis, J. (1990) *Partnerships for Profit: Structuring and Managing Strategic Alliances*, Free Press, New York.

Nonaka, I. and Takeuchi, H. (1995) *The Knowledge Creating Company. How Japanese Companies Create the Dynamics for Innovation*, Oxford University Press, Oxford.

10

Strategic alliances and intellectual property

Introduction

In strategic alliances firms co-operate out of mutual need and share the risks to reach a common objective. Strategic alliances provide access to resources that are greater than any single firm could buy. This can greatly improve the ability to create new products, bring in new technologies, penetrate other markets and reach the scale necessary to survive in world markets.

Intellectual property concerns the legal rights associated with creative effort or commercial reputation. The subject matter is very wide indeed. The aim of this chapter is to introduce the area of intellectual property and to ensure that managers are aware of the variety of ways in which it can affect the management of innovation and the development of new products.

Learning objectives

When you have completed this chapter, you will be able to:

● Recognise the reasons for the increasing use of strategic alliances
● Provide an understanding of the risks and limitations of strategic alliances
● Explain how the role of trust is fundamental in strategic alliances
● Explain how the prisoner's dilemma game can be used to analyse the behaviour of firms in strategic alliances
● Examine the different forms of protection available for a firm's intellectual property
● Identify the limitations of the patent system
● Explain why other firms' patents can be a valuable resource.

Defining strategic alliances

Faced with new levels of competition many companies, including competitors, are sharing their resources and expertise to develop new products, achieve economies of scale and gain access to new technology and markets. Many have argued that these strategic alliances are the competitive weapon of the twenty-first century. One of the main factors preventing many firms from achieving their technical objectives, and therefore their strategic objectives, is the lack of resources. For technology research and development (R&D), the insufficient resources are usually capital and technical critical mass. The cost of building and sustaining the necessary technical expertise and specialised equipment is rising dramatically. Even for the largest corporations, leadership in some market segments they have traditionally dominated cannot be maintained because they lack sufficient technical capabilities to adapt to fast-paced market dynamics.

In the past, strategic alliances were perceived as an option reserved only for large international firms. Intensified competition, shortening product life cycles and soaring R&D costs mean that strategic alliances are an attractive strategy for the future. Moreover, Slowinski *et al.* (1996) argue that strategic alliances provide an opportunity for large *and* small high-technology companies to expand into new markets by sharing skills and resources. They argue that it is beneficial for both parties, since it allows large firms to access the subset of expertise and resources that they desire in the smaller firm, while the smaller company is given access to its larger partner's massive capital and organizational resources.

Chan and Heide (1993) define a strategic alliance as follows:

A strategic alliance is a contractual agreement among organizations to combine their efforts and resources to meet a common goal.

It is, however, possible to have a strategic alliance without a contractual agreement, so a more accurate definition would be:

A strategic alliance is an agreement between two or more partners to share knowledge or resources, which could be beneficial to all parties involved.

Vyas *et al.*, (1995)

For many firms the thought of sharing ideas and technology with another company is precisely what they have been trying to avoid doing since their conception. It is a total lack of trust that lies at the heart of their unwillingness to engage in any form of co-operation. The element of trust is highlighted later through the use of the prisoner's dilemma.

Technology partnerships between and in some cases among organisations are becoming more important and prevalent. From 1976 to 1987, the annual number of new joint ventures rose sixfold; by 1987, three-quarters of these were in high-technology industries (Lewis, 1990). As the costs, including risk associated with R&D efforts, continue to increase, no company can remain a 'technology island' and stay competitive.

The term strategic alliance is used to cover a wide range of co-operative arrangements. The different forms of strategic alliances will be explored later in this chapter.

The fall of the go-it-alone strategy and the rise of the octopus strategy

Businesses are slowly beginning to broaden their view of their business environment from the traditional *go-it-alone* perspective of individual firms competing against each other. The formation of strategic alliances means that strategic power often resides in sets of firms acting together. For example, the success of the European Airbus strategic alliance has been phenomenal. Formed in 1969 as a joint venture between the German firm MBB and the French firm Aérospatiale, it was later joined by CASA of Spain and British Aerospace of the UK. The Airbus A300 range of civilian aircraft has achieved great success in the 1990s, securing large orders for aircraft ahead of its major rival Boeing.

Even IBM has forsaken the go-it-alone strategy. It has teamed up with Nippon Telephone and Telegraph, Japan and with Toshiba, Japan to develop liquid crystal display (LCD) screens (Nordwall, 1991).

The so-called octopus strategy (Vyas *et al.*, 1995) gets its name from the long tentacles of that creature. Firms often develop alliances with a wide range of companies. Figure 10.1 shows the alliances that IBM has formed to strengthen elements of its business strategy. Arguably, JVC adopted an octopus strategy to try to ensure that VHS technology became the industry standard in the VCR industry. It entered alliances with Sharp, Toshiba and RCA.

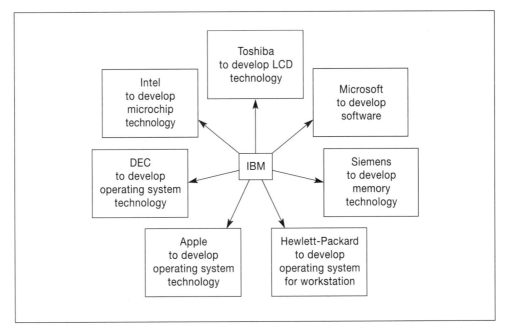

Figure 10.1 : The alliances formed by IBM

Source: Nordwall (1991)

Forms of strategic alliances

Strategic alliances can occur *intra-industry* or *inter-industry*. For example, three US automobile manufacturers have formed an alliance to develop technology for an electric car. This is an example of *intra-industry alliance* and in response to US legislation requiring a certain percentage of US cars to be gasoline free by 2000. The UK pharmaceutical giant Glaxo-Wellcome has established many *inter-industry* alliances with a wide range of firms from a variety of industries; it includes companies such as Matsushita, Canon, Fuji and Apple.

Furthermore, alliances can range from a simple handshake agreement to mergers, from licensing to equity joint ventures. Moreover, they can involve a customer, a supplier or even a competitor (Chan and Heide, 1993). Many of these technology co-operations were discussed in Chapter 8. Faulkner (1995) identifies three generic types of strategic alliance:

- joint ventures
- collaboration (non-joint ventures)
- R&D consortia.

Joint venture

A joint venture is usually a separate entity, with the partners to the alliance normally being equity shareholders. With a joint venture, the costs and possible benefits from an R&D research project would be shared. They are usually established for a specific project and will cease on its completion. The intention of establishing a joint venture is generally to enable that organisation to 'stand alone'.

Collaboration (non-joint ventures)

The absence of a legal entity means that such arrangements tend to be more flexible. This provides the opportunity to extend the co-operation over time if so desired. For example, many manufacturing firms are increasingly entering into long-term relationships with their component suppliers. Often such agreements are for a fixed term, say five years, with the option of renewal thereafter. British Aerospace adopts this approach when negotiating component suppliers for its aircraft.

Consortia

A consortium describes the situation where a number of partners come together to undertake what is often a large-scale activity. Chapter 8 gives a more detailed explanation of this form of strategic alliance.

Motives for establishing an alliance

Alliances will frequently have multiple objectives. For example, an alliance may seek to access technology, gain greater technical critical mass and share the risk of future technology development. The European Airbus is a good example of an alliance that has multiple objectives. Table 10.1 lists the most common reasons cited for entering a strategic alliance.

Table 10.1 : Reasons for entering a strategic alliance

	Reasons	Examples
1	Improved access to capital and new business	European Airbus to enable companies to compete with Boeing and McDonnell Douglas
2	Greater technical critical mass	Industry alliance formed between US microchip manufacturers to compete with Japanese
3	Shared risk and liability	GEC-Alsthom, a joint venture between UK and French power generator manufacturers
4	Better relationships with strategic partners	European Airbus
5	Technology transfer benefits	Customer supplier alliances, e.g. VW and Bosch
6	Reduce R&D costs	GEC and Siemens 60/40 share of telecommunications joint venture GPT
7	Use of distribution skills	Virgin Cola and Tesco
8	Access to marketing strengths	NMB, Japan and Intel; NMB has access to Intel's marketing
9	Access to technology	IBM gained access to Apple's user interface technology
10	Standardisation	Attempt by Sony to get Betamax technology as industry standard
11	By-product utilisation	Glaxo-Wellcome and Matsushita, Canon, Fuji
12	Management training	Rover management general expertise from experiences with Honda

Sources: Vyas *et al*. (1995); Chan and Heide (1993)

Research by Morrison and Mezentseff (1997) suggests that strategic business alliances will only achieve a sustainable competitive advantage if they involve learning and knowledge transfer (*see* Chapter 9). They have designed a framework to help such partnerships develop a co-operative learning environment to achieve long-term success. The emphasis on learning helps to develop individual and organisational intelligence, thereby ensuring the future success of the strategic alliance.

The process of forming a successful strategic alliance

The formation of a strategic alliance is a three-step process (*see* Figure 10.2). It begins with the selection of the right partner. This will clearly depend on what is required and the motivation for the strategic alliance. This is usually followed by negotiations based on each partner's needs. The third and final stage is management towards collaboration. This last step encompasses a wide range of activities, including joint goal setting and conflict resolution. Moreover, the last stage needs constant work to keep the relationship sound. Aside from collaborative management, the success of a business alliance depends on the existence of mutual need and the ability to work together despite differences in organisational culture.

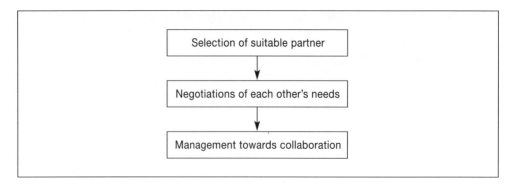

Figure 10.2 : The process of forming a strategic alliance

Risks and limitations of strategic alliances

So far we have addressed only the potential benefits to be gained from strategic alliances. However, a strategic alliance also has its downsides. It can lead to competition rather than co-operation, to loss of competitive knowledge, to conflicts resulting from incompatible cultures and objectives and to reduced management control (Chan and Heide, 1993).

The literature on the subject of technological co-operation presents a confusing picture. There is evidence to suggest that strategic alliances may harm a firm's ability to innovate. Arias (1995) argues that inter-firm networking may result not only in desired outcomes but also in negative consequences. The creation of closely structured networks of relationships may produce increased complexity, loss of autonomy and information asymmetry. These hazards may ultimately lead to a decreased ability to innovate and participate in technological change.

To avoid these problems, management should anticipate business risks related to partnering, carefully assess their partners, conduct comprehensive resource planning and allocation of resources to the network, and develop and foster social networks. All parties should also ensure that the motives for participating are positive, that the networks are as formidable as the alliances within them, and that there is a perception of equal contribution and benefits from the parties. Lastly, there should be communication, data sharing, goals and objectives.

The level and nature of the integration appear to be crucial factors. In some cases the alliance is very tight indeed. For example, Motoman, a robotic systems supplier, and Stillwater Technologies, a tooling and machining company, share the same facility for their offices and manufacturing and their computer and communications systems are linked (Sheridan, 1997). For other firms a loose alliance is far more comfortable.

In a review of the literature on strategic alliances, Vyas *et al.* (1993) identify three barriers to successful strategic alliances:

1 Failure to understand and adapt to new style of management required for the alliance.

2 Failure to learn and understand cultural differences between the organisations.

3 Lack of commitment to succeed.

The formation of strategic alliances by definition fosters co-operation rather than competition. This has major implications for the theory of competition. Economists would stress the importance of competition for the development and growth of a healthy economy. Government departments of trade and commerce around the world need to be aware of the extent to which firms that co-operate are also capable of manipulating the price of products.

The use of game theory to analyse strategic alliances

Research using game theory has suggested that some alliance structures are inherently more likely than others to be associated with a high opportunity to cheat, high behavioural uncertainty and poor stability, longevity and performance. Parkhe (1993) argues that maintaining robust co-operation in inter-firm strategic alliances poses special problems. This study looked at 111 inter-firm alliances. The findings suggested the need for a greater focus on game theoretic structural dimensions and institutional responses to perceived opportunism in the study of voluntary inter-firm co-operation.

The development of the VCR industry is littered with strategic alliances formed by various businesses to try to help ensure that they gain access to the relevant technology. Unfortunately, not all of the alliances were successful. Sony embarked on several strategic alliances with competitors in an attempt to try to make its Betamax technology the industry standard. When JVC, Toshiba and others refused, the alliance existed in name only (Baden-Fuller, 1996). There are many other examples of alliances failing – some soon after inception, others after a long and successful relationship.

The issue of trust is a critical element in any strategic alliance. By its very nature an alliance, like a marriage, is dependent on all parties working together so that the total outcome is greater than any one party can achieve on its own. It is important to note that trust is usually established over a long period, in much the same way as courtship prior to marriage involves understanding one another and building confidence in the relationship. Before one can lose trust, however, one must have gained it in the first place. A more serious problem is that firms may enter a strategic alliance with a lack of trust in the other party. The issue of trust is the underlying theme of the prisoner's dilemma, which is discussed in the next section.

Game theory and the prisoner's dilemma

The extent to which two companies are going to co-operate is a key question for any strategic alliance. This can be examined using the prisoner's dilemma. It graphically highlights the options facing companies when they embark on a strategic alliance. It illustrates that co-operation is the mutually advantageous strategy, but that non-co-operation provides high-risk opportunities to both parties.

The basic form of this game is known as the prisoner's dilemma. It gets its name from the following scenario. Suppose that two criminals get arrested for drug dealing. The local police chief arrests them both and takes them to the cells for interrogation. They are placed in separate cells and face fierce questioning. The police chief, however, does not have sufficient evidence to gain a conviction. The chief asks Detective

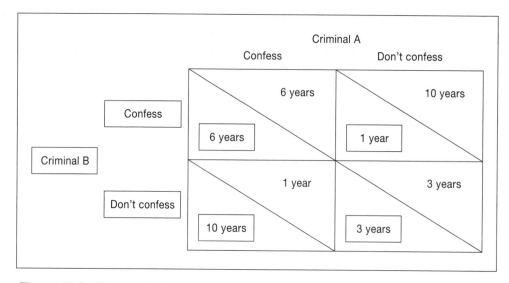

Figure 10.3 : Prisoner's dilemma

Holmes to offer a deal to both criminals. If either confesses, he will receive a minimal sentence for becoming an informer and helping the police. If neither confesses, they will both receive a sentence based on some other lesser charge for which the police chief does have evidence. If they both confess, the court will take this co-operation into account and will probably pass a lighter sentence on both. The game matrix is represented in Figure 10.3, with the relevant years of sentence to be expected.

Both criminal A and B have a dominant strategy. No matter what the other does, both are better off if they confess. The option of 'don't confess' carries with it the risk of spending 10 years in prison. The maximum sentence for confessing is 6 years, with a possibility of only 1 year. Given this pay-off matrix both criminals should confess. This is the classic form of the prisoner's dilemma.

It has a close relative, the repeated game. This is a more realistic interpretation of reality, as few business relationships are one-off events. For example, BMW competes with Volkswagen in a variety of markets. With the knowledge that one is to repeat any game played the options are likely to be different. To return to the criminals locked up in prison: if they both realise that 'squealing' on a fellow prisoner may bring with it some form of revenge, such as death, from the prisoner's friends, the range of outcomes changes significantly. The dominant solution is now to play 'don't confess'. Figure 10.4 shows the repeated game matrix.

Intellectual property

The notion of two or more separate organisations working together to achieve a common aim is laudable in itself. One needs to remember, however, that those same organisations are also independent and autonomous. There will be areas where they choose to co-operate and other areas where they choose not to. A firm will have knowledge it wishes to share and knowledge that it does not. Furthermore, what happens to

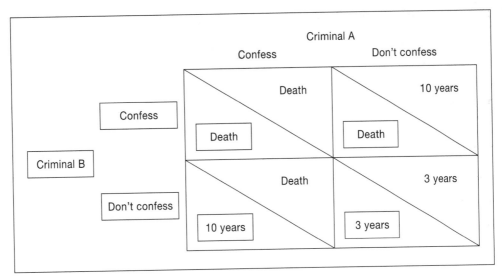

Figure 10.4 : The repeated game

knowledge that results from the alliance? Clearly, this needs to be clarified before entering an alliance. In virtually all alliances intellectual property issues are high on the list of points for discussion. Intellectual property is the subject of this section.

If you happen to come up with a novel idea, the simplest and cheapest course of action is to do nothing about legal protection, just keep it a secret (as with the recipe for Coca-Cola). This approach prevents anyone else from seeing it or finding it. The owners can take their intellectual property to their grave, safe in the knowledge that no one will inherit it. This approach is fine unless you are seeking some form of commercial exploitation and ultimately a financial reward, usually in the form of royalties.

One of the dangers with trying to keep your idea a secret is that someone else might develop a similar idea and apply for legal protection and seek commercial exploitation. Independent discovery of ideas is not as surprising as one might first think. This is because research scientists working at the forefront of science and technology are often working towards the same goal. This was the case with Thomas Edison and Joseph Swan, who independently invented the lightbulb simultaneously either side of the Atlantic. They formed a company called Ediswan to manufacture lightbulbs at the end of the nineteenth century.

Table 10.2 shows an overview of the different forms of intellectual property and rights available for different areas of creativity.

The issues of intellectual property are continually with us and touch us probably more than we realise. Most students will have already confronted the issue of intellectual property, either with recording pre-recorded music or copying computer software. The author is always the owner of his or her work and the writing of an academic paper entitles the student to claim the copyright on that essay. The submission of an academic paper to a scientific journal for publication requires the author to sign a licence for the publisher to use the intellectual property. Patenting is probably the most commonly recognised form of intellectual property, but it is only one of several ways to protect creative efforts. Registered designs, trademarks and copyright are other forms of intellectual property. These will be addressed in the following sections.

Table 10.2 : An overview of the main types of intellectual property

Type of intellectual property	Key features of this type of protection
1 Patents	Offers a 20-year monopoly
2 Copyright	Provides exclusive rights to creative individuals for the protection of their literary or artistic productions
3 Registered designs	As protected by registration, is for the outward appearance of an article and provides exclusive rights for up to 15 years
4 Registered trademarks	Is a distinctive name, mark or symbol that is identified with a company's products

Trade secrets

There are certain business activities and processes that are not patented, copyrighted or trademarked. Many businesses regard these as trade secrets. It could be special ways of working, price costings or business strategies. The most famous example is the recipe for Coca-Cola, which is not patented. This is because Coca-Cola did not want to reveal the recipe to its competitors. Unfortunately, the law covering intellectual property is less clear about the term trade secret. Bainbridge (1996) argues that there is no satisfactory legal definition of the term.

An introduction to patents

The article on DNA chip patents from the front page of the *Financial Times* dramatically illustrates the importance of patents to the business world. A patent is a contract between an individual or organisation and the state. The rationale behind the granting of a temporary monopoly by the state is to encourage creativity and innovation within an economy. If the individual or organisation discloses in the patent sufficient details of the invention, the state will confer the legal right to stop others benefiting from the invention (Derwent, 1998). The state, however, has no obligation to prevent others benefiting from it. This is the responsibility of the individual or organisation who is granted the patent. And herein lies a major criticism with the patent system. The costs of defending a patent against infringement can be high indeed. This point is explored later.

The UK Patent Office was set up in 1852 to act as the UK's sole office for the granting of the patents of invention. The origins of the patent system stretch back a further 400 years. The word patent comes from the practice of monarchs in the Middle Ages (500–1500) of conferring rights and privileges by means of 'open letters', that is, documents on which the royal seal was not broken when they were opened. This is distinct from 'closed letters' that were not intended for public view. Open letters were intended for display and inspection by any interested party. The language of government in medieval England was Latin and Latin for open letter is

Rivals in dispute over DNA chip patents

Oxford professor and US biotechnology company both claim credit for discovery

by Roger Taylor

A US biotechnology company is challenging Oxford University in a legal wrangle over ownership of one of the most powerful medical innovations of recent years.

The issue is who invented the DNA chip – a device for rapidly analysing human genetic make-up using silicon chips containing bits of DNA.

Potential revenues from the new chip are large, as experts predict it will form a key platform for future research. It has the potential to uncover connections between genes and disease, diagnose people's susceptibility to different illnesses and devise new therapies.

Affymetrix, a US biotechnology company 34 per cent owned by Glaxo Wellcome, is one of the leading developers of the new technology. The loss-making company, which has a market value of over $500m, has already begun marketing chip products in the US.

However, plans to expand into Europe have met an obstacle in the form of Professor Ed Southern of Oxford University, who claims to have invented DNA chips and has a Europe-wide patent.

The patent is currently assigned to the university, which has agreed to assign it to Oxford Gene Technology, a newly formed biotechnology company owned by Professor Southern and the university.

Several companies, including Roche of Switzerland and Abbott Laboratories in the US as well as Affymetrix, have registered objections to the patent, but it could be years before a decision is made and in the meantime Professor Southern's patent stands.

To overcome this obstacle, Affymetrix has now begun discussions with the professor to agree a licensing deal. The company said: "We greatly respect Professor Southern and hope to be able to settle this amicably."

Oxford Gene Technology is close to launching its own product, but Professor Southern said he intended to grant licences to other companies in order to encourage competition. "It would be wrong for one company to try and exploit this" he said.

He is aware that if his patent is upheld its value would be enormous: "The business of genetic testing is likely to be very big and this could be the core technology," he said.

He has also filed a patent in the US which he hopes will be issued soon.

Affymetrix has objected to Oxford Gene Technology's European patent on the grounds that it is not sufficiently inventive. It says the idea of DNA chips was relatively obvious and claims its own scientists came up with the idea independently.

The skill, it argues, was in discovering a way to manufacture chips. Both companies have patents on their different approaches to manufacturing chips. Professor Southern says he is confident of beating off any challenges.

Oxford Gene Technology is likely to start marketing its first product soon and is talking to potential investors about further development.

Source: *Financial Times*, May 6 1997

litterae patente. As English slowly took over from Latin as the official language, the documents became known as 'letters patent' and later just 'patents'.

The earliest known English patent was granted to John of Utynam in 1449. The patent gave Mr Utynam a 20-year monopoly for a method of making stained glass that had not previously been known in England. For a patent to benefit from legal protection it must meet strict criteria:

- novelty
- inventive step
- industrial application.

Novelty

The Patent Act 1977, section 2 (1), states: 'An invention shall be taken to be new if it does not form part of the state of the art'. A state of the art is defined as all matter, in other words publications, written or oral or even anticipation (*Windsurfing International* v *Tabar Marine Ltd* 1985), that will render a patent invalid. In *Windsurfing International* v *Tabar Marine Ltd*, the Court of Appeal held that a 12-year-old boy who built a surfboard and used it in public for a few weekends at a caravan site at Hayling Island in Hampshire, had effectively anticipated a later patent for a surfboard which was declared invalid for want of novelty (and also because it lacked an inventive step). Bainbridge (1996).

Inventive step

Section 3 of the Patent Act states: 'An invention shall be taken to involve an inventive step if it is not obvious to a person skilled in the art'.

Industrial application

Under the patent act an invention shall be taken to be capable of industrial application if it can be a machine, product or process. Penicillin was a discovery which was not patentable, but the process of isolating and storing penicillin clearly had industrial applications and thus was patentable.

Monopoly for 20 years

Patents are granted to individuals and organisations who can lay claim to a new product or manufacturing process or to an improvement of an existing product or process which was not previously known. The granting of a patent gives the 'patentee' a monopoly to make, use or sell the invention for a fixed period of time, which in Europe and the US is 20 years from the date the patent application was first filed. In return for this monopoly, the patentee pays a fee to cover the costs of processing the patent, and more importantly publicly discloses details of the invention.

Annual fees required

The idea must be new and not an obvious extension of what is already known. A patent lasts up to 20 years in the UK and Europe, but heavy annual renewal fees have to be paid to keep it in force.

Patent agents

The role of a patent agent combines scientific or engineering knowledge with legal knowledge and expertise. It is a specialised field of work. Many large companies have in-house patent agents who prepare patents for the company's scientists. They may also search patent databases around the world for relevant information.

Exclusions

Discoveries (as opposed to inventions that have an industrial application), scientific theory and mathematical processes are not patentable under the Patent Act 1988. Similarly, literary and artistic works and designs are covered by other forms of intellectual property.

The patenting of life

Rapid scientific developments in the field of biology, medical science and biotechnology have fuelled intense debates about the morality of patenting life forms. Until very recently there was a significant difference between the US patent system, which enabled the granting of patents on certain life forms, and the European patent system, which did not. Essentially the US system adopted a far more liberal approach to the patenting of life. This difference was illustrated in the 'Harvard oncomouse' case (Patent No: 4581.847). The Harvard Medical School had its request for a European patent refused because the mouse was a natural living life form and hence unpatentable. The European approach had serious implications for the European biotechnology industry. In particular, the R&D efforts of the biotechnology industry could not be protected, so there was a danger that intellectual and financial capital could flow from Europe to the US, where protection was available. The other side of the argument is equally compelling: the granting to a company of a patent on certain genes may restrict other companies' ability to work with those genes. On 27 November 1997 the European Union agreed to Directive 95/0350(COD) and COM(97)446, permitting the granting of patents on certain life forms. This has particular significance in the area of gene technology.

The subject of cloning new life forms from existing cells is emotive for many people. When it was announced that Dolly had been created from cells taken from other sheep it generated enormous controversy and publicity. This was especially so for a group of scientists from the Roslin Institute, a publicly funded institute, and PPL Therapeutics, a biotechnology company, that had developed Dolly. The debate about the ethics of the science continues and related to this is the intellectual property of the gene technology involved (*see Financial Times* (1997) and Rowan (1997) for a full discussion of this debate).

The configuration of a patent

For a patent to be granted its contents need to be made public so that others can be given the opportunity to challenge the granting of a monopoly. There is a formal registering and indexing system to enable patents to be easily accessed by the public. For this reason patents follow a very formal specification. Details concerning country of origin, filing date, personal details of applicant etc. are accompanied by an internationally agreed numbering system for easy identification (see Appendix 1). The two most important sources of information relating to a patent are the patent specification and patent abstract. Both of these are classified and indexed in various ways to facilitate search.

The specification is a detailed description of the invention and must disclose enough information to enable someone else to repeat the invention. This part of the document needs to be precise and methodical. It will also usually contain references to other scientific papers. The remainder of the specification will contain claims. These are to define the breadth and scope of the invention. A patent agent will try to write the broadest claim possible, as a narrow claim can restrict the patent's application and competitors will try to argue that, for example, a particular invention applies only to one particular method. Competitors will scrutinise these claims to test their validity.

The patent abstract is a short statement printed on the front page of the patent specification which identifies the technical subject of the invention and the advance that it represents (*see* Appendix 1). Abstracts are usually accompanied by a drawing. In addition, these abstracts are published in weekly information booklets.

It is now possible to get a patent from the European Patent Office which covers the whole of Europe. This can be granted in a particular country or several countries. The concept of a world patent, however, is a distant realisation. The next section explores some of the main differences between the two dominant world patent systems.

Patent harmonisation: first to file and first to invent

Most industrialised countries offer some form of patent protection to companies operating within their borders. However, while some countries have adequate protection, others do not. Moreover, different countries are members of different conventions and some adopt different systems. The European patent system and the US patent system have many similarities, for example a monopoly is granted for 20 years under both systems. There is, however, one key difference. In the US the patent goes to the researcher who can prove they were the first to invent it, not – as in Europe – to the first to file for a patent.

The implications of this are many and varied, but there are two key points that managers need to consider:

1 In Europe, a patent is invalid if the inventor has published the new information before filing for patent protection. In the US there are some provisions which allow inventors to talk first and file later.

2 In Europe, patent applications are published while pending. This allows the chance to see what monopoly an inventor is claiming and for an objection to be made to the Patent Office if there are grounds to contest validity. In the US the situation is quite different; applications remain secret until granted.

The issue of patent harmonisation has a long history. The Paris Convention for the Protection of Industrial Property was signed in 1883, since when it has received many amendments. At present its membership includes 114 countries. European countries have a degree of patent harmonisation provided by the European Patent Convention (EPC), administered by the European Patent Office.

The sheer size of the US market and its dominance in many technology-intensive industries means that this difference in the patent systems has received, and continues to receive, a great deal of attention from various industry and government departments in both Europe and the US.

Some famous patent cases

1880 – Ediswan

It is rare for identical inventions to come about at the same time. But that is what happened with the electric lightbulb, which was patented almost simultaneously on either side of the Atlantic by Thomas Edison and Joseph Swan. To avoid patent litigation the two business interests combined in England to produce lamps under the name of Ediswan, which is still registered as a trademark.

1930 – Whittle's jet engine

While Frank Whittle was granted a patent for his jet engine, his employers, the RAF, were unable to get the invention to work efficiently and could not manufacture it on an industrial scale. It was left to the US firms of McDonnell Douglas and Pratt and Witney to exploit the commercial benefits of the patents.

1943 – Penicillin

Alexander Fleming discovered penicillin in 1928. On 14 October 1941, thirteen years later, researchers at Oxford University filed Patent No. 13242. The complete specification was accepted on 16 April 1943.

BTG

Penicillin was discovered in a London hospital by Alexander Fleming in 1928. It was to take another 12 years (1940) before a team working at Oxford University discovered a method of isolating and storing the drug. However, as a result of World War II, which drained much of its financial resources, Britain did not have the capability to develop large-scale fermentation of the bacteria. Help was sought from the US and the success of the technology is well known.

The UK government was concerned that it had given away valuable technology. By way of a response to this, following the end of World War II, it established the National Research Development Corporation (NRDC) in 1948 to protect the intellectual property rights of inventors' efforts which had been funded by the public sector. This included research conducted in universities, hospitals and national laboratories.

From its very beginning the NRDC began generating funds. Oxford University developed a second generation of antibiotics called cephalosporins. They were patented worldwide and the royalties secured the financial base of the NRDC for many years.

The NRDC changed its name to the British Technology Group (BTG) and has continued to be successful in arranging and defending patents for many university professors. In 1994 BTG became an independent public limited company.

Historically BTG was only involved in UK intellectual property issues, but its activities have expanded. It was recently involved in litigation with the US Pentagon for patent infringement on Hovercraft. It also became involved with another case involving Johnson & Johnson, a US health-care group. BTG was so successful in this case that Johnson & Johnson asked it to manage a portfolio of nearly 100 inventions to try to generate royalties.

Patents in practice

There are many industrialists and small business managers who have little faith in the patent system. They believe, usually as a result of first-hand experience, that the patent system is designed primarily for large multinational corporations who have the finances to defend and protect any patents granted to them. The problem is that applying and securing a patent is only the beginning of what is usually an expensive journey. For example, every time you suspect a company may be infringing your patent, you will have to incur legal expenses to protect your intellectual property. Moreover, there are some examples of large corporations spending many years and millions of dollars in legal fees battling in the courts over alleged patent infringement. One of the best-known cases was Apple versus Microsoft, where Apple alleged that Microsoft had copied its windows operating system. The case lasted for many years and cost both companies many millions of dollars in legal fees.

Many smaller firms view the patent system with dread and fear. Only 10 per cent of the UK patents granted in 1997 were to small firms. Yet small firms represent 99 per cent of companies (*Guardian*, 1998).

In theory it sounds straightforward – £225 to apply for a UK patent. In practice, however, companies should be considering a cost of £1000–£1500. Furthermore, protection in a reasonable number of countries is likely to cost more like £10 000. The example James Dyson highlights many of the limitations of the patent system.

Effective patents depend on the depth of your pocket!

James Dyson, responsible for designing and developing the 'bagless' vacuum cleaner, he is critical of the patent system. From personal experience argues that it is prohibitively expensive. He explains that when he was filing for patents for his vacuum cleaner he did not have enough money to patent all of its features. Also, the costs of taking patents out in several countries is very expensive. Many of the costs involved are hidden. For example, there are translation fees to pay for different countries and languages. According to Mr Dyson, the cost of taking out a patent in five countries is between £50 000 and £60 000. In addition, there are renewal fees to pay.

Source: Graham (1998)

Patent expiry

Much has been written on the subject of patent application and the benefits to be gained from a 20-year monopoly. There is, however, much less written about the subject of the effects of patent expiration. In other words, what happens when the patent protecting your product expires? A glance at the pharmaceutical industry reveals an interesting picture.

For any firm operating in this science-intensive industry, the whole process of developing a product is based on the ability to protect the eventual product through the use of patents. Without the prospect of a 20-year monopoly to exploit many years of research and millions of dollars of investment, companies would be less inclined to engage in new product development. (The case study at the end of Chapter 8 explores new product development in the pharmaceutical industry.) On expiry of a patent competitors are able to use the technology, which hitherto had been protected, to develop their own product. Such products are referred to as generic drugs (a generic sold on its chemical composition). When a generic drug is launched, the effect on a branded drug which has just come off patent can be considerable. For example, when ICI's drug Tenormin came off patent in June 1991 its market share fell by almost 75 per cent (*see* Figure 10.5). Remarkably, market share falls of 85 per cent are typical (*Chemistry & Industry News*, 1995). A generic drug is cheap to produce as no extensive research and development costs are incurred and pharmaceutical drugs are relatively easy to copy. It is in effect a chemical process. The principal forms of defence available to manufacturers are brand development and further research.

Developing a brand requires long-term investments. Pharmaceutical companies with a product protected by patents will usually have between 10 and 20 years to develop a brand and brand loyalty. The aim is that even when the product goes off patent customers will continue to ask for the branded as opposed to the generic drug. In practice, companies adopt a combination of aggressive marketing to develop the brand and technical research on existing drugs to improve the product still further, and file for additional patents to protect the new and improved versions of the product.

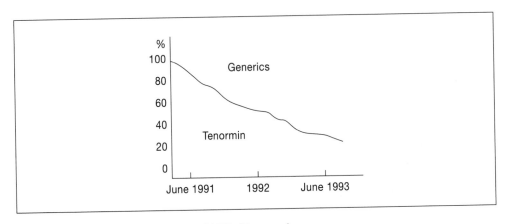

Figure 10.5 : % market share of ICI's Tenormin

Source: Economics Review 1994

The use of patents in innovation management

Patent Offices in each country house millions of patents. There are over two million British patents. All this information is available to the public. Each publication, because of the legal requirement that details of patents be disclosed, is a valuable source of technological knowledge. Indeed, the information-provision activities of the patent office have increased. For example, scientists working in a particular field will often search patent databases to see how the problems they face have been tackled in the past. They will also use previous patents to identify how their current area of work fits in with those areas of science and technology that have been developed and patented before. Very often patents can provide a valuable source of inspiration.

In addition, many firms also use the patent publication register to find out what their competitors are up to. For example, a search of the worldwide patent databases may reveal that your major competitor has filed a series of patents in an area of technology that you had not previously considered. Armed with prior knowledge of the industry and the technology, it may be possible to uncover the research direction in which your competitor is heading, or even the type of product line that it is considering developing. All of this industrial intelligence can help research teams and companies develop and modify their own strategy or to pursue a different approach to a problem.

Trademarks

Trademarks have particular importance to the world of business. For many businesses, especially in less technology-intensive industries where the use of patents is limited, trademarks offer one of the few methods of differentiating a company's products. Coca-Cola is an example. Trademarks are closely associated with business image, goodwill and reputation. Indeed, many have become synonymous with particular products: Mars and chocolate confectionery, Hoover and vacuum cleaners and Nestlé and coffee. The public relies on many trademarks as indicating quality, value for money and origin of goods.

Significant changes have been made to trademark law in the UK. The Trade Marks Act 1994 replaced the Trade Marks Act 1938, which was widely recognised as being out of touch with business practices today. The UK now complies with the European Commission Directive on the approximation of the laws of member states relating to trademarks and ratifies the Madrid Convention for the international registration of trademarks.

The law relating to trademarks is complex. For example, what is a trademark? Bainbridge (1996) offers a comprehensive review of the law surrounding intellectual property. The following section offers a brief introduction to some of the key considerations for product and business managers.

The Trade Marks Act 1994, s 1(1), defines a trademark as:

being any sign capable of being represented graphically which is capable of distinguishing goods or services of one undertaking from those of other undertakings.

This can include, for example, Apple Computer, the Apple logo and Macintosh, the name of some of the company's products, all of which are registered trademarks. Some of the first trademarks were used by gold- and silversmiths to mark their own work. The first registered trademark, No 1, was issued to Bass in 1890 for their red triangle mark for pale ale. The example below of the Mr Men offers an example of the effective and successful use of trademarks.

There are certain restrictions and principles concerning the use of trademarks. In particular, a trademark should:

- satisfy the requirements of s 1(1)
- be distinctive
- not be deceptive
- not cause confusion with previous trademarks.

Satisfy the requirements of s 1(1)

The much wider definition of a trademark offered by the 1994 Act opened the possibility of all sorts of marks that would not have been able to be registered before. Sounds, smells and containers could now be registered. A number of perfume manufacturers have applied to register their perfumes as trademarks. Coca-Cola and Unilever have applied to register their containers for Coca-Cola and Domestos respectively.

Distinctive

A trademark should be distinctive in itself. In general, this means that it should not describe in any way the product or service to which it relates. Usually words that are considered generic or descriptive are not trademarked. In addition, it should not use non-distinctive expressions which other traders might reasonably wish to use in the course of a trade. For example, to attempt to register the word beef as a trademark for a range of foods would not be possible since other traders would reasonably want to use the word in the course of their trade. It would, however, be acceptable to use beef in association with a range of clothing because this would be considered distinctive. Laudatory terms are not allowed, for example the word heavenly for a range of cosmetics would not be possible since it is a laudatory term.

Non-deceptive

A trademark should also not attempt to deceive the customer. For example, the attempt in 1900 to register Orlwoola as an artificial fibre was not possible, since the very word could persuade people to believe the material was made of wool.

Not confusing

Finally, a trademark or service mark will not be registered if it could be confused with the trademark of a similar product that has already been registered. For example, Velva-Glo was refused as a trademark for paints because it was judged to be too near the word Vel-Glo which was already registered.

Mr Hargreaves and the Mr Men

Many of you are probably aware of the children's book and cartoon characters the Mr Men. Since 1973 Mr Happy and his colleagues have appeared on everything from yoghurt pots to a Japanese commercial for a gas company. That is not including the TV series or the millions of books sold. All the characters are registered trademarks. After all, if you want to stop someone stealing your ideas it's an advantage if you can prove that you own them. That's why Roger Hargreaves registered his drawings with the UK Patent Office. To date the Hargreaves family has received over £1.5 million pounds for use of the characters.

Source: Patent Office

Duration of registration, infringement and passing off

Under the Trade Marks Act 1994 the registration of a trademark is for a period of 10 years from the date of registration. This may be renewed indefinitely for further 10-year periods. Once accepted and registered, trademarks are considered to be an item of personal property.

The fact that a trademark is registered does not mean that one cannot use the mark at all. In the case of *Bravado Merchandising Services Ltd* v *Mainstream Publishing Ltd*, the respondent published a book about the pop group Wet Wet Wet under the title A sweet little mystery – Wet Wet Wet – the inside story. Wet Wet Wet is a registered trademark and the proprietor brought an injunction against the use of the name. The court decided that the trademark had not been infringed because the respondent was using the mark as an indication of the main characteristic of the artefact which, in this instance, was a book about the pop group (Bainbridge, 1996).

Where a business uses a trademark that is similar to another or takes unfair advantage of or is detrimental to another trademark, infringement will have occurred. This introduces the area of passing off, the common law form of trademark law. Passing off concerns the areas of goodwill and reputation of the trademark. In *Consorzio de Proscuitto di Parma* v *Marks and Spencer plc* (1991), Lord Justice Norse identified the ingredients of a passing-off action as being comprised of:

- the goodwill of the plaintiff
- the misrepresentation made by the defendant
- consequential damage.

The article about copycats highlights many of businesses' concerns about what they see as unfair competition. This area of law has many similarities to trademark law and is considered to be a useful supplement to it (*see* Bainbridge (1996), for a full explanation of the law of passing off).

On the prowl for copycats

Neil Buckley reports on the battle to stop retailers from selling products identical to famous brands

Consumer goods manufacturers in the UK are fighting to stop retailers selling own-label products that look almost identical to well-known brands.

A dozen of the biggest names have formed the British Producers and Brand Owners Group to press for a change in the law – which they say lags far behind those in other European countries when it comes to protecting their products from 'copycat' competition by retailers.

Members include Allied Lyons, Gillette, Guinness, Grand Met, ICI Paints, Kellogg, Mars, Nestlé, Procter & Gamble, SmithKline Beecham and Unilever.

They say own-label products are being designed deliberately to resemble manufacturers' brands – using similar bottles or packs, colours and typography, even similar names. But while manufacturers spend millions of pounds on research, development and marketing of brands, it costs retailers very little to copy them.

The issue, says Michael Mackenzie, director-general of the Food and Drink Federation, which represents manufacturers, is not so much that consumers might mistake the own-label product for the manufacturer's brand. Rather, look-alike brands may 'give the impression that the manufacturer of the proprietary brand has made the own-label product'.

Brand manufacturers may have contributed to the confusion in the past by actually making own-label products for supermarkets, but most no longer do so. Kellogg recently ran an advertising campaign based on the fact that it does not make cereal for anyone else.

While the big names believe the problem has worsened, they have nevertheless been reluctant to speak out. This is because their relations with retailers are delicate. 'The worst thing you can do is to pick a fight with your biggest customers,' says Mackenzie. 'But the customers are giving them no option.'

What has prompted manufacturers to move now is the prospect of changing the law through the government's Trade Marks Bill, which was introduced first into the House of Lords and reached the report stage last week. It will get its third reading in about 10 days' time.

The bill is designed to harmonise UK laws on unfair competition with those in other EU countries, based on the Paris Convention on intellectual property. It aims to make it easier to register trademarks, as well as certain shapes, words and logos on packaging.

But manufacturers say it does not go far enough. They want protection against look-alike brands which imitate the overall appearance of their own brands, without directly copying logos or designs. Lord Reay last week introduced an amendment on behalf of the brand owners group extending such protection.

After a debate in the Lords last Thursday, Lord Reay withdrew his amendment when the government promised to review the issue, but the group may re-introduce its amendment if the government does not act during the passage of the bill.

Paul Walsh, partner at Bristows, Cooke & Carpmael, a law firm specialising in intellectual property, says the UK is out of line with most of Europe in not giving brands proper statutory protection. Germany has a statute on 'protection of get-up', and there are similar laws in France, Benelux and Greece.

▶

The problem of look-alikes is particularly sensitive in the UK because supermarkets have worked hard to change consumers' perceptions of own-label products from inferior imitations to quality alternatives. Retailers make much higher margins on own-label products because they do not bear the same development costs as manufacturers. The big three UK grocers – Sainsbury's, Safeway and Tesco – have pushed own-label sales to more than 50 per cent of turnover, far higher than elsewhere in Europe.

But opponents of the amendment argue that the bill as it stands, coupled with existing safeguards, is adequate. The British Retail Consortium, which represents more than 200 retailers, says manufacturers are attempting to restrict shops' ability to introduce own-label products.

'Shoppers are not confused,' the consortium said. 'they are very canny and read the label carefully.' The Consumers Association found in a survey last month that shoppers showed a preference for many own-label products in blind tastings. It warns that tighter restrictions on own-label products could lead to narrower choice for consumers.

Source: Financial Times, March 20 1994

Registered designs

A new product may be created that is not sufficiently novel nor contain an inventive step which satisfies the exacting requirements for the granting of a patent. This was the situation faced by Britain's textile manufacturers in the early nineteenth century. Manufacturers would create new textile designs but these would later be copied by foreign competitors. The Designs Registry was set up in the early 1800s in response to growing demands from Britain's textile manufacturers for statutory protection for the designs of their products. Today, designs that are applied to articles may be protected by design law. There are two systems of design law in the UK. One is similar to that used for patent law and requires registration. The other is design right and is provided along copyright lines. There is a large area of overlap between the two systems.

The registered designs system is intended for those designs intended to have some form of aesthetic appeal. For example, electrical appliances, toys and some forms of packaging have all been registered.

A design as protected by registration is the outward appearance of an article. Only the appearance given by its actual shape, configuration, pattern or ornament can be protected, not any underlying idea. The registered design lasts for a maximum of 25 years. Initially the proprietor is granted the exclusive right to a design for a fixed term of five years. This can be renewed for up to five further five-year terms.

To be registered, a design must first be new at the date an application for its registration is filed. In general a design is considered to be new if it has not been published in the UK (i.e. made available or disclosed to the public in any way whatsoever) and if, when compared with any other published design, the differences make a materially different appeal to the eye. For example, if a company designed a new kettle that was very different to any other kettle that had been made before, the company could register the design. This would prevent other kettle manufacturers from simply copying the design. Clearly, the kettle does not offer any advantage in terms of use, so a patent cannot be obtained, but a good design is also worth protecting.

Copyright

This area of the law on intellectual property rights has changed significantly over the past few years, mainly because it now covers computer software. Computer software manufacturers are particularly concerned about illegal copying of their programs. The music industry has also battled with the same problem for many years. It is common knowledge that this is an exceptionally difficult area of law to enforce.

For the author of creative material to obtain copyright protection, it must be in a tangible form so that it can be communicated or reproduced. It must also be the author's own work and thus the product of his or her skill or judgement. Concepts, principles, processes or discoveries are not valid for copyright protection until they are put in a tangible form such as written or drawn. It is the particular way that an idea is presented that is valid for copyright. This particular point, that ideas cannot be copyrighted, often causes confusion. If someone has written an article, you cannot simply rephrase it or change some of the words and claim it as your own. You are, however, entitled to read an article, digest it, take the ideas from that article together with other sources and weave them into your own material without any copyright problems. In most instances common sense should provide the answer.

Copyright is recognised by the following symbol © and gives legal rights to creators of certain kinds of material, so that they can control the various ways in which their work may be exploited. Copyright protection is automatic and there is no registration or other formality.

Copyright may subsist in any of nine descriptions of work. These are grouped into three categories:

1 Original literary, dramatic, musical and artistic works.
2 Sound recordings, films, broadcasts and cable programmes.
3 The typographical arrangement or layout of a published edition.

Each of these sections has more detailed definitions. For example, films in Section 2 includes videograms, and 'artistic work' in Section 1 includes photographs and computer-generated work.

The duration of copyright protection varies according to the kind of work. In the UK, for literary, dramatic, musical and artistic works copyright expires 70 years after the death of the author; in other cases 50 years after the calendar year in which it was first published. The period was 75 years in the US (now 50 years for all works created after 1978), but this issue is currently causing concern for one of the best-known organisations in the world, as the Mickey Mouse case explains.

Mickey Mouse will soon be 75 years old and out of copyright

Mickey Mouse will soon be 75. At this point, the first Mickey Mouse cartoon will be publicly available for use by anyone. *Plane Crazy* was released in May 1928 and will slip from the Disney empire's grasp in 2003. In autumn 1928 Disney released *Steam Boat Willie*, the world's first synchronised talking cartoon, and soon after it copyrighted the film.

At first glance one might be tempted to have some sympathy for the Disney organisation. However, Walt Disney wisely registered Mickey Mouse as a trademark, recognising from an early date that he had value far beyond the screen. So the use by others of the character on numerous products provides large licensing revenues for the Disney corporation, and trademarks can be renewed an indefinite number of times.

Source: Langton (1998)

Remedy against infringement

There are some forms of infringement of a commercial nature, such as dealing with infringing copies, that carry criminal penalties. HM Customs has powers to seize infringing printed material. Also a civil action can be brought by the plaintiff for one or more than one of the following:

- damages
- injunction
- accounts.

Damages

The owner of the copyright can bring a civil case and ask the court for damages, which can be expected to be calculated on the basis of compensation for the actual loss suffered.

Injunction

An injunction is an order of the court which prohibits a person making infringing copies of a work of copyright.

Accounts

This is a useful alternative for the plaintiff in that it enables access to the profits made from the infringement of copyright. This is useful especially if the amount is likely to exceed that which might be expected from an award of damages.

Security Systems of Denmark (SSD) and the development of a new security product[1]

This case study explores the development of an exciting technology for a potentially large market opportunity. Most of the company names used are fictitious. It is, nonetheless, based on an original piece of research (Heddegaard, 1998) and helps to illustrate some of the problems of managing strategic alliances. In particular, it illustrates the importance of trust in a strategic alliance and what can happen when this trust is missing.

Introduction

SSD, as the name suggests, is a Danish security firm with operations in cash-in-transit services and residential security services. The company's headquarters is on the outskirts of Copenhagen, where it employs a relatively small team of staff. For the year ended 1997 the company showed profits of $3.6 million on sales of $20 million. The company has grown rapidly over the past 10 years; this growth is reflected in the wider security industry. Figure 10.6 shows the sales figures for the past five years. Unlike many other industries, the security industry has not experienced a recession or fall in demand during the past 20 years. Indeed, larger security firms like Group 4 and Securicor have shown remarkable growth and profit figures during this period. This case study tells the story of how SSD formed a strategic alliance to exploit a business opportunity.

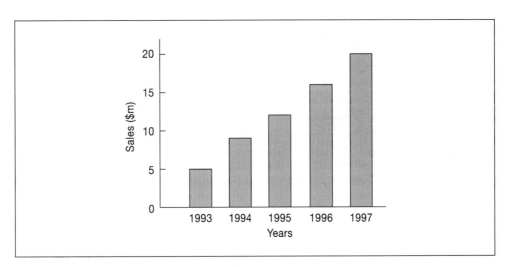

Figure 10.6 : SSD sales over the past five years

---

[1] This case study has been written as a basis for class discussion rather than to illustrate effective or ineffective managerial or administrative behaviour. It has been prepared from a variety of published sources, as indicated, and from observations.

SSD operations

The Copenhagen site is also the home of the company's control centre, from where it receives and delivers all its information relating to the business's operations. Many operations are provided by local contract staff or through franchise agreements with small security companies spread across Denmark. SSD is considered by business analysts to be a technology pioneer. It has been at the forefront of applications of technology in Europe in general and Denmark in particular. It was one of the first security companies in Europe to develop the idea of a control centre and the first to install remote engine-immobiliser switches to its cash-in-transit vehicles.

The cash-in-transit business

The cash-in-transit business was SSD's original business activity. Like most other security businesses it has witnessed steady growth over the past 15 years. Despite many analysts' and commentators' protestations that the cashless society would remove the need for the transport of cash, the demand and use of cash have continued to rise and with them the services of security, delivery and collection of cash. The business's largest customers are in the retail sector. Three years ago SSD introduced revolutionary new additional security technology to its cash-in-transit vehicles. In the event of the theft of a vehicle the SSD control centre can isolate the engine remotely. A password system was introduced using an in-vehicle telephone so that the control centre could confirm that the alarm had not been activated by accident.

Residential security business

The technology and service skills developed for the cash-in-transit business provided the basis for entry into residential security. Four years ago SSD took the strategic decision to enter what it believed to be a rapidly growing market. The product offered by SSD is aimed at large residential properties and small to medium-sized business premises. Large business premises tend to employ their own security guards and systems. The product can be tailor-made to suit a customer's particular requirements, but the nominal product comprises the installation of a standard hard-wired security system including alarm and closed-circuit television (CCTV) cameras with a picture feed back to SSD control centre.

Several franchise agreements have been established over the country to ensure that guards are geographically located for those areas covered by SSD. The operations are similar to that undertaken by the car breakdown services of the AA, Green Flag and the RAC.

It is well known in the security industry that 98 per cent of alarms are triggered accidentally by the owners. To overcome this, SSD has set up a password system that enables it to contact the property by telephone to check whether the owner is at home and has accidentally set off the alarm. If the correct password is given SSD will not process the breach of security any further. If, however, there is no reply to the telephone call, a guard will be sent to the property to check whether there is a fault or a genuine breach of security. The information received from the CCTV and the guard will inform the control centre whether it is necessary to inform the police.

The SSD security product and accompanying service is not a low-cost item and is targeted at small to medium-sized businesses and large residential properties. Payments are made on a monthly basis and the cost is typically $50 per month for a mid-range system.

Uncovering a new security business opportunity

It was during discussions with an existing residential customer that SSD uncovered a new security business opportunity. The owner of a large residential property in Copenhagen was explaining to an SSD salesperson the problems he was experiencing trying to get insurance for his new Saab motor car. It seemed that very few companies were willing to offer insurance against theft. Most insurance companies did quote for third-party insurance and fire. Those that did offer insurance for theft were quoting annual premiums of 5–10 per cent of the value of the car, so the annual premiums on a $50 000 Saab were as high as $5000. The SSD sales-man retold the story to his colleagues. A small team was established to investigate the situation further to see if a business opportunity existed and whether SSD could exploit it.

The vehicle security market

Following enquiries to a variety of insurance companies and other car vehicle security manu-facturers, it seemed that there was a genuine interest in a comprehensive vehicle security system. The team was able to confirm that the insurance industry considered high-value vehi-cles to be a high risk, hence many either charged high premiums or did not offer an insurance product for this category of vehicle.

The existing vehicle security market was divided into three main categories:

1 in-car portable security devices
2 retail alarms and immobilisers
3 factory-fitted alarm systems.

It is important to note at this point that it is the view of industry observers that all security systems are fallible and all can be conquered by a determined thief. Nonetheless, the insur-ance industry expressed interest and consumers were very intrigued by a security system that could track, locate and immobilise a stolen vehicle. Early investigations recommended a more detailed analysis.

The prototype product and service

The security product idea that SSD was considering would be based around its existing strengths. The product would utilise the company's knowledge of the service for its residential security business and the technology of its cash-in-transit business. The control centre would be at the heart of the product. It would incorporate satellite surveillance technology to track the vehicle and in the case of theft would enable immobilisation of the vehicle's engine from SSD's control centre. In addition, the product would have to be linked to a mobile phone system. Given that the vast majority of alarms are false and usually triggered accidentally by the owner, a system is required that would provide for a check on authenticity. In the event of the alarm being activated the control centre would contact the car's mobile phone and ask for a security password. If the correct password is not given the control centre would immobilise the car, and using the on-board tracking system send a security guard to collect the vehicle.

Technology development and the strategic alliance

The product would require several different elements of technology and a combination of existing technology from a variety of industries. SSD did not envisage any new technological research. The product would be based on reconfiguring existing technology linked to the service provision of SSD's control centre. The key areas of technology were:

- cellular telecommunications
- satellite navigation technology
- car security technology
- SSD's residential security systems service.

A local mobile telephone component manufacturer and supplier, Advanced Telecommunications (ATC) in Copenhagen, was contacted. ATC employed some of the best telecommunications technologists in Denmark and had built a reputation for developing advanced technology products for a wide range of telecommunications companies across Europe. Following extensive discussions over a period of three months, the two companies agreed that each had expertise that the other required and decided to set up an alliance to bring the product to market. The agreement and contract established that SSD would provide ATC with the necessary information to enable it to develop the technology for a product that would be operated by SSD's control centre.

During a period of two years the two companies worked together to develop an appropriate product. Input from the insurance companies was gathered and provided by SSD. Unfortunately, vehicle manufacturers expressed very little interest in the product idea. Indeed, they were dismissive of the idea and preferred to concentrate on their own vehicle security products. One R&D manager from one of Europe's largest car manufacturers suggested: 'This is big technology for big companies. We will develop our own technology'.

One of the technology areas that caused most concern was satellite navigation. These systems, however, have been under development for many years and are now appearing in many luxury car models such as Jaguar, Mercedes and Saab. So, the technology was available from a variety of component manufacturers.

After 12 months a prototype product was available for consideration. It now looked as if the product concept would reach the market. SSD, however, was not entirely happy with the final product. The technology worked but additional features and styling changes were required. Further months passed during which time SSD made further changes and modifications. ATC was showing signs of frustration and began questioning SSD's commitment to the project. SSD reassured ATC and made it clear that it was its project and it would do as it wished. ATC reluctantly agreed, but began negotiations with other security companies to discuss opportunities for developing similar technology. The enthusiasm for the technology shown by three security companies encouraged ATC to begin projects with these companies who were competitors of SSD.

Despite the popular belief that R&D activities are highly secretive and competitors have no idea what others are doing, in reality most scientists and R&D managers are aware that there is a great deal of cross-communication between laboratories. SSD eventually discovered that its competitors were also in negotiation with ATC. This was partly in breach of the strategic alliance contract that both parties had signed.

SSD broke the alliance with ATC and decided to take all its marketing research studies, R&D studies and prototype products to another component supplier. It also began litigation for damages from ATC. SSD also informed all other security companies in the industry of why the strategic alliance between itself and ATC had collapsed.

ATC continued to develop technology for the other security companies. One of the security companies decided not to pursue negotiations further. The other two continued to work with ATC to develop satellite security products. They are, however, proceeding with increased vigilance and have tightened their project contracts.

Discussion

This case study illustrates virtually all the aspects of innovation management that have been covered in this book. In particular, the role of external technological development and external societal changes is captured in the development of the security business opportunity. It is also a good example of technology transfer and the use of the external acquisition of technology via a third party.

The primary purpose of this case, however, is to illustrate the importance of trust in any strategic alliance. Arguably, trust is necessary in all business activities, but strategic alliances make it explicit. It must surely be the case that litigation is an unsatisfactory outcome for all parties involved. Its purpose is primarily to act as a threat so the companies keep to the terms of the negotiated contract. The terms are not revealed in this case and one must question whether the intellectual property rights were actually clarified. Furthermore, the case study highlights one of the main weaknesses of using third parties to conduct R&D, that is, the potential for leakage of technology and intellectual property. The questions raised in Chapter 8 concerning the degree of control over the technology seem particularly pertinent.

Chapter summary

This chapter has explored the role of strategic alliances and how firms are increasingly recognising that alliances provide access to resources that are greater than any single firm could buy. The main purpose was to highlight their growing importance within the world of business.

Linked to the issue of co-operation is the question of intellectual property. The chapter has examined the different forms of protection available to a firm. It also made it clear that the patent system has fierce critics, largely due to the associated costs involved in defending a patent against infringement. However, the patent system was also highlighted as a valuable source of technological knowledge used by many companies.

Questions for discussion

1 Explain why many research organisations are against the patenting of life forms.

2 Why are some government departments concerned about the increasing use of strategic alliances?

3 What is an octopus strategy?

4 Discuss the wide range of reasons for entering a strategic alliance.

5 Explain why the repeated game of the prisoner's dilemma is considered to be more useful than the single form in predicting behaviour.

6 Discuss the main forms of intellectual property protection available to companies.

7 Explain why discoveries are not patentable.

8 Discuss some of the limitations of the patent system.

9 Explain with the use of examples when it would be appropriate to use trademarks and copyright to protect a firm's intellectual property.

10 What other business opportunities might be available to firms that operate control centres?

11 Are there any justifications for ATC's actions?

12 Discuss the potential success for the new vehicle security product.

13 If there were a strategic alliance between the competitors in the security industry for the development of this new technology, what are the strategic issues for these firms once that technology becomes available?

References

Arias, J.T.G. (1995) 'Do networks really foster innovation?', *Management Decision*, 33(9), December 15, 52–7.
Baden-Fuller, C. and Pitt, M. (1996) (eds) *Strategic Innovation*, Routledge, London.
Bainbridge, D.I. (1996) *Intellectual Property*, 3rd edn, Financial Times Pitman Publishing, London.
Chan, P.S. and Heide, D. (1993) 'Strategic alliances in technology: key competitive weapon', *Advanced Management Journal*, 58 (4) 9–18.
Chemistry & Industry News (1995) http://ci.mond.org/9521/952107.html.
Derwent (1998) *Derwent World Patents Index*, Derwent Scientific and Patent Information: www.Derwent.com.
Economics Review (1994) 'Monopoly profits and patents', 12, (1).
Faulkner, D. (1995) *International Strategic Alliances*, McGraw-Hill, London.
Financial Times (1997) 'Gene is out of the bottle', October 30, 15.
Graham, N. (1998) 'Inventor cleans up with profits', *Sunday Times*, March 1, 4, 16.
Guardian (1998) 'Keep your ideas to yourself', February 17, 22.
Heddegaard, E. (1998) 'The development of a new product at Dansikring', final year dissertation, BABS, Business School, University of Portsmouth.
Lewis, J. (1990) *Partnerships for Profit: Structuring and Managing Strategic Alliances*, Free Press, New York.
Longton, James (1998) 'The mouse up for grabs', *Sunday Telegraph*, February 15, 23.
Morrison, M. and Mezentseff, L. (1997) 'Learning alliances: a new dimension of strategic alliances', *Management Decision*, 35(5/6), May/June, 351–8.
Nordwall, B.D. (1991), 'Electronic companies form alliances to counter rising costs', *Aviation Week and Space Technology*, June 17, 151–2.
Parkhe, A. (1993) 'Strategic alliance structuring: a game theoretic and transaction cost examination of interfirm cooperation', *Academy of Management Journal*, 36(4), August, 794–830.
Rowan, D. (1997) 'Signing up to a patent on life', *Guardian*, November 27, 19.
Sheridan, J. (1997) 'An alliance built on trust', *Industry Week*, 246(6), March 17, 67–71.

Slowinski, G., Seelig, G. and Hull, F. (1996) 'Managing technology-based strategic alliances between large and small firms', *Advanced Management Journal*, 61(2), Spring, 42–8.

Vyas, N.M., Shelburn, W.L. and Rogers, D.C. (1995) 'An analysis of strategic alliances: forms, functions and framework', *Journal of Business & Industrial Marketing*, 10(3), Summer, 47–61.

Further reading

Bainbridge, D.I. (1996) *Intellectual Property*, 3rd edn, Financial Times Pitman Publishing, London.

Lewis, J. (1990) *Partnerships for Profit: Structuring and Managing Strategic Alliances*, Free Press, New York.

Parkhe, A. (1993) 'Strategic alliance structuring: a game theoretic and transaction cost examination of interfirm cooperation', *Academy of Management Journal*, 36 (4), August, 794–830.

Rowan, D. (1997) 'Signing up to a patent on life', *Guardian*, November 27, 19.

Walters, B., Peters, S. and Dess, G.D. (1994) 'Strategic alliances and joint ventures: making them work', *Business Horizons*, July–August, 37 (4) 5–11.

Appendix: Guinness patent

(12) UK Patent Application (19) GB (11) 2 183 592 (13) A

(43) Application published **10 Jun 1987**

(21) Application No **8529441**

(22) Date of filing **29 Nov 1985**

(71) Applicant
Arthur Guinness Son & Company (Dublin) Limited,

(Incorporated in Irish Republic),

St. James's Gate, Dublin 8, Republic of Ireland

(72) Inventors
Alan James Forage,
William John Byrne

(74) Agent and/or Address for Service
Urquhart-Dykes & Lord, 47 Marylebone Lane,
London W1M 6DL

(51) INT CL⁴
B65D 25/00 5/40

(52) Domestic classification (Edition I)
B8D 12 13 19 7C 7G 7M 7P1 7PY SC1
B8P AX
U1S 1106 1110 1111 B8D B8P

(56) Documents cited
GB 1266351

(58) Field of search
B8D
B8P
Selected US specifications from IPC sub-class B65D

(54) **Carbonated beverage container**

(57) A container for a beverage having gas (preferably at least one of carbon dioxide and inert (nitrogen) gases) in solution consists of a non-resealable container 1 within which is located a hollow secondary chamber 4, eg a polypropylene envelope, having a restricted aperture 7 in a side wall. The container is charged with the beverage 8 and sealed. Beverage from the main chamber of the container enters the chamber 4 (shown at 8a) by way of the aperture 7 to provide headspaces 1a in the container and 4a in the pod 4. Gas within the headspaces 1a and 4a is at greater than atmospheric pressure. Preferably the beverage is drawn into the chamber 4 by subjecting the package to a heating and cooling cycle. Upon opening the container 1, eg by draw ring/region 13, the headspace 1a is vented to atmosphere and the pressure differential resulting from the pressure in the chamber headspace 4a causes gas/beverage to be ejected from the chamber 4 (by way of the aperture 7) into the beverage 8. Said ejection causes gas to be evolved from solution in the beverage in the main container chamber to form a head of froth on the beverage. The chamber 4 is preferably formed by blow moulding and located below beverage level by weighting it or as a press fit within the container 1 by lugs 6 engaging the container walls, the container being preferably a can, carton or bottle. The chamber 4 may initially be filled with gas, eg nitrogen, at or slightly above atmospheric pressure, the orifice being formed by laser boring, drilling or punching immediately prior to locating the chamber 4 in the container 1.

The drawings originally filed were informal and the print here reproduced is taken from a later filed formal copy.

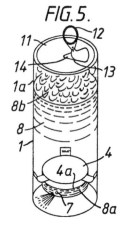

FIG. 5.

Reference to UK Patent Application 2,183,592A is made with kind permission of Guinness Brewing Worldwide Limited and their Patent Attorneys, Urquhart-Dykes & Lord.

29 NOV 8529441

2183592

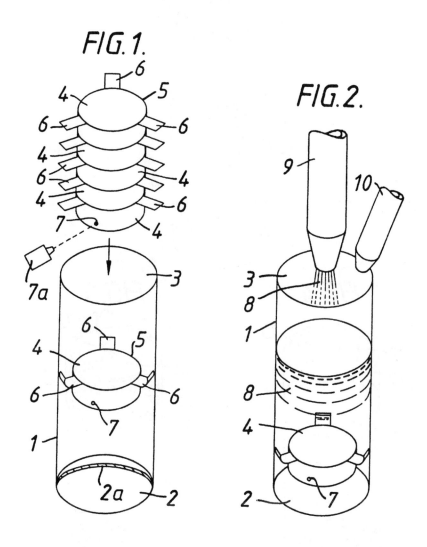

FIG.1.

FIG.2.

29   Nov 85 29441

2/2   2183592

FIG. 3.

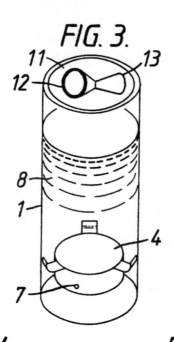

FIG. 4.

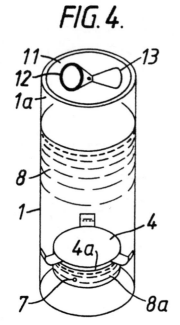

FIG. 5.

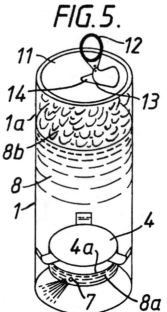

SPECIFICATION

A beverage package and a method of packaging a beverage containing gas in solution

5   *Technical field and background art*

This invention relates to a beverage package and a method of packaging a beverage containing gas in solution. The invention more particularly concerns

10   beverages containing gas in solution and packaged in a sealed, non-resealable, container which, when opened for dispensing or consumption, permits gas to be evolved or liberated from the beverage to form, or assist in the formation of, a head or froth on the

15   beverage. The beverages to which the invention relates may be alcoholic or non-alcoholic; primarily the invention was developed for fermented beverages such as beer, stout, ale, lager and cider but may be applied with advantage to so-called soft drinks

20   and beverages (for example fruit juices, squashes, colas, lemonades, milk and milk based drinks and similar type drinks) and to alcoholic drinks (for example spirits, liquers, wine or wine based drinks and similar).

25   It is recognised in the beverage dispensing and packaging art that the characteristics of the head of froth which is provided on the beverage by the liberation of gas from the beverage immediately prior to consumption are an important consideration to the

30   consumers enjoyment of the product and are therefore of commercial importance. Conventionally beverages of the type discussed above containing gas in solution and packaged in a non-resealable container (such as a can, bottle or carton) provide a

35   headspace in the container within which gas is maintained under pressure. Upon opening of the package, the headspace gas is vented to atmosphere and the beverage is usually poured into a drinking vessel. During such dispensing of the beverage it is

40   usual for gas in solution to be liberated to create the froth or head. It is generally recognised that when dispensing a beverage as aforementioned, the gas is liberated as a result of the movement of the beverage over a surface having so-called gas nucleation or ac-

45   tive sites which may be the wall of the drinking vessel into which the beverage is poured. There is therefore a distinct possibility with conventional beverage packages that upon opening of the container after storage and until the beverage is poured there-

50   from, the beverage will have little or no froth or head - such a headless beverage is usually regarded by the consumer as somewhat unattractive and unappealing especially where the beverage is to be drunk directly from the container. Admittedly it may be pos-

55   sible to develop a head or froth within the container by agitating or shaking the package (so that the movement of the beverage over the interior surface of the container causes the liberation of the gas in solution) but this is clearly inconvenient once the

60   container is opened and is inadvisable if the package is shaken immediately prior to opening as the contents tend to spray or spurt on opening.

There is therefore a need for a beverage package and a method of packaging a beverage containing

65   gas in solution by which the beverage is packaged in a non-resealable container so that when the container is opened gas is liberated from the beverage to form or assist in the formation of a head or froth without the necessity of an external influence being

70   applied to the package; it is an object of the present invention to satisfy this need in a simple, economic and commercially viable manner.

Statements of invention and advantages

75   According to the present invention there is provided a beverage package comprising a sealed, non-resealable, container having a primary chamber containing beverage having gas in solution therewith and forming a primary headspace comprising gas at

80   a pressure greater than atmospheric; a secondary chamber having a volume less than said primary chamber and which communicates with the beverage in said primary chamber through a restricted orifice, said secondary chamber containing beverage

85   derived from the primary chamber and having a secondary headspace therein comprising gas at a pressure greater than atmospheric so that the pressures within the primary and secondary chambers are substantially at equilibrium, and wherein said package is

90   openable, to open the primary headspace to atmospheric pressure and the secondary chamber is arranged so that on said opening the pressure differential caused by the decrease in pressure at the primary headspace causes at least one of the beverage and

95   gas in the secondary chamber to be ejected by way of the restricted orifice into the beverage of the primary chamber and said ejection causes gas in the solution to be evolved and form, or assist in the formation of, a head of froth on the beverage.

100   Further according to the present invention there is provided a method of packaging a beverage having gas in solution therewith which comprises providing a container with a primary chamber and a secondary chamber of which the volume of the secondary

105   chamber is less than that of the primary chamber and with a restricted orifice through which the secondary chamber communicates with the primary chamber, and charging and sealing the primary chamber with the beverage to contain the gas in solution and to

110   form a primary headspace in the primary chamber, and charging the secondary chamber with beverage derived from the primary chamber by way of said restricted orifice to form a secondary headspace in the secondary chamber whereby the pressures in both

115   the primary and secondary chambers are at equilibrium and gaseous pressures in both the primary and secondary headspaces are at a pressure greater than atmospheric so that, when the container is broached to open the primary headspace to atmos-

120   pheric pressure, the pressure differential caused by the decrease in pressure at the primary headspace causes at least one of the beverage and gas in the secondary chamber to be ejected into the beverage of the primary chamber by way of said restricted ori-

125   fice and the said ejection causes gas to be evolved from solution in the beverage in the primary chamber to form, or assist in the formation of, a head of froth on the beverage.

The present invention is applicable to a wide range

130   of beverages of the type as previously discussed and

where those beverages contain gas in solution which gas is intended to be liberated to form or assist in the formation of the head or froth on the beverage. Understandably the gas in solution must not detract
5 from, and should preferably enhance the characteristics required of the beverage and be acceptable for use with food products; preferably therefore the gas is at least one of carbon dioxide and inert gases (by which latter term is included nitrogen)
10 although it is to be realised that other gases may be appropriate.

   The present invention was primarily developed for the packaging of fermented beverages such as beer, ale, stout, lager and cider where among the desirable
15 qualities sought in a head are a consistent and regular, relatively fine, bubble size; a bubble structure which is substantially homogeneous so that the head is not formed with large irregularly shaped and random gaps; the ability for the head or bubble
20 structure to endure during a reasonable period over which it is likely to be consumed, and a so-called "mouth-feel" and flavour whcih may improve the enjoyment of the beverage during consumption and not detract from the desirable flavour characteristics
25 required of the beverage. These desirable qualities are of course equally applicable to non-fermented beverages, for example with so-called soft drinks. Conventionally, beverages of the type to which the invention relates are packaged in a non-resealable
30 container which when opened totally vents the headspace to atmosphere, contain carbon dioxide in solution and it is the liberation of the carbon dioxide on opening of the package and dispensing of the beverage into a drinking vessel which creates the froth or
35 head; however, the head so formed has very few of the aforementioned desirable qualities - in particular it is usually irregular, lacks homogeneity and has very little endurance so that there is a tendency for it to collapse after a short period. It has been known for
40 approximately 25 years and as discussed in our G.B. Patent No. 876,628, that beverages having in solution a mixture of carbon dioxide gas and inert gas (such as nitrogen or argon) will, when dispensed in a manner whereby the mixed gases are caused to
45 evolve to develop the head or foam from small bubbles containing the mixture of carbon dioxide and, say, nitrogen gases, provide the desirable qualities for the head as previously discussed. Commericially the formation of the head by the use of mixed
50 gases as aforementioned has been widely employed in the dispensing of beverage in a draught system and on demand from a bulk container (such as a keg or barrel) where the gases are caused to evolve by subjecting the beverage to intense shear forces in
55 passing it under pressure through a set of small holes. Beverages, particularly stout, having a mixture of carbon dioxide and nitrogen gases in solution and dispensed in draught using the aforementioned technique have met with considerable commercial
60 success and it was soon realised that there was a need to make available for consumption a similar beverage derived from a small non-resealable container suitable for shelf storage and retail purposes.
   Research has indicated that to achieve the initia-
65 tion of a head on a beverage containing carbon

dioxide and inert gas such as nitrogen in solution it is necessary to provide so-called "active sites" which are regions where the beverage is subjected to a high local strain (such a strain being higher than the
70 cohesive force of the beverage). In these conditions the beverage prefers to generate a bubble of mixed gases instead of "bending around" the active site. It was found that an active site could be solid, liquid or gas such as granules, restrictor holes, rapid streams
75 of liquid or bubbles and the like. It was also found that ultrasonics could produce a "ghost" active site by the formation of extreme pressure gradients. There has however been a problem in providing an "active site" in a beverage packaged in a non-
80 resealable small container in a manner which is commercially and economically acceptable. During the past 25 years considerable expenditure has been devoted to research and development in an attempt to overcome the aforementioned problem. For ex-
85 ample, our G.B. Patent No. 1,588,624 proposes initiating the evolution of mixed carbon dioxide and nitrogen gases from a beverage by subjecting the beverage to ultrasonic excitement, by injecting a gas, liquid and/or foam into the beverage by use of a
90 syringe-type device, or by pouring the beverage over an excitation surface such as polystyrene granules. Although these latter proposals were successful in achieving the desired head formation, the necessity to use ancilliary apparatus had commercial dis-
95 advantages (for example, it is unreasonable to expect a retail customer to have available an ultrasonic signal generator; also the steps required to effect initiation of the head following opening of the beverage package involved an inconvenient discipline and
100 time factor). In a further example our G.B. Patent No. 1,266,351 relates to a non-resealable package containing beverage having mixed carbon dioxide and inert gases in solution; in this disclosure a can or bottle has two chambers of which a larger chamber
105 contains the beverage while the smaller chamber is charged under pressure with the mixed gases. On opening of the can or bottle to expose the larger chamber to atmosphere, its internal pressure falls to atmospheric permitting the pressurised gas in the
110 small chamber to jet into the beverage by way of a small orifice between the two chambers. This jet of gas provides sufficient energy to initiate the formation of minute bubbles and thereby the head from the evolution of the mixed gases in the beverage
115 coming out of solution. By this proposal the small gas chamber is initially pressurised with the mixed gases to a pressure greater than atmospheric and from a source remote from the beverage; as a consequence it was found necessary, particularly in the
120 case of cans, to provide a special design of two chambered container and an appropriate means for sealing the smaller chamber following the charging of that chamber with the mixed gases (such charging usually being effected, in the case of cans, by injec-
125 ting the mixed gases into the small chamber through a wall of the can which had to be sealed). Because of the inconvenience and high costs involved in the development of an appropriate two chambered container and the special facilities required for
130 charging the mixed gases and sealing the container,

the proposal proved commercially unacceptable.

The container employed in the present invention will usually be in the form of a can, bottle or carton capable of withstanding the internal pressures of the
5 primary and secondary chambers and of a size suitable for conventional shelf storage by the retail trade so that, the overall volume of the container may be, typically, 0.5 litres but is unlikely to be greater than 3 litres.
10 By the present invention a two chambered container is employed as broadly proposed in G.B. Patent No. 1,266,351; however, unlike the prior proposal the secondary chamber is partly filled with beverage containing gases in solution and the bever-
15 age in the secondary chamber is derived wholly from the beverage in the primary chamber so that when the contents of the primary and secondary chambers are in equilibrium (and the primary and secondary headspaces are at a pressure greater than atmosphe-
20 ric) immediately prior to broaching the container to open the primary headspace to atmosphere, the pressure differential between that in the secondary headspace and atmospheric pressure causes at least one of the beverage and the headspace gas in the
25 secondary chamber to be ejected by way of the restricted orifice into the beverage in the primary chamber to promote the formation of the head of froth without the necessity of any external influence being applied to the package. The pressurisation of
30 the headspace gas in the secondary chamber is intended to result from the evolution of gas in the sealed container as the contents of the container come into equilibrium at ambient or dispensing temperature (which should be greater than the tem-
35 perature at which the container is charged and sealed). Consequently the present invention alleviates the necessity for pressurising the secondary chamber from a source externally of the container so that the secondary chamber can be formed as a
40 simple envelope or hollow pod of any convenient shape (such as cylindrical or spherical) which is located as a discrete insert within a conventional form of can, bottle or carton (thereby alleviating the requirement for a special structure of can or bottle as
45 envisaged in G.B. Patent No. 1,266,351).

Although the head or froth formed by pouring wholly carbonated beverages tends to lack many of the desirable qualities required of a head as previously discussed; our tests have indicated that by
50 use of the present invention with wholly carbonated beverages (where the head is formed by injection of gas or beverage from the secondary chamber into the primary chamber) the resultant head is considerably tighter or denser than that achieved solely by
55 pouring and as such will normally have a greater life expectancy.

The beverage is preferably saturated or supersaturated with the gas (especially if mixed carbon dioxide and inert gases are employed) and the
60 primary chamber charged with the beverage under a counterpressure and at a low temperature (to alleviate gas losses and, say, at a slightly higher temperature than that at which the beverage freezes) so that when the container is sealed (which may be
65 achieved under atmospheric pressure using con-

ventional systems such as a canning or bottling line), the pressurisation of the primary and secondary headspaces is achieved by the evolution of gas from the beverage within the primary and secondary
70 chambers as the package is handled or stored at an ambient or dispensing temperature (greater than the charging temperature) and the contents of the container adopt a state of equilibrium. As an optional but preferred feature of the present invention, following
75 the sealing of the container, the package may be subjected to a heating and cooling cycle, conveniently during pasteurisation of the beverage. During such a cycle the gas within the secondary chamber is caused to expand and eject into the primary
80 chamber; during subsequent cooling of the package, the gas in the secondary chamber contracts and creates a low pressure or vacuum effect relative to the pressure in the primary chamber so that beverage from the primary chamber is drawn into the sec-
85 ondary chamber by way of the restricted orifice. By use of this preferred technique it is possible to ensure that the secondary chamber is efficiently and adequately charged with beverage and has the desired secondary headspace.
90 The restricted orifice through which the primary and secondary chambers communicate is conveniently formed by a single aperture in a side wall of the secondary chamber and such an aperture should have a size which is sufficiently great to alleviate
95 "clogging" or its obturation by particles which may normally be expected to occur within the beverage and yet be restricted in its dimensions to ensure that there is an adequate jetting effect in the ejection of the gas and/or beverage therethrough from the sec-
100 ondary chamber into the primary chamber to promote the head formation upon opening of the container. The restricted orifice may be of any profile (such as a slit or a star shape) but will usually be circular; experiments have indicated that a restricted
105 orifice having a diameter in the range of 0.02 to 0.25 centimeters is likely to be appropriate for fermented beverages (the preferred diameter being 0.061 centimetres). It is also preferred that when the package is positioned in an upstanding condition in which it is
110 likely to be transported, shelf stored or opened, the restricted orifice is located in an upwardly extending side wall or in a bottom wall of the secondary chamber and preferably at a position slightly spaced from the bottom of the primary chamber. It is also
115 preferred, particularly for fermented beverages, that when the contents of the sealed package are in equilibrium and the package is in an upstanding condition as aforementioned, the restricted orifice is located below the depth of the beverage in the
120 secondary chamber so that on opening of the container the pressure of gas in the secondary headspace initially ejects beverage from that chamber into the beverage in the primary chamber to promote the head formation. It is believed that such ejection
125 of beverage through the restricted orifice is likely to provide a greater efficiency in the development of the head in a liquid supersaturated with gas than will the ejection of gas alone through the restricted orifice; the reason for this is that the restricted orifice
130 provides a very active site which causes the bever-

age to "rip itself apart" generating extremely minute bubbles which themselves act as active sites for the beverage in the primary chamber, these extremely minute bubbles leave "vapour trails" of larger initia-
5 ted bubbles which in turn produce the head. Since the extremely minute bubbles are travelling at relatively high speed during their injection into the beverage in the primary chamber, they not only generate shear forces on the beverage in that chamber
10 but the effect of each such bubble is distributed over a volume of beverage much larger than the immediate surroundings of an otherwise stationary bubble.

A particular advantage of the present invention is
15 that prior to the container being charged with beverage both the primary and secondary chambers can be at atmospheric pressure and indeed may contain air. However, it is recognised that for many beverages, particularly a fermented beverage, prolonged
20 storage of the beverage in contact with air, especially oxygen, is undesirable as adversely affecting the characteristics of the beverage. To alleviate this possibility the secondary chamber may initially be filled with a "non-contaminant" gas such as nitrogen (or
25 other inert gas or carbon dioxide) which does not adversely affect the characteristics of the beverage during prolonged contact therewith. The secondary chamber may be filled with the non-contaminant gas at atmospheric pressure or slightly greater (to allev-
30 iate the inadvertent intake of air) so that when the container is charged with the beverage, the non-contaminant gas will form part of the pressurised headspace in the secondary chamber. As previously mentioned, the secondary chamber may be formed
35 by an envelope or hollow pod which is located as a discrete insert within a conventional form of can, bottle or carton and such a discrete insert permits the secondary chamber to be filled with the non-contaminant gas prior to the envelope or pod being
40 located within the can, bottle or carton. A convenient means of achieving this latter effect is by blow moulding the envelope or pod in a food grade plastics material using the non-contaminant gas as the blowing medium and thereafter sealing the envelope
45 or pod to retain the non-contaminant gas therein; immediately prior to the pod or envelope being inserted into the can, bottle or carton, the restricted orifice can be formed in a side wall of the pod or envelope (for example, by laser boring). Immediately
50 prior to the container being sealed it is also preferable to remove air from the primary headspace and this may be achieved using conventional techniques such as filling the headspace with froth or fob developed from a source remote from the container and
55 having characteristics similar to those of the head which is to be formed from the beverage in the container; charging the primary chamber with the beverage in a nitrogen or other inert gas atmosphere so that the headspace is filled with that inert gas or nit-
60 rogen; dosing the headspace with liquid nitrogen so that the gas evolved therefrom expels the air from the headspace, or by use of undercover gassing or water jetting techniques to exclude air.

Although the secondary chamber may be con-
65 structed as an integral part of the container, for the

reasons discussed above and also convenience of manufacture, it is preferred that the secondary chamber is formed as a discrete insert which is simply deposited or pushed into a conventional form
70 of can, bottle or carton. With cans or cartons such an insert will not be visible to the end user and many bottled beverages are traditionally marketed in dark coloured glass or plastics so that the insert is unlikely to adversely affect the aesthetics of the package. The
75 discrete insert may be suspended or float in the beverage in the primary chamber provided that the restricted orifice is maintained below the surface of the beverage in the primary chamber on opening of the container; for example the insert may be loaded or
80 weighted to appropriately orientate the position of the restricted orifice. Desirably however the insert is restrained from displacement within the outer container of the package and may be retained in position, for example at the bottom of the outer con-
85 tainer, by an appropriate adhesive or by mechanical means such as projections on the package which may flex to abut and grip a side wall of the outer container or which may engage beneath an internal abutment on the side wall of the outer container.
90

Drawings
One embodiment of the present invention as applied to the packaging of a fermented beverage such as stout in a can will now be described, by way of
95 example only, with reference to the accompanying illustrative drawings, in which:-
Figures 1 to 4 diagrammatically illustrate the progressive stages in the formation of the beverage package in a canning line, and
100 *Figure 5* diagrammatically illustrates the effect on opening the beverage package prior to consumption of the beverage and the development of the head of froth on the beverage.

105 *Detailed description of drawings*
The present embodiment will be considered in relation to the preparation of a sealed can containing stout having in solution a mixture of nitrogen and carbon dioxide gases, the former preferably being
110 present to the extent of at least 1.5% vols/vol and typically in the range 1.5% to 3.5% vols/vol and the carbon dioxide being present at a considerably lower level than the amount of carbon dioxide which would normally be present in conventional, wholly car-
115 bonated, bottled or canned stout and typically in the range 0.8 to 1.8 vols/vol (1.46 to 3.29 grams/litre). For the avoidance of doubt, a definition of the term "vols/vol" is to be found in our G.B. Patent No. 1,588,624.

The stout is to be packaged in a conventional form
120 of cylindrical can (typically of aluminium alloy) which, in the present example, will be regarded as having a capacity of 500 millilitres and by use of a conventional form of filling and canning line appropriately modified as will hereinafter be described.
125 A cylindrical shell for the can 1 having a sealed base 2 and an open top 3 is passed in an upstanding condition along the line to a station shown in Figure 1 to present its open top beneath a stack of hollow pods 4. Each pod 4 is moulded in a food grade plastics
130 material such as polypropylene to have a short (say 5

millimetres) hollow cylindrical housing part 5 and a circumferentially spaced array of radially outwardly extending flexible tabs or lugs 6. The pods 4 are placed in the stack with the chamber formed by the
5 housing part 5 sealed and containing nitrogen gas at atmospheric pressure (or at pressure slightly above atmospheric); conveniently this is achieved by blow moulding the housing part 5 using nitrogen gas. The volume within the housing part 5 is approximately 15
10 millilitres. At the station shown in Figure 1 the bottom pod 4 of the stack is displaced by suitable means (not shown) into the open topped can 1 as shown. However, immediately prior to the pod 4 being moved into the can 1 a small (restricted) hole 7
15 is bored in the cylindrical side wall of the housing part 5. In the present example, the hole 7 has a diameter in the order of 0.61 millimetres and is conveniently bored by a laser beam generated by device 7a (although the hole could be formed by punching or
20 drilling). The hole 7 is located towards the bottom of the cylindrical chamber within the housing part 5. Since the hollow pod 4 contains nitrogen gas at atmospheric pressure (or slightly higher) it is unlikely that air will enter the hollow pod through the
25 hole 7 during the period between boring the hole 7 and charging of the can 1 with stout (thereby alleviating contamination of the stout by an oxygen content within the hollow pod 4).
   The hollow pod 4 is pressed into the can 1 to be
30 seated on the base 2. Conventional cans 1 have a domed base 2 (shown by the section 2a) which presents a convex internal face so that when the pod 4 abuts this face a clearance is provided between the hole 7 and the underlying bottom of the chamber
35 within the can 1. It will be seen from Figure 1 that the diameter of the housing part 5 of the pod 4 is less than the internal diameter of the can 1 while the diameter of the outermost edges of the lugs 6 is greater than the diameter of the can 1 so that as the pod 4 is
40 pressed downwardly into the can, the lugs 6 abut the side wall of the can and flex upwardly as shown to grip the can side wall and thereby restrain the hollow pod from displacement away from the base 2.
   The open topped can with its pod 4 is now displa-
45 ced along the canning line to the station shown in Figure 2 where the can is charged with approximately 440 millilitres of stout 8 from an appropriate source 9. The stout 8 is supersaturated with the mixed carbon dioxide and nitrogen gases, typic-
50 ally the carbon dioxide gas being present at 1.5 vols/vol (2.74 grams/litre) and the nitrogen gas being present at 2% vols/vol. The charging of the can 1 with the stout may be achieved in conventional manner, that is under a counterpressure and at a temperature of
55 approximately 0°C. When the can 1 is charged with the appropriate quantity of stout 8, the headspace above the stout is purged of air, for example by use of liquid nitrogen dosing or with nitrogen gas delivered by means indicated at 10 to alleviate contamina-
60 tion of the stout from oxygen in the headspace.
   Following charging of the can 1 with stout and purging of the headspace, the can moves to the station shown in Figure 3 where it is closed and sealed under atmospheric pressure and in conventional manner
65 by a lid 11 seamed to the cylindrical side wall of the

can. The lid 11 has a pull-ring 12 attached to a weakened tear-out region 13 by which the can is intended to be broached in conventional manner for dispensing of the contents.
70 Following sealing, the packaged stout is subjected to a pasteurisation process whereby the package is heated to approximately 60°C for 15-20 minutes and is thereafter cooled to ambient temperature. During this process the nitrogen gas in the hollow pod 4a
75 initially expands and a proportion of that gas passes by way of the hole 7 into the stout 8 in the main chamber of the can. During cooling of the package in the pasteurisation cycle, the nitrogen gas in the hollow pod 4 contracts to create a vacuum effect
80 within the hollow pod causing stout 8 to be drawn, by way of the hole 7, from the chamber of the can into the chamber of the pod so that when the package is at ambient temperature the hole 7 is located below the depth of stout 8a within the hollow
85 pod 4.
   Following the pasteurisation process the contents of the can 1 will stabilise in a condition of equilibrium with a headspace 1a over the stout 8 in the primary chamber of the can and a headspace 4a over the
90 stout 8a in the secondary chamber formed by the hollow pod 4 and in the equilibrium condition. With the sealed can at ambient temperature (or a typical storage or dispensing temperature which may be, say, 8°C) the pressure of mixed gases carbon dioxide
95 and nitrogen (which largely results from the evolution of such gases from the stout) is substantially the same in the headspaces 1a and 4a and this pressure will be greater than atmospheric pressure, typically in the order of 25lbs per square inch (1.72
100 bars).
   The package in the condition shown in Figure 4 is typically that which would be made available for storage and retail purposes. During handling it is realised that the package may be tipped from its up-
105 right condition; in practice however this is unlikely to adversely affect the contents of the hollow pod 4 because of the condition of equilibrium within the can.
   When the stout is to be made available for consumption, the can 1 is opened by ripping out the re-
110 gion 13 with the pull-ring 12. On broaching the lid 11 as indicated at 14 the headspace 1a rapidly depressurises to atmospheric pressure. As a consequence the pressure within the headspace 4a of the secondary chamber in the pod 4 exceeds that in the
115 headspace 1a and causes stout 8a in the hollow pod to be ejected by way of the hole 7 into the stout 8 in the primary chamber of the can. The restrictor hole 7 acts as a very "active site" to the supersaturated stout 8a which passes therethrough to be injected
120 into the stout 8 and that stout is effectively "ripped apart" to generate extremely minute bubbles which themselves act as active sites for the stout 8 into which they are injected. These minute bubbles leave "vapour trails" of larger initiated bubbles which dev-
125 elop within the headspace 1a a head 8b having the previously discussed desirable characteristics.
   It is appreciated that the headspace 1a occupies a larger proportion of the volume of the can 1 than that which would normally be expected in a 500 millilitre
130 capacity can; the reason for this is to ensure that

there is adequate volume in the headspace 1a for the head of froth 8b to develop efficiently in the event, for example, that the stout is to be consumed directly from the can when the tear-out region 13 is removed.
5 Normally however the stout 8 will first be poured from the can into an open topped drinking vessel prior to consumption but this pouring should not adversely affect the desirable characteristics of the head of froth which will eventually be presented in
10 the drinking vessel.

In the aforegoing embodiment the can 1 is charged with stout 8 (from the source 9) having in solution the required respective volumes of the carbon dioxide and the nitrogen gases. In a modification the can 1 is
15 charged with stout (from source 9) having the carbon dioxide gas only in solution to the required volume; the 2% vols/vol nitrogen gas necessary to achieve the required solution of mixed gas in the packaged stout is derived from the liquid nitrogen dosing of
20 the headspace in the can.

CLAIMS

1.   A beverage package comprising a sealed, non-
25 resealable, container having a primary chamber containing beverage having gas in solution therewith and forming a primary headspace comprising gas at a pressure greater than atmospheric; a secondary chamber having a volume less than said primary
30 chamber and which communicates with the beverage in said primary chamber through a restricted orifice, said secondary chamber containing beverage derived from the primary chamber and having a secondary headspace therein comprising gas at a pres-
35 sure greater than atmospheric so that the pressure within the primary and secondary chambers are substantially at equilibrium, and wherein said package is openable, to open the primary headspace to atmospheric pressure and the secondary chamber is arran-
40 ged so that on said opening the pressure differential caused by the decrease in pressure at the primary headspace causes at least one of the beverage and gas in the secondary chamber to be ejected by way of the restricted orifice into the beverage of the primary
45 chamber and said ejection causes gas in the solution to be evolved and form, or assist in the formation of, a head of froth on the beverage.

2.   A package as claimed in claim 1 in which the container has a normal upstanding condition with an
50 openable top and said secondary chamber has an upwardly extending side wall or a bottom wall within which said restricted orifice is located.

3.   A packaged as claimed in either claim 1 or claim 2 in which with the pressures within the
55 primary and secondary chambers substantially at equilibrium the restricted orifice is located below the depth of the beverage within the secondary chamber.

4.   A package as claimed in any one of the preced-
60 ing claims wherein the secondary chamber comprises a hollow and discrete insert within the container.

5.   A package as claimed in claim 4 in which the insert floats or is suspended in the beverage in the
65 primary chamber and means is provided for locating

the restricted orifice below the surface of the beverage in the primary chamber.

6.   A package as claimed in claim 5 in which the insert is weighted or loaded to locate the restricted
70 orifice below the surface of the beverage in the primary chamber.

7.   A package as claimed in claim 4 wherein means is provided for retaining the insert at a predetermined position within the container.
75   8.   A package as claimed in claim 7 wherein the container has a normal upstanding condition with an openable top and said insert is located at or towards the bottom of said container.

9.   A package as claimed in either claim 7 or claim
80 8 wherein the insert comprises a hollow pod or envelope having means thereon for retaining it in position within the container.

10.   A package as claimed in claim 9 wherein the retaining means comprise flexible tab means which
85 engage a side wall of the container to retain the insert.

11.   A package as claimed in any one of claims 4 to 10 wherein the insert comprises a hollow moulding.

12.   A package as claimed in claim 11 when
90 appendant to claim 10 in which the container has a side wall and the moulding is substantially cylindrical with radially extending tabs engaging the wall of the container.

13.   A package as claimed in any one of claims 4 to
95 12 in which the container has a base on which the insert is located and said restricted orifice is located in an upwardly extending side wall of the insert spaced from said base.

14.   A package as claimed in any one of the pre-
100 ceding claims in which the beverage has in solution therewith at least one of carbon dioxide gas and inert gas (which latter term includes nitrogen).

15.   A package as claimed in claim 14 in which the beverage is saturated or supersaturated with said
105 gas or gases.

16.   A package as claimed in any one of the preceding claims in which the container is in the form of a can, bottle or carton.

17.   A package as claimed in any one of the pre-
110 ceding claims in which the restricted orifice comprises a circular aperture having a diameter in the range of 0.02 to 0.25 centimetres.

18.   A package as claimed in any one of the preceding claims and comprising a fermented beverage
115 having in solution therewith carbon dioxide in the range 0.8 to 1.8 vols/vol (1.46 to 3.29 grams/litre) and nitrogen in the range 1.5% to 3.5% vols/vol.

19.   A beverage package substantially as herein described with reference to the accompanying illust-
120 rative drawings.

20.   A method of packaging a beverage having gas in solution therewith which comprises providing a container with a primary chamber and a secondary chamber of which the volume of the secondary
125 chamber is less than that of the primary chamber and with a restricted orifice through which the secondary chamber communicates with the primary chamber, and charging and sealing the primary chamber with the beverage to contain the gas in solution and to
130 form a primary headspace in the primary chamber,

and charging the secondary chamber with beverage derived from the primary chamber by way of said restricted orifice to form a secondary headspace in the secondary chamber whereby the pressures in both
5 the primary and secondary chambers are at equilibrium and gaseous pressures in both the primary and secondary headspaces are at a pressure greater than atmospheric so that, when the container is broached to open the primary headspace to atmos-
10 pheric pressure, the pressure differential caused by the decrease in pressure at the primary headspace causes at least one of the beverage and gas in the secondary chamber to be ejected into the beverage of the primary chamber by way of said restricted ori-
15 fice and the said ejection causes gas to be evolved from solution in the beverage in the primary chamber to form, or assist in the formation of, a head of froth on the beverage.
   21.   A method as claimed in claim 20 which com-
20 prises subjecting the sealed container to a heating and cooling cycle whereby gas within the secondary chamber is caused to expand and eject by way of the restricted orifice into the primary chamber and subsequently to contract and create a low pressure ef-
25 fect in the secondary chamber relative to the primary chamber to draw beverage from the primary chamber into the secondary chamber by way of said restricted orifice.
   22.   A method as claimed in claim 21 in which the
30 heating and cooling cycle comprises pasteurisation of the beverage.
   23.   A method as claimed in any one of claims 20 to 22 in which the container has an upstanding condition with an openable top and which comprises
35 locating the restricted orifice within an upwardly extending side wall or bottom wall of the secondary chamber.
   24.   A method as claimed in any one of claims 20 to 23 which comprises charging the secondary
40 chamber with beverage from the primary chamber to the extent that the restricted orifice is located below the depth of beverage in the secondary chamber.
   25.   A method as claimed in any one of claims 20
45 to 23 which comprises forming the secondary chamber by a discrete hollow insert located within the primary chamber of the container.
   26.   A method as claimed in claim 25 in which the hollow insert is to float or be suspended in the bever-
50 age in the primary chamber and which comprises loading or weighting the insert to locate the restricted orifice below the surface of the beverage in the primary chamber.
   27.   A method as claimed in claim 25 which com-
55 prises retaining the insert at a predetermined position within the container.
   28.   A method as claimed in any one of claims 25 to 27 which comprises forming the hollow insert having the restricted orifice in a wall thereof and loc-
60 ating the insert within the primary chamber prior to the charging and sealing of the primary chamber.
   29.   A method as claimed in any one of claims 25 to 28 which comprises forming the hollow insert by blow moulding.
65   30.   A method as claimed in claim 29 which com-

prises blow moulding the hollow insert with gas for dissolution in the beverage so that said gas is sealed within the secondary chamber, and forming said restricted orifice in the wall of the insert immediately
70 prior to locating the insert in the primary chamber.
   31.   A method as claimed in claim 30 which comprises sealing said gas in the secondary chamber at atmospheric pressure or at a pressure slightly greater than atmospheric.
75   32.   A method as claimed in any one of claims 25 to 31 which comprises forming the restricted orifice in the hollow insert by laser boring, drilling or punching.
   33.   A method as claimed in any one of claims 25
80 to 32 in which, prior to it being sealed, the container has an upstanding condition with an open top through which the primary chamber is charged with beverage and which comprises locating the insert through said open top to provide the secondary
85 chamber within the container.
   34.   A method as claimed in claim 33 when appendant to claim 27 which comprises press fitting the insert within the container so that during its location the insert engages with a side wall of the container to
90 be retained in position.
   35.   A method as claimed in any one of claims 20 to 34 which comprises, prior to sealing the primary chamber, purging the primary head space to exclude air.
95   36.   A method as claimed in any one of claims 20 to 35 in which the gas comprises at least one of carbon dioxide gas and inert gas (which latter term includes nitrogen).
   37.   A method as claimed in claim 36 in which the
100 beverage is fermented and has in solution carbon dioxide in the range 0.8 to 1.8 vols/vol (1.46 to 3.29 grams/litre) and nitrogen in the range 1.5% to 3.5% vols/vol.
   38.   A method of packaging a beverage as
105 claimed in claim 20 and substantially as herein described.
   39.   A beverage when packaged by the method as claimed in any one of claims 20 to 38.

110 _____

Printed for Her Majesty's Stationery Office by
Croydon Printing Company (UK) Ltd, 4/87, D8991685.
Published by The Patent Office, 25 Southampton Buildings, London, WC2A 1AY,
from which copies may be obtained.

Index

Books are to be returned
the last date be

HAVERING COLLEGE